D0427783

THE FOUR
GOLD KEYS

Robert B. Clarke

THE FOUR
GOLD KEYS

*Dreams, Transformation
of the Soul, and the
Western Mystery Tradition*

HAMPTON ROADS
PUBLISHING COMPANY, INC.

Copyright © 2002
by Robert Clarke
All rights reserved, including the right to reproduce this
work in any form whatsoever, without permission
in writing from the publisher, except for brief passages
in connection with a review.

Cover design by Marjoram Productions
Key photo © copyright 2002 by
PhotoDisc/PictureQuest/Glenn Mitsui
Background photo © copyright 2002 by
RubberBall Productions/PictureQuest/Alan Pappe

Hampton Roads Publishing Company, Inc.
1125 Stoney Ridge Road
Charlottesville, VA 22902

434-296-2772
fax: 434-296-5096
e-mail: hrpc@hrpub.com
www.hrpub.com

If you are unable to order this book from your local
bookseller, you may order directly from the publisher.
Call 1-800-766-8009, toll-free.
Library of Congress Catalog Card Number: 2001095579
ISBN 1-57174-313-8
10 9 8 7 6 5 4 3 2 1
Printed on acid-free paper in the United States

*This book is dedicated to the memory
of my parents and sister.*

TABLE OF CONTENTS

ACKNOWLEDGEMENTS

I would like to thank the following for their help and cooperation in various ways with this book: Anne Franklyn and Andrew Smith for some original typing; Chris Nocetti at Burslem Development Trust; all at Burslem and Hanley Libraries; Sally Sweet and Annemieke Dolfing at ITPS; Princeton University Press; the Theosophical University Press; Richard Leviton, Frank DeMarco, and all at HRPC; also Tracy Mosley, Stephen Rowe, Ernie Bourne, and Peter Heath.

My special thanks to Colin Wilson, whose heart is as great as his talent. Many aspiring writers have benefited from his help. My own debt to him is very large.

My greatest thanks to Jung, for his works of profoundest wisdom in the outer world, and for his guidance through the unconscious.

FOREWORD

Most writers receive a dozen or so letters a week from strangers, commenting on their work or offering advice. A few of these, inevitably, are from religious cranks who feel that the answer to all life's problems can be found in the Bible. When I receive one of these, I usually throw it straight in the waste paper basket.

So it was fortunate that, when in April 1997, I received a long handwritten letter from a correspondent in the Midlands describing a kind of religious conversion, I went on reading to the end.

What he was explaining was how the discovery of the analytical psychology of Jung had brought about a profound change in his outlook, and made him aware of the true meaning of religion. And the sincerity of the letter, and the obvious intelligence of the writer, made such an impression on me that I immediately picked up the phone and rang him at his home in Stoke on Trent, the heart of the district known as "the Potteries."

The man who answered had a Staffordshire accent—which, for the benefit of American readers, is not unlike Yorkshire—and we had a long conversation. I told him that I had been moved and excited by his account of his childhood, and his long, miserable period as a laborer and office worker, because it resembled in many ways my own experience. And I advised him to settle down and write a book.

Now, it is something of a responsibility for a writer to advise someone to write a book, for they assume that you will be able to find them a publisher. And at that time, I had no idea of who might be interested. But I could see very clearly that this was what Robert Clarke needed to do—to express the ideas that were obviously boiling inside him, and get them out of his system. This was the obvious priority, and looking for a publisher could wait.

As far as Robert was concerned, there were major obstacles to be surmounted. At that time he could not even type. But in a short time he not only taught himself to type, but bought a computer and got himself on to e-mail. And in due course I received the early chapters of his book, with a delightful account of his happy childhood, when he set out in life with the expectation that, whatever the future held, it was going to be exciting and fulfilling. Then he left school, and "shades of the prison house" began to close, leading to the disheartening anticlimax of a succession of jobs he detested. The feeling that life meant well by him faded away, and, in effect, he began a long prison sentence that lasted until his unconscious mind provided release in a nervous breakdown.

Now, this was a problem that had always preoccupied me, and that had led me to write my first book, *The Outsider*, in 1955. Like Robert, I had been born into a working class background in the Midlands, the son of a factory worker. Like Robert, I had been a good student at school, and no one had any doubt that I could get the necessary scholarships to go on to higher education. But in my case, an unexpected obstacle intervened. At the age of sixteen, I suddenly lost interest in science—of which I had intended to make a career—and decided I wanted to become a writer.

What had happened was that, after I left school in 1947 at the age of 16, I discovered that I lacked the credit in mathematics that I needed to take a science degree. That meant taking the maths exam again, and that could not be done for several months. In the meantime, I took a laboring job in a wool factory—the first job the employment exchange offered me—and began working a nine-hour day. I found the work boring and exhausting, and used to cycle home at six o'clock in a state of exhaustion and depression.

But I had discovered an excellent antidote to gloom—poetry. I would go to my bedroom, climb into bed—it was a cold winter and this was the best way of keeping warm—and plunge into my favorite poets. These included Keats, Wordsworth, Milton, Poe, W. B. Yeats, and T. S. Eliot. And gradually, a mood of calm and relaxation would replace the depression, and after a couple of hours I had been restored to my usual mood of cheerful optimism.

The problem was that these nightly infusions of poetry were like de Quincey's opium eating, and made physics and mathematics seem more and more disagreeable. And although this made no difference during the remaining months I worked in the factory, it proved to be a major drawback when I passed my maths exam and was offered a job as a laboratory assistant at my old school.

A year earlier, this offer would have fulfilled all my dreams, for it would have meant that I could work in a congenial environment while I studied for a science degree, and took the major steps towards becoming a nuclear physicist or cosmologist (which is what really interested me). But Keats and Shelley had spoiled me for all that. Now I wanted to write plays like Bernard Shaw or novels like H. G. Wells (both were still alive at the time), and devote my life to literature and philosophy. (I had been introduced to the latter by the writings of "Professor" C. E. M. Joad.)

So when I took my end-of-year exams, and it became apparent that I had done no work in physics or analytical chemistry, the headmaster sacked me from the lab-assistant position, and I had to look around for a new way of earning a weekly wage packet. Still detesting the idea of any regular occupation but writing, I ended as a civil servant, working at the Collector of Taxes, but—predictably—found that even more boring and depressing than the school laboratory.

At this point, national service in the Royal Air Force intervened. I found the initial period of "square bashing" unexpectedly invigorating, but soon lost interest when I was given a clerking job. At this point I set about "working my ticket," and succeeded so well in convincing a medical board that I was temperamentally unsuited to service life that I found myself discharged after a mere six months as an airman.

There would be no point in describing the various jobs I accepted—and lost—during the next four years, for this introduction is supposed to be about Robert, not about me. Suffice it to say that I worked as a farm laborer, navvy (ditch digger), plastic molder, filing clerk, laundry hand, and washer-up in a coffee bar before I wrote The Outsider at the age of twenty-three, and found myself hurtled into a dubious notoriety as an "Angry Young Man" when I was still twenty-four. But, for a long time after I moved to a Cornish village to write books, I woke up having nightmares of being back in a factory.

So when Robert wrote to me outlining a career that sounds depressingly similar, I was naturally sympathetic. "Left school at 15—1957—to work in office of tile factory—hated it. I didn't realize it, but education stopped just when I had come fully awake to knowledge. I was to further work at a small printers setting type, as trainee manager at pottery ware-house, assistant at car-spare warehouse, shop assistant selling electrical goods, driver's mate, filling cylinders at color works, mixing coke dirt and tar (twelve-hour shifts), shoveling basalt rock into a furnace (twelve-hour shifts), preparation work in a fish-and-chip shop, stacking saggers (pottery vessels) in a bottle oven (one day, but it seemed like a year), and other laboring jobs in factories."

It can be seen that, compared to Robert, I had a fairly easy time of it. Yet I had contemplated suicide during my period as a lab assistant, and actually went to the analytical chemistry class one evening with every intention of drinking cyanide.

If I had killed myself, of course, I would have been following in the footsteps of so many "Romantic Outsiders," like Kleist, Beddoes, and Chatterton. But if I had been forced to spend another decade working at uncongenial jobs, I think it quite possible that I might have taken the fatal step—or at least, had a nervous breakdown, as Robert did at the age of twenty-eight.

Robert's collapse was obviously a deep unconscious revolt against our society and the life it was forcing him to lead. Jung had experienced the same thing at the age of twelve, and he describes it in *Memories, Dreams, Reflections*. Like Robert, Jung had been fascinated by the romance of archaeology, and wanted to become an archaeologist. But for the son of an impoverished Protestant pastor, this was out of the question. Jung's father had remarked: "The boy is interested in everything. but heavens knows where he'll end up." And as Jung became increasingly depressed about his prospects, he became accident-prone, and one day, a boy pushed him so hard that he fell and banged his head on the pavement. He lost consciousness for a moment, and the thought flashed through his mind: "Now I shan't have to go to school any more." And from then on, he began having fainting fits.

One day, sitting behind a shrub in the garden, he heard his father speaking about him to a friend about his illness. ". . . they think it might be epilepsy. It would be dreadful if he were incurable. I have lost what little I have, and what will become of the boy if he cannot earn his own living?"

Suddenly filled with guilt, Jung hurried off to his father's study and took out his Latin grammar. After a short time, he had a fainting fit and fell off the chair, but desperation forced him to go on working. He had a second blackout, but still pressed on. An hour later, he fainted again, but made himself go back to work. Then suddenly he felt better than he had since the attacks began. And, in fact, they ceased.

That experience taught Jung a little about the terrible power of the unconscious mind, and how gloom and negativity can influence the body.

Something of the sort, I believe, happened to Robert when he was twenty-eight. He had become utterly depressed—not merely with himself, but with the world around him. He spent every free moment reading, but could find nothing that seemed to offer a glimmer of a solution. The teachings of Freud had struck him as totally negative. Then he came across a best-selling book by a foreign professor, declaring that man is an accident that should never have happened, and that where evolution is concerned, humanity has no future. (Robert cannot remember the title of the book, but I wonder if it might have been Jacques Monod's 1970 bestseller *Chance and Necessity*.) His own deepest instincts told him that all this was nonsense, but this certainty only increased his sense of standing alone.

An unhappy, unfulfilled love affair did nothing to improve things, and in 1970 he had the breakdown which effectively put an end to his career as a reluctant laborer.

It was about five years later that he saw a television program about Jung, which came as a revelation. Long before that, he had noted the vividness and strange symbolism of his dreams, and felt that they were trying to teach him something. Now, suddenly, through the works of Jung, he began to understand what that was.

The result was a mental revolution that dragged him back from the abyss. He began to keep a dream diary, and used the collected works of Jung to help him interpret them. And as he realized that his dreams were offering him insights into the collective unconscious, he knew he had found what he had been seeking since he left school.

His whole world changed. He tells me that he suddenly ceased to be the misfit of the family, and became the one who made decisions.

He had also, at some point, stumbled upon my own writings, and recognized immediately that I was also in revolt against the pessimism that has dominated our culture for more than two centuries. This is why, in 1997, he decided to write to me. He accepted my suggestion that he should begin the book with a long autobiographical section, and this is what, some time in 1999, he sent to me on disk. I was enthusiastic, but could see that his major problem was going to be how to move from his own personal story to a study of the development of the ideas of Freud and Jung, and to the quarrel between them that led to Jung's own mental breakdown in 1914, and to the development of the idea of the collective unconscious. Still less could I see how he could find room for his own "dream diary."

Fortunately, I mentioned Robert's project in an e-mail to my friend Frank DeMarco, one of the two founders of the publishing house of Hampton Roads. Frank asked to see the uncompleted book, and to my delight, decided that it was publishable, and that a good editor—in this case, Richard Leviton—could solve the problems that had left me baffled. He was right, and the result is the present volume.

And here, I realize, I should start winding up this introduction. Yet I have a deeply frustrating sense that there is something important that I have simply failed to say. Let me take a deep breath, beg the reader's indulgence, and try again.

In the 1960s, I was sent a book called *Evolution for Beginners* by a writer called Michael Byrom. (I have put a portrait of Michael into an early novel of mine called *The Violent World of Hugh Greene*.) The book seemed to me basically Shavian in spirit, but written with a wit and incisiveness that was entirely his own. I replied to Michael, and discovered that he lived alone in a cottage at Bovey Tracey, near the edge of Dartmoor. I drove over one day to see him.

I was expecting to meet someone as combative and pugnacious as Shaw, and was surprised to meet a pale, quietly spoken young man, who seemed rather shy. The cottage belonged to his mother, who allowed him to live there rent free, and he devoted his days to drawing and writing. He was a brilliant cartoonist whose work owed something to Max Beerbohm, and he enjoyed presenting Punch and Judy shows for children. Concealed behind a stage and puppets, his shyness vanished.

But what amazed me most about Michael was that he was a natural puritan. (Shaw had said the same thing about himself, so perhaps this was not so surprising.) In spite of being an evolutionist, his philosophy made a sharp distinction between "this world" and the world of reality—the world of the spirit, and he felt strongly that the prophets of the evolution of mankind to a higher stage are all distinguished by a sense of revulsion that they feel for "this world." He liked quoting a work called *The Dwarf* by Par Lagerkvist, in which the protagonist declares "I delight in nothing." Michael would spit out this last word with an abyss of contempt.

His attitude to sex was also puritanical. He told me that he had recently seen an old man and woman standing at a bus stop, both slightly drunk, dancing a little jig together. This brought out his contempt. "They should have outgrown that kind of thing long ago!" And when I said that I thought it sounded rather charming, he shook his head in bewilderment, as if to say, "I thought you and I had something in common."

The point of this story is still to come. Michael had written a play set in Ruritania, about a prince who is next in line for the throne. But, the prince detests the idea of becoming king and ruling the country. His main interest is training fleas for his flea circus, which is the joy of his life. That is why he hates the idea of becoming king: He would have to give up his flea circus.

Michael explained that the flea circus was a deliberately trivial symbol of this "other world," the world of evolutionary purpose. He had rejected the idea of making the heir apparent a musician or painter or heroic figure. He wanted to emphasize that the evolutionary impulse is basically a dislike of all the things that "this world" offers us. He might have expressed it like Villiers de L'Isle Adam's Axel: "As for living, our servants can do that for us."

But with his symbol of the prince and his flea circus, Michael was adding another layer of meaning to Axel. The person who is driven by that obscure urge to evolve towards a higher type of man may not have the slightest idea what this evolution is all about. He is not at all sure what he *does* want. He only knows very clearly that he doesn't want the kind of life that seems to content the vast majority of his fellow humans. He cannot grasp that his real problem is his deep sense of dissatisfaction with humanity as it exists.

Somerset Maugham wrote about the same problem in *The Moon and Sixpence* and *The Razor's Edge*, but by making his hero an artist or a natural ascetic, he is blurring the outline of the problem, which is that an immense majority of the "higher evolutionary types" have no idea why they find everyday life so dreary and repellent. They feel themselves to be outsiders or misfits, doomed to an unhappiness that seems to have something to do with being born into the wrong world.

The credit for creating the first of these outsider-misfits should probably go to Shakespeare with Hamlet. Goethe with Young Werther came a century-and-a-half later, and launched the Romantic movement, with its "world rejection." Those early "outsiders," from Hoffmann and Byron to Yeats' "tragic generation" of the 1890s, felt that the answer lay in accepting that life is a kind of tragic joke, like someone blundering on to a stage set while the play is in progress; the best thing the unhappy misfit can do is to make his apologies and back out as soon as possible.

Michael Byrom may have been a "world rejecter," but he saw that the underlying problem is the "misfit's" evolutionary urge. It is a desire for another type of consciousness, connected to the deeper meaning of the universe.

It is because Robert Clarke's story encapsulates this whole tremendous issue so perfectly that I feel his work has something deeply significant to say to the present time.

—*Colin Wilson*

PREFACE:

Opening Up to the Experience
of the Archetypal Depths

And the Son of God is dead, which is worthy of belief because it is absurd. And when buried He rose again, which is certain because it is impossible.

Tertullian, De Carne Christi

I discovered psychologist Carl Jung quite by accident, though at a critical time when he was of the greatest necessity, of the greatest urgency, to my woeful existence.

My life had developed into a very troubled one since being a relatively happy young teenager, and I eventually suffered a nervous breakdown, followed by years of dismal depression. Though having causes connected to personal disappointments to a degree, the breakdown was due in the main to a loss of deeper meaning in reality itself, which is really loss of soul. This existential problem of feeling lost and isolated in eternity is a common enough malady in the modern world, but was greatly intensified in my own case. My discovery of Jung was to have a tremendous effect upon my life, for he was responsible for the transformation that eventually occurred both within myself, and in full reality itself, although nothing could have happened without the participation of the world of the unconscious, that other realm we experience through dreams.

We are all of us two people, whether we know it or not, in that we have outer and inner selves—I am not referring to the unconscious Higher Self here—and the distance between the inner and outer selves varies with the individual. The face we show to the world, known in psychology as the persona, the mask worn, does not necessarily match the way we think with our deeper, hidden personality. There is usually nothing intentionally false about this, it being rather that we have to share our environment with others, and so must find common ground with them, keeping what we consider private thoughts, or thoughts unacceptable to others, to ourselves.

My own inner self was always very deep, being constantly occupied with the most serious questions of existence, and so I seldom showed this face to the world, to the people in my own environment, who frankly would not have been so interested in any case. However, what follows here in this book is mostly concerned with that inner self, the face not shown to the world, though it is true to say that in my case this has developed and become much stronger over the years, replacing the more shallow outer aspect to a large degree. The latter could be of no interest to the world, as nothing of any consequence ever happened to me in everyday life; but inwardly, I came to live what is known as the symbolic life, and that is quite something else again.

I was fated to make long journeys through that other, unconscious, reality that exists behind the known conscious universe. This is the source, as I was to discover, of all of the world's myths and true religions, as well as the substratum upon which consciousness itself rests. The record of my years of experience of those archetypal depths is, I believe, certainly worth the telling, and that is what you will find in *The Four Gold Keys*.

These first few pages may become somewhat negative and depressing as they progress, but this has to be, because such was the state my life had tumbled into before my discovery of the wider, archetypal reality that is attached to our dull and heavy material world. But then, it is experience of—or at least, belief in—that other reality of spirit and soul that has always enriched mere physical existence for mankind, which is why the loss of it in the modern West will have catastrophic consequences for culture unless we quickly find it and our true selves again.

But I must begin more or less at the beginning, to relate very briefly the personal sickness and near soul-chaos that I had gradually fallen into when I first discovered, quite by chance, the remedy for all sick souls.

Nevertheless, this book is not primarily about myself, but rather concerns that other realm of the unconscious itself, where the Higher Self in all of its opposites resides, and where even the Great Mother, the World Soul, and the God of Spirit may also be ultimately experienced. If things sound a little contradictory at times, that is because we often think from different sides of ourselves, particularly when we are young or are somewhat lost, desperately trying to find our way.

My childhood was very happy, despite poverty and what is today termed social deprivation. They were joyful years, and most of the people I know from those days say the same. The 1940s in Britain was a very positive era, as the earlier decades of the twentieth century had also been, for a rich spirit of the age seemed to illumine everywhere. If ever there was a time of the ordinary, decent man, which gave him a distinct measure of nobility, this was it. Many German people opposed Hitler and the Nazis in those times and paid the price for it, but the difference between the cultural spirits in Britain and Germany in the thirties and forties was enormous—diametrically opposed, in fact.

The spirit in Britain was what we could only call essentially Christian, in deed if not in word; in other words, essentially decent and moral, whereas in Germany the old pagan god of the depths, Wotan, had resurged, and in his darkest and most dangerous aspect. There is a saying now that you could leave your front door open all day and night in those days, and nothing would be touched, and that is the truth of it. This despite the fact that most people were poor and more or less on the breadline. When my father was ill for two years, unable to work, the neighbors would bring us what little food they could spare, and that was the general rule. That is how the people thought and lived. It was not the generals and the politicians who really defeated the evil of the Nazis, but these ordinary decent people: British, American, and many others of the nations of the world, the good of man defeating the evil of man.

At school I was a good scholar, possessing a romantic bent and a very vivid imagination, but cold science was always my worst subject. Such things as The Arabian Nights and Schliemann digging up Troy were of prime importance to me, whereas the scientific spectrum, from quantum theory to electrical circuits, could not hold my attention for five seconds. However, Einstein and Darwin with their respective theories of relativity and evolution did fascinate me because they had a philosophical aspect involving the mystery of the universe, and therefore of God.

The times were hard in many ways, but I loved them, and it is warm and humorous to reflect on a memory long ago of eating lard on bread for Sunday dinner because there was nothing else in the house, and you could laugh heartily about it. If your stomach was full with anything in those days you were grateful and considered yourself fortunate. I loved music, but I only knew half of the popular songs of the day because we had to sell the radio so often, and then later buy another one secondhand.

All of this taught me an extremely important lesson in life, that happiness does not depend upon money as long as you are healthy and the poverty is not so severe that you actually starve. What is far more important is to have a good family around you, decent friends, a healthy framework of orientation in which to grow and develop, and certainly of high priority, that "rich spirit of the age" that is positive and noble. I grew up in the midst of all these things, and so material prosperity, or the lack of it, was never of high priority in my life. I have nothing against wealth and would greet it cordially if it came, but I have known those other things in that other time, and they are the *real* treasures of worldly existence (apart from the spiritual ones, of course).

At Christmas—I tell this because it is an essential part of the story, of the foundations that I lost and had to rediscover and reestablish—my sister and I would make decorations out of cotton wool, colored paper, or anything else we could find available, though some years we were able to buy a few cheap decorations. But we enjoyed Christmas all the more, perhaps, because we had to work for it and contribute toward it.

This, as I said, was in the mid-1940s when I was quite young. I never could quite believe it when Christmas Eve arrived because it was so magical to me, and it was not just a matter of receiving presents, which were, of necessity, few and inexpensive in our circumstances. It was rather the pure magic of it all, the birth of the divine child, the visit of the shepherds and the wise men, the stars sparkling above in the beautiful night sky—it was a truly holy night. It was always breathtaking to me, and I somehow felt that this was a larger and truer reality than the normal, everyday one, more real in a strange way. It always struck a chord very deep within me, touching on what I now know are the archetypal depths, of which I knew nothing then, but which I was fated to experience one day as actualities of wider and truer reality.

I had a dream just a couple of nights ago in which I was a young boy of about four or five years of age again, just coming into life and beginning to learn about it, finding it all magical and wonderful. This may sound rather sentimental, but the dream was deadly serious and had an important message. In the dream I had this wonderful feeling, and I hold hands with my sister as we sing the old hymn, "There's a Friend for Little Children above the Bright Blue Sky." I then realized, in the dream, that at that early age God was certain and unquestioned to me, and was there in His Heaven, making life and reality immensely secure. It was the loss of God later, and all that He represents (that higher, magical reality), as I reached adulthood, that brought all the insecurity and disturbance in my life.

That is another reason why the material treasures of the world never meant a great deal to me; they cannot soothe and quell that inner insecurity, that longing for the state of mind I knew as a child. This is not a wish to return to childhood in any way, but of reaching a state of mind again, a state of being, that sees reality in the same breathtaking and magical way because that is its true nature.

We lose so much when we leave childhood that should be found again, though in a higher, more mature way, and this must involve the spirit in some form. Behind all outer, material reality lies the hidden mystery of existence, the divine source, the magic fountain of healing that is able to restore true health and security to both the individual and society, and if we search for it and have luck, we may even find it. I know that now, but it was many long years before I did.

Jung says somewhere that the authority of the personal father over us as children should be replaced by the authority of God over us when we become adults. He could have added that the magical, fantasy world of fairy stories that we know as children should be replaced by the irrational stories of myth and the magical symbols of religion when we become adults, so that we step easily from a childhood reality that is not chained entirely to gross matter into an adult one that is similarly free.

This step has always happened with man until our neurotic and dissociated modern times, when we grow up to a society that has everything to offer but the magic of myth and the miracle of religion. This is a very severe lessening of the meaningful reality we are meant to inhabit, and so we should not be too surprised when we display all sorts of neurotic and psychotic symptoms that eventually drive us and our culture into soulless chaos.

I eventually left school at the age of fifteen, still happy and enthusiastic about life, but with an ever-growing thirst for learning that the string of mundane jobs, from office to shop work, from frying potato chips to digging ditches, could do nothing to satisfy. I had a love of the arts, though chiefly for the traditional forms, and I also loved history and somehow felt grounded in centuries past.

Nevertheless, my greatest love was philosophy—though not necessarily what modern man means by the term. To me, it meant that hidden meaning behind life itself, involving religion in the wider sense, and therefore wisdom in some way, though I naturally knew very little about these things and certainly lacked whatever wisdom is. The very word "wisdom" always stirred something deep in me, starting a warm, spreading glow. Nevertheless, being young and energetic and fresh to life, I was naturally drawn to the outer world, and this preoccupation mostly dominated at that time.

As the next few years passed, though it was all very vague at first, I came to feel progressively lost and insecure, the need for deeper meaning growing stronger and more definite the more I failed to find it, until it all developed into the great passion of my inner life, eventually coming to dominate everything else. Though the gradual loss of God and meaning was impelling me to find a way to soothe the ache and fill the gap, a thirst for wisdom and truth for their own sakes had grabbed solidly hold of me, and I fully realized that this could not be quenched by any mundane answers or material rewards.

However, though very shy by nature, my outer personality enjoyed going to the pubs and after a few drinks meeting the girls, and this was always such a welcome escape from my unhappy working life. I perhaps appeared more or less the same as other young people I mixed with. Furthermore, I was a good dancer and even won a dancing competition, and so with this and many other activities, my outer life was not always devoid of pleasure and satisfaction. But I knew by then that I was carrying a great disturbance within myself, part of my powerful secret inner life that the other young people did not seem to have, nor the older ones, come to that. At least, if they did, it did not seem to trouble them, for they were carried away with the ordinary things of life and with the crowd in a way that I could not be. Having these very deep inner problems eventually set me apart, and I knew it only too well.

Still, I managed to mask it and went on dates like the rest, but as time passed, I came to feel more isolated and alone, my inner search for deeper meaning growing correspondingly stronger, and it came to dominate my life. As for the girls, I always felt a certain warmth for them, as well as a very strong physical attraction, but then I have always had great admiration for womankind generally, though my shyness, sensitivity, and inner disturbance were very much of a problem in actual relationships.

I liked to be alone at times because I could ponder the deeper truths, the possibility of God, His possible nature, as well as the possibility of His non-existence. I recall walking along the street, aged about sixteen, very surprised to have suddenly realized that the majority of people do not reflect every day about God and the nature of truth as I did. In fact, it was the first time that I became aware that I actually did this myself, every day, and even when the time came that I lost belief in all spiritual reality, even in the wider sense, I still reflected frequently and deeply upon these things.

However, this was later. In the meantime, my studies and searchings were not giving me answers that were in any way satisfactory. Though I particularly appreciated Tolstoy, Dostoyevsky, and Dickens—the latter being a far more serious writer on the religious problem of man than he is usually given credit for—for their warnings of what would happen to man if he should surrender his soul to atheism, scientific rationalism, and business worship, they gave me nothing more substantial than their own ideas and beliefs. These were interesting and perfectly true, and certainly more valid than most philosophers of the last couple of hundred years, but I needed more.

Modern philosophy bored and depressed me, and still does, with its materialistic stance, splitting of hairs, and big words to cover holes as big as craters. A couple of years ago, I thumbed through a seven-hundred page book of modern philosophy after searching the comprehensive index trying to find the word "wisdom," but could discover no trace of it.

Though love of wisdom is the very essence and meaning of philosophy, the modern form of official philosophy is little more than a dissociated split-off, like music without the melody, which is what modern "music" is, of course. So although I felt myself to be a lover of philosophy, I hated the modern variety. Of the older variety, I liked Plato, Heraclitus, and Spinoza, though they did nothing to soothe the ache or halt the growing sense of threatening chaos that I felt welling up from within.

Gradually, as the years passed, I fell more and more into my lost and neurotic state, doubts and fears replacing to a large extent the optimism and hope that I had felt when younger, and although nothing I studied helped, I suppose I educated myself to a degree, if it can be called that. I now came increasingly to mostly negative conclusions concerning the ultimate questions, for while a child of eight could point out to you the impossibilities of orthodox religion if taken literally, I had also come to lose belief in spiritual truth in the wider sense.

Of course, and as said above, I was not engrossed in negative moods all of the time, but these had come to dominate, and formed my total world view. I eventually became what I can only call a negative personality, seeing no real meaning to the life process, and as with the German philosopher Nietzsche, this loss of soul made all the difference to my already depressed mental condition.

Like Nietzsche, I realized only too well that you cannot say, "God is dead" in the same way and with the same meaning as you say, "The fly on the floor is dead," for with the death of God, rivers flow upstream and dry up, mountains shake violently and crumble to dust, worlds rotate contrary-wise and explode, and stars wail and finally blacken out. Man is then lost and alone in the middle of meaningless eternity, the one hope for real meaning gone, and as Nietzsche says with trembling emotion, "Gods too decompose. God is dead. God remains dead. And we have killed him." I cannot say at what moment I finally lost God, but it was a gradual process, and some time later, when I first began to find my answer, an old teacher of mine, a religious man, appeared in a dream and asked of me, "You poor boy, don't you have God?"

Yet despite feeling inwardly shaky and unsound in what had now become a cold and soulless universe, I nevertheless found a little security in the past for a time, for man has undoubtedly produced some beautiful and worthwhile things, though inversely, human history is nevertheless overflowing with cruelty, brutality, and stupidity. But it was very depressing to me to see the old culture forms and values gradually being abandoned in the modern world, for they were not being replaced by others of a more positive nature, or even by any at all.

I could feel in my bones that the loss of culture and positive values in society—which meant, therefore, the beginnings of chaos—were due at bottom to the same causes responsible for the deep disturbance within myself, for that same loss of God and loss of meaning. As with society, reality had become mere materiality to me now. Though it was not in the usual manner we apply the term "materialist," for while a successful banker or businessman would probably be happy enough in his state of atheistic materialism, my own condition was by now beginning to break me up, causing a deep fear, and it was certainly starting to make me ill.

When the "permissive society" and the new "pop culture" hit Britain in the 1960s, I again felt a deep inner disturbance, due partly to my own conscious thoughts perhaps, but I felt these more strongly as effects from the lower collective depths of the unconscious. I was always extremely sensitive to this sort of thing. (German expressionist art of the early twentieth century always upset me, which I now know is because it expresses that chaos of soul which produces holocausts. I felt it shudder through me long before I knew precisely why.) I knew that the culture shift in the sixties meant a movement towards chaos, rather than towards the construction of new foundations or further development of the old ones. The new permissive age, with its discord and its non-music (dis-chord?), was joining the ranks of modern art with its disintegration and destruction of forms, and I felt the basic instability of the new permissive age like a cold, chilling draft.

It all fell in line with Nietzsche's predictions that with the death of God and religious forms, mankind would suffer a giant fall, and art itself would die. This is why he felt it was imperative for a new type of man to be constructed. The trouble is, his Superman, "beyond good and evil" and compassion, is an aberration of what any normal human individual should be, let alone a Superman, so God help the world if such a monstrosity is ever produced.

Nietzsche also came up with his theories of will to power, "yea-saying," and ecstatic abandonment, though, mostly unconsciously, he was gripped by the pagan spirit of Wotan that was beginning to resurge at that time in Germany. Losing the spirit, he endeavored to glorify matter, not as an unemotional scientist might do, but rather as a dancing Earth-worshipper lost in the ecstasy of abandonment.

But I knew none of this at the time. I felt only a deep emotional reaction to certain trends, and not being very wise and finding no answers, I eventually sank into a morose and very negative state. The truth is, I always hated and feared the forces of disintegration, whether in art, society, or anything else, and I could see those forces at work in the modern world to a large extent. Science had spent the twentieth century, following on from the nineteenth, dissecting reality and reducing everything down to its constituent parts, so that a creature or an object is not what it is, but is what it consists of, the sum total of its parts. In this way, reality slips away from us because nothing is real, as it can be reduced to its parts, and those parts, in turn, can be reduced to their parts, and so on.

I personally felt, partly as a reaction to all of this, a definite need to find or to reach the other extreme, where the whole of something is the truth of it, possessing a quality and a reality that the mere sum of its accumulated parts does not. I was to learn years later that the processes of the unconscious, and life itself, strive to reach a state of wholeness that was laid down from the beginning of time. In this way, the whole state is the true one, possessing a quality and a reality that all of its added parts do not. As an old man, Jung spoke of the need for art that is infused with a "whole-making spirit," adding that he could not bear to look at modern art any more with its themes of disintegration. That is precisely how I felt, long years before I knew anything of Jung and the unconscious.

However, this did not prevent me from viewing nature from the lowest and most negative aspect. The one law of life was obviously the survival of the fittest, where the big fish swallow the little fish, and though I was merely a little fish myself, it was as bad, or worse, to be the big fish. There was no worthwhile nobility of existence in any of this. All I could see now was that life on Earth survives by devouring other life, which is not a very pleasant basis for a world life-system, and which is, in fact, quite ugly when you think about it, which I constantly did. I reached the stage where the whole universe seemed cold, cruel, stark, threatening, and pointless. Who wants to get up in the morning to such a reality?

Yet all of this is perfectly valid; this is how a reality without God and any real higher meaning should make us feel. Nietzsche realized it only too well, and finding no immediate answer or remedy, tumbled into years of nihilistic despair. He proclaimed "God is dead" in some of the most emotionally poetic words ever written, for he knew the devastating effect this would have upon man and culture. I had always asked the same questions as Nietzsche, and felt the same fears, concerning not only the existence of God, but of the validity or non-validity of truth and morality in eternity. I therefore felt that he and I were close in certain ways, and that was the crux of it, apart from the question of God's existence.

Are truth, morality, and compassion valid in eternity, or are they only provisional and expedient in Man's somewhat ephemeral existence? If the latter, this would mean ultimately that there is no real solid foundation for our morality and compassion, for they would not be lasting values in themselves. Nietzsche concluded that, like God, they exist only while Man believes in them, which is why he believed we can go beyond them, taking God's place as amoral (which really means immoral) gods ourselves.

Nietzsche called himself a yea-sayer, but he was really a nay-sayer, for he said no to any extension beyond physical and biological existence, to any otherworldly reality. I could see that Nietzsche's ideas were highly dangerous, leading in the end to the total collapse of truth and morality upon which all true civilization must rest, and to which it must aspire. Yet I believed, and feared, that he may well be right, and this is why I had no solid ground beneath my feet. If we watch a movie where in the end the bad guys and evil win, it leaves us with a bad taste in our mouths, for we feel instinctively that right and justice must be substantiated in the end—the same goes for truth, morality, and compassion—as eternal values.

If Nietzsche is right, it would mean that all the best of existence, of reality itself, has no permanence and ultimately fades to nothingness, and is therefore an illusion. God, truth, morality, compassion, even love, could not then be solid, lasting foundations, either for individuals or for culture as a whole. They could only be provisional, and this is why I was relentlessly impelled, against hope, to search for values that *cannot* fade, even in eternity. So again, Nietzsche and I were completely absorbed with the same fundamental problems, though whereas he was fated to deny the eternal things, I was trying desperately to establish them. (Which I managed to do eventually.)

In other words, I had to find an answer to Nietzsche and all the other materialists, but not just a set of beliefs; rather, something definite that can be experienced and proved, and which Armageddon itself cannot even vaguely wobble. In a sense, it boils down to the reestablishment of the secure childhood state, but on a higher level.

When we are children the world around us seems permanent, as though it will never change. The values of our parents, those we are taught at school, those we learn at church or in the tribal mythos, those we pick up from society in our framework of orientation, all seem right and everlasting to us. Then we grow up and begin to question all we formerly took as right and lasting, coming to realize that many things do indeed change and are not as permanent as we believed.

However, as Jung says, the permanent values that myth and religion teach normally provide solid foundations in eternity that sustain both ourselves and our culture. At least, this is the case as long as the myth holds, which may nevertheless be for thousands of years. But modern Western man lost his myth; not because it is basically untrue, not because it is old and outworn, but because he never understood it. It is our understanding of our religious heritage, of its meaning, that is old and outworn, not religion itself. The Higher Self, evidence of which will be featured throughout this book, is immortal, being ultimately son of the Great Mother and of God, and being timeless, cannot be outworn. So again, it is our understanding of this phenomenon in the West, always on the simplest of levels, that must be updated and greatly widened.

The ancient Egyptians are instructive in this. They placed tremendous emphasis on the goddess and concept of Maat, wisdom, truth, righteousness, and right order, not just in their society, but throughout the whole universe as the very basis of reality itself. They knew the tremendous power of chaos and the forces of destruction. They knew that it is of no use for man himself to try to establish Maat on the merely human level, as we today try to establish culture on mere intellectual concepts. The gods themselves had to live in Maat because such is eternal law, and only if Maat ruled throughout the whole of infinity and eternity, could society and culture ever be stable.

The Hebrew prophets felt exactly the same in their great insistence upon fundamental righteousness, which meant not only the people leading decent individual lives, but the establishment of universal right order that came from God. This too was the essence of ancient Egyptian culture. Yet it is these things that Nietzsche pulled down, eternal truth and morality, and indeed, God Himself, smashing the old tablets and values.

And here was I, a shy, nervous young man, uneducated in the normal way, but burdened with the enormous problem of the death of these things, trying desperately to reestablish them—not merely in myself, not merely in my society, but in and throughout the whole of reality itself.

The old movies, books, and so forth that had formed part of my framework of orientation as I grew up, had Maat to a tremendous degree. Disorder and evil come to threaten, otherwise there could be no movie, but Maat is reestablished by the end because that is the natural order of things throughout reality. Nobody says this; it is just automatically taken to be so. Part of my problem now was that not only could I see it slipping away from modern life, but I feared deep down that Nietzsche could have the truth of it. I was to learn later by direct experience that Nietzsche was wrong on almost all counts, as I hope my book will demonstrate, but he was right concerning the devastating effects of the death of God and the loss of truth that is eternal, and in his perception that man would suffer a massive fall into chaos as a consequence. Nietzsche did at least see that much.

On the one hand, I merely wanted everything to be right—in Maat as it had been when I was a boy—so that I could get on with my life; but on the other, I realized that a human life is a mere moment in eternity, suddenly conscious and aware, baffled and alone. Who and what am I? What is this I am part of? What is its meaning, if any?

The average, intelligent person asks these questions, but with me it meant everything, for everything depended upon the answers—if there were any. Nevertheless, I gradually sank lower and lower into a morass until all I could see was the cruelty of nature and of life, and as a reaction I even strove for a time to be unfeeling, believing that it was necessary to be hard and callous in order to survive, as Nietzsche had partly suggested.

In reality, it is in this way we destroy what is best in the human personality, denying the soul its right to develop in beauty and light. Life at the level of man needs the higher qualities of love, compassion, and humility in order to develop and expand in a way that it otherwise cannot. Had Nietzsche's Superman possessed these qualities then he would have been not so much a Superman as a worthwhile human being, and that would have been sufficient. St. Francis of Assisi was not a Superman, just very humble and human, and therein lay his greatness. Had Nietzsche understood this, in all probability he would not have become insane, for he would not have become so inflated that his mind burst.

I recently came across something that I wrote all those years ago as a young man, and I will quote a small part of it here as it reveals plainly my deeper thoughts at that time:

We are born, we live out our brief life spans, we die. This is the fate of all living creatures. Even so-called dead matter has its cycle of existence/non existence. The great question is, does life have any meaning beyond the mere fulfillment of the needs of everyday existence? This is not to belittle the great struggle it often is just to stay alive, but human beings, due to their ever-increasing conscious awareness, are only beginning to live when their basic physical needs have been satisfied.

As I sit here writing this, my dog is lying stretched out on the floor in front of the fire. He has no need or desire for meaning, for deep purpose, because his level of conscious awareness is much lower than mine. He does not need answers because his mind does not and cannot ask questions. So which of us is the more fortunate, I or the dog?

If I can find lasting significance for all existing things then higher consciousness will become the greatest of blessings. But, if I cannot, then consciousness is a curse, life is a sick joke, and he may have been better had man not come into being. Then I envy not only the dog, but perhaps more so the wooden floor upon which it lies, for as far as I know, wooden floors do not have to think and feel at all, even less so than dogs, and they too do not have to ask these questions. Already this search for meaning has taken me into many subjects, or taken me further into them, and into many facets of life, and though to a degree these subjects are enjoyable in their own right, they have not as yet led me to any real meaning. The search gives a degree of meaning, though it is a sort of substitute meaning, a substitute for real meaning itself, and so ultimately does not satisfy.

I remember reading Victor Frankl's *Man's Search for Meaning* in which the psychologist tells of prisoners (himself and others) in the Nazi concentration camps. He says that the ones best able to survive were those who had—or could find— some meaning in all of the suffering. Even those who could only force themselves to go on because of hatred for their persecutors and the consequent need for revenge, had found at least temporary purpose. All of this is quite understandable in the special or abnormal circumstances of the horrors of the concentration camps, but what about when life returns to what we call the normal? Hatred and vengeance are then no longer a means to substitute meaning, and we once again have to extend our horizons to search deeper, higher, and wider.

All my life, even as a young boy, I have sat looking up at the night sky, watching the stars. It has always given me a wonderful feeling, and I somehow know that great meaning is there. Yet at other times, when I am merely reflecting upon universal truth, not looking up at the stars, the universe then seems cold and threatening. It is a strange contradiction, and perhaps one day I shall find the answer to this puzzle.

These were, to me, the great questions and problems that dominated my thinking and engulfed my young adult life. I had as yet found no answers, and before I could, I was to reach—and perhaps *needed* to reach—the depths of despair, culminating in my nervous breakdown. I well remember the day when everything came to a crisis point as I walked along a busy street. I felt so distraught and in a state of panic that I just had to try and get home to escape from the world. As I walked in an increasing state of shock, all of the negative side of life became magnified in my mind, so that all I could think of were carnivorous animals devouring their prey, and human beings as brutal ape-men. I could see it all in my head, so to speak, it seeming to be the only real truth of life. I felt really ill and traumatized, though I still tried to act as calmly and as normal as possible. Finally I arrived home, but though it was a great relief to be off the street, I still felt broken up and anguished inside. Anyone who has suffered this state himself will know just how horrible and devastating it is.

That night, as I sat trying to watch television, the figures started to come out of the screen and into the room, so that I was forced to close my eyes tightly to shut them out, though I could not shut off the horrible feeling of being torn apart inside. No words can convey the torture of the fragmentation that I felt. I was breaking up and was frightened and lost, not frightened in a physical way, but afraid of my own thoughts. I could not face so ugly a reality and feel such anguish any longer. I somehow made it to bed and lay in the darkness, closing my eyes tightly again, not wanting to look at the world, even though I was lying in darkness. And then it occurred to me that that was the answer. If I were blind, then I would not have to face any of it again; it would be blessed release from my suffering.

So I prayed to go blind, and meant it from the bottom of my heart. I kept praying and praying for it, and even if there were no God, I hoped I could perhaps bring about the blindness by psychosomatic means. I knew that people can bring on all sorts of illnesses unconsciously in this way, so maybe I could do so consciously. I finally fell asleep hoping and praying for my wish to be granted, and then had the most frightening nightmares. But when I awoke, I found that I could see as plainly as ever.

Obviously, if a person seriously wishes blindness upon themselves they must be in a state of much suffering, and that was indeed the case. It may seem from all of this that I am just a morose and negative sort of person who merely concentrates on the gloomy aspects of existence. That is not the case at all, and the opposite is actually the true situation. I had loved life and believed in it so much as a child and young adolescent, yet later, when I could find no real meaning and permanence and feared that life had no true and solid foundations, everything began to slip away nonetheless.

The real basis of my illness was that very same fall into the bog of matter that has afflicted modern man, though he seems largely unaware of it. If there is only material reality, then man is no more than an animal, and the basis of animal life is the devouring of other forms of life in order to survive. I am a lover of animals and this is not any sort of condemnation of animal nature itself, but we are all caught up in the same brutal process, though only man knows it due to his more highly developed consciousness. Yet because of this, man can reach up and know the truth of the spirit as no other creature can; man can know God, and can know his own soul.

Without desiring it or even thinking about it too much, the debased purview of life, of mere animal existence in a universe that is matter only, became the basis of reality for Western man in the twentieth century, replacing the higher, nobler belief in God and spiritual causation that man had always known. It was a total switch from something beautiful and meaningful to something ugly and meaningless. Of even greater significance, as I was to discover, is the fact that it was the switch to a *false* way of thinking, and to a very dangerous one too.

I saw psychiatrists during and after my breakdown, but, most modern psychiatry and psychology being on the same shallow level as modern philosophy, they understood nothing of the real cause of my problems, and their sole resource was drugs. They had no inkling that the sickness of the individual may be connected to (and have the same basic cause as) the sickness of the culture. Society is after all composed of individuals, and the way they think and act determines the nature of the culture.

Of course my personal circumstances were involved to a degree; I hated the thought of working in an office or factory for the rest of my life because it was like being contained in a small, stifling box. I needed to exist in a wider, fuller reality, connected with the things I was always studying, and so I felt extremely frustrated. It was not a question of financial needs at all, for I have always been content to live frugally—a can of baked beans is all I need for a meal, if necessary. It was always food for the soul that I craved.

Furthermore, I always liked the people I worked with—decent working class ones as it happened—but I could not share my deeper thoughts or needs with them. So while the very limiting conditions of my personal life did play a small part in my breakdown, they were not by any means the main cause. I can now happily dig ditches because I have the spiritual treasures of the unconscious, whereas if I lost them and gained great worldly wealth, I would nonetheless be utterly desolate.

After my breakdown I managed to pull myself up and improve somewhat, despite the doctors, though this was due to time the healer more than anything else. I suppose people I knew considered me more or less returned to health, but the true picture of my inner state was an entirely different story. Depression and a type of fear still engulfed me, for my well being depended on so much more than my mere personal problems. The truth is, I fully realized that while I could not be truly well in a sick and meaningless universe, I could far better be sick in a healthy and meaningful one, for that would be no more than our illnesses as children when we recover in a happy, secure home. I realized the consequences for mankind as a whole, as well as for myself, if the mysteries of the soul and of God are mere illusions, if truth and morality are merely provisional. Then, life is ultimately a sick joke and the world a madhouse.

I read Freud at this time and he depressed me so much that I still wonder how he ever cured anyone. Maybe he didn't. Maybe his patients just became used to their problems and managed to readjust and to cope to a degree. This often happens. But Freud's insistence on a sexual basis to all problems of the human psyche, and to life itself, and the consequent denial of spirit and soul, must have done harm to many of his patients. Indeed, the main problem of modern man is that he has become far too possessed by sexuality and other forms of materiality, so that his soul is forced to rebel in utter despair.

I found Freud's reductionism far worse than Nietzsche's, for while the latter did at least *ask* religious questions, trying to find a greater answer than mere man himself, Freud declared all such ponderings neurotic, infantile, and essentially futile. Freud could not have cured me had I been his patient, though he may well have killed me, pushing me over the edge. I needed precisely the opposite, not only to his theories on the human mind, but to his views on the whole of reality itself. It is true that I came to find the answer to my great problem largely through dreams, and that Freud's world-renowned first work was *The Interpretation of Dreams*, but there any similarity ends.

My family was always close-knit, and so was a marvelous haven in which to find some comfort during my "sick period," allowing me to lick my wounds. I was living with my parents and brother, and they, very decent, caring people, tried to help me as much as they could. Nevertheless, I could not share the fundamental causes of my malady with them. I knew that in the end I could only sort out my great problems myself, though it involved sorting out God and the whole universe to accomplish this.

I also had a lifelong friend, who died just a couple months ago. While I am deeply introverted by nature, he was a great extrovert, loving and living life to the full. While he was always there as a friend, he was too busy living life to question it too deeply, and so I kept my own deepest questions, worries, and fears to myself. We were like heads and tails of the same coin, of the same personality, but while he went to extremes in the outer world, I was fated to eventually explore the unknown depths of the inner one.

One further thing I should mention is that for years a terrible feeling of dread would suddenly overwhelm me, and this often occurred when I encountered most modern art, philosophy, music, and architecture. I recall standing before the shelves of the philosophy and psychology section in my local library, and the thought of the contents of some of the books brought on such sudden, terrible emotion that I wanted to scream at the top of my voice. I always knew somehow that the real cause of these attacks was the nature of modern reality itself, what we have made of it, and I now know that I was experiencing the collective neurosis, the acute psychic dissociation, of modern man—getting the full blast, so to speak.

One of the best expressions of this in art is Edward Munch's painting *The Scream*, where an eerie, phantom-like figure, with round sockets for eyes and mouth, has his hands at his cheeks to cry out in neurotic, agonized despair. Munch himself suffered a nervous breakdown not long after he painted the picture, and the painting reveals why. Jung speaks of "the whole-making spirit," that synthesizes opposites into harmony, and great art is full of this, expressing health and vibrancy. Only dissociated modern man could produce the art of chaos, pay vast sums of money to acquire it, and hang it up on the wall to admire it. Yet the collective unconscious works in opposition to chaos, its one desire being to synthesize all opposites into wholeness and harmony. This is why the true holy man, who has united all opposites within himself, within the Higher Self and within God, lives in a state of perfect peace.

Writer Colin Wilson says that many creative people have experienced the terrible, fearful attacks that once assailed me, driving certain nineteenth century Romantics to even commit suicide. But it is a fairly modern phenomenon, arising with Western man's spiritual dissociation and capture in the embrace of matter. What I was to experience in the years that followed, as I explored the depths of the unconscious through dreams, eventually healed the neurotic dissociation within myself, even though the collective neurosis of Western civilization not only remains, but is becoming an even more dangerous psychosis.

My grandfather, who served in the trenches in France during the first World War, seeing many true horrors, always remarked that you can get used to anything, even to the horrors of the trenches, and that is what happened with myself. I got used to my depressed state so that it seemed normal, going hand in hand with the rest of depressing reality. Nevertheless, two events, connected to a large degree, were about to occur that not only changed my life completely, but the whole of reality itself. I was to eventually learn that miracles do happen and that all I had lost since childhood would be restored, though in a far higher way now. I was to learn that wisdom, truth, love, and all that we hold (or did hold) as noble and good are indeed eternal values in God. Though counter-matched by their negative aspects as well, mine were quite contrary to Nietzsche's conclusions. It was a long while before my transformation took place, and I had to travel a deep, dangerous, and sometimes tortu-ous path for many years, but it eventually happened, all stemming from two events.

As to the first, I sat watching television one Sunday evening, trying to recover from a heavy hangover. I was drinking heavily at the time as an escape from my woes, and for solace. A program came on about Jung and his work. This was the first of two hour-long programs by Laurens van der Post, the writer who had known Jung for some years. I had vaguely heard of Jung though knew very little of his work, but from the beginning of the program I was hooked, and when film footage was shown of Jung himself, I was mesmerized.

All my adult life I had been vaguely aware of a "wise old man" fig-ure within my depths, connected with the wisdom that I mentioned ear-lier, and I would sometimes unconsciously doodle him on scraps of paper—at times he was the only comfort I had in my darkness—and now he seemed to be here before me in the figure of Jung on the televi-sion screen. Jung spoke enthusiastically of the spirit and of the soul as living realities, but it was not just his words that sank into me. It was also the way his eyes sparkled, the way he spoke, even the shape of his head. Something immensely profound and somehow wonderful was tak-ing place, and although I could not have known it then, at least con-sciously, it was the beginning of something great for myself.

After this experience, I acquired a couple of Jung's books from my local library, though I had to request them, as there were none on the shelves. When the books finally arrived, I found much of the material difficult to understand, but I persevered and was struck by his basic pos-itive attitude, not only to his subject of depth psychology, but to reality itself. It was quite different from other authors I had been reading on these subjects for some years, in particular Nietzsche, Freud, and the modern philosophers I mentioned earlier. Jung was completely opposite to these, and was nothing less than a revelation to me.

Colin Wilson once compared my first encounter with Jung to St. Paul being struck down by his vision on the road to Damascus, and that pretty well describes it. Fairly soon I realized that I would have to study all of Jung's works in depth, hoping that one day I would be able to understand more fully, but it was something positive and even breathtaking to aim at with the rest of my life—a life's work, in fact. All these years later it still seems somewhat unreal that such good fortune could happen to me, to come to find a way out of my terrible, negative morass. But it did happen, and although it involved much suffering and self-sacrifice, overall my discovery of Jung was nothing less than a miracle.

The second event that was to have a profound effect on my life occurred not too long after the television program on Jung. One night I went into a local pub with a friend and saw a young woman working there who affected me in the same mesmerizing way as Jung had. Jung says that fate sometimes arranges these events when we are ready for them, and he may well be right. It certainly seems to have been the case here. Being an intensely shy and nervous man by nature, especially in those days, it was only after a few drinks that I spoke to the woman, and we then exchanged a few pleasant words, and that was it. But something magical had happened to me, and not just the conventional love at first sight, though that may in itself be mesmerizing enough. There was somehow more to it. From that night on I thought about the woman, whom I will call Julie, constantly; she kept invading my thoughts so much that I started going to the pub a few nights of the week just to see her.

Gradually, I got to know her better, and she fascinated me in a way that no other woman ever had. Before long I realized I was falling for her. The trouble was, she possessed all the wrong attitudes and values—though that was part of the fascination—and said all the wrong things, which belied her beautiful and very gentle looks. I had met people with her low, almost non-existent values before, but with her it was different. It was as though she should not have been that way, but had become possessed by a sickness and a madness that was causing her to act completely opposite to her true nature. Or perhaps it was because I had fallen for her that her lack of right values made her appear possessed. Whatever the case, I was captivated—or should I say captured?

I came to learn—as she eventually confided to me—that she was secretly the girlfriend of a local businessman, and the fact that he was married did not worry her in the slightest. In today's world this is not unusual, but this was some years ago when standards were a little higher, so that if a woman did go with a married man, or vice versa, it

21

was mostly for deeper feelings, rather than just for kicks. However, in Julie's case it seemed that she was immoral by nature and had no conscience, not just over this affair, but generally, and the businessman was not her first married lover and apparently would not be her last.

This would not have concerned me at all with any other woman, and I was not altogether an innocent when it came to women myself, but there was something numinous and magical here. Julie had such a beautiful, angelic face that it all seemed like the corruption of an angel, or of the Virgin Mary herself. Something was wrong and upside-down somewhere, and that is what intrigued me partly, though I was also shocked and disappointed because of my feelings for her.

In my search for meaning, to find solid foundations to prevent myself and my world from sinking beyond recovery, I had by now become even more deeply involved with the ideas of truth and morality and their eternal validity or otherwise. However, I had taken a somewhat opposite position to Nietzsche, and needed desperately to sustain it. I needed the eternal values that he had rejected to form unshakable foundations, because I realized the danger to both myself and human culture generally if they are entirely lost. This formed a large part of the philosophical framework of reality that I was trying to develop as a sort of unassailable fortress, and to me, every action had become a moral question, or had strong moral implications. Is it right or is it wrong? Not just, "is it profitable?" or "does it give pleasure?"

It seemed to me that we must ask the moral question in a state of higher conscious awareness, and that it is our obligation to do so, and that the stability of culture depends largely upon it. This is one of the reasons we have developed higher consciousness, to build more worthwhile personal lives, and indeed, whole civilizations, to rise above animal selfishness and self-seeking, and to bring right and justice to the world.

But Julie now brought the whole business, the problems that both Nietzsche and I had faced, to full prominence and urgency, though she herself was completely oblivious to them. Julie seemed to consider only what was profitable and pleasurable to her personally, here and now. Right and wrong would not enter into it, and it even appeared that she enjoyed sin without scruples, enjoyed the excitement of it. I knew how attractive and exciting forbidden fruit can be to us all, but it threw me off balance with Julie because it seemed so out of place, so unexpected.

I now found myself in another turmoil, and I knew that all that I have spoken of up until now—the philosophical framework, the unassailable fortress of lasting values that I was trying to construct and maintain—would henceforth be under severe attack, and might well topple in this newly arisen situation. I thought I might just say to heck with it all and follow Julie wherever she led, because the attraction was so powerful, so overwhelming, that anything could happen.

Yet it was obvious that Julie would not return my feelings because I was not the type of man she would be interested in. I was a bachelor, and her interest seemed to be married men. And, while I am a philosopher by nature, in the original meaning of the word, and while I knew that I must somehow establish the things I have spoken of, Julie lived her life quite happily without them. She would neither admire nor be attracted to me in what had become my quest; in fact, she was attracted to men of the opposite character, men who were shady dealers, who cheated on their wives—and others—and who would be oblivious to truth even if it pounced on them.

This turmoil added itself to that other feeling of neurotic dissociation I experienced at times. In fact, this new pain was so intense that it replaced, to a degree, everything else. Though I had had strong feelings for women before, they had never been anything like this. It was an upheaval that shot right through to my foundations, and it was even worse than my breakdown. As bad as that had been, the need for truth, for right and wrong, had remained clear to me, whereas now, in my new disturbance, it all became questionable and uncertain. It was not now a case of whether truth and morality are eternal values, but whether I should live by them. The pain became like an unbearable toothache, such that I would do *anything* to get rid of it. Something had to be done.

I go into all of this more deeply with the dream processes that follow, so I will just add briefly here that Julie, although I was unaware of it, was a real life woman upon whom I was projecting my own *anima*, my feminine counterpart in the unconscious. Such a woman always has a magical quality for a man because the anima herself is connected to the eternal archetypes of the unconscious. It is mightily ironic that a woman such as Julie makes an excellent receptacle for such a projection, for it is also such a woman who, though she may never know it, may lead a man to the greatest spiritual truths, and even to God directly—the very things I had been hitherto seeking.

Julie had activated an archetype of soul within me, on the one side, while Jung had activated an archetype of spirit on the other side, the "wise old man," the "personification of spirit," who exudes hidden knowledge of other planes of being. Jung now became my one hope for all of my seemingly unsolvable problems, and there was no other way for me to go but to follow him into the unconscious processes. So Jung and Julie on the outside, and their archetypal counterparts in the unconscious, formed the classic symbolic pairing of spirit and soul. The "wise old man" and the anima well known to mythology and the Bible, led me eventually to inner transformation. I had found in Jung and Julie an archetypal pair corresponding to Jethro, the "wise old man" who teaches Moses the hidden wisdom, and Zipporah, the anima figure with whom Moses marries, (i.e., unifies). I was now to lead the symbolic life for many years, the quest for the divine essence through the unconscious, the alchemists' Philosopher's Stone, the Holy Grail of medieval Europe, or the ancient archetype of the "god of the four quarters," though I was not aware just what was happening for some time.

It eventually became nothing less than a mission to rebuild Western culture itself on foundations of the values I had experienced. If I can experience transformation through these processes, then so too can other people—the whole of society, in fact. This was not a conscious intention for some years, but was rather the hidden intention of the unconscious itself. This is the meaning of the Grail quest, for the Fisher King's sick Kingdom must be respiritualized to be restored to health. However, I was not altogether successful in my quest at the final stage, though the fight still continues, but this is true of almost all who attempt the quest, for which of us is perfect? And yet, if enough people aim for the goal and come close, then Western culture may indeed be renewed, and the "evolution of the religious spirit" that Jung speaks of may take place.

It was at this point that I began to study my dreams. There was no other way for me to go but inwardly, for I did not have God and eternal values, and I certainly did not have Julie, so I was in deeper desperation than ever. But I did have Jung and my newly discovered unconscious, and if the outer world gave me no answers and seemed to constantly cause me suffering, perhaps the inner world would be a different matter.

I knew it was dangerous, and Jung warns us not to try to make the inner journey alone, but I was so desperate, so unhappy, and so lost that

I was willing to risk all danger. I even sat down and wrote a letter to the unconscious, informing it that I was coming down to its depths. I wanted to start the ball rolling, and it worked. This is where my dream processes, my quest, begin, and I was eventually led to the greatest truths possible, the record of which follows shortly. But first I have one or two further things about this book to explain, and one more biographical fact.

I was still living with my parents and brother, though things now became changed-around, as it were. I had been the sick one, but now my mother suffered two heart attacks that disabled her, my father developed emphysema which eventually killed him, and my brother also had a very severe nervous breakdown, from which he never fully recovered. This should have placed us in an impossible position, and yet by this time I was feeling some of the healing effects of the individuation processes, and I found that it gave me such strength that I could look after us all, even the dog.

It is impossible to say just how much reality was changed for me, though I hope the dreams that follow will demonstrate it. Later, I developed physical illness, due to hereditary weakness mostly, and still the effects of archetypal reality continued to sustain me, inspiring me to write this book. For if we strive in the unconscious and in our lives for the things which Nietzsche denied eternal validity—wisdom, truth, humility, love, morality—then the unconscious pays us back in kind.

My own dream processes cover a period of over twenty years and comprise at least 14,000 dreams. Out of these I have chosen some of the most highly symbolical and meaningful, although all dreams have meaning, no matter how seemingly trivial. Not only are dreams messages from the personal unconscious, they also connect us to the collective unconscious, that other reality of spirit and soul existing behind the material universe, extending to infinity and eternity, and even to God Himself.

Jung established beyond all doubt that processes involving the collective unconscious may produce the Higher Self (or written simply as capitalized "Self"), and that this figure, at its highest level and fullest meaning, is, or may equal, the Anthropos or "Christ within" of the Gnostics, the Son of Man figure of the Biblical prophets, ultimately the Son of God. As I say throughout the book, the phenomenon has been known since earliest times across the world, at various levels of development and understanding, and we find a large amount of evidence for it in the myths and religions of history.

Alchemy, for example, with the many names for its ultimate treasure, including the philosophical gold, the elixir, the Philosopher's Stone, and the *filius macrocosmi* (son of the macrocosm) was mostly a development of the lower Spirit of Mercurius. Then, certain alchemists found to their amazement that this paralleled the higher Son, the *filius microcosmi* (son of the microcosm), which led to them positing the lapis-Christ parallel, the paralleling of their "stone" to Christ. Exactly the same happened with the Golden Flower of Chinese alchemy, the mandala that is also a Taoist symbol.

The main symbol of the Higher Self for Western civilization has been Christ, for the last two thousand years, but always as an *outer* phenomenon. It was never realized that the individual human psyche is connected to, and is actually part of, the immortal inner man, and that furthermore, this figure could be experienced at the culmination of certain inner processes. Jung believed fervently that this is the main and most urgent problem facing Western man today, the extremely urgent "evolution of the religious spirit," as he put it. He also said that the West must now follow the East and develop the inner Self, but in the mode of Christ.

He points out that an abyss of difference exists between the ultimate Western religious experience of Christ, the woeful carrier of the cross, and the Golden Flower of the East. It is therefore our future task to develop the Self in the Western form of Christ, in order to bridge the chasm that has grown so wide. If this can be achieved, the state of spiritual enlightenment long known in the East will be attained in the West. This will mean a state of more highly evolved consciousness, which could eventually lead to the respiritualization of Western man (Jung 1968).

As a matter of fact, that is what I became involved in myself, largely without realizing it, as I journeyed further and further through the unconscious, following wherever it led me. The unconscious even informed me in a dream that my record in its depths is phenomenal, and designated me a "trailblazer" and "frontiersman," stating that I had traveled where no man had been before. I am only repeating the statements of the unconscious here, to help prepare the way for what is to follow.

One morning I awoke after a dream, a "night vision," amazed to realize that I had just encountered the Higher Self as a Son of Man figure on the clouds, and further, that he was looking up and addressing God as "Father." This seemed to show that I had accomplished the task described by Jung, the development of the inner man, the Self, the Golden Flower, into a Christ parallel, or even equivalent. Or perhaps I should say that I came very close to accomplishing it, or that I accomplished it for a time but failed to sustain the phenomenon. This was apparently not only the lower Son, the *filius macrocosmi*, but also and primarily, the higher Son, the *filius microcosmi*, as he was clearly Son of the Father.

I should perhaps further explain that while the full and ultimate Self is the supreme totality containing both part of God and part of the World Soul, eternal masculine and feminine spirits within his nature, there is also the lower version of the Self that is of the lower depths alone. This may be positive or negative, depending on which side is brought forth. The son of the lower spirit is only part of the full Higher Self, and is, as said, Son of the Mother, the feminine depths of the unconscious. We find the lower Son in mythology in various forms, but in ancient Egypt, Osiris was the light aspect of this, and his twin, Set, the dark. To the alchemists Mercurius was "son of the Old Great Mother," and he too was dual-natured. The dreams that follow will demonstrate the phenomenon of the Self and how it unfolds.

I had not intended to go so far myself as to develop the Higher Self to full realization, but I should have realized what track I was on because of the extremely meaningful symbolic contents that flowed through during the years of the processes. One of the earlier dreams, in fact, was where a dying Jung asked me what I saw forming out of thin air before my eyes, and when I answered, "Four golden petals," he replied, "Good. It is finished."

I then received four gold keys, on a gold key ring, which I now know meant that I had taken on the task of furthering Jung's work, involving the development of the inner Self, the Golden Flower, into the parallel Christ figure. This was, to some extent, the further development of the royal line, which stretches back through Christ and the Old Testament prophets, to ancient Egypt with their Osiris-Horus experiences. It is imperative that the line be appreciated and continued today, for we have no other real, fundamental foundations upon which to sustain our civilization.

A dream appears later in which a giant-size Jung is above in the air with his arms outstretched to span a river of blue blood. This the royal bloodline of Higher-Self instances that have occurred through the unconscious since earliest times. They involve human initiates developing the inner Self, and on the spirit side amount to incarnations of God. This is why Jesus, or rather the higher Christ, is of the seed of King David—a physical line of worldly kings is not meant, but the line of spirit and soul through the unconscious. The bloodline refers therefore to the spiritual blood, not the mundane.

However, the line became stuck with Christ and was not further developed and continued. The Grail Knights on their quests represent attempts by initiates to develop the line, though they would not have been fully aware of this consciously. The writers of this material must have gone a long way on the quest, but none ever brought forth the Higher Self. The divine child does make brief appearances in the tales, but is not recognized as such and soon fades.

The modern books about the royal bloodline project it all into the world so that the child is the son of Jesus and Mary Magdalene, beginning a bloodline of monarchs of France. But the actual marriage was through the unconscious, and the product was the divine child, Christ, whose kingdom was "not of this world."

As to the four gold keys on the key ring, they form a symbol that is very ancient. It represents the squaring of the circle, the unification of spirit and matter (soul), but there are also associated meanings. The circle is the symbol of spirit, of Heaven, and even of God, while the number four represents matter—the Earth with its four corners or directions. So the unification of these in a symbol means, as said, the marriage of Heaven and Earth. This is seen in the *ankh* cross of the ancient Egyptians, the cross within the circle of the Gnostics, or even Christ upon the cross.

However, the symbol also alludes to unlocking the gateway to the inner mysteries through the unconscious, of spirit/soul reality. A medieval alchemical text states that the door to the treasure is opened with the four keys. These were not said specifically to be gold, whereas the keys that I receive are, so perhaps the meaning for me is even higher than in alchemy. Gold was always the most precious metal of mankind, and so was designated the substance of the gods. The most sacred spiritual symbols were therefore usually fashioned in gold.

All of this may sound very strange and somewhat incredible to those not familiar with depth psychology, and perhaps even to some who are.

Nevertheless, it is now my intention to prove that the Higher Self is a real phenomenon by giving both the evidence of my dream processes and the historical evidence of Higher-Self examples in the royal line that reaches back to ancient Egypt.

Much of the symbolic material reported in this book is what we would call original Christian, (Gnostic, if you like) although the collective unconscious also clearly supports the Church, despite the fact that it is in dire need of further development and renewal. Other material here is alchemical, while "treasure" in ancient Egypt is also frequently referred to, but, all in all, a picture of balanced wholeness within a Christian framework emerges. This is how it was given to me, though I was not a Christian as such at the outset, like the majority of people in the West today.

The foundations of the Church reach back to the original experience of the Higher Self of the man Jesus, the last example as far as we know of the divine incarnation of God on the royal line at that level. There is nothing else in Western culture by which to symbolize this tremendous phenomenon, so the Church, despite its many failings, is still valid and necessary for us as carrier and caretaker of the monumental mystery. The unconscious, and the spirit realm itself, clearly see Christianity and the Church as representing the divine drama adequately, and even excellently, though the processes of the lower depths are nevertheless largely missing from dogma. This, partly, is what my own unconscious processes compensate and restore. But as Jung says, if the West loses the Christian mystery, rather than understanding, renewing, and transforming it, then the West will fall into a barbarism and chaos that will eventually destroy it.

The dreams, as will be seen, take the path of the archetypal hero and his quest, and they go all the way to direct experience of God Himself. As we know, historically anyone who claims to have had experience of God has always been under the gravest suspicion of charlatanism or insanity. The world ever abounds with false prophets and rogue messiahs, but it is mostly the genuine ones who are given a hard time of it, and even Moses moaned to God that the people will never believe that the Lord has spoken to him. However, my dream processes, though religious texts in the truest sense, are nevertheless also scientific investigations, experienced and studied under the most stringent rules and conditions, for safety's sake as much as for anything else. I am, furthermore, quite sure that nothing that appears in them would fail to have Jung's fullest support and approval.

The Higher Self in ultimate form usually occurs at critical times in history, when the living spirit is fading or dying, and when the people are lost and falling into all sorts of ailing states, from nervous breakdowns to moral degeneracy and corruption. At such a time, the worst side of man comes out, and may gradually destroy the culture. Then, an appropriate human being is chosen in whom God can incarnate. Many persons may be tried before one extra-special individual is found. When the divine incarnation is accepted by the people, there is renewed growth and a flowering of culture, and all over the world there are myths of the figures who bring this about, Horus/Osiris, Marduk, Quetzalcoatl, Vishnu, Kwan Shi Yin, Oannes, Christ, and so forth. When he is denied, however, and the contact with eternal spirit broken, the disease sets in, and a great flood of filth and evil from the negative unconscious realm deluges the land hence the flood legends around the world.

Kwan Shi Yin was chiefly male originally, though he had his feminine side. He was "Self manifested," "Son of the Father," "The Universal Savior of all living beings," the "Son identical with his Father," all marking him out as the Higher Self. He was also known as Kwan Shai Yin and Kwan Yin, but the latter usually referred to the feminine side. Later in China, this feminine side, which had originally been a sort of Shakti companion to Kwan Shi Yin, became all-dominant as a Great Mother of All, the male side fading to a large extent.

Horus and Osiris are really the two aspects, higher and lower, of the full Higher Self. The Egyptians said there were two Horuses, one son of Ra and Hathor, and one son of Osiris and Isis. The priests of Ra and Osiris argued for many centuries whether Horus was son of the one or the other. The higher Horus was known as Horus the Elder, and the lower Horus as Horus the Child, which only confuses matters more because Horus the Elder was the divine child himself as son of Ra and Hathor, the Sky Goddess. In yet another myth, Horus the Elder himself was father of Horus the child.

The lower Horus follows on from Osiris and is even said to be Osiris resurrected. But ultimately Horus is the manifestation of Ra himself, which is why both are falcon-headed, the Father manifested as the Son. Pharaoh, who was the human incarnation of Horus, died as Osiris and resurrected as Horus.

The Egyptians were trying to cover all aspects of the Higher Self by this, even the human aspect before transformation into the god. Osiris was said to be human originally, and Horus has his human and immortal aspects. So from the one angle Horus is Osiris of the Underworld continued, while from the other, he descends from Ra above as higher counterpart to Osiris.

The culture-hero is brought forth from the human side through an individuation or process of inner transformation towards wholeness which has the Self as its center, and this has its own needs and follows its own route. Material as high as God and as low as the devil (or the dragon) and everything in between may be experienced eventually, though all are connected to the central point, as we discover. The journey through the processes is the quest for the Holy Grail, the Golden Fleece, Heaven as a House, and as an individuation process, it is similar to a fairy tale, though a deadly serious one. You may be devoured by the bear, swallowed by the serpent, or you may finish up god-like in insanity. Very rarely, you may taste from the Holy Grail and survive. This, fortunately, is what happened in my case.

Jung knew that God must be further developed at times and the old form of religion renewed, which is to say that our understanding of God and religion must develop. Colin Wilson says in *Alien Dawn:* "Jung had spoken of the major changes that might be expected with the coming of the Age of Aquarius (due around the year 2000). In fact, he felt that the human race was on the point of a leap to a new phase of psychic evolution" (Wilson 1998).

This may be so, but like myself, Jung had doubts and fears that man has traveled too far along a negative road with his reductionism and materialism. Perhaps in consequence he will sink before he can make that most urgent and necessary leap forward, as other societies have done in the past. I speak of Western man here, of course, because he leads the caravan at the moment, and the rest of the world seems to follow blindly.

Jung says that we are now at the time for a "metamorphosis of the gods," as the Greeks termed it, which really means a higher development of our own understanding. However, we must be acutely aware of this, or we could well destroy the whole planet through our ignorance and irresponsibility. An enormous task is being placed upon our shoulders, ultimately a religious task, for the gods must always be renewed rather than abandoned. Jung feared we are in danger of losing the "life-preserving myth" that the Church has maintained over the centuries, and wondered if we are at all aware that the lost and denied Christ can, in the end, only lead to catastrophe (Jung 1964).

That inner man is the Higher Self of which I speak throughout this book. The Higher Self extends through the collective unconscious into eternity, though it is very difficult to get people to understand or form an adequate concept of the collective unconscious. Indeed, it is difficult to ascertain where this ends, if at all, and the "other reality" continues, or whether it should all be termed the collective unconscious, or the "other reality," the Pleroma, as the Gnostics termed it.

But whatever we decide, the fact is that spirit reality does exist behind the physical universe, and furthermore, it can be, is, and always has been, experienced by man. Jung even says that we do not know whether God is indistinguishable from the collective unconscious or is in some way part of its contents, but after twenty or so years of my own experiences of this phenomenon, I can say that whatever the situation, it is all quite definitely a matter of *fact*.

This other reality of spirit and soul has no physical forms of its own, and so in order to convey itself to us has to assume appropriate forms that we may recognize and understand. The collective unconscious therefore possesses, in that sense, its own skies and outer space, its own worlds, and its own sea depths, as symbols of real, though non-material contents. We thus find that the ancient Egyptian Amenta, the Underworld, contained all of the things found in worldly reality, and even Heaven and Hell included, clearly showing that the Egyptians had full knowledge of the collective unconscious. They did, in fact, construct their whole civilization largely on those foundations. Modern man, in stark contrast, has become almost totally dissociated from those foundations, which is a highly dangerous and precarious way to exist, as Jung warned. (As A.E. Wallis Budge, authority on the Egyptian myths, states, Amenta was really the "Other World," or the "Other Reality" for the Egyptians.)

As it was contact with and experience of the archetypal contents of the unconscious that healed the dissociation in myself, by the same token, those contents can heal the whole of society, and indeed, the whole of mankind. As the archetypal contents are of spirit and soul nature, involving God and the Great Mother ultimately, the cure for mankind is therefore a religious one, which should not surprise us too much as the religious view of reality is precisely what modern man has lost.

In *From Atlantis to the Sphinx*, after evaluating some of Giorgio de Santillana's theories about how the myths of the world have their origins in astronomy, Colin Wilson comments: "He needed a large and extremely dense book to convey what he wanted to bring to our attention: the incredible richness of world mythology, and the fact that it seems to point to some way of apprehending the universe that, in our age of written information and sound-bytes, we have long forgotten" (Wilson, 1997).

Precisely! And in *Fingerprints of the Gods*, Graham Hancock (1995) wonders if an ancient intelligence has somehow managed to speak to us through myths across the ages, posing unsolved questions that we can perhaps now answer.

Jung solved that puzzle many decades ago, and it seems at first incredible that so few people who study myths consider Jung's discoveries at all, though his works are full of so much evidence of their true meaning and origin. But then, not too many people know of the collective unconscious, and even fewer understand its true nature. Mythologists, for the most part, do not study depth psychology, and psychologists, of most types, do not study mythology.

Most of the many books that have appeared over the last few decades concerning these mysteries are marvelously entertaining, being both informative and fascinating. But they nevertheless invariably come to the wrong ultimate conclusions because they lack the key that the special knowledge of depth psychology, and of the origins of myths in the collective unconscious, would give them. That other reality always affects man and works through him, either knowingly or unknowingly, consciously or unconsciously, for good under certain circumstances—or, if man is not heedful, for ill.

A dream written down is always so much less than the dream itself, which, while it is occurring, is thought to be conscious reality itself. Recorded later, it is naturally somewhat less than the dream experience, and along with certain details possibly being forgotten, the literary gifts of the dreamer, plus his mood, must be taken into consideration. So the dream as retold is always so much less, especially for other people who hear or read it. That has to be the case with many of the dreams that follow. Furthermore, I have omitted certain details that are nonessential, to make what remains more concise and easier to read, although even the smallest details in a dream may have meaning. But I have added absolutely nothing to them, so that the dreams remain pure products of the unconscious processes, which ultimately produced the Higher Self.

As to the main sources of my material, the first to be mentioned is the unconscious itself, for without its years of supply of processes in dreams, I would not be writing this book now. Next, though perhaps he should come first, is Jung, my guru and teacher over a lot of years. Without him and his great knowledge I would never have understood the vast amount of material that has always flowed up from the depths of the unconscious. I mention Jung throughout this book, and he is ever with me in spirit. As Kipling had one of his characters say, "Thou and I be of one blood, Mowgli." My debt to Jung can never be repaid, but I hope that the work can do at least something to prove the great truth and immense value of Jung and his discoveries. The unconscious itself insists in my dreams that Jungian depth psychology must be our new pathway to religious understanding.

I have obtained much of my information concerning Egypt from the nineteenth-century mythologist, Gerald Massey, who was a master in his own right. Also from A. E. Wallis Budge, another great authority on the Egyptian myths. Massey understood the myths of Egypt as no one has since, and recognized the very close connection between those and the Bible texts, stating that much Biblical material is actually Egyptian myth, which in no way lessens the validity of either, rather the opposite. But more than this, Massey realized that the Egyptians meant their myths to take place "in spirit," in some other realm beyond the earthly, yet connected to it. We know today that this is the collective unconscious, that other reality that extends out to eternity.

Twentieth-century scholarship became all science, and eventually technology—all very precise and clinical, but the real spirit of the myths was thereby lost, and along with it, any real understanding of them. Though Massey was something of a genius, his works were nevertheless rejected by the newer, down-to-earth experts. Massey was a spiritualist who claimed that the original mythmakers were spiritualists, and he became forgotten as the early twentieth-century progressed. It is true that some of Massey's ideas on the spread of cultures are now out of date, but his intensely detailed work on the myths is phenomenal.

Yet, like H. P. Blavatsky, whom I shall discuss in a moment, Massey saw no conflict whatsoever between the creation and evolution theories, stating that evolution is growth in matter at one end of the spectrum, while spirit and God are at the other end, these touching and forming one total reality. We find today that Massey's works fit in very well with the discoveries of depth psychology, particularly his realization that the divine Father/Son archetype, usually with the World Soul as Great Mother somehow, was not new with Christ, but reached back through the Bible to the beginnings of Egyptian culture.

Massey has been silenced for a hundred years, but his work should be assessed anew, and I am proud to let the man speak himself occasionally here. He may be wrong in certain details, as I must be, and indeed, as we all are, but essentially he is right and possesses knowledge of the myths of the ancient world that no other scholars, especially modern ones, can begin to approach.

I also quote H. P. Blavatsky, that other nineteenth-century mythologist, spiritualist, and medium, who herself quotes Massey on occasions. Though a Buddhist, she recognized the full validity of Christ as a Higher Self phenomenon, classing him with other Sons of God around the world. Colonel Olcott, H. P. B.'s fellow Theosophist, writes that they both became Buddhists in America, and then later underwent "official" Buddhist ceremonies in India. Blavatsky was well aware that through inner processes the immortal Self may descend into the mortal initiate at the very highest level of attainment, and that the Christ had so descended into the man Jesus. When we consider the narrow writings of other nineteenth-century philosophers, scientists, churchmen, etc., we can only be amazed at the scope of Blavatsky's vision. As with Massey, some of her ideas seem ridiculous to us now, with the benefit of modern knowledge, but I know the processes of the unconscious and find that her profound writings on the Higher Self fit precisely with what I have experienced. It is a pity she remained a Buddhist, for the West could never really understand Buddhism or accept it *en masse*; after all, it had not understood Christianity in two thousand years!

As Jung says, if the West as a whole is ever to really understand religion it must be through the Christ myth, for our roots are sunk deeply in this through the collective unconscious, and all the way back to the beginnings of Egypt.

INTRODUCTION:

The Importance of Dreams
in the Individuation Process

At the beginning of *The Interpretation of Dreams*, Freud states that although the ancients believed dreams may contain divine revelation, it was now his task to show how completely wrong this idea was. He mentions Aristotle who, true to type, also debunked any notion that there could be meaning to dreams beyond the human personality. Now, over a hundred years after Freud's book was published, it is my hope to prove how wrong Freud and Aristotle were, and consequently, how right were the ancients. As Jung tells us, Freud did not know how to deal with religious dreams with archetypal contents. Nevertheless, Freud was instrumental in the discovery that the direct *link* between the conscious and unconscious realms is the dream, and both Freudian and Jungian psychological systems were to depend to a large extent on dreams as the key and the gateway to the unconscious depths.

Man in the past always placed the highest importance on dreams, not only going back to the earliest civilizations, but also to primitive man in remote times. In cave paintings and rock drawings we find symbols and abstract depictions, some of which cannot express outer reality as such and can only be products of the unconscious as experienced by primitive man in dreams, visions, and trances.

37

For example, a film I saw about the Australian desert contained an ancient Aborigine rock-drawing of a wavy horizontal line making its way towards the center of a circular spiral. We find this same symbol produced by the unconscious today. It may be said that this is merely an expression of sexual union, but as the findings of depth psychology reveal, the collective unconscious itself produces these symbols to represent the union of opposites at a much higher level than the merely personal and physically sexual. There is also, Jung states, a Rhodesian rock drawing that displays a double cross within a circle, a symbol that is found in one form or another in virtually all of the cultures of the world, including the Christian. It even appears in cultures in which the wheel as such had yet to be invented, and so could not express a wheel from outer reality. These symbols of the unconscious would have been experienced largely in dreams, although it is also natural for human beings to produce them spontaneously in the conscious state, being affected unknowingly by the unconscious.

To the primitive mentality, reality was always magical and demonic, and this is certainly nearer to its true nature than the rationalistic and dissociated view of it in our modern mode of thinking. The members of a primitive tribe would sit around together and relate the dreams they had experienced, which is actually the sharing of unconscious life. If those dreams happened to contain magical and demonic contents, then this was taken to be the revelation of the will of the gods or even the appearance of the gods themselves. As my own dream experiences show, there is a large amount of truth in this, if we understand the contents to be the *symbolic* expressions of a reality totally different in nature to our conscious one.

The myths of the tribe—their religious and *real* life—were based largely on such dreams, and it is a well-known fact that primitive societies soon go to pieces if they lose their mythic foundations, as do great civilizations. We should have realized long ago that the myths which originate in and through the psyche of man express the hidden unconscious life. The East, so much wiser in these things than the West, has always known that spirit reality is inexorably intertwined with the deeper processes of the human psyche.

The shaman/medicine man figure has been known all over the world, and his supposed powers are legendary. Not only is he a dreamer of dreams, but going into a state of ecstasy, the shaman is said to be able to travel through both the material world and the "land of the dead" and is claimed to possess powers to influence spirits, demons, even the gods themselves. Possessing powers to cure the sick, they are also said to accompany the souls of the dead to the afterlife. The processes involved in becoming a shaman are so painful, both physically and mentally, that they often result in the initiate becoming permanently injured psychically. This fits in with the "wounded savior" and "wounded healer" motif known in many religious mysteries, including the Christian.

In one of my dreams, as I lie sobbing on my knees unable to carry on, the figure of the wounded Christ comes to me, his arms and hands dripping blood from his wounds. After laying his hands on my head, Christ then walks out of the dream and into higher reality again. This has the same basic meaning as the wounded shaman who heals, and it also means that the inner, spiritualizing processes can now bring that healing, possibly conferring a state of grace. Shaman, true priest, prophet, mystic—they all are deeply involved with processes of the collective unconscious, the apparently eternal reality of spirit and soul that exists behind—surrounds—the physical universe.

Having made many journeys through the unconscious myself, I can understand how shamans are said to travel through the "land of the spirits" and the "land of the dead." The widespread belief that they are able to turn themselves into animals, however, is due to the inevitable magic and miracles that always become attached to such figures, plus the fact that they activate archetypal spirit and animal-soul contents in the collective unconscious, which may be experienced by more than one person in the tribe or group.

Dreams were so important to certain ancient civilizations that they had special temples devoted to them. These had resident priests whose function was not only to interpret dreams for others, but to have revelations in dreams of the will of the gods. In Egypt these priests were called "Masters of the Secret Things." Even in other temples, special beds were provided for priests whose main, or even sole, function was to have dreams in which the powers of the other world would manifest and make their will known.

As well as in Egypt, these special temples flourished in Greece, and they are known to have existed in Israel; but it is a safe bet that they were known in many cultures. And it was not solely, or primarily, a case of personal dreams of the individual. Whole societies, large and small, depended upon dreams to a large extent for their spiritual lives as the chief means of communicating with the otherworldly reality of the spirits and the gods. So temples were associated with dreams and visions, although only the priests and other initiates were allowed into the secret mysteries that grew therefrom.

Jung mentions the case of the sixth-century B.C. Babylonian tyrant, Nebuchadnezzar, who had a warning dream of impending doom. He dreamt of a great, fruitful tree that canopied the whole earth, and which stretched right up to Heaven. But then an angel descended and commanded that the tree be chopped down, and that Nebuchadnezzar's heart be changed to that of a beast, so that he would graze in the fields like cattle. His dream thus foretold the fall of his mind into insanity, and his empire into ruins. Jung states that this was to be Nietzsche's fate, his conscious mind inflating to take the place of the gods, only to betray its all too human frailty by the collapse into insanity.

The ancient world is full of such tales of prophetic dreams and warnings, some of which must be true, while others are obviously allegorical and symbolical. Yet there is something of greater importance than these individual stories. The truth is, although modern scholars fully realize that myths and religion played a large, dominating role in ancient civilizations, and indeed, were the very foundations of cultures both large and small across the world, no one seems to have realized that they were based on processes of the unconscious. This despite the fact that it is eighty years and more since Jung first made the discovery and informed the world. But the world listened mostly to Freud, rather than Jung, and in consequence the immensely important knowledge of the origins of myths and religions in processes of the unconscious has largely been missed.

The renowned Egyptologist, A. E. Wallis Budge, stated many years ago that the Book of the Dead cannot be the product of a primitive mentality, and then contradicted this by saying that the Egyptians believed that the gods literally took animal forms in worldly reality. Another writer, Lewis Spence, even claimed that the Egyptians were incapable of abstract modes of thinking. However, though scholars today now know that this is far from being the case, they nevertheless still fail to realize by just how far this is so. The truth is, the Egyptians (and other ancient and not-so-ancient cultures) had an association with the collective unconscious that was very highly developed; much of the symbolism we find in their myths would have been experienced through dream processes.

The psychic origin of myths should not be understood merely in the limited sense of, say, Freud's interpretation of the Oedipus myth, or even of Joseph Campbell's understanding of the sea-journeys of Odysseus around the Aegean. Both are limited to the personal unconscious. We must rather see it, to give an example, in terms of the whole mythos of ancient Egypt, which was based on direct experience of spirit and soul reality directly through the human psyche, i.e. through the personal unconscious.

Kingship was based on the connection between the psyche of the human individual, in this case Pharaoh, and the immortal entity in the unconscious realm that Jung termed the Higher Self. That is why Pharaoh was both man and god and son of the High God. The East has known of this phenomenon for thousands of years, calling the super figure Self, Atman, Purusha, Aja, Kshetrajna, and other terms, while the West failed to grasp the fact that the figure of Christ also symbolizes the same phenomenon.

Jung discovered the psychological facts, plus many historical examples, which prove that this is indeed the case. Yet few understood the meaning and full implications of his discoveries. Having undergone similar processes in the unconscious myself, I can fully substantiate Jung's findings and statements. To me, these are *facts* of direct experience, and whosoever has direct experience of something, *knows*. When that experience is of inner reality, it is the direct knowledge the ancients called *gnosis*. This gnosis of the unconscious processes that we find in myths and religious mysteries can only have come about by certain individuals making the long journeys through the psychic depths, and this must be true of all cultures, as they all have corresponding myths.

Returning to dreams, in the Greek world there were the temples of Asklepios, and those wishing to have deeper, more meaningful dreams would be required to abstain from sexual intercourse and then sleep in a special room that contained harmless snakes. These measures, far from being ridiculous, would have "turned up" the unconscious, perhaps bringing forth dreams from the deeper levels that would contain more powerful contents. Sexual abstinence reverts the unused libido back into the unconscious, where it activates the deeper layers; snakes being one of the main symbolic contents of the deeper unconscious, would have set the mood, as it were. It is the worldwide experience of mankind in the esoteric-religious mysteries that sexual abstinence increases direct experiences of spirit, visionary dreams, and so forth, which is why serious initiates, priests, monks, and prophets have almost always been required to be celibate.

The Roman Artemidorus studied dreams and their meaning in what can only be termed a scientific way, collecting old manuscripts and all the other information he could find, then classifying all the material. His treatise called *Oneirocritia*, has the same meaning as Freud's famous work, *The Interpretation of Dreams*. Artemidorus tried to link the dream to the personality of the dreamer, and perhaps has more claim to the title of "Father of Psychology" than anyone else. On the other hand, as the secret wisdom of the Sumerians, Egyptians, Babylonians, Hindus, Buddhists, and in fact, all peoples of the world, was based largely on dream processes, these earliest cultures, or rather their initiates into the mysteries, were the real fathers of psychology, and indeed, of religions. These were the true "Masters of the Secret Things."

The Bible contains quite a number of dream incidents and in the New Testament, Joseph, the father of Jesus, has a dream concerning Mary's pregnancy with the baby Jesus. Then after the birth and the wise men's visit, they also have a dream warning them not to return to Herod. Joseph in Egypt, Gideon, Mordecai, Pilate's wife, and others, have significant dreams, and Daniel tells us himself that his vision of four beasts rising up from out of the sea, followed by the coming on the clouds of "one like the Son of man," were due to dreaming "in the night visions."

In India, Queen Maya, the mother of the Buddha, has a dream of pregnancy in which a beautiful white elephant comes down into her womb for the special birth of the "great soul" (an elephant is a well-known symbol of the Higher Self). In the Arab world, the founding of Islam by Mohammed was due to the religious dreams that the prophet experienced. In Persia, God in the form of Ahura Mazda gave the prophet Zarathustra the drink of omniscience, after which Zarathustra dreamt of a tree with four branches, made of gold, silver, steel, and iron, which corresponds to the *arbor philosophia*, the metallic tree of the alchemists. These, and so many other mythic accounts, are experiences of archetypal contents and processes, including those of divine spirit, of, in, and through the realm of the collective unconscious.

As we know, every culture from primitive tribe to high civilization had myths, forming the links between conscious and unconscious realities, and the shamans, priests, and prophets were always the keepers of the sacred teachings. Certain initiates became the heroes who fought the Great Dragon, the unconscious depths in negative form (involving also a battle with themselves), to win the spiritual treasures to enrich, and even to found, their cultures. They did this without being overwhelmed and destroyed by the powerful archetypal contents, spiritual as well as chthonic. But it would all have depended very largely on dreams, as they are the surest means of direct contact with the unconscious, and therefore with spirit and soul reality.

Of course, the ordinary people would not have been allowed into the secret doctrines based upon the original experiences, only into the religious rituals that expressed them. But primitives doing sacred dances around the campfires and congregations taking part in the Mass or church service all express the same processes of the unconscious looked at from the human or psychological standpoint. Viewed from the collective unconscious, they are ultimately processes of God and the Great Mother. In other words, we may assess the world of the unconscious rationally and scientifically, but in itself it is a vast, numinous, religious complex that stretches out to eternity, and our own worldly reality is just an aspect of it. Only if we think in religious terms can we ever hope to obtain some insight into its true nature and meaning.

I should perhaps try to give some explanation of the nature of the collective unconscious here, or at least, of some of the functions and contents that we can experience and perhaps come to understand. This may give the reader an elementary idea of that other realm. We have to distinguish between the personal and collective unconscious. The personal unconscious inwardly corresponds to outer ego-consciousness, and the collective unconscious inwardly corresponds to the outer reality of the world, and indeed, to the whole universe. In other words, the human psyche, with its conscious and unconscious sides, is in between two opposite realities, even though they are two aspects of one greater reality.

When a symbolic vision, or some other non-material manifestation, is experienced in conscious reality as an outer event, it may actually be occurring in the collective unconscious. It is either breaking through into conscious, outer reality, or is being projected into it; in both instances it is from the unconscious realm. It is no less real in any way because of that. On the contrary, it may even be more real than anything in consciousness. This is because while the latter means constant change, so that nothing remains in the same state permanently, spirit reality is unchanging and timeless, and is constancy itself. Only by coming through to physical reality, apparently, can change be brought about.

The vision of St. Paul (originally as Saul) on the road to Damascus can only be understood in this light, as can visions of St. Bernadette at Lourdes and those witnessed by the children at Fatima and Pontmain. Their visions would have been actual events occurring in, or through, the unconscious, breaking through the curtain and experienced as outer events. A lowering of consciousness may be involved in certain instances, so that unconscious contents are then able to rise up, or rather to come through, allowing the two opposite realities to merge. However, this apparently only occurs with certain individuals, for with others nothing happens and they see nothing.

The collective unconscious is therefore another reality that actually exists *behind* the physical universe, or surrounding it. The way to it is through the personal unconscious, although at times it may break through into matter as outer events. Such visions may pass through the psyche of human individuals, or may manifest as purely outer phenomena, like a ghost materializing. In the latter case, the activity could still break through even if no human individual were there to witness it (though there would then be no point). Though a lowering of human consciousness may be involved at times, it seems that on certain other occasions it is not. Jung's "active imagination," in which conscious and unconscious realities merge, is a voluntary method of achieving contact with the unconscious, and involves a partial lowering of consciousness.

Projection is a well-known phenomenon of the human psyche and occurs frequently, mostly without our knowledge. It is a fact that even though we may come to realize we are making the projection, it may still continue. The picture on a movie screen may seem to be happening on the screen itself, but is actually a projected image from the movie projector; certain visions and supernatural phenomena seem to be of the same nature. But I must emphasize that these projections are not from the personal unconscious, but from beyond, from the collective levels, which ultimately constitute another, eternal reality. Projections from the personal level of the unconscious occur all the time, and though limited to personal contents, are nevertheless based on the same principle.

There appear to be various sides and levels to the collective unconscious, and to begin with it is the answer to what lies behind such enigmas as telepathy, clairvoyance, and precognition. In fact, "what lies behind" is a phrase that could be used to sum up the nature of the collective unconscious. Telepathy does not pass across empty space from one person to another in the outer world, but travels through the collective unconscious, which all humans share. Clairvoyance is possible because, as Jung says, in the unconscious, the future is already prepared (Jung 1995). However, this is understating it, for the future may also be experienced. Again this is due to the fact that the collective unconscious is out of time and all events in it are simultaneous. This seems impossible for us to comprehend from our position *in* time, but even many scientists believe that it is nevertheless likely to be so.

The collective unconscious is also the "void" which the spirits of the dead pass through to "go over"; and to return again at times. Jung stated that the term collective unconscious, which was his own, is an inadequate one. The term unconscious means "that which is not conscious or of the conscious" and so could apply to anything that is "other" and that lies beyond consciousness. Jung also wondered if God equals the unconscious realm itself, or whether He is a content of it, but concluded that we can never know this. (Jung stated on a number of occasions that he *knew* that God exists, but would then usually qualify the statements by referring to the "god-image" in the human psyche. However, anyone who travels far enough through the individuation processes, as Jung himself did, comes to realize that God is a definite reality.)

We may also encounter spirit in the form of aliens and spacecraft in dreams, as I have several times, although it is not a holy kind of spirit. However, higher, holy spirit itself can be experienced there, and may take the form of holy visions with varying degrees of numinosity.

Paracelsus and very many others realized there is indeed the higher spirit, of holiness and God, although he personally concentrated on the lower spirit, the soul of matter (World Soul or *Anima Mundi*). It is the latter with which we would associate the occult mysteries, alchemy, magic, and so forth, though alchemy led certain alchemists to the higher spirit. Modern man mostly lost contact with these forces when he became fascinated by scientific materialism, but now that fascination is fading as conventional science reveals itself wholly inadequate to bring meaning to people's lives and they turn to the irrational side of things again. Having lost belief in traditional religious forms, they are looking for answers in all kinds of supernatural phenomena, revealing the deep psychological and spiritual need of our age. This search ranges from telepathy and regression hypnosis to ghosts and UFOs; even the great interest in Atlantis and pre-existent cultures is due to the same deep need.

The latest development is the growing fascination with ancient and secret wisdom. Certain scientists and scholars are now beginning to believe that full reality itself must extend to other realms of actuality, though these are nevertheless considered to be other forms of matter; hence spirit itself is still denied as a reality.

Alchemy, which originated in ancient Egypt along with many of the world's myths, religions, and legends having their foundations in the unconscious, also investigated the lower psychic depths. As Jung comments, visions are at the bottom of the other reality, experienced in dreams breaking through into worldly reality; alchemy was based largely upon dreams and visions. In fact, visions of all kinds would inundate the alchemists, so much so that madness was often the great danger, and not a few alchemists became insane (Jung 1958).

The Gnostics, who drew from many ancient esoteric and mythological traditions, and also from the Christ phenomenon itself, investigated the processes of the unconscious in search of the Anthropos figure, the "Christ within." And the Bible is actually the record of a royal line of unconscious Higher-Self experiences in which the Anthropos figure, as Son of Man, is brought forth from the other reality of the collective unconscious by various individuals, including Jesus the man. All of these would have involved dreams to a very large extent.

Many writers have been inspired by dreams, including Robert Louis Stevenson with his famous story *Dr. Jekyll and Mr. Hyde.* This was the result of a dream in which the doctor was transformed into Mr. Hyde (Jung's "shadow figure") after taking a potion. This imagery fits with what Plato said about a wild beast nature in men appearing in dreams. Charles Dickens is also known to have used dream material in his works, but the most interesting and significant instance of all is Goethe's *Faust.* This was based on dream processes occurring over a period of many years, corresponding, in fact, to Jung's "individuation process," the end result of which may be the bringing forth of the Higher Self.

However, whereas Christ symbolizes the light side of the Self, Mephistopheles, the figure brought forth by Faust, represents the dark, negative side. This tells us that Faust's, and therefore Goethe's, alchemical dream processes must have gone disastrously wrong, otherwise he would have brought forth a positive savior figure rather than Mephistopheles. So while Mr. Hyde represents the shadow side of the human Dr. Jeckyll, Mephistopheles is the lower shadow of the Higher Self, rather than of the man Faust.

Another example of the individuation process occurring in an individual is Nietzsche, most evident in *Thus Spoke Zarathustra*. We know that Nietzsche always paid a lot of attention to his dreams. However, it is again a negative example of the processes, happening to some extent without his conscious awareness. Negative results in these processes are brought about by selfish, inflated, and likewise inferior motives of consciousness. It is imperative in the work that the goals and aims of consciousness are the highest.

The pursuit of wisdom and truth, and wanting to help God and mankind to come together in harmony will do to start with. The alchemists insisted that they were good Christians and made a long list of all the virtues necessary for positive results in the *opus,* that is, the great work of inner transformation. They were well aware of the great dangers, and stated "Not a few have perished in our work." Whatever the personal fates of all these figures we know they relied on dreams in their work.

Dreams that agree completely with the attitude of consciousness are rare, as dreams are mostly complementary and compensatory and at times may totally oppose, and even violently contradict, consciousness. When people believe, therefore, they have told themselves what to dream, the true situation is more complicated than that. Suppose I told myself to dream of a train. I may do so that very night, but close inspection of the details and nuances would reveal the unconscious' own message and meaning. I may miss the train, which would possibly mean a missed opportunity with the processes, or I may catch the train, which would have the opposite meaning. Or, I may be on the tracks with the train approaching, which would obviously mean danger. Yes I have dreamt of a train, as I told myself to do, but the unconscious has provided the meaning. Consciousness has to learn that it is not the authority of the psyche, for that lies with the "great man" (the Anthropos, or Higher Self), of whom consciousness is a mere part.

Benedictus Pererius, writing in 1598, states that God ". . . inspires dreams where he will, when he will, and in whomsoever he will." He also says, "Many (dreams) are natural, some are of human origin, and some are even divine." Pererius belonged to the Church, which, while admitting that dreams may be divinely inspired, nevertheless never encouraged their occurrence, always claiming the right to pronounce on their validity, or otherwise, whenever they do occur.

As Jung says, the unconscious is independent to the highest degree, and St. Augustine thanked God that he was not responsible for his own dreams. The fact is, the unconscious produces mythological material in dreams which, if reduced to the merely personal unconscious, builds up consciousness to an inflated extent, thus increasing an apparently already existing dissociation from the unconscious. Mythological contents cannot be derived from the personal level, and indeed, may at times ultimately be religious statements from God.

The Dream Visions:
A Record of Transformation Processes

In a dream, in a vision of the night, when deep sleep falleth upon men, in slumberings upon the bed; Then he [God] openeth the ears of men, and sealeth their instruction.

Job 33:15-16.

It will be remembered that I was suffering from long years of depression after a nervous breakdown, hating my meaningless life, and indeed, hating meaningless reality itself, when I first encountered Jung and his work in a television program. My anima figure, Julie, onto whom I had unknowingly made the projection of the unconscious content, was also causing me considerable pain, so that I thought I must go mad, there seeming to be no way out of my torment. It was then that I had my first important dream.

I am in a lost and forlorn state as I find myself walking down a dark back alley. Suddenly, to the left I see a doorway, and over it is the white, ghostly head of psychologist C. G. Jung, and this speaks to me, saying in French, *"Avec Moi."* Knowing that this means "Come with me," I go through the doorway to find myself in a small workshop. Everything is made of pink stone, including the walls, shelves, and workbenches, and there are large blocks of the pink stone that are to be worked on as sculptures. This is not just cold, lifeless stone, but warm, living stone that is alive with spirit, which is why it is pink. With this, I realize that everything in the universe is in some way alive, even what we call dead matter, and even empty space itself seems to have life. I say, "Everything that exists is alive. There is no such thing as death, only change." I am now extremely happy and I want to carve shapes out of the stone myself.

By this time, the workshop has become the Royal Doulton china factory at Nile Street, though a smaller version, which is situated about a mile away from where I live in real life, in Stoke-on-Trent, the "Potteries," in the middle of England. I see an elderly man wearing an apron, chipping away at one of the blocks of stone. Going up to him, I find that it is Jung himself. "Please teach me how to carve in the stone," I ask him, and when he does not reply, I continue, "You don't have to pay me anything at all. In fact, I'll pay you. But please, teach me." Still he does not reply, but he grins broadly and knowingly.

Right away this first dream was in direct contrast to my conscious way of thinking. While I had become pessimistic, rationalistic, morose, and depressed in consciousness, the dream is meaningful, otherworldly, mystical, and magical, with a ghostly head, stone vibrant with living spirit, and the concept of "no such thing as death, only change."

Being lost down a dark alley reflects the state of meaningless existence in which I was sunk in real life at that time, and not only was I lost, I was also in torment and could see absolutely no way to turn or to go. But suddenly the doorway appears to the left with the ghostly head of Jung over it telling me to go with him. There was no neck or shoulders, just the head, which was rather like a skull. It is significant, perhaps, that when the doorway suddenly appeared as my way out it was to the left, as "left" has always been considered secret, mysterious, sinister.

Only the *secret* way of the unconscious is now open to me, appearing suddenly when all other roads are closed and all seems lost. I had seen the name of a racehorse, *Avec Moi*, on a newspaper recently, and had thought, that meant "Come with me," so the dream was now using this to convey part of its message to me.

As I was to learn later, in alchemy and certain other esoteric mysteries, a head, sometimes a skull, was regarded as the "vessel of transformation," and in ancient times there was the symbolical Head of Osiris. In one aspect in the Mysteries, Osiris was termed "the headless," while the head itself was said to have crossed the waters, "indicating resurrection," as Jung puts it. When Isis, wife of Osiris, recovered the fourteen parts of her husband's body, dismembered by Set, at different nomes, or cult centers of Egypt, the head was found at Abydos, where the gateway to Amenta, the Underworld, was situated. This meant the gateway to the resurrection mysteries of the soul, for the Underworld was really the realm of the collective unconscious, as I shall demonstrate later in this work. The head thus became highly symbolical in the resurrection and transformation mysteries of the ancient world; indeed, of those that came later.

At the time of Zosimos of Panopolis, the third-century A.D. Gnostic alchemist, Greek alchemists generally called themselves "Children of the Golden Head," and "Sons of the Golden Head," referring to the transformation processes that were ultimately of the unconscious depths. To the medieval alchemists, the head, as a round, containing vessel equaled the *rotundum, arcanum,* or *vas hermeticum,* in which the magical *opus* could occur with the separation and mixture of the base substances, which would ultimately produce the true "gold": the *lapis,* or "stone." Zosimos speaks several times of the "whitest stone, which is the head," and was known in ancient Egypt, where each new initiate into the mysteries received a white stone. This imagery is repeated in the Book of Revelation where a white stone is given to "him that overcometh."

So the stone obviously equals the head and vice versa, and both are connected with rebirth and transformation of the personality. Jung tells us of a certain Gerbert of Rheims (d. 1003), who became Pope, and to whom it was rumored a golden head spoke. Jung also mentions that the original Rabbinic teraphim of the Hebrews was traditionally believed to have been a decapitated human head of a firstborn that had been plucked of hair. Afterwards, it would answer any questions of those who knelt before it and asked.

The teraphim seems to have been a dummy head, though it may originally have been real. We find it in the Bible where the wife of King David, Michal, puts a teraphim in his bed to deceive the messenger of King Saul. It is known that human heads were sometimes used in the Mysteries, and in the year 765 A.D., the priests of Harran, in Mesopotamia, were severely punished for using decapitated heads. In some circumstances the head was a contact with spirits, or could perhaps ward off unwelcome ones, while in the Hermetic and alchemical mysteries it was the symbolical vessel of transformation, comparable to the *vas* or *rotundum*. The Jewish teraphim itself seems to have been in general use, though said to be connected with the priesthood as the "Rabbinic teraphim."

The mysterious head of Baphomet worshipped by the Knights Templars certainly had origins in the unconscious, and in fact part of the charges against them that brought about their destruction was the blasphemous worship of the head. In their book *The Temple and the Lodge*, Michael Baigent and Richard Leigh list some of these charges, stating also that when officers burst into the Paris Temple of the Templars in 1307 they found a silver reliquary that contained the skull of a woman. The list of charges included: the keeping of heads as idols; the worship of the heads; the belief that they could be redeemed by the heads; that they could cause the vegetation to flourish; and that they could make them rich (Baigent and Leigh 1990).

For similar reasons, the head played a considerable role in alchemy, and as a transformation was about to commence within my own personality, it is fitting that in the dream, the ghostly head of Jung, who was to become my guru on my long journeys through the unconscious, should appear to me. It is particularly fitting since alchemical symbolism, having become constellated in the collective unconscious, often appears in our dreams today during individuation processes. It may also be symbolically relevant that Christ was crucified on a hill called Golgotha, which means "The place of the skull." This seems too meaningful for it to be coincidence, for the head of Osiris was involved in the resurrection mysteries, and after the crucifixion, Christ too was resurrected.

In old Celtic tales, Bran the Blessed is wounded in the foot by a poisoned dart, and so instructs his seven male followers to cut off his head to stop his suffering. The head is taken to the White Mount in London, which is reminiscent of the head equaling the "white stone" of Zosimos. In other tales, the Green Man cuts off his own head, and the Green Knight does the same in his conflict with Gawain. This is interesting because Perceval cuts off the head of the stag, and this is the animal form of the god Kernunnos, who is really the Green Man, the spirit of green vegetation.

The head of John the Baptist naturally has its symbolical meaning in the Mysteries, and in an ancient Gnostic text, Christ states that nothing will be understood until the head of John the Baptist is understood. It is believed by some scholars the magical head of the Templars', Baphomet, derives from the contraction of "Baal," the old Canaan god, and "Mohamet," the earlier form of Mohammed. But I would think that "Bap" comes from the head of John the Baptist.

Once inside the dream-workshop, I find that everything is made of pink stone, and the stone is almost pulsating with living spirit. This suggests blood, the age-old symbol of soul and spirit, which I shall explore with the next dream. As for the pink stone, because of its qualities of endurance, it has always been used the world over to symbolize the religious and the eternal: the secret mysteries of Masonry, for instance, reaching back to ancient Egypt. In fact, the Hittite city of Boghazkoy, one of the very earliest sites of human communal habitation, had cuneiform texts which stated that the son of the father-god was a stone.

To the Kabbalists, the stone of Bethel marks the union of Tifereth and Malkhuth, the symbolic male and female opposites, therefore spirit and soul as *Beth-El* means "feminine abode of God." Jung says that despite associations with Christ, stone cannot symbolize spirit alone as its very nature is solid, earthly, and concrete. It therefore symbolizes not just an incarnation of God, but also a "materialization" and "concretization" of him. It also symbolizes that part of God that is deeply sunk in matter, the lower triad of the three-headed Mercurial serpent that is the counterpart to the higher Holy Trinity.

The alchemists sought their magical Philosopher's Stone, and the legendary Ostanes wrote, "Go to the waters of the Nile and there ye will find a stone that hath a spirit." This is probably why the workshop is in Nile Street in my dream, and in fact, Egypt is frequently referred to throughout my twenty years of dreams. Alchemy, Christianity, Judaism, and Islam all have their roots in Egypt. In his quest for paradise, alchemist Michael Maier had crossed three continents in three directions when he was advised (by the feminine anima) to journey to the seven mouths of the Nile to find Mercurius. The spirit Mercurius is really the lower aspect of the Higher Self, the "age-old son of the Mother," She being the World Soul, the collective feminine unconscious, the soul force that apparently animates matter throughout the whole universe, apparently in counterbalance and contrast to the masculine spirit.

However, the stone in the workshop is pink, which is the combination and unification of red and white, and these colors represented the opposites in both alchemy and Egyptian mythology. The Pharaoh's crown was red and white, or really two crowns in one, symbolizing the Two Lands of Upper and Lower Egypt unified. Ultimately, all of this represented the unification of the eternal opposites of matter and spirit, or more specifically, soul and spirit, this world and the "other world," as the Egyptians called it. Even today, the appearance of red and white in our dreams symbolizes the very same opposites. The pink stone in my dream, therefore, corresponds to the "living stone" of the alchemists, and also of the New Testament where it states ". . . like living stones be yourselves built into a spiritual edifice" (1 Peter 2:5).

The original goal of alchemy was the transmutation of base metals into gold, and so it remained with perhaps the majority of the alchemists, but there were also those who came to realize that much more was involved than mere matter. Until relatively recent, the nature of matter was unknown, and it was, therefore, a suitable receptacle for the projection of unconscious contents and processes. The alchemists, who made projections of their own psychic processes into matter, believed that the wondrous transformations were being caused by their laboratory work, though certain of them were wise enough to realize that the transformation was due to processes occurring within the depths of themselves, where the base and material man could be spiritualized.

Their work was, in reality, profoundly religious, as through it they could unite the opposites of matter and spirit in their magical "stone." This was a symbol that the unconscious produced for the Higher Self, the Anthropos figure of which Christ is also a symbol for Western man. The alchemists were led to posit their stone, or lapis, as a Christ parallel. The stone did not equal Christ, but rather countermatched him, because Christ is of the higher spirit, the Son of the Father, while the stone equaled Mercurius, the spirit of the soul depths, the "age-old son of the Mother," who in successful processes *copies* Christ.

This is why Jung said that the alchemists took the place of Christ in the unconscious processes, though it is perhaps more correct to say that they replaced the man Jesus, as they became initiates undergoing similar spiritualizing processes themselves. But alchemy was really too matter-bound in its concepts and aims, and the Philosopher's Stone is not the Son of God. Yet, at the same time, it is—both ultimately imply the Higher Self, though at different levels, the *filius macrocosmi* and the *filius microcosmi*. Nevertheless, the alchemists experienced much of the symbolism involved in developing and bringing forth the Higher Self, and so came near to bringing forth a Christ parallel, though none ever achieved it, as far as we know.

There is some confusion over the terms macrocosm and microcosm, but basically the macrocosm is connected with the circumference that surrounds and the microcosm with the point in its center. Jung speaks of the *filius macrocosmi* being identified with the lower spirit Mercurius, citing examples, and then mentions those who identified the *filius microcosmi* with Christ. The *filius macrocosmi* is also identified with the lapis so that it clearly refers to the lower son. In these instances the *filius macrocosmi* is identified with the "Son of the Great World," whereas the *filius microcosmi* is the single point in which all things are unified, as with Christ.

H. P. Blavatsky cites the macrocosm as being, in one meaning, the whole universe, while the microcosm refers to man, or to his solar system. That is what we would expect, but it seems that the alchemists interpreted the two "worlds" in their own ways to match specific circumstances. However, the *filius macrocosmi* was chiefly the lower son, and the *filius microcosmi* the higher.

The *filius sapientiae* is the son of Sophia, allegorical goddess of wisdom, found in ancient, alchemical, and Gnostic texts alike. Jung identifies the sun-woman in Revelation with Sophia, so the son of the Sun Woman is really the *filius sapientiae*. This figure is also *homo altus*, the "mysterious Man" found in alchemy who is sometimes identified with the lapis. This would be the equivalent of the Anthropos of the Gnostics, which means that at least a few alchemists were experiencing something higher than the Philosopher's Stone itself.

Speaking of how alchemy characterizes its "child" as the stone, on the one hand, and as *filius sapientiae*, or *homo altus* on the other, Jung comments that the latter figure appears as the "son of the sun-woman" in the Apocalypse, and that furthermore, the birth of this child is a repetition, in a sense, of Christ. This was experienced to a degree by various alchemists, so that, as Jung wrote in *Mysterium Coniunctionis*, the ones who continued to search for the lapis as a material product abandoned their mystical terminology, while those who were engrossed with the lapis-Christ parallel ceased their work with material substances (Jung 1963, 223).

I had no inklings of any of this at the time of the dream of course, but in the dream I nevertheless begged Jung to teach me to carve the stone, which symbolizes the learning of the special knowledge, the secret wisdom of the unconscious processes. Some years later I was to learn that the Aramaic word in the scriptures that was translated into the Greek as "carpenter" can mean "carver in stone." There is no doubt that the man Jesus was steeped in the mysteries of the unconscious, and Victorian mythologist, Gerald Massey, a scholar of no little knowledge and profundity, states that "carpenter," along with "builder," "potter," "architect," and so forth, was a title used by the ancients to designate the creators of the world and civilizations, actually spirit powers connected with the seven powers of the Higher Self, and that the Buddha was called "carpenter" in his own mythos.

Depicted on the walls in the cave-tomb of pharaoh Tuthmosis III, we find an example of the "journey through the Underworld," the unconscious. Here the god-king contends with all the forces of the Underworld, of the Tuat, or Amenta, in order to be born anew; that is, to reach the reborn, spiritualized state. It actually depicts a version of Jung's individuation process at its highest and most archetypal. Furthermore, Tuthmosis III was great-grandfather of the heretic pharaoh Akhenaten. It was this Akhenaten's dynasty, the eighteenth, that reintroduced the Aten cult, which had existed well over a thousand years earlier at the sacred city of Annu, or Iunu, the Biblical On, referred to as Heliopolis today. Aten was without doubt a Higher-Self figure for these Egyptians, though they rightly called him a god, and for Akhenaten he became the High God Himself.

With this dream I became the apprentice of Jung, the master workman, the disciple to his guru. Not only has a way been opened up for me in my lost state, but the way of the unconscious and the secret wisdom in which God Himself is the ultimate truth. With Jung and his works in the outer world—works which I devoured feverishly—and Jung in the inner unconscious processes, where he appeared as the "wise old man," between them they fashioned me, teaching me the secret knowledge, the gnosis, of the unconscious. This transforms both the individual personality and reality itself, and would eventually place the burden of a profound cultural task heavily upon my shoulders, which, though meaning much sacrifice and suffering, I nevertheless enthusiastically accepted.

Most of the contents of this dream and its interpretation may seem to suggest the occult and the supernatural, but the cultural task of which I speak turned out to be a highly religious one, concerning both Gnostic and Biblical Christianity to a high degree—the *real* spirit of Christianity. But all true religions are originally due to *direct* experiences of the unconscious processes in one way or another. This is not to say that the archetypal material does not occur as outer phenomena as well, for spirit reality may be experienced inwardly or outwardly, in the latter case when the two realities seem to merge. I knew with this dream that I had touched on something very special, something magical, or perhaps I should rather say that something very special and magical had touched me.

One final point is that after having now spent well over two decades experiencing the unconscious processes, I would say that the head of Jung in the dream is really the Holy Spirit in the specific form of the "wise old man," the "personification of spirit," as Jung puts it. Later dreams will show that the spirit of Jung appears to me on a number of occasions, and though it *seems* to be Jung himself, his spirit, it is quite possible, or even probable, that Jung's personal spirit has become merged with the Holy Spirit in higher reality.

> I am ill, suffering with anemia. What I need is blood, and a good deal of it, so my sister takes me to a bucket full of it.

This second dream goes right to the heart of the problem and pinpoints exactly what has been wrong with me for so many years. I am bereft of spirit, soul, and God as realities of my life and as pillars upholding the framework of orientation into which I, my society, and my universe must fit. As I was to learn, these religious values are natural to man, to his psyche and well-being, and it is the dissociation from them that causes such great disturbance both within the individual and in society itself. Religious symbols have always been needed to express man's association to these things because he is part of their reality, and they his.

The two sides of full reality are matter and spirit, the eternal opposites, and from the earliest times these were symbolized by flesh and blood. (The two sides are really three, body, soul, and spirit, for the soul inhabits the body to animate it, while the spirit redeems the soul with higher meaning.) The flesh is solid and the blood liquid, and the blood brings life to the flesh, so they are very apt symbols for matter and the spirit that livens and redeems it. Some primitive cultures even ate the one and drank the other in their religious rituals, it seems. Flinders Petrie, for example, uncovered human bones from early Egypt that could only have been gnawed by human teeth, the marrow from the bones also having been extracted. We must ask that since the flesh was eaten, was the blood also drunk?

The first type of worship was matriarchal, and women victims, so Gerald Massey tells us, were sacrificed and ritualistically devoured in what has been called "god-eating." This has been known all over the world, at least, in symbolical form. We find bread and wine being used as substitutes quite early, though in ancient Egypt it appears to have been bread and beer more often than bread and wine. The Egyptian ritual in the Book of the Dead says, "Give me bread and beer. Let me be made pure by the sacrificial joint, together with white bread." As with manna, the bread here is considered a spiritual, or spiritualizing, substance.

In the Old Testament, the mysterious priest-king Melchizedek brings the bread and wine to Abraham, and it is most probable that Melchizedek, "having neither beginning of days, nor end of life, but made like unto the Son of God," according to Hebrews 7:3, was the Higher Self of Abraham. Later Jews believed Melchizedek to be an incarnation of the Logos, making him a prefiguration of Christ. In the New Testament, at the Last Supper Christ tells the disciples that the bread is his body and the wine his blood. To take them together is to unite matter and spirit, which at the same time is also the integration of the god, i.e. the higher immortal, the Higher Self. Jesus himself says (John 6:53-6):

> . . . Verily, verily, I say unto you, Except ye eat the flesh of the Son of Man, and drink his blood, ye have no life in you. Whoso eateth my flesh, and drinketh my blood, hath eternal life; and I will raise him up at the last day. For my flesh is meat indeed, and my blood is drink indeed. He that eateth my flesh, and drinketh my blood, dwelleth in me, and I in him.

It was therefore said of Christ, "Thou art a priest for ever / after the order of Melchizedek," (Ps 110:4, Heb 7:17) and Christ's blood has become the redeeming blood. Christ is the vine and also the blood of the grape, whose followers therefore drink his blood. It was said that in drinking the wine, Christ drank his own blood. The full quotation from Hebrews 7:3 is: "Without father, without mother, without descent, having neither beginning of life, nor end of days; but made like unto the Son of God; abideth a priest continually." This clearly qualifies Melchizedek—who is the first Messiah figure (and therefore Higher Self figure) in Israel—to be the Higher Self of Abraham. Furthermore, Abraham almost certainly learns the secret wisdom processes from the Egyptians, as Moses was to do.

In the dream, I am ill with anemia and need plenty of blood myself. In other words, my mental attitude, my state of being, my whole life, exist far too much on the material side, so that I am in great need of a transfusion of spirit. My illness was being caused by the heavy surfeit of matter, and as matter is too real, spirit as the compensating medicament had to be just as real. Ordinary belief or faith would not do the trick; only direct experience would suffice. My sister in the dream represents an aspect of my feminine unconscious, the anima in Jungian terms. One of the main functions of the anima is to take male consciousness down to the archetypal depths of the collective unconscious, where both spirit and soul may be experienced directly. That is why it is my sister who takes me to the bucket of blood.

An alchemical text called the *Turba Philosophorum*, states: ". . . for the body incorporates the spirit through the tincture of the blood: for all that has spirit, has also blood" (Zosimos 1593b). One of the many names the alchemists used for the spirit Mercurius was *sanguis,* or blood, and George Ripley took blood to symbolize the higher spirit. Blood was also the red tincture, an earlier stage of the lapis.

The sun-god historically was usually associated with blood, partly because it symbolized spirit, and partly because of the blood produced by torture and suffering, which the god, what we would call today the Higher Self, must undergo in his mythic processes. The blood of the Persian Anthropos figure Gayomart was said to have turned into seven metals—the seven powers of the Higher Self—after soaking into the Earth. Primitive man symbolized the soul by the blood, and a certain Mithraic rite involved being covered with the blood of a slain bull, after which a sacramental meal of bread and wine was taken.

In the previous dream there was a stone that was alive with spirit, while this dream concerns the spiritual blood. In the *Theatrum Chemicum,* the

Christian alchemist Gerard Dorn says that the alchemical philosophers produced a "dark, red liquid, like blood" from the alchemical vessel that sweated out as drops. This blood brought healing and freed men from disease, and similarly in the last days a "pure man" will descend to earth sweating the bloody drops, come to save the world. Only the prophets of God can know this secret, and this according to the spirit Mercurius himself.

The legends of the Holy Grail are full of blood symbolism. The sick Fisher King, or Grail King, has been wounded with a lance by a heathen adversary, and not only does the king become sick, but so has the whole kingdom, so that the heathenism can only be healed by a respiritualization. The lance itself drips the blood and it flows into a silver vessel, along a golden pipe, and into another silver vessel. The Grail is not only the cup from which Christ drank at the Last Supper, but also the vessel that caught his blood as it flowed from the wound in his side, caused by the lance, as he hung on the cross. From then, the Grail has held Christ's blood, his divine essence or spirit, and it is this that brings the healing. The metal of the Grail as it catches the blood is not mentioned in most books, but according to Emma Jung's and Marie-Louise von Franz's *The Grail Legend* (1960), which reviews the history of Grail symbolism, it is given as silver. In its later appearance it is pure gold, of course. But then, earlier it is only a worldly cup; later it is a holy vision.

In certain doctrines of the Church in the Middle Ages, the blood flowing from Christ on the cross was more important than the crucifixion itself. The bleeding heart of Christ, whereby the lance of Longinus has pierced not only Christ's side but also his heart, is likewise highly symbolical, and there are depiction's of this in medieval art. In one woodcut (shown in *The Grail Legend*) two angels kneel beneath the cross holding a chalice between them in which Christ's blood is caught. There is a symbolic heart at each corner, a central heart replaces Christ's lower half on the cross, thus forming a mandala.

The heart represents feeling, primarily a feminine attribute, and while the blood is thought to indicate soul itself, the life essence, it more specifically symbolizes the spirit. In the Mass, the wine in the chalice means Christ's blood is infused with the Holy Spirit. The Fisher King's realm is sick and ailing because it has lost all spiritual values, not just beliefs and ideas, but *contact* with living spirit through *direct* experience. The redeeming blood of Christ, caught in the Grail vessel, will restore the lost spirit and health to the ailing kingdom.

In fact, it is difficult for us to imagine now just how precious and holy the symbolic holy blood became in the Middle Ages, but this was so because it represented the divine spirit itself, which would bring true redemption *as an actuality*, not just as an ideal. This is the meaning of the blood in my dream; i.e. it is the healing spirit. It would be a serious mistake to believe that all of this symbolism was invented by conscious man; it is rather that he *experienced* it, or most of it, through unconscious processes in the same way that I am now doing, though certain basic archetypal contents would have been developed and amplified. I had watched an old Bob Hope movie some weeks earlier in which there was a tavern called "The Bucket of Blood." with a large bucketful of blood hanging up outside. The unconscious had remembered this and was now using it to convey a very large quantity of blood.

> I am helping load a lorry with goods, but when I pick up a side of beef, my legs almost buckle under me with the weight, it is so heavy. It is a great strain to carry it, but I finally manage to throw the beef onto the wagon. My sister says to me, "The reason it is so heavy is that it is lifeless. It is white." I then pick up a gallon bottle containing blood and I say, "This is what it needs."

As often happens, the dream repeats exactly the same message as the last dream but in somewhat different images. The beef is so anemic it is white, and it is this that makes it such a burden to carry. In other words, the flesh needs the blood; that is, the mortal man needs the soul and the spirit to give him true life and meaning. Then the flesh, the world of heavy, meaningless matter, will no longer be such a burden, and this is why my own life has been weighing me down so much. The world of matter also propelled Nietzsche into catastrophic measures.

I was to find soul and spirit and the greatest meaning possible through the unconscious processes, and then the burden that is life would no longer be so heavy to carry. But mankind as a whole must realize this. Society itself cannot exist without the living spirit, for the floods of chaos soon deluge the culture. My sister represents the anima again, of course. The gallon container expresses the same meaning as the bucket, a very large amount.

> I am running down the street with a lion chasing after me, but I manage to run into the house where I live, and I slam the door just in time. However, the lion starts to push the door open, so that I have to push it shut again, and there ensues a great struggle, with both the lion and myself pushing hard from either side of the door. I am afraid that if I let the lion in, it will devour me.

Now things are really moving and the archetypal contents from the collective levels have begun to appear, the lion being one of the most well-known and important symbols of the collective unconscious. For the alchemists, the lion represented Mercurius, the double-natured power of the *prima materia*, for the "unclean body," and also for a certain stage of the transformation processes, though it is often encountered in some of the world's myths. The *prima materia* is really the unconscious itself, the material to be worked on to produce the "philosophical gold." The "unclean body" is its most raw, dangerous state. It really means the cold-blooded dragon, the basic collective lower spirit or soul-essence of matter, in a more developed, warm-blooded form. Though more acceptable than the dragon, nevertheless the lion is just as dangerous potentially.

So usually, the lion appears in alchemy when the dragon is dismembered, meaning that a higher stage has been reached in the opus though it may also appear earlier, as in my dream here. The alchemists stated that the lion's paws must be cut off to render it relatively harmless.

When Samson slays the lion in the Bible at almost the beginning of his story, he is slaying the dragon depths of the unconscious. Then "the Spirit of the Lord came mightily upon him," which means the power of the immortal Self. Samson sees a swarm of bees and honey coming from the carcass of the dead lion, and so he eats of the honey, also giving some to his parents. Later he sets a riddle for the hated Philistines concerning the lion: "Out of the eater came forth meat, and out of the strong came forth sweetness" (Judges 14:14). But although the Philistines ponder it for three days, only when Delilah wheedles it out of Samson on the seventh day do they obtain the answer. "What is sweeter than honey? and what is stronger than a lion?" (Judges 14:18).

However, the real meaning in terms of the inner processes is that the lion represents the dual-natured collective unconscious, out of which both highly dangerous and highly beneficial contents flow, and Samson, by slaying the dangerous lion-dragon side, has now partaken of the highly beneficial, honey side.

Herakles' wearing of the lion-skin has a similar meaning, namely, the defeat of the lion, of the unconscious, and the taking on of its power. He slays the Nemean lion after being given fifty wives, the daughters of King Thespius, and they symbolize temptation from the instinctual depths. But then the moon-harlot Omphale strips Herakles of his great strength by taking from him his club and lion-skin, and wearing the latter herself. Herakles has to wear female attire because he has been overcome by the feminine unconscious. Bacchus, the god of wine and ecstatic frenzy, very significantly became crazy when the furies of Hell sprang at him in the form of a lion, again the lower forces of the unconscious, which may well overwhelm consciousness during the processes.

The lion is a symbol of Christ, of Vishnu in India, and of Horus and Iu-em-hetep in Egypt, all Higher-Self figures. Sekhet in Egypt, consort to Ptah, "the grandfather of the gods" was the lioness, or lioness-headed goddess, the Great Mother. It also is a symbol of the Antichrist, for as 1 Peter 5:8 says, ". . . your adversary the devil, as a roaring lion, walketh about, seeking whom he may devour." There is also a lion of Mithras that has seven stars above its head, the seven powers of the Higher Self, of which I shall speak in depth later. Dionysus, in a solar aspect, is a lion termed "the roarer," while again in Egypt, Atum was two lions on top of the sacred Mound, the old lion and the young lion. This almost certainly referred to the divine Father and Son, and the archetype is similarly expressed in the two asses upon which the Messiah had to ride into Jerusalem. When Christ does this it is an allusion to this same divine Father and Son archetype.

So although the lion usually symbolizes the spirit Mercurius in dreams, it has in the past also meant the solar aspect. We find this several times in the Old Testament when God Himself is likened to a roaring lion. Hosea (11:10) says: "He (God) shall roar like a lion." Jeremiah (25:30) says: "He (God) shall roar from on high." While Amos (3:8) tells us: "The lion hath roared, who will not fear? The Lord God hath spoken, who can but prophesy?" And Hezekiah (Isaiah 38:13) states: "As a lion, he (God) breaketh all my bones."

In my dream, the unconscious, the great collective depths, want to be "let in," but being very much afraid, I am determined to keep them out, for I am a raw novice as yet, and know nothing. Jung remarks that the rose-colored blood, which was significant to the last dream, appears in many alchemical texts. He mentions Khunrath saying that the alchemical lion, signifying all and conquering all, had rose-colored blood, and that the stone, blood, and lion, which have been the main features of these first three dreams, are connected with Christ as the perfect healer. However, the Redeemer figure of which alchemy speaks is not said to be Christ himself, the *filius microcosmi*, but his parallel; the lower Self, the *filius macrocosmi:* Osiris, rather than his son Horus.

> It is night as I lie as if dead on a slab in a mortuary. Suddenly, I awake and declare, "What is this? I am not dead. Why does everyone think I am dead?" I get to my feet and go to the door, but find that it is locked. I then spot a hammer and chisel lying on the floor, and picking them up, I start to knock a hole in the wall. I say, "This will be my way out."

For much of my adult life up to that time I had gradually fallen into living a dead life, if that is not too much of a contradiction. From being a lively young teenager, I had eventually sunk into a morbid, neurotic state, drinking heavily at times as an escape, and then suffering my breakdown. I did recover to a degree and was even trying to build up a structure of positive values, but these were bad times when I could see little hope. This was because I could see little hope for life itself, there being no real meaning and deep purpose to it. With the loss of God and spiritual values in the twentieth century, man was left alone and soulless in a cold, unfriendly universe, and though you could try to have faith, it never really worked because reason and scientific knowledge were against it.

As I have said, the possibility that Nietzsche might be right was my greatest fear, and that, in the end, I could not take. For me, reality must have truth that is eternal and right; wisdom and justice *must* be the foundations of the universe, as well as of the culture to which I belong. Above all, God must be real in some way in order for all these things to be secure and for all to be right with the world. But I had lost my way, as the first dream shows, and I was moving very shakily between vague hope and despair. On the surface, I was trying to build up the structure of unshakable values, but my heavy drinking at the time reveals my true inner state.

On top of this, and this was gnawing away at me personally, was the fact that everything must fade and die—the best, greatest, and most beautiful things, the people and things we love—so that there is nothing permanent. We lose everything as it slips through our fingers like sand. I knew I had to find an answer to Nietzsche, to his answer. This meant finding truth that, contrary to his beliefs, is everlasting, finding morality that exists even when there are no people to know it, finding pity and compassion that are natural to the universe because they are a valid part of eternal truth.

Modern intellectuals who see deeper and higher meaning in Nietzsche and his answer are the most deluded people of all, for they substitute twisted, dissociated thinking for hard reality. Let they, themselves, be victims of stark evil and cruelty and then let us see if they still agree with "beyond good and evil" and "beyond compassion."

Now, like a miracle, this dream suggests I have stumbled upon the solution, and it is an awakening as though from the dead. I have discovered Jung and the collective unconscious, and there is suddenly hope, and my heartbeat quickens. Now, with the awakening, a way has been pointed out to me that may lead to some kind of permanence and eternal meaning, which an awakening from the dead must be, though I must hack my way through to it.

Indeed, in the very first dream, the unconscious has caused me to say, "There is no such thing as death, only change." As it turned out, I was to find meaning and purpose beyond my wildest dreams, and find them as a matter of experience, rather than any kind of vague faith. Put simply, I was to find the Higher Self and God as *realities* of the collective unconscious, that other reality that lies behind the material universe.

What the dream amounts to is the beginning of the transformation processes known in the ancient world and in alchemy, which in Egypt occurred in Amenta, the Underworld, or the depths of the collective unconscious. On the one hand, the resurrection processes meant Osirification, which was promised to the deceased at death if he had lived a righteous and blameless life; but on the other hand, these resurrection processes were founded on the unconscious processes which lead to spiritual rebirth. But these involved much suffering and "dismemberment" of the psyche, in order for it to be reassembled in an unassailable way. Because this process involves the Higher Self, the immortal structure to which the conscious personality is connected, a sense of immortality is also experienced by consciousness, as it seems to share in the immortality of the Higher Self. Or, to quote Ephesians 5:14, "Awake, O sleeper and arise from the dead, and Christ shall give you light."

> There is a huge dinosaur, a tyrannosaurus, attacking the city. It crushes buildings under its feet, and picks up the people who are scattering and trying to escape and devours them. There is great panic everywhere, the crowds screaming and running in all directions, and I realize that it is up to me to try to kill the monster. I have only a short sword, and I am terrified, but nevertheless determined to make a fight of it.
>
> As I face the monster, the blade of my sword suddenly drops off and I am left helpless. The creature then lifts me up with its front claws and I think it is going to tear me to pieces and devour me. Instead, it looks at me and smiles. This makes me realize that it can be friendly and harmless, if it so wishes, and that I am safe with it—at least, for now.

I have just begun my journey into the unconscious and so now confront the dragon, which symbolizes the terrible side of the instinctual depths of the World Soul. The fact that the blade falls off my sword means that, as a simple novice, I am woefully inadequate to fight the collective unconscious in its negative aspect.

In the Grail legends, based on actual transformation quests through the unconscious, the special sword plays an important role, as does Excalibur with King Arthur. But when, in one version, the Grail Knight Perceval receives his special sword and it is broken, the imagery has the same meaning as in my dream here. Perceval is just starting his quest and he has much to experience and learn before he is fit to be the hero who battles the tremendous negative forces of the unconscious depths.

The broken sword reflects, in this way, the shattered state of the values of consciousness, fragmented and somewhat weak and useless. Only when consciousness has learned to think in a more spiritual and unified way towards its great goal will the sword become whole and be a cutting and thrusting force for the hero on the quest, which ultimately is always a moral and religious one. The reassembled sword also means the unified Self, and in the Galahad version of the story, when the sword is reassembled there is yet a small crack remaining. This means that for whoever's individuation process the tale was based upon, it was not quite completed. There still remained some small weakness in the man's character, be it ever so small.

As to my dream, just as I believe I am going to be devoured, the monster smiles at me, proving that it can be friendly, if it so wishes. It all depends on the attitude and aims of consciousness towards the unconscious, which in my case is to seek wider truth and deeper meaning. This will give the unconscious due recognition and let it through from the darkness to the light of consciousness, which it partly wants, although another aspect of it fights against it.

I have not experienced the higher spirit side yet, and when I do, I shall be deeply influenced by it. This will mean that when I face the lower instinctual side again with definite spiritual values—definite because they have been experienced—it will cause the lower unconscious to show its ferocious, negative side, because spirit, being the eternal and diametrical opposite to the chthonic depths, is anathema to it. There will then ensue my fight with the dragon, which I will undertake on behalf of spirit, which actually forms the basis of the myth of the hero-dragon fight that is found in cultures all over the world from earliest recorded times. Thus, in the Babylonian myth, Marduk fights and slays the great serpent-dragon Tiamat on behalf of the sun-god; in Canaan, Baal slays Yam; in Egypt, Horus slays both Apep and Set; in Scandinavia, Sigurd slays Fafnir, and so on.

Many of the heroes are gods, but initially human ego-consciousness has to descend to the unconscious depths to slay the dragon, and this allows the Higher Self to develop and come forth, ultimately as a god and savior (as a fact of the unconscious, of course). Jesus the man had to defeat Satan, "that old serpent," in his temptation, in order to bring forth the Son of Man who, in highest form, is the Son of God. This process, at its ultimate fulfillment, always amounts to God's incarnation, though it may be of the dark side rather than the light, depending on the values and aims of consciousness. Jung says that although the dragon, and reptiles in general, symbolize the instinctual depths, they are nevertheless the forerunners of the Higher Self.

This is why in legends and fairy tales the dragon or serpent always guards the treasure. They do not, however, "guard" the treasure in reality, but rather, they represent the first, lower, chthonic form of the Higher Self, and must be encountered and defeated for the treasure of the

Higher Self to be attained. The serpent is sometimes three-headed, representing the lower Trinity, or sometimes seven-headed, which represents the dark lower side of the seven powers that are found with Higher Self figures all over the ancient, and not so ancient, world.

In Egypt, the seven-headed crocodile dragon, Sevekh, (Sevekh means "sevenfold"), was son of the Great Mother, Apt, the World Soul as Dragon Mother. She was called the "Great Mother of him who is married to his mother." These symbolize the lower, feminine collective unconscious, the World Soul. This World Soul brings forth the lower side of the Higher Self, the "Son of the Mother," in dark form, as contrasted with the lighter form (Sophia, for example) who has seven sons that countermatch the seven-headed dragon. These in turn countermatch the Higher Self as Son of the Father, the Christ figure, who in Revelation is sevenfold in several ways. In alchemy, the dragon, or sometimes the lion, must have its paws cut off, and both lion and dragon devour themselves in the process. The dragon is also cut up and dismembered, taking the form of a man who must have his limbs and head cut off, which reminds us of the dismemberment of Osiris and his golden head.

The myth of the hero always concerns the perilous descent of ego-consciousness into the depths of the unconscious, where it may well perish unless it can face the menacing onslaught and not only survive, but thrive on the experience. There is an illustration in the 1590 alchemical text *Rosarium Philosophorum* of a lion devouring the sun (the light), which symbolizes only too well the highly perilous situation. Another motif is becoming tied fast to the rocks at the bottom of the sea or in Hades, unable to rise to the fresh air of the surface again, to the world of consciousness.

But the theme may be that the would-be hero is swallowed, like Jonah, or scorched to death by the dragon, or blinded, like Samson. He triumphs at first by slaying the lion, but Samson later loses due to his weakness for women. The dragon must be faced, fought, and endured for the treasures of the spirit, of the Higher Self, to be attained; these treasures have been expressed as the great jewel, the Paradise of Peace, and by sundry other terms. Though the danger is often from the watery depths, alchemically it involves the intense heat of the retort, and the shaving of the head by priests in many religions was originally done to represent the scorching of the initiate, in which his hair is symbolically burnt off.

In Revelation, the red dragon appears from out of Heaven to devour the divine child of the pregnant Sun Woman as soon as it is born, which causes the Archangel Michael and his angels to fight the dragon and its angels in defense of mother and child. The dragon has ten horns and seven heads, with seven crowns upon the heads. No side slays the other, but the dragon and his dark angels are cast out of Heaven and "into the Earth" for his evil intentions.

> There is a dangerous lion about and it suddenly approaches. However, before it can bite me, I grab it at the back of the neck with one hand, while with the other hand I slowly cut off its head with my penknife. All the while, the lion is trying to break loose, but finally the task is done and the lion is rendered harmless. Some teenagers close by are somewhat critical of my actions but I say, "It had to be done."

Here is the lion again, the highly dangerous unconscious, but I render it harmless by cutting off its head, which is a variation of the alchemical cutting-off of the lion's paws. As I say in the dream, this has to be done to begin my real task in the unconscious, and the processes could not continue otherwise. I will just add that the severing of the head of the spirit of the Earth, which is what the lion represents ultimately, runs right through the Western Mysteries from ancient Egypt, as intimated in the earlier dream. A giant sometimes represents the dragon in mythology, so when David slays Goliath and cuts off his head, it has the very same meaning as severing the lion's head in my dream above. The decapitation of John the Baptist, the Green Man, and so on, is the same. The cutting off of the lions paws is a variation of this, meaning the defeat of the lower Earth spirit, or at least, rendering it harmless, or even amicable. Gawain cuts off a lion's head in the quest for the holy lance.

> There is a knock at my front door and when I answer, a very presentable young man, who seems to be a Jehovah's Witness or a Mormon, confronts me. However, I can see through his pose and I know that he is an agent of the devil. "You can't fool me," I say, "I know you are a demon." He replies, "Well, you are one of us now. You reject God and Christ."
>
> "That is only because I am unable to believe," I answer, "but I don't follow you. I still believe in right and good." At my words, he changes

into his true shape, horns and all, and he attacks me. A terrible fight
ensues, but I am not at all afraid because I know that I am the stronger
and that the demon will not defeat me. I pick up a wooden spar to hit the
demon with; the spar has a horizontal piece loosely attached to it, and
when I raise it up, a cross is formed. Lightning flashes, casting the
shadow of the cross onto my adversary, and as I speak the Latin words,
Omnia bene vici, which I keep repeating, this causes the demon to fall to
the ground, where, screaming in agony, he crumbles to dust.

We humans are illogical creatures, quite often contradicting ourselves
in our thinking, and this was largely the case with myself at this time. It
was imperative that I should find spiritual meaning, to help construct my
unassailable fortress of values. Though periodically I had been able to
force myself to take God on trust, as a sort of philosophical postulate, it
would all come crashing down again at other times. I would argue with
myself hither and thither, from one side to the other, from hopeful belief
to rationalistic disbelief, though it is true that when I heard the negative
arguments put forward by others, they seemed quite naïve and limited.

Some of these unbelievers were philosophers and scholars, considered to possess great minds, but to me they always seemed to lack
deeper wisdom—though at that time I had no notion what deeper wisdom was. However, I did know that it was not concerned with intellectualism and rationalistic powers of reason, which the philosophers and
scholars possessed in abundance and which lead to nowhere, but rather
was concerned with the mysteries of the soul and of God, if these
existed.

Yet more than this was involved. I had projected my feminine counterpart in the unconscious, my anima, onto the real-life woman Julie,
and because a love relationship was not really possible and was causing
me the greatest torment, I was now blindly blaming God for the suffering. My attempts to build my philosophical framework seemed not only
unimportant now, but even detrimental to my emotional involvement
with her. This did not fit in with her own likes and needs, and in consequence I was resolving to give up my search for lasting truth to go her
way. Furthermore, maybe she was right, and maybe Nietzsche was right;
maybe I had been wrong all along.

Maybe I was a naïve idiot for caring so much about establishing
"truth in eternity," which seemed of paramount importance to me.

Maybe I should live, then, rather by the Will to Power, by "yea-saying," beyond good and evil and morality in answer to the suffering that is life. Although all this was way above Julie's head, she had nevertheless become bound up with the great existential problems that had for so long been so important to me.

The truth is, my yearning for Julie was *intended* by the unconscious and had great purpose. It meant the overwhelming desire to be united with my feminine anima, and beyond that, ultimately with the Higher Self. It forced me on and on through the unconscious searching and hoping, for it was the only way that I could turn. Julie would appear in my dreams as someone unattainable, although I just might be able to win her if I fought long and hard enough, and even then it would take a miracle. I had to win her from the clutches of the dragon depths, to put it mythologically, as the individual soul is part of the great World Soul. It never occurred to me that winning Julie in the unconscious was not the same as winning her in outer reality, but as it was the projection of the archetype from the depths that was causing the intense and numinous attraction in the first place, I was actually getting to the root of the problem in my unconscious quest, I was therefore getting to the root of my suffering.

The reason I digress with this is that for a time I blamed God for my suffering—bitterly so—though, I had lost my belief at this time. This is what I mean when I say we are illogical. While I had searched for God, truth, and meaning for years, I now came to reject Him and His way, though His existence was extremely doubtful in any case. The devil then saw his chance, or thought he did, and came to befriend me in the dream. A person may certainly turn to evil through suffering—at least, for a time—but it was not the case with myself. I was quite easily able to fight the evil off, as the dream shows.

What surprised me was the fact that it was a cross, the main symbol of Christianity, that helped me to defeat the demon; and there was also the flash of lightning, the thunderbolt of the gods, signifying the power of God, or so the dream was saying. As for the words I repeated, *Omnia bene vici*," though I do not know Latin, I could just about figure them out to mean, "All good conquers." This dream of defeating evil with the symbol of Christ, the cross, plus the lightning from above, impressed me deeply at the time, especially since it was precisely these things I was deciding to reject.

The symbol of the cross overflows with tremendous meaning, and many times over the years I have defeated evil in dreams with a cross. The valedictory words of St. Peter, supposedly spoken as he was crucified upside down, express this beautifully. I need only quote the first few sentences here.

> O name of the cross, hidden mystery! O grace ineffable that is pronounced in the name of the cross. O nature of man that cannot be separated from God! O love unspeakable and indivisible, that cannot be shown forth by unclean lips! I grasp thee now, I that am at the end of my earthly course. I will declare thee as thou art, I will not keep silent the mystery of the cross, which was once shut and hidden from my soul.

For Peter, there is a deeper meaning to the cross here, a hidden secret, which we now know involves other realities that may be reached through the unconscious. That secret involves the immortal who is the Son of God, the "god of the four quarters," known in some form to all peoples at all times, as the Higher Self in its fourfoldness. The fourfoldness of the cross symbolizes the four emanations of the Higher Self, often expressed as a 3 + 1 structure, as do the four sons of Horus, the four dogs of Marduk, the four hollow places of Enoch, the fourfold wheel of Ezekiel, and so on. The true cross is also one of the main symbols of true order as it counterbalances itself from all directions. And as I show elsewhere, the wholeness of the human psyche, of the Higher Self, and of God, are fourfold in nature. The cross, as some of the dreams that follow will show, is a very powerful symbol of great holiness to the unconscious, as indeed, the symbol of the Son of God, and of God Himself, must be.

> I had a number of dreams in which I am with two men and a woman, symbolizing the quaternity structure of the human psyche, and this one has some significant details.
>
> I am with two men and a woman at a registrar's office at a town hall, and we sit with the elderly female registrar in front of us. One of the men I am with is marrying his woman companion, and so the other man and myself are witnesses.

Suddenly, an angelic choir above starts to sing heavenly music and the registrar asks if anyone knows a poem. Surprising myself, I begin to quote scripture.

"Let not your heart be troubled, ye believe in God, believe also in me. In my Father's house are many mansions; if it were not so, I would have told you."

Then I think of Judas Iscariot, confusing him with "doubting Thomas," who actually comes in the text (John 14) a couple of verses later. Still, I am highly surprised by all of this.

At this time I was continuing in the state of spiritual disorientation, though desperately searching for answers as well as considering Nietzsche's way, but Christianity was still dead to me now, despite recent dreams. Like many other people, I found the literal acceptance of the stories of the Bible absurd, and had felt so since about ten years of age, yet the unconscious in this dream is now not only insisting on a religious solution to my lost state in these dreams, but to a decidedly Christian one. Why this is so will become clear, but the text that the unconscious has me quote here is where Christ basically states, "Let not your heart be troubled, believe in me." I did not know it at the time, but Christ is the main symbol in the West for the immortal that lies within us all, the divine Self, and this is what the dream is saying: Believe in Christ, in the Higher Self.

Jung has been accused of all sorts of neuroses and complexes for proposing the "feminine fourth," as well as the "recalcitrant fourth," as realities of both the personal and collective unconscious, but I had many dreams at this time of myself with two men and a woman, forming a 3 + 1 structure. As I came to realize, the human psyche consists of a fourfold structure that has a primary function in consciousness, opposed by an opposite fourth function that is sunk in the unconscious, with two auxiliary functions in between. One auxiliary function is closer to the primary function, while the other is closer to the fourth function.

The fourth is always opposite in nature to the primary function, and so while the two auxiliary functions may with some difficulty be won over to the primary conscious function during the processes, the fourth is always recalcitrant, the "odd man out" that is apt to go off on its own, wildly opposing consciousness. This aspect is always far more difficult to win over, and as it tends to become contaminated by the repressed shadow, it may therefore be felt to be the very devil by consciousness.

However, the fourth may be represented as a woman to the male consciousness, and presumably by a man in the female. The four functions are sensation, which tells us that something is there; thinking, which tells us what it is; feeling, the emotional tone and value of it; and intuition, the "sixth sense" which may bring us added insight into it. Any of these may be the primary function, and so thinking, for example, will be opposed by undeveloped feeling, and so forth.

Here in the dream, the woman represents the fourth function, unified with its auxiliary function, although all four are really united, including myself as the primary function that is in consciousness, unified to a degree with the rest of the psyche. Christ is brought into the dream because he symbolizes the Higher Self, the Anthropos, the inner Great Man to whom the psyche is attached. Yet I must add that Christ himself is also alluded to, and not just the Higher Self, as future dreams will show.

One final point is that "doubting Thomas" could refer to myself, my state of mind at this time, though why I confuse him with Judas Iscariot is still something of a puzzle to me even now. I wonder if Judas represents the "recalcitrant" one to the totality of Christ?

A priest takes me into an inn, though he soon disappears when we enter. In the middle of the room is the bar, which has four sides forming a square. Inside of this is an androgynous Christ, serving the customers, acting as a sort of barman. Sitting over by the wall are the spiritual elders with their long, white beards, about a dozen of them, watching over the situation. Christ comes over to serve me in a friendly manner, but I grab him by the arm and demand, "Why isn't your religion more practical?" By this I mean why does not Christianity act as Communism is supposed to, taking the wealth from the rich to help the poor, and so be more socially reforming? But Christ is very perturbed by my words, and breaking from my grasp, moves away.

I then turn to the elders and shout, "Don't be fooled. Ask yourselves why this religion isn't more practical." This disturbs them, and they seem shocked. I then leave, and as I walk down the street I am followed by two government agents who stop me and demand my assurance that I will not spread my subversive ideas, which would be highly dangerous. So I

give my assurance, out of cowardice partly, but also, perhaps, because I
have the feeling deep down that I am wrong.

The fact that it is a priest who takes me into the inn presumably
means the dream concerns religious matters. The central bar has four
sides, making a square, and as it contains Christ, it therefore forms a
mandala with a god at the center, the "god of the four quarters," a very
ancient archetype. This represents the Higher Self in its fourfoldness,
again, four denoting wholeness. It has the same meaning as the Buddha
on his podium with a pillar at each corner, the prophet Daniel's Son of
Man with four beasts rising from the sea, the Babylonian god Marduk
with his four dogs, or Horus with his four sons.

Jung states that of all the many hundreds of mandalas he had seen
produced by his patients, there was never a deity in the center. He says
in *Psychology and Religion:* "The center . . . is a star, a sun, a flower, a
cross with equal arms, a precious stone, a bowl filled with water or
wine, a serpent coiled up, or a human being, but never a god."

Jung concluded that this was due to the peculiar psychic condition
of modern man, but all I can say in reply is that from the beginning of
my own dream processes it was usually Christ who appeared in mandalas, and this for a while when I was a nonbeliever, when Christianity
was dead and buried for me, when I did not know its hidden meaning.

These mandala visions, and ones of Christ, should have told me that
something special was in the cards, but I was a raw recruit, a novice just
setting out on my quest in the vast unconscious, and I still had a tremendous amount to learn. A fundamental transformation had to occur
within my personality before I could come to understand the deeper
meaning of the processes and their symbolism, and although this was to
happen eventually, it was a long and gradual process.

Now in the dream, Christ is hermaphroditic, male and female, and
as Jung points out, so is the Original Man in mythology. For example, in
the Vedas this man unites with his own feminine half, having produced
her himself, and this is the same meaning as Eve coming from the rib of
Adam. The Self is a *complexio oppositorum,* a complexity of opposites
and a totality *par excellence.* It is therefore both male and female, as well
as containing all other opposites.

That is why the Pharaoh Akhenaten was sometimes depicted with certain feminine characteristics; being a god in his divine aspect based on the

phenomenon of the Higher Self, he was androgynous. Certain modern scholars, not knowing the real basis of the god-man in mythology, put it all down to Akhenaten being effeminate himself, suffering from Frolich's syndrome, despite the fact that there are other depictions of him with a normal male shape. There are early depictions of Christ himself where he is portrayed with a number of feminine characteristics, breasts, and so forth, and even as feminine and masculine Wisdom combined, so that the figure is the goddess Sophia with the beard and other male features of Christ.

As a novice in the dream I have no knowledge of any of this as yet, and the real meaning of Christ is lost on me, so that I expect him to be some kind of social reformer or revolutionist. I am also irreverent, abusive, and arrogant in my attitude, so that the "agents" have to extract from me the promise not to spread my subversive ideas around. My attitude also causes Christ to retreat, perturbed.

I completely fail to understand that Christ, and therefore the Higher Self, is so much more than a mere social reformer. Though having different levels, ultimately, He is the Son of God, the immortal to whom we mortal human beings are attached. He represents everything that is eternal and holy, and is the true link making the connection between Man and God. This is psychic from the human side, but a spiritual reality as the Self. Christ, or the Self, is the direct link, for we are part of the self, and He is part of God. He has more meaning and light than any mortal being could ever wish for, and in this way saves and redeems mankind. As physical beings we need bread in our bellies, and we must ensure that everyone receives it, but Christ, the Higher Self, is the eternal bread and wine for our souls. However, the Christ in the dream expresses the fourfold nature of the Self as well as his male/female nature.

Jung says that the light inherent in Christ would not have been perceived by human consciousness had there not been a correspondence and attraction between the Christ figure and the archetype of the savior within the unconscious. This latter is the Higher Self, the true authority of the human psyche, which in ultimate form became a worldly phenomenon in the figure of Christ (Jung 1959a).

All I remember of this dream is that I see a white ape.

The ape symbolizes the sub-human, instinctual part of the human personality, or psychic structure, which is still there in the depths of the psyche. Jung tells us that the conscious attitude must be changed to accommodate the reconstruction of the instinctual part of the psyche, symbolized by the ape, within the structure of consciousness.

In other words, the instinctual part of the psyche must be made conscious and integrated, as must all other parts, in order to develop the Higher Self, and to bring to him all parts that rightly belong to him. In the long run they do not belong to consciousness; rather consciousness is one of the parts that belong to the Self, though a very important one, being the agent of the Self in the world of matter.

The Gnostic demiurge, who created the lower world of matter, was said to be the "ape of God," and Zosimos of Panopolis, the Greek alchemist of the 3rd century A.D., also called the devil the "ape of God."

> I am walking along the seashore with a young woman when a sailing ship comes in from across the sea. A man disembarks who wants to kill the girl, saying that she must die because she has caused so much trouble. However, I protect her, stating that a lot of great and important things depend upon her. When I try to touch the man, my hand goes right through him, showing that he is spirit. He remarks, "No, Nietzsche was wrong."

The seashore is where land and sea meet, and so symbolizes the meeting point between the conscious and unconscious realms. The girl represents the feminine element in my unconscious, the anima, and she is obviously in a very negative state as she has been the cause of much trouble. This means that in my conscious life, some of the moods of depression, listlessness, and gloom have been due to her negative effects, though by no means all. The anima can certainly pull a man down to gluttony, greed, lechery, and so on, and may even drive a man to suicide.

The man sailing across the seas, who is apparently spirit/soul manifested, comes from the collective unconscious and seems to be the agent of the Self, as the sea implies the collective depths. Though he intends to kill the girl, I protect her, because she must be redeemed and integrated rather than killed (stifled), for only then can the processes involving the Higher Self develop to the higher stages. The Self must have all of its parts for wholeness, including the anima.

The man says that Nietzsche was wrong, and this is a good sign. I had been playing with the idea of following Nietzsche in his selfish will to power, and notions beyond good and evil, though this was never at all serious. This struggle had some influence on the unconscious, as my battle with the demon in the earlier dream showed, when it thought I had joined the ranks of evil. However, Nietzsche and his way are now rejected. (Nietzsche was not evil, but his "way," if followed far enough, ultimately leads to evil.)

Rejecting spirit reality and Christian values and setting up the Superman and the will to power in their place, Nietzsche eventually went insane. Though his madness is generally believed to be due to syphilis, Jung states that quite simply, his mind burst. The small, frail mind of man is tiny before the eternal mystery of God, and it is wiser and safer to remember this. The collective unconscious, the "other reality," stretches out to infinity, and we are smaller than specks of dust before it. Modern man, without realizing it and without necessarily wishing to do so, has followed Nietzsche to no small degree, and will pay dearly for it. Modern man is not altogether to blame for the way he thinks, but then, neither was Nietzsche, but the catastrophe in culture and consciousness still occurred.

Jung comments that when the non-personal power of the unconscious in positive form, represented by Christianity, is brought into conflict with the inflated and bloated pride of individual human consciousness, seen to no small degree in Nietzsche with his Superman, the human personality may ultimately be destroyed in the conflict. We saw this happen on a grand scale in Nazi Germany (Jung 1958).

> There is a knock at the front door and when I go to answer it, I find that it is Julie, representing my anima in a romantic aspect, my "ladye soule," for whom I have fallen so deeply. We exchange a few pleasant words, though she stays outside, and then I say to her, "You know, one day you will marry me." To which she replies, "Yes, I think I shall." She then leaves, while I go indoors again to my family. My mother asks, "Who was that?" to which I reply, "Oh, it was only Julie," as though it is the most natural thing in the world for her to call.

She had in reality never been to our house, and none of my family knew her. This dream promises that my anima-soul, represented by Julie, will one day be unified with consciousness in the syzygy, in this context, meaning the unification in the psyche of male and female. Though my family do not know her in real life, in the unconscious she is well known. However, future events were to reveal that the winning of the anima is no easy task. There are different aspects of the anima, and Julie represents just one of them, though an extremely important one.

"Julie" represented my feminine side in the unconscious, yet not just the twin of consciousness, but the deeper aspects of the anima that are connected to the collective unconscious and eternity. Every man has this feminine counterpart in the unconscious, just as a woman has her male counterpart, known as the animus. The anima has various aspects, both personal and collective, and we see many examples of the archetype in the literature, myths, and legends of the world, where she is the Beatrice of Dante, the Ariadne of Perseus, and the Helen of Simon Magus. In her more negative form, she is Circe, Delilah, and Melusina.

A man may unknowingly project his anima onto a real-life woman and become infatuated with and besotted by her, and although he may come to realize that she is largely a projection from within himself, it makes no difference, the projection continues. Certain Jungian writers have stated that once the projection is realized and understood, it is broken, the fascination and libido then being turned entirely inwards, but in my own experience this is not the case. I was still mesmerized by Julie for some years even after I discovered the source of her power and her meaning in the unconscious, where she was necessary to the individuation processes themselves. The Julie outside remained as magical and mesmerizing as the Julie inside.

Because she ultimately belongs to the lower soul-depths of the unconscious, the anima, or soul-image, has a strong tendency to become lost in base materiality. So a woman of low morals makes a suitable receptacle for the projection. In the Christian myth we find her as Mary Magdalene. Although she represents the anima, she may also have been the real-life woman onto whom Jesus the man projected his feminine soul, and whom he won over to higher spiritual values by casting out her seven devils. The Virgin Mary represents not only the purified aspect of the anima, but the World Soul itself in highest meaning, as *Theotokos*, "god-bearer." As Jung says, the Virgin Mary is actually Sophia, goddess of Wisdom, and we could even say that the Virgin Mary is Mary Magdalene in a collective aspect and purified.

Certain other women in the Bible, though portrayed as wives, are actually anima figures, including, Sarah, Rebekah, Rachel, Asenath,

Bathsheba, and the Woman of Samaria. These figures represent the collective feminine soul. Simon Magus is said to rescue the prostitute Helen from a brothel, and she too turns out to be the collective anima who has become sunk in base materiality, in need of rescue and redemption. When the alchemists spoke of the incestuous marriage between the brother-sister pair, it symbolized the unification of ego-consciousness with the anima. In a version of the Grail legends, the Fisher King is told to marry his son and daughter to one another, to restore fertility to the barren Fisher Kingdom. That story has the same meaning as the preceding examples.

The anima is found in myths and legends all over the world, sometimes connected with a lake or pool, water being the main symbol of the feminine depths of the unconscious. She may bring a man much inner light, as she can lead him to the depths and heights of the collective unconscious wherein dwell the eternal forces of spirit and soul, the unification of which is the goal of the inner quest.

There are reckoned to be four stages of the anima. The first stage is the purely biological, physically sexual; the second stage the romantic love interest; the third stage the religious, represented by the Virgin Mary; and the fourth stage, the highest form of the feminine spirit, represented by Sophia, goddess of wisdom. However, these are not always so definite and clear. As I said above, Jung equates the Virgin Mary with Sophia, and this is so, as Mary is the World Soul raised and purified to her highest meaning, ready to receive the seed of God.

Julie, who affected me so deeply, represented my own feminine soul in the depths of the unconscious, the anima at the personal level. Jung states that such a woman can bring great upheaval to a man, but may also lead to spiritual transformation. My yearning for Julie was the yearning for my own feminine soul, and also for that "other reality" to which she could lead me, although Julie herself as a woman was a very strong attraction. But I knew nothing of this for some time, for I knew very little of Jung and depth psychology, which would be my way to knowledge, to enlightenment, and to transformation. As yet, I was still in a state of torment, darkness, and disorientation.

Small of stature but well proportioned, Julie had a face that was beautiful, angelic almost, with large deep eyes and a slightly upturned nose. She looked so innocent, like a little girl at times, and yet was very sensuous and voluptuous, so that a man would have mixed emotions and conflicting desires concerning her. You could not imagine her being married, living a normal married life, not as she was; it just did not fit her. I would sometimes wonder what she would do as she grew old. She was surrounded by men now, usually other women's husbands, and this would continue into her middle-age, when she would be even more beautiful, if possible. But what would she do when she was old? However, we are not meant to live our lives solely on considerations of our old age, for life must be lived now.

Julie was a disturbing force, a cause of great inner earthquakes, a "Disturber of the Peace," as Jung calls this type, and it would be possible for her to wreck any number of marriages in the world, because she was able to affect and disturb a man so deeply in the unconscious. Julie was not just any woman upon whom I had projected my anima; she was *the* archetypal anima-figure.

According to Jung, this type of woman is the result of a mother complex in which the daughter has a negative reaction to an overly-maternal mother, which may result in the extinction of the maternal instinct in the daughter. This extinction automatically results in over-development of the sexual instinct, usually with an unconscious, incestuous relationship with the father. She is, of course, a victim of complexes over which she has no knowledge or control, and so while many a wife would wish to kill her, she deserves sympathy and understanding.

It is ironic that while I was the one man who understood these complexes at work in Julie, and therefore could have helped her and given her real support, I was also the one man she did not want. This was by far for the best in the long run from my point of view, as I was forced to search for and attempt to win Julie through the unconscious, where she was my anima-soul. This led to my hero's quest for the Holy Grail, the Philosopher's Stone, or whatever else by which you may wish to symbolize the Higher Self. She faded a little in time when my real task of the Higher Self took over. Ironically, I had thought Julie would lead me away from my need to find spiritual values, but to a degree she led me directly to the divine source. She and Jung, that is, for this pair form the archetypal situation as old as the hills: Asenath and Potiphera with Joseph in Egypt; Rachel and Laban with Jacob; Zipporah and Jethro with Moses, and so forth.

When Joseph interprets dreams successfully for Pharaoh, he, Joseph, is greatly honored and rewarded, being made a sort of vizier and second only to Pharaoh in all the land of Egypt. He is also given Asenath, daughter of Potiphera, high priest of On (Annu, Heliopolis) as a wife. This is actually part of the individuation process, and Potiphera is the "wise old man," while Asenath represents the anima, the latter in collective as well as personal aspect.

A little earlier in the Bible, Joseph's father, Jacob, meets his mother, Rachel, at a well (the unconscious). She is the daughter of Laban. Rachel and Laban are these same archetypal figures of anima and "wise old man." Jacob also marries Rachel's sister, Leah, and there are complicated symbolic reasons for this that I need not go into here.

Moses, after slaying the Egyptian, flees to the land of Midian, and he too sits down by a well. Immediately, the seven daughters of the priest Jethro appear, one of who, Zipporah, Moses marries. Jethro also teaches Moses the secret wisdom. So here again are examples of the "wise old man" and anima archetypes.

All of these stories are parts of individuation processes. The Bible is full of them, and most of the hero/initiates experience the Higher Self, God, or both.

As Jung also says, a woman of Julie's type makes an excellent anima-figure for she has positive aspects as well as negative ones. She is able to set alight a furnace within a man's unconscious, possibly leading him to the divine source of his being and ultimately of all being if he has it in him to become an initiate on the heroic quest. For this reason Jung calls the anima a "deliverer and redeemer"; he says ". . . the glare of the fire she ignites both illuminates and enlightens all the victims of the entanglement" in *The Archetypes and the Collective Unconscious* (1959b).

I was a single man, deeply philosophical by nature, seeking higher wisdom and deeper meaning. An ordinary, physical affair with Julie would not have forced me forward in my quest in the unconscious; I would merely have been led to the outer world by her, instead of to the inner. On top of this I was still neurotic and lost in chaotic turmoil, which placed me in such a depressed state at times that I probably would not have been up to so serious a love affair. I was lost, no doubt about it. In fact, my tortured longing for Julie was not mostly of a biological nature, being rather magical and mystical, even spiritual in the wider sense (though it took a while for me to realize this). I knew her only for about a year, but she had done her work, having lit up in me both the personal and collective unconscious. Years later, I still encounter Julie in dreams now and then.

I saw her on the street about a year ago, after a period of many years. From a distance, she looked exactly the same as when I last saw her. She can have no inkling of the journeys I have made through the unconscious since we last met, and of the transformation, both within myself and of outer reality itself, that have occurred in the interim.

A man loves his anima-figure so completely because she represents his own missing part, but he does not necessarily like her so much as a human being. I have often wondered whether I greatly liked Julie, though I greatly loved her. I certainly disapproved of much of what she did, despite being able to understand her psychologically. She was lost but was she bad? And if so, just how bad was she? Beautiful women can be just as bad as their plainer sisters, but they are far more dangerous, and while many a saint has not possessed physical beauty, many a villainess has made the trees sway with her allure. Furthermore, I must ask just how much of what I saw was the real Julie and how much my projected anima? Even now, when I see things more objectively, I cannot answer these questions.

Had I not made the projection onto her and become so completely smitten because of it, Julie's affairs would not have caused me any concern whatsoever. It was my captivation that made all the difference. Few of us would be unconcerned if the one we love had been having secret affairs with married people, for we hope the one we love is better than that. Even in a society that has become as morally disoriented as our own, this perhaps still applies to the majority of people. Whatever the situation, in my own case her immorality hurt a great deal.

Yet it had the desired effect, which was total upheaval. Julie lit fires within my depths which, though like the flames of hellfire at the time (after all, it was the Underworld, the lower depths of the collective unconscious, that were involved) were nevertheless the source of the highest enlightenment. It was the beginning of something great for myself. Together with my discovery of Jung and the unconscious, Julie was nothing less than a Godsend. Jung and Julie led me to truths and to the certain answer that Nietzsche had denied the reality of, had declared did not and could not exist.

We are perhaps still a little too set and limited in our concepts of the anima, especially in her more personal aspects. The anima may appear as the sister or mother of the man as often as she does the loved one, and I have seen my mother, sister, and Julie together in the same dream, all apparently aspects of the anima. But there are other women I know who appear in my dreams, as well as many who, as far as I know, are not of real life. Some of these are also aspects of the anima, so the anima is obviously of manifold variety and not just the love interest or sister-mother. Jung believed the male counterpart to the anima in a woman, the animus, to be multiple and varied, but not so much the anima. Yet in my experience the anima seems to be multiple in the same way, or many-aspected.

I have observed occasionally that a real life woman will do or say something, or take an attitude that I have witnessed before in a dream, although this also happens with men sometimes. This may mean that it is the souls, the inner essence, of those people I have witnessed in the dreams; that what we call the unconscious is largely the soul of outer reality, and that outer reality the expression and concretization of inner reality. So Julie in the unconscious, for example, is not merely part of my own soul essence, but part of the real Julie herself, so that she seems to form part of what I take to be my soul essence.

We are all thus intertwined with one another in the unconscious, connected to the same pool as we are outwardly. Ah, you may protest: The unconscious of a woman is largely male, as a man's is largely female, so the real Julie in the unconscious would be doubly opposite— male, not female. To this, I will answer that it is not so simple. Julie is a total psyche, and it may well be possible for me to experience the essence of her feminine consciousness, the part of her totality that appeals to me, and indeed, the masculine part of her unconscious would be of no interest to me. We simply cannot imagine the people we know as being of the opposite sex in the unconscious. In fact, I am not aware of Jung mentioning this.

There are many well-attested cases of people dreaming of other people and the dream coming true in some way, but it is not the opposite sex, anima or animus, that has appeared in the dream, but the conscious personality that is known to the dreamer. All I am trying to say is that the true situation may be a little more complicated than Jung and other depth psychologists have believed.

I am in Rome where the ghostly head of Cesare Borgia instructs me to construct a tall Renaissance building, which is to be quite ornate. This

I do, though I may rather paint it on the flat surface of a high cliff face. It is immediately accomplished, in fact, and on the top portion are painted three decorated circles, while below these are four squared panels. In one of the panels, a scene featuring Christ is painted, and the actual building, or painting of it, is a church or cathedral. It is a great and beautiful work of art, and the people come to view it and are awe-struck.

The Pope, (not the real life one, probably) is extremely pleased and invites me to a function as guest of honor. I attend with a girlfriend, and we sit high up on the balcony of a large round hall with the Pope. This too is part of a cathedral, though it is not clear if it is part of the one I have constructed. All the time, the unseen, spiritual presence of Cesare Borgia has been with me, to guide and direct me.

Rome, being once the center of the Roman Empire and the world, then became the center of Christendom, despite the fact that Jerusalem was said to be the center of the universe. Now, in the dream, I am in Rome, where I construct an awe-inspiring cathedral, or paint one, which here amounts to the same thing. This evokes the images of the ancient sevenfold temple or "Heaven as a House," symbol of the Higher Self, but here of a specifically Christian nature. I am instructed in this work by the spiritual presence of Cesare Borgia (c. 1476–1507. Duke of Valencia, illegitimate son of Pope Alexander VI, church and military leader), who is a positive entity in the dream, rather than the dark villain of history. At the time I was fascinated by Cesare, due partly to a projection of my own shadow, and also because of my love of the Italian Renaissance. He is, of course, a representative of higher spiritual forces in the dream, of the Holy Spirit, as was the ghostly head of Jung in the earlier dream.

The cathedral I construct consists of circles and squares, and these not only form the basis of Renaissance architecture in general, they also symbolize the opposites of spirit and matter in the unconscious processes. The "Great Bear Circle over the Four Quarters of the Horizon," and the "Circle of Heaven" supported by the "Four Pillars of Shu," are ancient Egyptian symbols, and we find this motif repeated with the Gnostic cross within the circle; almost certainly this was the origin of the Celtic Cross. All of these are mandala symbols, in this form holy wheels, usually with four, eight, or twelve divisions. Jung tells us that the circle means the roundness of Heaven where the God of spirit has his throne, while the square signifies the Earth where the Goddess of wisdom has her throne. Furthermore, in the structure in my dream there are three circles and four squares, and again, three symbolizes spirit and four matter, or soul, as we find throughout mythology, religions, and the esoteric mysteries.

In one of the squares is a scene containing Christ, which makes the whole structure a mandala with Christ at the center. He is the central theme of it, so to speak, and in fact, the mandala, and the whole dream, is very Christian in nature. Indeed, although I was not raised a Catholic and had no particular disposition towards that faith at the time, it nevertheless all seems to be highly Catholic.

As said earlier, the cathedral structure equals the sevenfold temple and mansion, symbolizing the Higher Self seen as seven stages. The mythical temple constructed by Iu-em-hetep in ancient Egypt was built upon seven pillars, and the early seven-stepped pyramids reflect this— the sacred Mound was seven-stepped, as were the Assyrian/Babylonian ziggurats. Solomon's temple was sevenfold in many ways and may actually be taken from the Iu-em-hetep myths. The mystical sevenfold mansion of medieval Christianity has the same basis, and the archetypal house in Jung's early dream was seven-storied.

The structure here in the dream is a great cathedral containing Christ, set in Rome, still the center of Christianity. While the cathedral concerns me personally, it is mainly a collective matter, as the Higher Self ultimately is, concerning apparently the further spiritual development of Christianity through inner processes. In other words, I must develop and bring forth the Higher Self in accordance with our Western religious traditions. That is the only way to more or less safely bring forth the Higher Self, within the protective walls of a genuine religion; any other way would be dangerous and could lead to catastrophe.

The round hall, in which the girl (who represents the anima) and I sit with the Pope, also suggests a mandala, meaning that the anima and I as ego-consciousnesses are united in a syzygy within the Higher Self in a specifically Christian framework. Dreams like this change us and bring about a transformation of personality, altering our whole way of thinking, though there is as yet still a long way for me to travel with the processes.

The construction of the cathedral is the same as the building of the temple in the ancient world, "Heaven as a House" as it was known. This structure was sevenfold in some way, and here in the dream the three circles and four squares of my construction compose just that. The temples of Iu-em-hetep, of Adapa in Sumeria, and of Solomon were mythical symbolizations for the Higher Self, and whether outer temples were built to express the inner ones is beside the point here. The Hanging Gardens of Babylon were seven-stepped and known as "The Temple of the Seven Lights." The first pyramids were also seven-stepped, and the Great Pyramid was known as "The Seven Lights." The divine son, Horus, was Lord of the Seven Lights, the Higher Self with the seven Powers. All of these again match the sevenfold cathedral in my dream.

One further point of interest is that one name for the Seven Lights associated with the Hanging Gardens was "The Lumazi," and as the original Assyrians and Babylonians were Indo-European, such words as "luminous" would come from the same source.

> Everything is hazy except for a circle that I see in front of me, and in the center of the circle is a Nazi swastika.

The swastika is an ancient religious symbol that appears all over the world; it is the most sacred of all symbols, according to H. P. Blavatsky, the nineteenth century seeker after wisdom and truth. In Mongolia and Tibet, the swastika was, and perhaps still is, found depicted on the heart in the images of the Buddha, though also sacrilegiously on the headgear of sorcerers. It was similarly used by the priests and seers of ancient Troy, as discovered by Heinrich Schliemann in his excavations, and it has also been found with the Assyrians, Egyptians, Babylonians, Scandinavians, Peruvians, ancient Britons, and in the catacombs of Rome. In India it is depicted shining on the head of Ananta, the great serpent of Vishnu, which represents infinite time. In fact, Blavatsky states that the swastika was so sacred a symbol to the ancients that it is found on excavated sites all over the world.

The Nazis adopted it (and revised it) because it was one of the main sacred symbols of the Aryan peoples, but the Nazis perverted and befouled it to such an extent that it has now become the most hated symbol of all time. Nazism, as is becoming more realized, was fundamentally a religious movement, though of a negative, pagan kind. It totally rejected Christian love, compassion, and tolerance, functioning on the "love of power" principle, rather than on the "power of love." While the mandalas in previous dreams have been positive ones containing Christ, the swastika in this dream now expresses, being the modern, darkened version, the dark half of the Self. It is the law of the unconscious processes that if you experience one aspect of a content, you are then required to also experience the opposite side for wholeness.

> After a dream where I am desperately trying to escape an evil, maniacal Nazi killer—the dark side of the Self, or its representative, whose appearance was heralded by the swastika—I then have the following dream:
> I see a flower, which may be a rose, at the center of a hazy, empty space. At first, the petals are closed up, but then they gradually unfold, and I see shapes appear at the four corners of the hazy space, perhaps flowers also. I was singing an old song immediately prior to the vision in the dream, which goes: "A rose must remain, in the sun and the rain, for its lovely promise to come true."

The flower now replaces the Nazi swastika at the center of wholeness, and with a flower at each corner, reminds us of the medieval depictions of Christ at the center of the four Evangelists. They have precisely the same meaning, symbolizing the Higher Self at the center of his four emanations. (Ironically, one of the forms of the swastika was on the lotus of the Buddha, thereby having the same meaning in the East that the rose, or flower, has in this dream.)

The rose here is a symbol for the Self, although it has always been one of the main symbols of the Virgin Mary, perhaps the main one as the lotus is for the Buddha. In the dream, the flower gradually unfolds, which means that as I continue on the unconscious processes, the Self is developing and unfolding. Though, as the old song suggests, both sides, light and dark, must be experienced "for its lovely promise to come true." (Again ironically, the swastika on the lotus also means the unfolding of the lotus, that is, of the Buddha, the Higher Self.)

The rose also has a variety of symbolic meanings and Jung tells us that it is a spiritual representation of Mary, and that we can see clearly from the heavenly rose that appears in Dante's "Paradiso," that it has the meaning of a mandala. He says that the "mystique of the Rose" found its way into alchemy by means of the lapis-Christ parallel, and here it obviously has associations with the Higher Self. In Eastern symbolism, the god is symbolized by the lotus containing the Buddha, and in the same way, psychologically the unfolding from the center is represented by the unfolding flower itself. As I say, the significance of the central rose, or flower, in this dream is the Higher Self, rather than Mary, though she could represent the feminine aspect of the Self (Jung 1959b; 1968).

There is also the "crucified rose" of the old Rosicrucians, and one old-time writer on the Mysteries, Hargreave Jennings, a contemporary of H. P. Blavatsky, comments that the rose is the loveliest of flowers and is feminine. He says that the Rosicrucians, the "sons of wisdom," had the "martyred rose" as their symbol, and which they held in adoration. This was not just a rose, of course, but the "crucified rose." Jennings further comments that "the rose is Queen of God's Garden," this being the Virgin Mary (Jennings 1884, 141).

So it is primarily Mary who is connected with the rose in Christian and Rosicrucian symbolism, and the feminine side must be part of the total Self, but the structure here of the One at the center of the four denotes the Self as a totality. In fact, the flowers at the four corners of the empty space, with the main flower at the center have the same meaning, in a sense, as the rose on the cross, the fourfoldness of the central symbol. One further point is that the dream may have chosen a rose to symbolize wholeness and the Self because it is my favorite flower.

I am dressed as a medieval crusader with a white tunic that has a red cross on its front and back. A woman suddenly appears, dressed in clothes of the period of the Roman Empire, and I announce to her, "I am very sorry, but I must kill you." I then raise my two-handed sword high above my head, while the woman becomes a stone, and bringing the sword down, I cleave her from head to foot. I then cut her across, so that she has now been quartered. She then becomes a whole "woman" again, but weeps with sorrow as she says, "Then I must go. I must return to long, long ago." She then fades and I have no doubt that she is returning to Roman Britain. I then go to my sister's fridge where I pull out a tray, on which lie a number of tins of baked beans, forming a circle.

My crusader dress makes of me a knight with the colors of the opposites, red and white, united on the tunic; the cross is a symbol of unification and of Christ the fourfold god. The woman, in Jungian terms, is the anima, not the personal anima but the collective aspect, who, being timeless, seems to belong to the past and history. The figure appears to be from the Roman world, which would still be "alive" in a timeless reality.

In the earlier dream the "un-human" figure of a man came from across the seas to kill a woman who was responsible for a great deal of trouble, and this may not have been merely the personal anima. She may have been connected with the figure from the Roman world in this dream, but whatever the case, it is necessary to send her back to the past—to the collective sphere—from whence she came. Jung says that there is often something deeply ancient about the anima, but she is, after all, archetypal and is nearer to the eternal things, and even part of them. Why I slice her into quarters, for what purpose she becomes stone, is unclear (the four quarters of the World Soul?), but the cross I cut matches the cross on my tunic. My sister, from whose fridge I obtain the beans, represents my personal anima, and the circle of bean tins represents a mandala or state of wholeness. The theme of the cross and the circle is again strongly represented of course.

> I touch hands with Julie, my anima figure, and a magical force like electricity passes between us. This causes a man to appear, who I know is from the "other world" of the collective unconscious. He takes the form of the detective character from the TV series, *Charlie's Angels*, which strongly suggests that he is an angel. He sits on a chair and a young woman comes and lies across his lap, a gesture which seems to show his authority over her. He pays no attention to her, and says to me, "We have work to do. We must journey across the desert to find the treasure." All this takes place in Egypt, and the angel and I then begin a dangerous quest.

The touching of hands between my anima and myself means unification of the personal conscious and unconscious, the male-female syzygy. This causes the higher spirit figure, the "angel," to appear, and we must then seek the treasure on a dangerous quest. Throughout my quests in dreams, over many long years, the treasure is frequently said to lie in Egypt, for as already quoted, the legendary alchemist Ostanes advised: "Go to the waters of the Nile, and there ye will find a stone that hath a spirit." This is because the royal line through the unconscious, of which Christ was the ultimate development, began in the original Egyptian mysteries and was continued by the Biblical prophets, Gnostics, and the first Christians.

We know that the alchemists relied very heavily on dreams in their opus, and indeed, their grandiose aims of transmuting base metals into gold and producing a real stone, would have remained merely futile chemistry had not archetypal dream processes possessed the alchemists. Those dreams often told them that the "treasure hard to attain" lay in Egypt, just as the Gnostics and early Christian groups knew that the inner immortal, ultimately the god, could be found in the more ancient Egyptian wisdom texts and their dreams too would certainly have pointed to Egypt.

It may seem very strange and remarkable to us, but the unconscious processes that produced the gods, or experiences of them, are still alive in the unconscious realm because it is timeless and seemingly eternal. It may also seem curious to us that the alchemists, who were working with physical substances, became engrossed in religious, spiritualizing processes, but that is where their alchemical/dream processes led them.

I have encountered angels which represent the thoughts and wishes of God that float down to our experience in dreams over the years, though not often in winged form and never in waking life. Being spirit phenomena, they have no physical form as we understand it, and so take on shapes that are appropriate, though "human" ones usually.

Plato says: "The function of the wing is to take what is heavy and raise it up into the region above, where the gods dwell; of all things connected with the body, it has the greatest affinity with the divine." We might add that just as wings can raise things from below to up above, to the realm of the gods, they can also carry things down from the realm of the gods above, to mankind below.

A king cobra is about my house and I am very much afraid of it.

The snake, being a reptile, is a long way from human beings on the tree of life forms, and so symbolically represents unconscious contents that are far removed from consciousness. At the same time, the snake also represents contents which are far beyond the human, and so from most ancient times it has been considered the most spiritual of creatures, particularly since it sheds its skin and puts on a new one, signifying renewal or rebirth.

The serpent also symbolizes the dark half of the Higher Self in its lower, instinctual aspect, but in myths, legends, and fairy tales worldwide, it guards the treasure. This is probably because the dark side of the Higher Self has to be encountered—as the serpent—before the light side, and therefore the treasure, comes forth.

The dragon sometimes guards the treasure—often the maiden, the anima—but it is more usually the serpent. However, the meaning is the same. The earliest example I know of this is the Seven Boxes of Thoth in ancient Egypt. The boxes went smaller with each one, and so all were contained in the largest. The treasure was in the innermost, but a serpent guarded it, so that only a true hero could obtain it. This is the same symbolic formulation as the seven stages to the Higher Self found in Hinduism and Buddhism, and the sevenfold mansion of medieval European tradition.

I have lost count of the old movies where people are after a treasure and finally find it in a cave. Then suddenly, a menacing snake appears. The archetype springs up from the unconscious spontaneously, and the writers automatically put it in.

In ancient Egypt, the cobra formed part of Pharaoh's crown, surrounding it, partly to protect it. This was the positive uraeus serpent, whereas the negative, dangerous serpent that Horus, Ra, and others slay was Apep (or Apophis). There were two main forms of the serpent in ancient Egypt. One, the uraeus, was light and helpful, and the other, Apep, was very dark and dangerous. Naturally, help from the uraeus was sought, while Apep had to be slain. The uraeus represented life and renewal, and at times there were seven of them, so that they were worshipped as seven divinities. They were thus called, "The seven divine uraei of life," and represented the lower powers of the earth.

One of Egypt's Two Kingdoms was symbolized by the serpent, and the other by the vulture, both forming parts of Pharaoh's crown. The rod, or staff, is the symbol of God's authority, as we know from the story of Moses, where the rod changes into a serpent and back again; but the symbol is actually Egyptian, and there are depictions in Egyptian paintings which clearly show the rod and serpent combined. The snake, or serpent, therefore, while symbolizing the dark side of the Self, also represents wisdom: "Be ye therefore wise as serpents."

The Gnostic Ophites worshipped the serpent because it was identified with Christ, and as Jung tells us, transformation by means of the serpent is one of the oldest archetypes known to man. The Agathodaimon (good spirit) of the Gnostics was said to be a snake in form, and the "brazen serpent on the wood," known first to Moses, was identified with Christ as the Logos, the Word. Hippolytus reports that the Naassenes considered the serpent to be in all other creatures and in all things, the serpent here obviously having the same meaning as the later Mercurial serpent, the spirit, or soul force of the unconscious and which permeates all material existence.

Jung comments that Mercurius is a magician and god of magicians, and just like Hermes Trismegistus, he has his wand, the caduceus, with two serpents twining round it. But Blavatsky states that the caduceus was originally three serpents, without the central wand, and as Trismegistus means "thrice great," we can see why this would be so. The three serpents, therefore, allude to the lower, chthonic trinity, the counterpart to the higher Trinity of spirit. The alchemists report experiences of a dark, chthonic trinity, and we find it again in Dante. Jung says that the snake is a prefiguration of Christ because it symbolizes the unconscious in all of its aspects, and is a personification of the wisdom of the divine Mother. The Gnostic and alchemical snake is sometimes crucified which means the overcoming of the unconscious, although it must also have a similar meaning to Christ being torn between the four opposites at his crucifixion, and indeed, to the transformation of Mercurius, the spirit of the unconscious.

In ancient Egypt, not only was the snake itself a symbol of transformation, renewal, and rebirth, but so was the hole out of which it came symbolizing the unconscious depths, just as a cave, the "Earth-womb," does. Furthermore, the coiled circle made by the snake symbolized the same thing, and these were termed the Circle of Necessity, into which the initiate into the Mysteries was required to enter. The sloughing of its skin by the snake symbolized spiritual renewal, and the initiate would be stripped of his clothes and then re-clothed again to imitate this. The Agathodaimon serpent is depicted with either seven or twelve heads, these symbolic numbers being featured throughout myths, religions, and the esoteric mysteries.

In this dream I am very much afraid of the snake, which I must nevertheless face, as well as all other unconscious contents that cause fear if I am to be successful in my quest. Jung, while saying that the sacrifice of the serpent is to be understood as the overcoming of the unconscious, adds that it also means the mental attitude of a son who is unconsciously too attached to his mother. However, I am reluctant to agree here because the two interpretations do not mix.

In the sentence immediately before this, Jung said the snake symbol "characterizes Christ" as a totality representation of all of the aspects of the unconscious. The snake sacrifice must therefore parallel the Christ sacrifice, even if from the opposite position, as in the lower chthonic as opposed to the higher spiritual, and the feminine to the masculine. We would not, however, say that the Christ sacrifice also has a personal interpretation of a woman who is unconsciously too attached to her father. The meaning is beyond the personal level. When the brass serpent on a pole occurs in the story of Moses, can we then interpret this as Moses hanging too much on his own mother? Jung makes this mistake now and then, taking non-personal, transcendent situations to be problems of personal psychology.

In fact, I would go so far as to say that psychiatrists should abandon personal psychology altogether and lead their patients to the non-personal, or supra-personal, levels. Personal problems seem to fade and work themselves out automatically when the patient becomes engrossed in archetypal material. Jung himself says his patients began to make improvements when they touched upon the archetypal material beyond themselves. But this has always been the great value of the religions. If the focus of our lives is something beyond ourselves, in God, the god-man, or the World Soul, with all of the magic and meaning that this entails, then we are lifted out of ourselves into a greater, mystical framework of reality.

Yet we can do this by finding the wider reality through the unconscious, which in effect shifts the center of our being from the personal self to the Higher Self. The latter corresponds to the outer divine figure, whether this be Christ, Vishnu, or the Buddha. Jung knew all of this too well, so it is a puzzle why he occasionally reduces non-personal material and situations to the personal.

I am at a school where one of Shakespeare's plays is being enacted. It seems to sum up life, as a mere play, with everyone a two-dimensional, cardboard cut-out. I am aware of a medieval atmosphere, perhaps to do with King Arthur, and when I see a sword and pick it up, I find that it has magical powers, like Excalibur. I then fit a precious stone into the hilt as the pommel, and someone remarks, "The Stone of Scone."

There are courtiers about in medieval dress as I walk to some steps, which are on four sides, forming a pyramid. Going up the steps part way, I see a throne on top in the center, and on this sits a great king who is also a god, and yet who resembles me a little. He speaks to me, saying, "Do you understand why all of this is necessary? Without the Divine Spirit man is merely a beast, and then even a king is only a king of beasts. Man's most important part is his eternal spirit. It is this that raises him above the beast."

A school is a place of learning, and it has often been said that life is a school where we are meant to develop our souls. But in the modern world everything has become so flat that we are like cardboard cut-outs, desouled, having no real depth, performing in a sort of two-dimensional play. All our values have become material ones, so that we are not only obsessed with, but also possessed by, all the forms of matter: science and technology, big business, politics, sports, pop culture, and always sex. But even worse, in the past few decades the shadow side has gradually crept into these things so that everything now seems contaminated; nothing is clean or wholesome anymore.

It is good to be aware of the shadow side of reality, and particularly of our own shadows, but as Jung says, we must then amputate them and live otherwise, though always aware of them. Unfortunately, in the modern world, the shadow has become increasingly attractive so that we are in danger of individually and collectively falling captive to its power, which in the end will result in the collapse of civilization. It has happened to many cultures of the past and myths contain the record of it.

In the dream I have long been in a state where my own life has been flat and meaningless, a state of real despair, in fact. Now the unconscious is showing me the way to real life and true meaning on my quest. I receive the sword that, like Excalibur, has magical powers, and with it I can cut my way through to the divine source. In alchemy, the *regius filius*, the reborn or rejuvenated son of the King as Father, reminding us of Horus as the resurrected Osiris, is often depicted with a sword. Christ also says that he brings a sword, for a higher, moral state of consciousness divides good and evil and chooses correspondingly. Mercurius as the spirit of the unconscious must be pierced with a sword and sometimes he pierces himself. He is also the actual sword as the "penetrating spirit," so whereas Christ is the dividing sword, Mercurius is the piercing sword, or the spirit who must be pierced.

The alchemist Ostanes (1622) advises, "Take an egg, pierce it with the fiery sword, and separate its soul from its body." This expresses the way we must discover our soul essence in the individuation processes. In Norse mythology, Sigurd slays the dragon Fafnir, the representation of the dark unconscious, with a special sword. This reminds us again of the earlier dream where I confront the great dragon monster with a sword, the blade of which drops off. This I compared to the shattered sword in the Grail legends that is shattered. However, Perceval's sword later becomes whole and very special because he is now fitter for the task, although a girl, an anima representation, warns him that the sword can be treacherous. Similarly, things are happening which strongly suggest that I am on the Grail quest myself now, and I receive a sword the blade of which will possibly not drop off, for this too is a special, magical sword.

The precious stone I fit as the pommel is the equivalent of the Philosophers' Stone, which the alchemists posited as parallel to Christ, and therefore to the Higher Self. Jung states that though there may have been a thousand symbols for this greatest of all treasures, perhaps none expressed it better than the perfect stone.

The "Stone of Scone," the old Celtic legend upon which the Grail may be partly based tells of four heavenly beings who descend to Earth, to Ireland, specifically, bringing with them four magic gifts, each one from a different celestial city. These were the Lia Fail, the Stone of Destiny, which was later taken to Scotland to become the Stone of Scone, and later still to England by Edward I to become the Coronation Stone; an unconquerable sword; a magical lance; and a vessel known as the Cauldron of Dagda.

The Stone of Scone in my dream, as well as suggesting this, also implies that the throne on top of the pyramid of steps is the seat of kings, i.e., of the god-king—again, the Higher Self. I then find the god-king seated on top of the pyramid of steps, and he resembles me a little because I am eternally connected to him as one of his "parts"—at this moment, his agent in worldly reality.

There are comparisons with the Grail legends, for the Grail sword was connected with the Grail stone, and in Wolfram von Eschenbach's *Parzifal*, the Grail *is* a stone. Wolfram must have been familiar with alchemy, its symbolism, and with the unconscious processes, because the Grail and the Philosopher's Stone imply the Higher Self. The Grail, however, has a different and more spiritual emphasis: being a round containing vessel, it suggests the feminine side, yet roundness expresses totality of the Self nevertheless.

Emma Jung and Marie-Louise von Franz in their excellent book, *The Grail Legend* (1960), comment that to the alchemists, the sword was similar in nature to the "divine water" and the "stone," and that the sword represents the inspiration to growth that engenders perception of the Higher Self. (Wolfram's stone, incidentally, is said to have come from Heaven, while the Philosopher's Stone is the "stone of chastity.") Likewise, the Grail cannot be lifted by the sinful, for it distinguishes between the moral and the immoral, which is why it may only be carried by a pure virgin, the Bearer of the Grail. As Jung says, the individuation process, on which both the Grail and the Stone are based, is above all a *moral* task, for only those who reach the noble heights and are capable of self-sacrifice will ever realize the Higher Self.

While these match in part the contents of the Grail stories there are differences. The Stone and the vessel do not appear in the same versions, the Stone rather replaces the vessel, and the cup that holds the blood of Christ has more differences from the Cauldron of Dagda than similarities. Furthermore, the spear of Longinus which wounds Christ was a part of the earliest Christian symbolism from the Middle East. My dream produces the magical sword symbol and connects the jewel stone of the pommel with the Stone of Scone, these being pure products of the unconscious processes, entirely uninfluenced by consciousness.

The four-sided pyramid of steps with the god-king at the center means the same as Christ on the four-armed cross, Marduk with his four dogs, Ezekiel's Son of Man and the wheel with four faces, and so forth: that is, the Higher Self with its four emanations. At the beginning of Egyptian culture, at Annu, which the Greeks called Heliopolis and the Bible called On, the god Atum (or sometimes Ra, or Atum-Ra, and later Osiris) was said to sit upon his throne on top of the sacred Mound, which the original pyramids were constructed to represent. Atum and Ra sit on the heavenly throne, while Osiris has his seat on the Mound in the lower Amenta, the Underworld.

The Mound was a staircase to the throne, just as in my dream, and so the god-king sitting on his throne on top of the pyramid of steps in my dream is a similar representation. The god-king on his throne at the center of the fourfold pyramid of steps, is, therefore, the "god of the four quarters," the fourfold Higher Self, experienced by mankind from the earliest times. Jung says that on the one hand we can devalue such a symbol and claim it to represent the human psyche, but ultimately it refers to the fourfold aspect of the Second Person of the Godhead in His universal aspect. This is Jung's way of expressing the fourfold nature— usually 3 + 1—of the Higher Self. Not solely, however, in lower aspect, but also and primarily as the Second Person—exemplified by Christ—of the Holy Trinity; Father, Son, and Holy Ghost. However, the god-king in my dream seems to be more the lower aspect, the Osiris.

As a matter of fact, no god in ancient Egypt is depicted seated on his throne as often as Osiris. He is almost always seated on his throne, and frequently at the top of steps. In fact, one of his titles is "the god at the top of the steps," though, as said, this is in Amenta, the Underworld, the realm of the lower unconscious. At other times he sits on his throne on a platform resting on the waters, because water symbolizes the realm of the lower unconscious. Again, Osiris is understandably termed "Lord of the Water" and "the Shoreless." In his book *The Miraculous Birth of King Amen-hotep III*, Colin Campbell describes part of the *Heb-Sed* festival stating that there was a sort of pyramid with steps on four sides, which led to the pavilion on top. Pharaoh, carrying the emblems of the god Osiris, came out of a sanctuary below and ascended the steps to take his seat on the throne. Facing the four directions in turn, he then made offerings as priest, though as he was also the god; these were to himself. All of this was an enactment of the deification of Pharaoh, repeating the original resurrection of the mortal Osiris to the immortal state (Campbell 1912).

This ritual is obviously enacted to repeat archetypal experiences in and through the unconscious, as in my dream. Osiris is lord of the lower unconscious, and personifies the lower half of the Self, though in positive form. He is thus the light side of Mercurius, whereas his evil twin Set represents the dark side. Mercurius is "good with the good, and evil with the evil," the alchemical tradition says. Horus, by comparison, is the higher part of the Self, his name meaning "He who is above," and though son of Osiris in a sense, because he follows on from Osiris, he is really son of Ra the High God. All of these are aspects of the full and total Higher Self.

The god-king in the dream informs me that without the divine spirit man is merely a beast, so it should be no surprise to us that whenever a culture loses that divine spirit it soon begins to fall into bestiality. It is happening to the West at this moment, and anyone who fails to realize it is merely being carried along by the tidal wave, oblivious to the fact that it is such tidal waves that drown whole civilizations.

It is imperative that we do not lose that divine spirit completely, or if we have already done so, that we immediately recover it again, for as the god-king, the immortal Self, says in the dream, it is our most essential part, connecting us to otherworldly reality and to God Himself. Jung devoted his life to a further development and new understanding of these great truths of the collective unconscious, and the dream is perhaps showing me that I must do the same, and that I must cut and thrust my way through with the sword on my quest.

One final point is that the sword has magical powers, like Excalibur, and it is with the receiving of Excalibur that King Arthur receives his birthright and kingdom, and his power to rule. With his own sword made whole, Perceval gains the Grail. With division in the kingdom and the war that follows, which means division in the Higher Self, the magical sword must be returned to the Lady of the Lake, the feminine unconscious. In this way the sword would seem to be the power of the lower unconscious—Mercurius as the sword to the alchemists—while the Holy Grail in its full meaning represents the Higher Self: Christ's blood, the Host, the spirit, and the containing vessel, the soul.

> The devil comes out of the air to attack me, and though I am assailed on all sides, I am totally unafraid; I know that I cannot be harmed. I say the Latin words, *Ad Deum* though I do not know Latin. A male relative is also present, and he warns me of the great danger, but still I am unperturbed, as I know that I cannot be harmed.

Whether this devil is the dark counterpart to the god-king of the last dream, and therefore the dark side of the Higher Self, the Devil himself, or his agent is not clear; all I know is that I cannot be harmed. Jung says that the dark side of the Self would not be quite so bad as the Devil himself, though still quite terrifying, of course, but to those having the experience the difference matters little. In the unconscious processes, it is not evil as such that we must fear, but being influenced to do evil ourselves. Therefore, we need to be always scrupulously on guard. That is why Jung states that the individuation process is above all a moral task, one that must distinguish the right, the just, and the good, from the darker, opposite values (or nonvalues), since the Higher Self, the power behind the processes, must be developed in positive form. However, the dark forces themselves have to be experienced, fought, and endured for completeness, as well as for victory, which is one of the reasons I received the magical sword.

The Latin words I speak, "*Ad Deum,*" as a defense against the devil, mean, apparently, "To God," and perhaps this is why I am not afraid. Those who follow God—which I have now come to do—if it is done genuinely and truthfully, need have no fear of devils.

> I am down by the canal at night where I see some very large double-gates, like in the 1930's King Kong movie. The spirit of a woman comes through the gates and she starts to speak about my grandmother, who died many years ago. I ask where she is now, and the spirit tells me, to which I comment, "That is where she was born and raised." The spirit of the woman then says, "She never returned," meaning to the spirit world, and so my grandmother's spirit is therefore still earthbound.
>
> This causes me to reason that in order to "return," she must have existed somewhere else previous to her earthly life, otherwise how could she "return" there, though she apparently failed to do so. For the first time I begin to consider reincarnation seriously, for that is what the dream also implies, if somewhat loosely.

The canal is the dividing line between this life and the "other world," as I know from various other dreams. The large gates, reminding me of the huge ones in the original version of *King Kong*, out of which the great ape emerges, represent the place in the dream through which the spirits of new life emerge, to one day return again, though my grandmother apparently did not return. But why should the other-worldly visitor inform me of this unless it was true? I have not really thought about my grandmother for years, and it has been decades since she died which was in 1950.

However, I am now exploring the depths of the collective unconscious, and if certain things are facts there, then I am going to experience them. As the collective unconscious is another, apparently timeless reality of spirit and soul, extending out to infinity, then this sort of thing is going to occur, and I have to take it all very seriously. The unconscious does not lie; it has no need to, and may not even know how to. It can be brutally frank, and in certain circumstances may even destroy the conscious personality, but it is always completely honest (as far as I know).

The experiences that I was to have in the unconscious over the years since this dream convinced me beyond all doubt that reincarnation is a fact. That is how the system works; it is "just so," and it may as well be that way as any other. This does not imply survival as higher spirit, in a heavenly sort of way, but rather perhaps survival that is no more holy or higher than earthly existence. This is why many religions teach that survival to an eternal, heavenly state can only be won by perfection of character or through the heroic quest. Be that as it may, this dream was perhaps the first that made me consider life after death as a definite reality, and one maybe involving reincarnation—especially since the unconscious seems to take it all as fact here.

> I come out of an inn called The Star to see many people on a great trek, journeying to the Promised Land. There are white people, black people, and perhaps Jews, and I decide to join them. A voice of great authority then speaks from the clouds, singling out a blond woman who is somewhat old, stating that she must marry the man next to me, who may or may not be the biblical Lot. The voice then says that the woman will bear twins, and I think, "Ah, Jacob and Esau." Then the woman makes to kiss the man Lot, who is to be the father of the twins, and the kiss is the sign that he is the choice, but instead of him she kisses me.
>
> By this twist it seems that I am to be the father of the twins myself, and the voice then warns that they will be the cause of much trouble and suffering. I reflect that this must be because the woman will give birth so late in life, like certain Biblical women, and then the name "Jacob" comes to me again. The whole dream has a very pronounced Old Testament feel.

The inn I come out of is called The Star, and a star in mythology either heralds the coming of a special being, or indeed, is that special being in first form. In certain myths the star is associated with the birth of twins, as in a Native American tale in which a star falls to Earth and becomes twins, one good, one evil. The Dogon myth of the twins of Sirius is based on the same archetypal foundation, the psychic processes of the unconscious involving the Higher Self, which, being dual, has its light and dark aspects.

We could also mention Horus and Set, Cain and Abel, Jacob and Esau, Romulus and Remus, Krishna and Balarama, and so on, as examples of light and dark twins in mythology. The early divine Son of Egypt had a name, *Iu,* one meaning of which was "dual." In fact, there are depictions of Horus and Set as one body with their two heads attached to the same shoulders. Even Christ had to be countermatched almost immediately by Antichrist in the scriptures, though the divine birth itself was not of twins.

It is prophesied in Numbers (24:17) that ". . . there shall a star come forth out of Jacob," and the dream causes me to remember the names Jacob and Esau specifically. For the birth of the Persian Zarathustra, a star shone over the village for three days and nights, and the most famous star of all in Western culture, the Star of Bethlehem, the "Star in the East," is also concerned with a special birth, of course: the Higher Self as the Christ. Jung tells us that a star is always associated with the birth of a Messiah.

The blond woman is "somewhat old," matching certain Biblical women who are too old to bear children or are otherwise barren, meaning that they are unable to conceive now in the normal manner, so that they are then impregnated by God or Holy Spirit. The real meaning of this, however, is that a human child of flesh and blood is not involved, but a divine one of spirit. The child is the Higher Self, of whom ultimately God is the Father.

The many people of various types who are making the trek to the Promised Land in the dream are all the different contents, or souls, in the collective unconscious, their destination being the realization of the Higher Self, in whom all the contents share, and with whom all must come into harmony. This is the real meaning of the Exodus in the story of Moses, being part of his own individuation process, though the Jews apparently did leave Egypt *en masse* after a long sojourn there, perhaps after Pharaoh Akhenaten ceased to reign. The Promised Land the people are journeying to in both Exodus and my dream is the Paradise of Peace. This not only alludes to the coming forth of the Higher Self as Savior, but also to the kingdom of peace and harmony that he brings, and under whose influence culture flourishes. However, as to the significance of Lot in the dream, the unconscious alone knows.

> I see a white dog and a voice says, "The white dog covers (or conceals, or protects, or reveals—or maybe all four) the very, very precious stone."

In Goethe's *Faust*, Mephistopheles appears first in the form of a black poodle. Mephistopheles is the Higher Self of the man Faust in dark form, developed and brought forth through alchemical/dream processes lasting decades. Jung says that because it was a dog that first appeared and not a fish—the fish being an ancient symbol of the Higher Self as savior—the Higher Self would finally arrive in dark form. However, Jung was mistaken here.

What is significant is that the Self is in the form of a *black* poodle rather than a *white* one, black meaning, symbolically, evil and sinister. I have experienced the black dog any number of times over the years in dreams and it always forebodes much danger, because it is a representation of the dark Self in early form. If the light Self ultimately parallels Christ, then the dark Self must ultimately parallel Antichrist, or at least a Mephistopheles, as with Faust (or with Goethe himself).

It is, however, a white dog that I see in this dream, which means that the Self is developing in light form. The dog is well known in mythology, alchemy, and folklore, symbolizing again the spirit side of the Self at lower level, or first form. In ancient Egypt, Anubis, or Anup, the dog-jackal, is Horus in a certain aspect, as Heru-em-Anpu. Anubis is "opener of the way to the South" while another form of Anubis, Apuat, is "opener of the way to the North," that is, through the unconscious depths, the Underworld.

Osiris is guided by Anubis in the Underworld, and so too is Isis; while in Central America, Xolotl is the dog-headed god that accompanies Quetzalcoatl to the Underworld. In the Germanic Wotan myths, a black dog is said to lead the unearthly pack of hounds as they follow Wotan, as the Wild Huntsman, across the sky, causing terror in the hearts of mortals. One of the fears was that the black dog would be left behind when the hunt had passed.

The custom of burying a dog as spirit guide with a dead person was practiced in many parts of the world, including Egypt, though it does not seem to have been commonplace there. Some of the practices elsewhere are quite horrifying. In certain Far Eastern countries, a dog would be buried near to its master with just its head showing, and would then be slowly starved to death. Food would be placed close to the head, but just out of reach, so that the slow death would be even more tortuous. When in greatest agony, near death, the head would then be cut off, for it was believed that the spirit of the dog would now be sure to return. The dog serves as psychopomp, a guide through the Underworld or afterlife, just as Anubis and Apuat were guides and "Openers of the Ways" through the Underworld in Egypt.

While Anubis and Apuat are believed by many scholars to have been jackal-gods, it is possible that dogs, jackals, wolves, and foxes were all considered the same species by the Egyptians. In fact, the name for the wolf in Egypt, *anush*, was also one name for the dog. To gain passage through the Underworld, the Osirian adept would receive the head of a dog with which to pay the gatekeeper as a toll, though whether this was a real or symbolical head is unclear. Only if the initiate possessed the head would he be let through the gate. It has also been said that the Aztecs would kill a dog at a funeral and either burn it, or bury it with the deceased; again, to lead the way to the land of the dead. The Eskimo would at one time perform a similar act at the death of a child, cutting off the dog's head and laying it in the grave, to help the child to find its way in the afterlife. And perhaps the most well-known example of all was the placing of a dog at the feet of a dead Viking warrior, perhaps also to lead the way to Valhalla.

All of this is based on the psychological fact that in the unconscious processes, the Higher Self, in spirit aspect, appears in first form as a dog, as my own processes show. This could also be seen as a spirit component of the mortal man that connects him with higher contents that are ultimately of the Higher Self. Then the dog is intermediary, in a sense, between the mortal man and his immortal Self. It is doubtless that this fact gave rise to all of the myths and practices involving dogs, not the reverse. The unconscious did not begin using dog symbolism because of what man ritualized in the outer world; man arranged his rituals to accord with what he had experienced in his dreams and visions.

The dream says that the dog protects and conceals the "very, very, precious" stone, the latter also being a symbol of the Higher Self, at the higher, fulfilled stage. This demonstrates again the role of the white dog as sort of herald and vanguard of the higher immortal, though in my experience the dog itself must be protected by consciousness in that good actions help it to flourish, whereas bad actions injure it and help the black dog, the dark side, to flourish. Then the white dog will fade and disappear. As Faust exclaims, "So that's what was in the poodle!" It was Mephistopheles!

The dog comes in dreams as helper as well as guide, and certain symbolism in my dreams is similar to material found in the quests for the Holy

Grail. In one version, a white dog is companion and helper to Perceval, the Grail Knight. And in another version, Gawain is led to the grail castle by a white dog. (I shall have more to say about this in a later dream, where certain symbolism is similar to that encountered by Perceval.)

A short while after this dream I obtained a black and white border collie as a pet and he then became the "dog-spirit" in my dream processes, my helper and guide, as future dreams will show. In one of the first, he has a halo and my hand goes right through him when I try to touch him, because he is of that higher, spirit Self. The dog-spirit in the unconscious, therefore, takes on the form of my dog in real life.

> I think I have just awakened, though I am still asleep and dreaming, and my bedroom is exactly as it is in real life. I say to myself, "If Christ is true, the door will swing to and fro and he will appear to me." The room then becomes stone cold and the door begins to swing backwards and forwards. I then feel the presence of Christ. He may be standing in the doorway, though this is very hazy.

I awakened for real after the dream, fully expecting to see Christ in the doorway, but everything was normal and the room was warm. Jung says that if a dream reproduces real life situations and things exactly as they are, then we have to take the dream to be literally true, which is how it was with this dream, apart from the coldness. I have read a number of times that the temperature often drops sharply with the appearance of a spirit or ghost, and the dream was obviously using this to proclaim such a spirit appearance. I must obviously take it, therefore, that Christ, or his spirit equivalent, has paid me a visit. Perhaps this was not in outer, material reality, but in the reality that exists *behind* it, which we can experience through the unconscious in dreams, and which implies, therefore, that Christ is true as spirit.

At this time I was still a non-believer, or perhaps partly so, Christianity being long since dead for me. Dreams, however, were now startlingly opening my eyes. Though I had been desperately trying to construct my castle of eternal values, they did not include Christianity. Can you imagine, therefore, how I felt after years of depression and fearing that Nietzsche was right to now have dreams such as this? This is why I was willing to give the processes my all, no matter what, why I was ready to follow Jung to hell itself, if need be.

But was it Christ himself who came to visit? Was it a force of spirit from above taking his form? Was it the Higher Self? Or was there some other explanation? The Gnostics taught that the "Christ within," the Anthropos, brought forth through inner processes, and this certainly alluded to the Higher Self. St. Mechthild of Magdeburg was surprised to find that in her own vision of him, Christ was beardless, which shows that it was a genuine vision and separate from her own imagination and preconceptions. Had it been otherwise, Christ would have been bearded to fit the accepted traditional bearded image, which would have constituted her own image of him. In some of my own later dream visions, Christ was also beardless, perhaps to distinguish him from God the Father, who would apparently be bearded. These would be representational images, beardless and bearded, in order for us to distinguish between them.

The appearance of the white dog in the previous dream strongly suggests that it was the Higher Self that followed in the dream above, but I am not sure. Normally, the Higher Self develops gradually after long processes in the unconscious depths, but these early appearances are occurring *first*, before my long journeys. Jung comments in *Psychology and Religion:* "In unconscious humanity there is a latent seed that corresponds to the prototype Jesus . . . the archetypal image of the Self has been shown to occur in dreams even when no such conceptions exist in the conscious mind of the dreamer."

For her part, Blavatsky writes, ". . . Christos [Christ], or Logos, [is] the Spirit of true Divine Wisdom . . . the Higher Self, in short." And, ". . . that power which causes the Divine Self to enshrine itself in its lower self—man" (1888). It is difficult for us to imagine now that these words were written in the second half of the nineteenth century, for Blavatsky has grasped the real meaning and fundamental nature of Christ in a way that most people are still unaware of even today.

> Two young women bring a large python and, as this terrifies me, I run away, trying to escape. However, the python catches me, and shrinking to the size of a small snake, goes up my leg inside my trousers. When it reaches my private parts I feel pain, so perhaps it is castrating me.

Whenever I experience Christ or the Higher Self in a dream, in a following one I experience the serpent in some form, in accordance with the law of the unconscious processes, which states that if a content from one side appears in a dream, then its opposite from the other side must also appear, to make up the totality. If Christ is heads, then the serpent is tails, as it were, and both must be experienced for wholeness.

The first vision that St. Teresa of Avila experienced was of Christ, while the second was of a "loathsome toad," which is exactly the same sort of thing, Christ from above and the toad from below. There is no doubt that St. Teresa was undergoing the individuation processes herself, and we must expect to find this with certain saints and mystics, who "turn down the world" and therefore become open to experiences of spirit/soul reality.

But, as my dreams show, the serpent appears in several snake forms, in this one as the python, which means the devouring aspect of the unconscious, while the earlier appearance was as a king cobra. Consciousness itself may well be swallowed up by the unconscious during these processes, though here castration becomes the danger, which means the weakening and ultimate impotence of consciousness. This in itself, however, would be the "swallowing up" of the power of consciousness, so to speak.

In mythology, the Sun-god—or the hero who fights on behalf of the Higher Self—and the serpent (or dragon), are inexorably linked together, for both are contenders in the fight with the dragon over which side will rule not only the psyche, but the Higher Self itself. Baal slays Yam, Marduk slays Tiamat, Ra slays Apep, Vishnu slays Ananta, and so on. Interestingly, from the point of view of this dream, in one myth of Egypt the falcon god Horus (birds represent spirit) relieves the evil Set, who takes the form of a serpent, of his testicles. So to castrate in dream processes, as in mythology, means to severely weaken or take the power from.

Although the serpent is connected on the one hand with Satan, it is also one of the symbols of Christ, possibly originally to express Christ's, or the Higher Self's, fullness and wholeness. The serpent also represented Christ for the Templars, and to the Gnostics, it was the most sacred creature. But the python itself, or its equivalent, is the universal symbol of the chthonic depths that always threaten to rule the Earth. As the Chinese *I Ching* says: "The Flying Dragon (or the serpent), superb and rebellious, suffers now, and his pride is punished; he thought he would reign in Heaven, he reigns only on Earth."

The Greek sun-god Apollo slays Python, while the Egyptian Sun-god Horus slays Typhon, a form of Set, who has slain and dismembered Osiris. However, in certain forms the serpent was sometimes seen as a positive force by the ancients, as the source of wisdom, and initiates into its mysteries were known not only as "Sons of Wisdom," but as "Sons of the Serpent."

All in all, the snake seems to be more positive than negative in the unconscious processes, if taken as part of their wholeness, but the python itself is highly dangerous, being the great swallower, the devourer. Python as the dark counterpart to the Sun-god Apollo fits in with what I said above about the serpent appearing in my dreams immediately after ones of Christ or the Higher Self. As Blavatsky puts it, "[Set or Typhon] is simply the dark half of Osiris, his brother, as Angra Mainyu Ahriman is the black shadow of Ahura Mazda" (1888).

> I catch a glimpse of the real-life woman who is my anima-figure, and the yearning for her is so great and terrible that it even causes me physical pain.

When I awoke, the terrible feeling was nothing less than torture. It was the longing for my own feminine soul onto whom I had projected my anima, but perhaps also partly for the woman herself. Yet if the projection had stopped, so too would the magic that the woman held for me, and when I say "magic" I am not just speaking figuratively. The archetypal forces of the unconscious are not physical ones in any way, and are either connected to wider spirit and soul reality or are that reality itself. These are frequently experienced as numinous and magical because that is how their nature seems to us, though they have their corresponding dark and terrible sides.

Jung quotes a commentary on the Song of Songs by Honorius of Autun: "Thou hast wounded my heart, my sister, my spouse; thou hast wounded my heart with one of thy eyes, and with one hair of thy neck" (1844-64). But, Jung adds, there is also a dangerous reference in which Honorius says that Tirzah, the goddess Ishtar, though beautiful and "comely as Jerusalem," is "terrible as an army without banners." Jung's notes say that the translation would more correctly be "terrible as a host of armies."

Jung is actually talking about Luna and "the bride" in alchemy here, but this is certainly the effect that the anima exerts on consciousness in the processes. Jung continues to say that the bride is "witch-like and ter-rible" as well as innocent and beautiful, and that her specialty is magic and love-spells. She also brings madness and other maladies to her poor victims. We can see the hypnotic effects of the anima in both personal and collective aspects here, and it just about sums up my own enrap-tured/tortured state at this time.

> I am rowing a boat across the Atlantic Ocean from America to
> Britain, where my journey will be over. A voice from above proclaims,
> "Oarsmen come and go, but the ... lasts for ever."

In the dream, the surface of the sea represents conscious, worldly reality, and the other oarsmen who rowed across are the individual human lives that pass through it. The word for the depths of the sea, the waters, the great unconscious, is left blank in the dream because we have no appropriate term for it. Although Jung called it the "collective unconscious," it is inadequate, as Jung himself admitted.

It is an eternal, timeless, unchanging "other reality," one totally opposite to conscious reality, and yet both are parts of one ultimate real-ity. The sea with its fathomless depths symbolizes the collective uncon-scious in myths all over the world, usually the soul depths, but sometimes the whole of otherworldly reality, including the spirit realm. This is why in Egypt you had to go through the Underworld to reach Heaven. In *The Secret Doctrine*, Blavatsky says: "Water is the symbol of the Female Element everywhere. . . . It is the Universal Matrix or the Great Deep." So the great sea is the Great Mother, who in certain myths gives birth to all of reality.

The oarsmen who come and go may not refer to different human lives, but to the different incarnations of a single individual—in other words, to reincarnation. Or it may mean that the Higher Self has many recurring lives lived through its human agent, or agents, in worldly real-ity. Whatever the case, many of my dreams seem to show that reincar-nation is a fact. Man is mortal while the Higher Self is immortal; but man shares in that immortality, it seems.

> There are a lot of very black Negroes dotted about the street, in the
> middle of the road, as well as on the pavement. One of them, a woman,
> is a prostitute and she tries to get me interested in her, though I decline.

> I can actually see more than one street, as if from above, and all the
> spaced-out Negroes are walking along like zombies, like the living dead.
> Suddenly, they lift their heads to the sky and howl like wolves, only
> these are the eerie, unearthly howls of the undead, which send a great
> shudder through the night.

Let me say first of all that this dream has nothing to do with Blacks
whatsoever, but rather reflects the way that the unconscious symbolizes
its contents. The dream denotes the beginning of what the alchemists
termed the *nigredo,* the "blackening," the state of black melancholia in
which dark alien contents from the collective unconscious rise up and
threaten to overwhelm consciousness. It really does make everything
seem heavily black, and a feeling of utter terribleness, of dark melancholia, creeps slowly over mind and body. Then the true nature of reality seems to be blackness itself, all over the universe and for eternity,
and light seems to be false, or at best, a temporary visitor.

Some alchemists said that a black demon was hidden in the *prima
materia* that drives seekers in the depths insane, and we can well understand why. The unconscious opposites slumber until activated, at which
time they fly apart, and the more consciousness can see these things in
religious-mythological terms involving the much wider, non-personal
reality, then the more it can detach itself from them. Personal identification with the contents is a great and dangerous mistake.

I remember walking down the street on a lovely summer's day, with
the sun shining brightly overhead, but the *nigredo* had crept over me and
everything seemed blackened, even the sun. Actually, it was some time
before I realized what this horrible feeling was that kept creeping over
me, coming at any time. I was at a party one night and was feeling quite
tipsy and happy, but suddenly the terrible, black feeling crept all over
me, even through the drunken haze. However, this state would only last
about four days (the *nigredo,* not the drunken haze), and then it would
be gone for perhaps a week, and so was not continuous melancholia.
And it could be postponed, reasoned with, as the following example
demonstrates.

It was December 23, and I had been working on the processes all
through the year, but was now going to give it a rest over the holiday
period. I have always loved Christmas and always celebrate it fully, and
that was my intention this year. But suddenly, the horrible blackness

began to creep slowly over me, and I knew it would last for days, as it always did. This was going to ruin Christmas for me, so I said to the unconscious, "I have worked hard on the processes all year, so let me now have Christmas in peace. Please go away and we will carry on the work afterwards." And sure enough, the *nigredo* then slowly ebbed away, and I was left alone until after the New Year. This taught me that as long as you are reasonable with the forces of the unconscious and work along with them, they will be reasonable in return.

Jung tells us that the alchemists saw the *nigredo* symbolically as the sun being devoured by the new moon, or as the descent into the Mercurial fountain, or again, as the effects of a snake bite while being held by the moon. This imagery is connected to the feminine anima, for it is the mad passion for her that has brought ego-consciousness to become ensnared by the unconscious. This then rises up in its somewhat alien state, threatening to overwhelm ego-consciousness. It is all a terrible wounding, and as Jung comments, what is wounded is the sun, the light of higher consciousness. The alchemists frequently spoke in such terms as a "raging madness that can only be assuaged by the caresses of the dove" because that was the effect upon them, plus the fact that the unconscious itself uses such language.

However, I must say that as well as the melancholy and suffering, I also felt great enthusiasm, for now I was on my quest and knew that I had a special job to do. I was no longer lost, though I was traveling a different way to other people. In fact, no matter how much I suffered, I truly loved the work. Where before I feared nightmares while asleep, but hated to get up in a morning to face the day, I now awaited all my dreams with enthusiasm, the bad as much as the good, and I eagerly arose in the morning to search out their meaning in Jung's and other works. The black sun was part of a wonderful quest for me, but the alchemists say that while the initiate remains under the influence of the *nigredo* "burial," the feminine unconscious rules.

The *nigredo* is the first stage of the work, or rather it occurs when the processes are getting under way. As has been seen, my own processes also contained visions of Christ and the Higher Self, and so it may be asked what I was doing in the alchemical depths. The answer is that they represent the eternal opposites of higher spirit and lower soul that must be united in the processes. This is the ultimate goal, the *hieros gamos*, the sacred marriage of God and the Great Mother, the World

Soul. It is essential that the lower spirit of the Underworld does not capture the adept, otherwise the result will not be good, the sacred marriage will not take place. In fact, the opposites may well then fly apart, and war will break out again between them.

> I am on a stage in a theater and I start to sing to the audience. I sing four songs, or rather parts of them, or maybe just a line from each, in the following order: "(The Bells Are Ringing) For Me and My Gal;" "Up a Lazy River"; "Moonglow"; and "Stardust."

I did not know it at the time but the four songs represent the unification of the opposites in alchemy. The third and fourth songs, "Moonglow" and "Stardust," suggest Sol and Luna, two favorite symbols of the alchemists for the eternal opposites. The first song, "For Me And My Gal," is about a marriage of course, and "Up a Lazy River" denotes the eternal river, the way between the opposites.

Some time after this dream I acquired Jung's book, *Psychology and Alchemy*, in which I found an old alchemical engraving of the sun and the moon, and a river flowing between them. This is what the East means by Tao, the Way—that is, the way to unite what is separated. This is also the way that lies between them, as well as being the way to travel. Below another engraving in the same book Jung quotes an allegory of the psychic union of opposites from the *Rosarium Philosophorum* (1550): "O Luna, folded by my embrace, / Be you as strong as I, as fair of face. / O Sol, brightest of all lights known to men. / And yet you need me, as the cock the hen."

Alchemical symbolism has become constellated in the collective unconscious, just as Christian symbolism has (in the West), the one being the underside that complements the other. My dream processes contain many examples of both.

> I am in a dark land where I see reptiles about everywhere. Snakes, crocodiles, alligators, lizards, even dinosaurs. It is a horrible vision.

This is the realm of the terrible serpent-dragon, the World Soul in its lowest, most instinctual aspect, the direct opposite of the realm of the divine spirit in its celestial light. It is the world of the most bestial instincts, and it is naturally very disturbing. But as with all other contents of the collective unconscious, it must be experienced for wholeness. All parts and sides must be experienced by consciousness to make them conscious, just as the prophet Enoch has to experience the four hollow places of the Earth, the Underworld, and Daniel had to experience the four beasts rising from the sea. St. Teresa of Avila would soar to the heights of spiritual ecstasy, then later find herself in "hell," as she described it, a place of foul-smelling reptiles. She too was undergoing the individuation process, and some of the symbolism she reports is very similar to my own in this book. She was a very intelligent woman who tried to reason out her visions, as I do here.

I see a hare hopping along and I decide to look up its symbolic meaning in a book, probably one of Jung's.

Again, I did not know it at the time but the hare is a symbol of the Higher Self in a lower, animal aspect. Just as the Self has its godly and human aspects, it also has its animal forms, which partly constitute the lower side of its nature, the hare among them. This is why a hare is a symbol of Mercurius in alchemy, and Jung tells us that the hare is the "evasive" Mercurius as guide through the unconscious. This is the basis of the White Rabbit in *Alice in Wonderland,* clearly a story with foundations in the unconscious. Mercurius also symbolizes the collective unconscious itself and as such has dozens of aspects. He is both light and dark, good and evil, and may be counterpart to both Christ and Devil, being the "system of the higher powers in the lower."

In ancient Egypt, the hare in one form was regarded as a seer, because its eyes never close. This is also one of the reasons it became symbolic to the alchemists, Mercurius as guide through the unconscious. The symbol is actually produced by the unconscious itself, not invented by the alchemists. In fact, the hare appears in myths over half the world, often connected with the moon, which fits in with its associations with Mercurius. Sometimes it is the fox that is guide rather than the hare, as both have evasive and elusive natures and qualities. There are also Egyptian representations of Osiris as the hare-headed Un-nefer, the "Good Being" and "the Opener," literally "Beautiful Hare." Indeed, the hare appears in depictions from the very earliest times in Egypt. The first ideograph in the hieroglyphic name Un-nefer is that of a hare. As it was an Osiris equivalent I experienced on his throne in the earlier dream, it is perhaps not too surprising that it is one of his symbols, the hare, that appears here.

Egyptologist A. E. Wallis Budge tells us, in *The Gods of the Egyptians*, that there is an engraving of the heavenly Elysian Fields in which a god is portrayed with the head of a hare. In another depiction, at Dendera, the hare-god wrapped as a mummy is identified with Osiris. This, as said, is as Un-nefer. Budge also states that this title was perhaps applied to Osiris because he "sprang up like a hare," but it would have been the unconscious that chose the symbol of the hare in the first place; probably because of its elusive nature and predilection for the hidden.

Now all this is very interesting because Osiris is Lord of the Underworld, and therefore of the lower unconscious, just as Mercurius. And Mercurius is dual, having light and dark aspects, good and evil, which reflects Osiris with his dark twin, Set. Horus is the higher spirit counterpart to this lower twin spirit, Osiris/Set, and as such comes forth from Ra. Although Horus is seen as the son of Osiris, he is really the higher power that comes forth in response to the lower Osiris, the Son of God. Horus is also twinned with Set to reflect his own dark shadow in the lower unconscious, the mercurial serpent, of which Osiris is the light side.

> I seem to be an archaeologist and I dig up a gold ring that belongs to the Scandinavian goddess, Freyja. A voice proclaims, "The Ring of Freyja." It has eight square insets and in one of these is the portrait of Christ. I say, "They must have had Christ even in ancient times, before the time of the historical Christ."

Freyja, Nordic goddess of love and beauty, was the daughter of Njord, god of the sea—the lower depths of the collective unconscious— and she possessed a magical golden ring (or girdle, or necklace) that was a great treasure. In one account it was fashioned for her by four dwarves, and was so beautiful that other divinities would sometimes borrow it. Freyja paid for the necklace by sleeping with each of the dwarves for one night in turn.

In *Psychology and Alchemy*, Jung gives a series of dreams that form the individuation process of one of his patients. In one of the dreams, four children find a dark ring and Jung comments that "dwarf-gods bring the ring" in alchemy, apparently unaware of, or forgetting, the four dwarves who make the ring for Freyja. There is no doubt that he would have mentioned it otherwise. The symbol is also similar to one in a dream I had that follows later in this book, where I receive four gold keys on a gold key ring from Jung.

Although we know Freyja from later Viking mythology, she is ancient in origin, and the story of her special ring (or girdle) dates from the Bronze Age. She is the equivalent of the Egyptian Isis in some ways, and also of so many other ancient goddesses who represent the feminine World Soul.

There is no goddess in Christianity to represent the eternal feminine spirit although the Assumption of the Virgin Mary by the Catholic Church has gone some way toward rectifying this. So in this dream the unconscious chooses Freyja, as she fits the symbolism adequately with her ring, girdle, or necklace; but there is the added meaning of Christ in one of the eight square insets. With the circular ring and square insets, the opposites are united in the one symbol, as Freyja representing soul, and Christ the spirit. Usually the circle represents spirit and the square soul, or matter, but in certain circumstances this may vary: Christ on the Cross is fourfold, the round containing vessel in alchemy, the *vas*, is feminine, and so forth. Eight is the number of wholeness, known as the Ogdoad in ancient Egypt, where there were eight reigning Great Gods (Later nine when the Father God was added). As Christ is contained in one of the insets of the ring, the whole symbol forms an eight-rayed mandala with the sun-god, Christ, as the central feature, though united with the eternal feminine principle. Jung states that in all the mandalas he witnessed produced by his patients, there was never a god in the center, but here, as in other of my dreams, Christ is the center.

In the German epic tale, *The Nibelungenlied*, the Rhine Maidens guard the Rhinegold, left in their care by their father, in the deep waters of the Rhine River. It was said that whoever could form a ring out of the gold would receive magical powers. Dwarves called Nibelungs greedily hoarded up gold in the Underworld to no purpose, and one day the ugly dwarf Alberich spotted the Rhinegold and stole it from the Rhine Maidens. He then fashioned the Ring of Power from the Rhinegold, setting himself up as king in the Underworld, intending to rule the world with the magic powers.

Much happens that I cannot go into here, but Wotan wins the ring from the dwarf, and then the giant-cum-dragon, Fafnir, obtains it. So

Wotan's son, Siegmund, must defeat the dragon to recover the ring, but Siegmund is guilty of a sin concerning a woman, and eventually he is killed. Siegmund's son, Siegfried, both wins the magic ring and rescues the immortal Valkyrie, Brunhilde, who renounces her immortality to be with Siegfried. However, the magical golden ring is usually associated with Freyja.

In the Grail legends, both Gawain and Perceval receive special rings, Perceval receiving his from the daughter of Merlin. This latter ring contains a precious stone inset and is therefore a symbol of the Higher Self, or perhaps I should say the lower Self. Merlin is the equivalent of the spirit Mercurius, who is dual-natured, expressed in light form as Osiris in Egypt and in dark form as Set. Merlin is variously described as Antichrist and servant of Christ, which reflects the dual nature of Mercurius. As "wise old man" with his daughter—from whom Perceval receives the ring—he reminds us of Jethro with his daughter Zipporah in the story of Moses, which is about the unification of masculine and feminine wisdom in the unconscious.

King Arthur receives a ring from his half-sister, Morgan le Fay, which holds him prisoner in an enchanted forest. The ring causes him to lose both his memory and his mind, but these return when the ring is removed. The Pharaoh in Egypt takes off his ring and gives it to Joseph, then arraigns him in white linen and puts a gold chain around his neck. The high priest Potiphera then gives his daughter to Joseph in marriage, just as Moses marries the daughter of the high priest Jethro. Nietzsche experienced a golden ring, "the ring of return," which seems to have promised resurrection and life. But though Nietzsche had, in a sense, a highly religious soul, he consciously denied it. Whereas Joseph was a true prophet who must love morality, must love the spirit, must love God as eternal truths, Nietzsche was to deny them all.

St. Teresa of Avila received a gold necklace from the Virgin Mary in a vision, at the end of which hung the cross of Christ. This is basically the same mandala symbolism as my dream, though Freyja is mentioned rather than the Virgin in my dream. Christ, in another vision, also put a wedding ring on the finger of St. Teresa, to signify the mystical marriage of her with himself. But the gold necklace and ring, and Christ, is there in both visions, though the former is fourfold and the latter doubled to eightfold.

As to the final point of the dream, where I reflect that they must have had Christ before the time of the historical Christ, this is to say that the equivalent of Christ has been experienced since the earliest times, thousands of years before Christ himself. Jung states, in *Psychology and Alchemy,* "There is thus a 'pre-Christian' as well as a 'non-Christian' Christ, insofar as he is an autonomous psychological fact." It was this and many other similar dreams that were to bring about a transformation in my personality and alter my whole view of reality itself.

> I watch a scene on a screen of things that are happening in the depths of the sea, although it is also as if I am actually there. It should be very dark at such depths, but it is quite light. I see green seaweed that forms into some other green plant, and then I see a green fish that is extremely special. Then I hear the word "Ichthys" spoken from above.

The first and main symbols of Christianity were the fish and the lamb, and it was not until later that the cross replaced the fish. Christ was said to be, symbolically, "the fish drawn from the deep," as St. Augustine expressed it, but this was nothing new to the world as the fish had been widely known since much earlier times as the symbol of the savior. In Assyria-Babylonia, the Fish-Man was Oannes, the Annedotus, with the Seven Annedoti; in Nineveh, "Dag," meaning both "fish" and "savior," and "Oannes," were contracted into "Dagan," or "Dogon," the fish-god that centuries later became the fertility god of the Philistines. In the Talmud, the Messiah is frequently called the "Dag," the "Fish." The name of Nineveh, the Assyrian city, probably derives from Nina, who was the great Fish Mother, though one name of Ea, "the Sublime Fish," was Nin-a-gal, and so Nineveh may derive from him. Perhaps Nin and Nina were alternative names for the male and female fish. However, the king who laid the foundations of the city was Ninus, deriving his name from the god, as King Assurbanipal was named after the god Assur, again at Nineveh.

The Greeks called Adonis, whose mother was half fish, "Ichthys," and Orphos, or Diorphos, was worshipped as a fish in Lycia. Bacchus too was "the Fish." In India the fish of Manu is a savior, being an incarnation of Vishnu, and A. E. Wallis Budge says that the Oxyrhynchus fish was worshipped all over Egypt. Horus was the "fish of the inundation," and "the fish in the form of a man" and there was also the "An" fish of Egypt, possibly from the very ancient sacred center of Annu. Oannes, or Oan, is really a form of Ea, "the Sublime Fish," who had seven fins. Ea is also an extremely ancient god, known to the Sumerians as Enki.

The An fish of Egypt may originally have been the crocodile, and this is possibly because as the Higher Self comes out of the unconscious, symbolized by water, so the crocodile walks out of the waters onto dry land. In this sense the crocodile is an advancement on the fish, as it has legs and can walk onto the land. But the Higher Self in light aspect is a savior, a bringer of spiritual light to the world, so how can the crocodile, a dangerous killer, symbolize this? So though certain ancient cults of Egypt venerated the crocodile as Sevekh, and possibly as Horus the An fish, it was generally hated over the land as the terrible dragon-monster.

The story of Jonah and the fish—a whale is not mentioned in the Biblical account—is certainly a version of Oannes. The name Jonah itself was a form of "Oannes," the Jews obviously adopting the figure and his myth during their captivity in Babylon. Long before the time of Christ, the Jews referred to the expected Messiah to come as, symbolically, the Dag fish. So when Christ did arrive as the Fish, he was continuing the line that began with Ea perhaps thousands of years earlier. Though in most other respects, Christ fulfills the Egyptian traditions. The Jews have a belief that a "pure fish" will be caught by the Angel Gabriel at the end of the Age of Leviathan. It will feed the worthy and will apparently mean the coming of the Messiah. Mythology abounds with fish symbolism, for the fish is the savior who comes from the depths of the unconscious, symbolized by the sea.

As I say elsewhere, there are ancient depictions of certain divine Sons, Christ, Vishnu, Oannes, as coming out of the mouth of the Fish Mother. This is because although the fish represents the higher savior, it is nevertheless the symbol from the lower soul depths in the first phase. The Higher Self must be born twice, from both the spirit heights and the soul depths, reflecting the two sides, higher and lower, of the Self, Christ and Mercurius, or Horus and Osiris (whose dark aspect was Set).

I remember reading a book many years ago by a learned professor who kept asking throughout, "Why so often in mythology does the savior/culture-hero come from out of the sea?" The professor seemed to be a man of some knowledge, but he obviously did not know depth psychology, otherwise he would have been able to answer his own question. Just as a fish comes from out of the sea depths, so the savior, the Higher Self, is brought forth from the depths of the unconscious.

The fish, called the *Ichthys* in my dream, symbolizes that special archetype from the unconscious realm, parallels of which, as said, reach back to the ancient world, including Christ himself. In *The Grail Legend*

(1960), Emma Jung and Marie-Louise von Franz comment, ". . . that as a symbolic manifestation of the unconscious archetype, the fish expresses an aspect of Christ." I have now myself, in the foregoing dreams, experienced Christ or his symbols several times, and there will be many other instances to come, and so the fish, the Ichthys, in this dream is clearly connected with him.

There is an event in the Gospel of John (21:1-14) where seven fishermen (disciples) go out to catch fish in the sea of Tiberias, but have no luck all night. The next morning, Jesus appears on the shore and tells them to cast their nets on the right side of the boat, and then the nets are overloaded with fish. The Gospel continues (21:9-12): "As soon as they were come to land, they saw a fire of coals there and fish laid thereon, and bread. Jesus saith unto them, Bring of the fish which ye hast now caught. . . . Jesus said unto them, Come and dine. . . ."

In *The Grail Legend*, the authors point out that St. Augustine (in *Evangelium Johannis Tractalus*) also wrote of this: "At this meal, which the Lord gave to his seven disciples and at which he served them the fish they had seen on the fire of coals, together with the loaves of bread and the fishes they had caught, it was Christ who had suffered, who was in reality the fish that was broiled."

So again, Christ is the fish, and in the Church it is the fish that is eucharistically eaten, signifying the eating or assimilation of the god that reaches back to very ancient times. In fact, Prosper Africanus speaks of Christ as the fish that feeds the whole world.

Mentioning the Grail legends, the sick Fisher King, having been wounded by a lance, and with a wound that will not heal, can only spend his time fishing. What he is actually doing is fishing in the unconscious depths for the Redeemer, and although the fish in the Grail meal feeds all of those present, it is only the Host from the Grail—Christ's blood—that can heal the Fisher King and his kingdom. The fish is thus an important ingredient and stage in the holy quest, but is not the ultimate goal. That is Christ's blood, the divine essence, which is held by the Holy Grail.

In *The Archetypes and the Collective Unconscious*, Jung tells a story from the Koran, called "The Cave," which connects the seven powers, Seven Sleepers, whom Jung says are gods, with the Self and the fish. Here, in Jung's retelling, the Seven Sleepers fall asleep for 309 years in the middle of the cave, after which they awaken, renewed or transformed.

(The seven powers in various forms feature throughout ancient mythology, and they were, in fact, the seven disciples in the boat spoken of above.) The cave is the unconscious, the "Earth-womb," where marvels do happen and where men may even be transformed into gods.

Later, the story concerns Moses who is on a quest with his servant, Joshua ben Nun. Nun was the Egyptian god of the primordial waters, and was also sometimes associated with the fish. (Nun was originally in feminine form, though soon became masculine, and in this way may be connected to the Nin, as in Nina and Nin-a-gal that we find with the Assyrians.) On reaching their destination, Moses tells Joshua to bring their breakfast, a fish, but the servant had forgotten it, and it had miraculously come alive again, making its way down to the sea by way of a stream. Moses then says that they must return to the spot where they left the fish, and when they do, they find there the figure of Khidr, the Verdant One. Khidr is the Long-lived One, who at the end of time will be dismembered by Antichrist and then resurrected. In other words, he is the Higher Self figure whose first presence in the story was as the fish, whom he then replaces as Khidr, just as in my own processes the fish is Christ.

So in this story we have the seven powers, the fish, and the Higher Self, and both the cave and the sea represent the unconscious. Joshua, Jung says, is the shadow of Moses, who must be won over to ego-consciousness for the quest.

In some versions of the story—there are several, as well as the Egyptian original—including the one in the Koran, the Seven Sleepers are accompanied by a dog. Now, we find examples of the seven powers with a dog in ancient Egyptian mythology and elsewhere—they form the seven stars of the Great Bear with the Dog Star as the eighth, or the seven gods with the dog god Anubis (or Anup) leading them. (In the Irish myth of Finn MacCool, Finn's dog, Bran, leads a pack of seven hunting dogs.) These mythic contents are not taken from the stars, but are sometimes projections from the unconscious onto the stars. But it is remarkable that symbolism—the dog with the Seven Powers from the earliest texts of Egypt—may still appear in our dreams today with the same meaning.

In Exodus, Moses approaches the Promised Land with his companions, Joshua and Caleb. As just mentioned, Joshua is associated with the fish, for he is the son of Nun, whose symbol is the fish. Now, the scholar

Gerald Massey tells us that one meaning of Caleb, perhaps the main one, is "dog," so in a sense, Moses' companions are a fish and a dog. It would be appropriate because the Jews always humanized the Egyptian gods and symbols into historical figures. Not only do the fish and the dog figure into the tale above, they have also appeared in my dreams, and will appear constantly in future ones.

In other words, the Exodus, and the Egyptian myths, are individuation processes, and I was experiencing a similar one here. The man Jesus would also have undergone a similar process, continuing the line from Moses and the other prophets that eventually produced the higher Christ. Appropriately, the Talmud states, "Only the son of a man with the name of a fish could lead the children of Israel into the Promised Land, namely Joshua, the son of the fish (Joshua, the son of Nun)."

Relevant here is that Jung says in *Aion*, "In conclusion, I would like to emphasize once again that the fish symbol is a spontaneous assimilation of the Christ figure of the gospels, and is thus a symptom which shows us in what manner and with what meaning the symbol was assimilated by the unconscious." And again in *Civilization in Transition:* "Like the teacher of wisdom in Babylonian legend, Oannes, he (Christ) rose up from the sea, from the primeval darkness, and brought a world period to an end."

I am due to start work on a new job but feel so ill with my nerves that it is impossible to do so. As I walk down a street, I realize that I have forgotten my tinted glasses, which would help to protect my eyes from the world. I cannot face the world at the moment. A teenage girl comes along and I explain to her just why I cannot start the job, apologizing for it, and this causes her to weep on my behalf. My suffering and despair weigh so heavily on me that, falling to my knees, I too begin to sob. With head bent I say that my heart is broken and I cannot go on any further.

At that moment, Christ walks into the dream, wearing long white robes, his arms and hands bleeding, and walking up to me, he lays his hands on my head as I kneel. Now, not only am I on my knees in the dream, I am also watching all of this from a few yards away, just inside the line which divides the sleeping state from consciousness, so to speak. So I watch as Christ leaves the "me" who is on my knees, and walking right past me as I stand there, he walks out of the dream again. Though I see him very clearly from the front, I do not actually register his face.

For some time after this dream I kept asking myself what was different about it, different from normal dreams (as well as the appearance of Christ), but I just could not put my finger on it. Then it suddenly came to me one day when I was out in the fields with my dog. Christ had walked in and out of the dream as a real figure and was not just an image of the dream as such. I had watched the dream as though from conscious reality, and Christ had come from behind me (from higher consciousness, higher reality) not just from the world itself. The earlier dream had featured the special green fish, the Ichthys, the symbol of Christ as Savior, and now he had appeared in person.

As with appearances of Christ in other dreams, I have long wondered if this was the Higher Self as a Christ-equivalent, the original Christ himself, or the Holy Spirit taking the form of Christ. To be honest, I am still unsure. All I can say is that he must have the same basic meaning as the original Christ or he would not appear in that form.

All of these forms—the "Christ within"; Anthropos of the Gnostics; the Son of Man of the prophets Ezekiel, Daniel, and Enoch; Melchizedek with Abraham; Horus, Iu-em-hetep, and Khunsu in Egypt; the examples of Atman, Purusha, and Vishnu in India; Quetzalcoatl in Central America; Ahura Mazda in Persia; Vatea in Polynesia; and Kwan Shi Yin in China—are expressions of the Higher Self found around the world. Of Kwan Shi Yin, Blavatsky says in *The Secret Doctrine* (1888), "He is the Self Manifested: in short, the 'Son of the Father.' Crowned with seven dragons, above his statue there appears the inscription 'Pu-tsi-K'ien-ling, the universal savior of all living beings'." In China, the Dalai Lama is said to be one of his incarnations, for Kwan Shi Yin is identified with Avalokitesvara, of whom the Dalai-Lama is the earthly form. All of this applies equally to Christ, to the Anthropos, to the Son of Man, and to all of the other god-man, Higher Self figures. Just as Kwan Shi Yin is crowned with seven dragons, Christ has seven stars, Horus has seven lights, Vishnu has seven rishis, and so on.

In the dream, I am unable to go on and break down sobbing, which reflects my mental state at that particular time. In my suffering, the suffering Christ hears me and performs the "laying on of hands." As well as indicating healing, this could also perhaps mean to confer blessings and grace. Christ himself is bleeding in the dream, which reminds us of how Christ sweats blood in Luke's Gospel 22:44: "and his sweat was as it were great drops of blood falling to the ground." This recapitulates the image of *Osiris Tesh Tesh,* the god who, in this guise, suffers in agony and bloody sweat. Because blood is red, it is said that the red sun suffered his agony in the Underworld. The Sun-god Atum, as the sun, is symbolically set in a "red pool," intimating blood, and even the red, scarlet, or purple robe of Christ is connected with the blood caused by suffering.

Just as Christ is said to redeem the world by his "bloody sweat," so the alchemists believed that the blood sweated from their "stone" would produce a Redeemer. Not Christ himself, but his parallel, hence the "lapis-Christ parallel."

Jung comments in *Mysterium Coniunctionis* (1963b) that in the individuation process at ultimate level, the adept experiences a transformation that may be compared to the Passion of Christ. This is because the higher self attaches himself to the Christ image, so that it may even involve a correspondence to Christ, rather than an "imitation." Always the original experience in the depths is repeated anew, though this must involve self-sacrifice.

Hippolytus, one of the Church Fathers who wrote on the Gnostic sects, writes: "The Naassenes speak of a nature of man at once hidden and manifesting itself, which they say is within man, and is the kingdom of Heaven that is sought after" (1921). However, I have not developed the Higher Self as a Christ figure yet—that occurs with the processes later—so who is the figure in my dream? The original Christ, the Holy Spirit?

> I search for the woman I love, first in the Southern Hemisphere then in the Northern, but she is nowhere to be found.

Before I comment on this dream I will continue with the next, which follows on from this one.

> Again I search for the woman I love, only now I look in the Western world, and then move across to the East.

The woman for whom I am searching is my own feminine side in the unconscious, the anima, and I form a cross with my movements, up and down and across the world. What I am doing with my processes is experiencing and making conscious the four sides of the lower depths of the collective unconscious or World Soul, just as Enoch finds "four hollow places" in the Underworld, and Daniel sees four beasts rise up from out of the sea. Certain of the places which Herakles visits in his labors form a cross, again denoting wholeness achieved in the processes of the unconscious.

As I said previously, the collective unconscious functions on the law of compensation and complementation, so that the making conscious and therefore the bringing forth of the four sides of the World Soul will bring the Higher Self its totality on the lower side. Enoch, after bringing the "four hollow places" to consciousness, experiences the Son of Man, Metatron, who is at once ancient and bearded and a beautiful youth. Enoch, as the human initiate, merges with Metatron, for of him it is said, "[He] who was not, for God had taken him up."

> I am in a pub called the "Jolly Carter," usually referred to by local people as the "Carter." Going to a back room, I begin to dig up the floor. Eventually I discover an underground chamber filled with treasure, dating from ancient Egypt to the Victorian era. There are priceless objects here, and particularly stressed are those of the Egyptian and Victorian eras.

This is a recurring dream, where I find a great treasure buried in Egypt, or a priceless treasure from there. Sometimes the Victorian era is mentioned and this is probably because it was more or less then that the tombs began to be opened up and Egyptian civilization was rediscovered after thousands of years. Many of the Victorian scholars had a somewhat mystical view of reality and were therefore more in tune with the deeper meaning of the ancient religious mysteries. Gerald Massey is a prime example. In contrast, twentieth-century scholarship became all science and technology. Very admirable and able from that angle, to be sure, but the awe of the religious mysteries was lost along with the feeling that there might be some kind of mystical truth in them. Blavatsky realized just what that mystical truth was, and how utterly valid it was, though she herself became a Buddhist and therefore concentrated more on the Far Eastern forms of religion. However, the world largely saw her as a medium, and something of a charlatan at that. Can you imagine by any stretch of the imagination the scientifically trained Egyptologists of the twentieth century going by Blavatsky? Even Massey was rejected and then forgotten.

But then Jung opened up the collective unconscious and we can now understand the ancient religions, and much else, from that view and see the great truth of them, and such figures as Blavatsky and Massey become very important to us.

I see a crocodile that terrifies me so much that I try to run up the wall to escape it.

The crocodile symbolizes the terrible dragon, the lower instinctual forces of the collective unconscious in their darkest aspect. To the ancient Egyptians the crocodile was Sebekh (or Sevekh), the seven-headed dragon that we also see in the Apocalypse. (Sevekh means "seven"). For the Egyptians, and indeed, for all cultures, the dragon must be slain for right order to come to the world. This is understandable as the dragon (or serpent), symbolizing dark chaotic forces of the unconscious, must be defeated and chained up for civilization to grow and flourish. The crocodile, as a type of dragon was also well known in alchemy.

Egyptologist Gerald Massey says in his *Ancient Egypt* (1907) that the goddesses Neith and Apt were crocodiles in one very early form in Egypt:

> The same typical devourer has another figure in the judgement hall, where it is named Amemit. Here it has the head of a crocodile. Where we may speak of the jaws of death, hell, or destruction, the Egyptians said or showed the jaws of the crocodile. Those who are condemned to be devoured pass into the jaws of the devourer. Thus the crocodile is the devourer, the typical tyrant, the cruel, hard hearted monster who guards the gate of exit and will not let the suffering people go up from the land of bondage.

In another myth, the seven-headed dragon, or crocodile, with ten horns, comes up from the depths of the sea, which again is the unconscious symbolically. Jung says that the mother of the unconscious depths sometimes appears as cat, snake, or bear, and sometimes as a black underworld monster like the crocodile.

I am perhaps in a hazy, space-like reality where I see a boy contained in a cylinder that is rolling away. I somehow use a square to trap and stop the cylinder, and it then becomes a woodcut or engraving that depicts the birth of Christ surrounded by holy men—priests, or monks perhaps, of the Russian Orthodox church. I then take the engraving on a dark evening to a sort of monastery situated on a snow-clad mountainside.

The priests or monks in the monastery are similar to those on the engraving, and as I approach the walls, one of the holy men comes down to meet me. He has a long, black beard, and wears black robes. He takes the engraving from me. It is extremely precious and holy and must be kept safe in the monastery. Then others are present and they doubt that it concerns the birth of Christ, but an angelic choir begins to sing from above, and a voice, also from above—God's, in fact—says "This is indeed my beloved Son."

The boy in the cylinder is the divine child, the infant Higher Self, whom I have to trap with a square, which represents worldly and material reality, to bring him to Earth in time and space. Since the earliest times a circle, or roundness, has symbolized the spirit—Jung simply says that it is a well-known symbol for God—whereas the square usually represents the Earth. The birth is the equivalent to that of Christ and the dream even depicts it as Christ's birth itself.

I realize this will seem incredible to the reader, but it must be remembered that it was such processes of the unconscious that produced (brought forth) the Son of Man/Son of God within the man Jesus originally. Nor was it the first time that it had occurred in world history, as we know from many other examples in mythology and other religions, and neither will it be the last. The Son of Man figure experienced by Enoch, Daniel, and Ezekiel are certainly prefigurations of Christ, and the line stretches right back to early Egypt, which built its mythology and religion on those experiences.

The Higher Self who comes forth as the child at this level is what the ancient Egyptians called the *Iusa*, the "ever-coming son," and the cults of Horus and Khunsu also developed from similar experiences. Because the alchemists became involved in processes of the unconscious in their opus, which involved the Higher Self—and in which the man Jesus must also have been involved—they were replacing him as the initiate in the work. Jung says that when they praised the Philosopher's Stone as the Second Coming of the Messiah, they must have had something similar in mind.

In my dream, the monastery and the priest-monks seem to suggest the Russian Orthodox Church, and for some time I had been seeing these holy men appear in certain dreams. I had even bought a book on icon paintings, which captivated and fascinated me. I had become "possessed" by an archetype taking that specific form. The holy men in the dream may have been Bogomils, or a similar sect, who flourished in Bulgaria and parts of Russia, and who had their roots in Gnosticism (as did the Cathars). But having said that, the monastery and the monks nevertheless do seem to have something of Russian Orthodoxy about them. (Russian Orthodoxy has its roots in the old Greek Orthodox Church.)

Whatever the case, others in the dream doubt that the engraving concerns the birth of Christ, but the voice from above insists "This is indeed my beloved Son," which would seem to settle the matter. I immediately think of Matthew 3:17: "And lo a voice from Heaven, saying, This is my beloved Son, in whom I am well pleased." Similarly in ancient Egypt, Ra has said to the divine child, Horus, at his birth: "You are the son of my body, begotten by me."

From the point of view of depth psychology we know that all of this is possible. Consciousness is but a small part of the total Higher Self, the mortal attached to the higher immortal, and the latter, in turn, is part of God. In Jung's individuation process, the Higher Self at the ultimate level breaks away from God to come through to the world as the Son, as a fact of the unconscious, this is to say, in a reality that lies behind the physical universe. There is initially a lower form of the Self that is restricted to the lower sphere, but which is ultimately part of the total Higher Self, the *filius macracosmi* as part of the *filius microcosmi,* The ultimate Higher Self is mediator between man and God, just as Christ was, and is: "No man cometh unto the Father but by me," as Christ states.

Man, as part of the Higher Self, and the Higher Self as part of God, is as a second is to a day, and as a day is to eternity. Man is a brief life in time and space, whereas God is the infinite and eternal All. Nevertheless, man can know God directly, through the Higher Self, and Jung insisted that it is God's desire to incarnate and become man which he does as the Higher Self.

Jung comments that the Church never made a lot of the phenomenon of the Holy Ghost, and that it was continued rather by the alchemists. Through the inner presence of the spirit of procreation, God may be incarnated within the human individual, who becomes caught up in the Trinitarian process as the Paraclete descends upon him. Similarly, the alchemical text *Aurora Consurgens* states: "The fullness of time shall come, when God shall send his son, as he hath said whom he hath appointed heir of all things, by whom also he made the world, to whom he said of old time. Thou art my Son, today I have begotten thee, to whom the Wise Men from the east brought three precious gifts."

It's important to note that God Himself claims the divine child to be his own in the dream, which means that it is not just a product of the collective depths of the unconscious. It is the Higher Self as Son of God the Father, or the divine birth of Him, and this is further substantiated by the fact that he came from the skies, from space, and not from the depths of the sea. The Son of the Mother comes from the sea, for as the sea can symbolize the total other reality, the spirit Self may also symbolically come from the sea. However, the birth of the divine child is exactly that, the birth of the Higher Self in the human individual, and he must be helped to develop and grow into his fullness. This is an extremely difficult and dangerous task for consciousness, and it is no wonder whatsoever that the task almost always ends in failure.

> I see the golden balance wheel of a clock on the sill just inside a window. Outside the window I can see the sun in the sky, and it shines down specially on the balance wheel.

The golden balance wheel is a mandala, one of the main abstract symbols of the Higher Self. A window in dreams means the dividing line between this world and the otherworldly reality, so the balance wheel being this side of the window in my dream means that the Higher Self has come through to my experience. The sun, as we know, has been the symbol of God from the very earliest times, so we can say that in the dream God the Father looks down on the Son who has incarnated into the material world, even if only as a fact of the unconscious. This substantiates what occurred in the previous dream, which was the birth of the divine Son witnessed by the Father from above.

The mandala is a very ancient symbol of totality and we find it all over the world, from simple circles, or even squares, with some kind of inner markings, to the great and complex world-wheels of Buddhism. A mandala is basically a balance of opposites around a center, and it expresses the situation in the unconscious. The squaring of the circle is sometimes involved, or the unification of three and four, and one of the earliest forms of this is the Great Bear Circle with the Four Quarters of the heavens from ancient Egypt.

> I go into a certain church where I find four statues carved in stone; they have also been painted. They bear figures of saints, three men and a woman, and I suddenly realize that they are, in fact, living spirits, and they even smile at me.
>
> I then see a man I know with his son, and as the father is named Joseph, I think of the Biblical Joseph and his son, Jesus. Then I hear the words, "Out of the Father comes the Son." The son in the dream has now become Jesus, but then changes again and becomes a white dog. Then I realize the figures of the four saints have also become animals.

The dream represents the birth of the Higher Self as a Christ parallel, with the four spirit figures being the four emanations, the fourfold structure of the Higher Self. These are of the 3 + 1 nature, three males and one female here in the dream. We find this historically and mythologically with Horus and his four sons, three animal- and one human-headed—these were originally three males and the fourth as female. We also find it with Daniel's four beasts rising from the sea, one a "recalcitrant fourth"; his four figures in the furnace, three men and a "Son of God"; and Christ with the four symbols of the Evangelists, three animal and one human (imagery which will be discussed shortly); again, all examples being of a 3 + 1 structure.

In my dream, the four figures represent the higher, spiritual side, but at the finish they become their symbolic forms as animals, just as we find with the four animal symbols of the four apostles, Matthew, Mark, Luke, and John, being those that appear in the symbol with Christ.

In the first chapter of Ezekiel, "four living creatures appear." The man, lion, ox, and eagle are of the fourfold structure, making them a similar formulation to the four sons of Horus. Then a wheel appears for each of the "four living creatures" and later commentaries interpreted these as the chariot, the Merkabah. This four-wheeled structure appears again in chapter 10, with four cherubim, but they are now cherub, man, lion, and eagle. The cherub has now replaced the ox of the first vision, though Ezekiel nevertheless says that they are the same he saw in the original vision. However, the cherub may itself be part ox, or bull.

The four creatures later became the symbols of the four Evangelists: man = Matthew; lion = Mark; ox = Luke; eagle = John. In medieval times these were portrayed at four corners with Christ at the center, again, the fourfold structure of the Higher Self. My earlier dream of a flower at each corner, with the rose at the center is similar, though not so developed. But the earliest symbol of this I know is Horus with his four sons.

"Out of the Father comes the Son," the dream says, and in keeping with the incarnating Self, the boy first becomes Jesus, or Christ, and then becomes the white dog, the dog-spirit that is the early symbol of the Higher Self. We are forced to think here of Mephistopheles, the dark Self in Goethe's *Faust*, whose first appearance was as a black poodle, and of Anup (Anubis), Xlolotl, Bran, and other dogs of myth and folklore. But I emphasize that all these dreams reveal that the Higher Self at the ultimate level is a god and Son of God. As Jung says: ". . . since Christ, as a man, corresponds to the ego, and as a god, to the Self. . . ." (1959a). Furthermore, the dream substantiates yet again that a divine Son has arrived—the Higher Self as divine child.

> I look out the window with my mother and sister and we see that although it is dusk, the sky has also become dark with clouds. A particularly dark cloud, round in shape, moves across the sky, and at the center of it is a gold spot, like an eye. From this radiates a beam of golden light, which shines through the window like a spotlight. It is searching for me, but being afraid I move into a hidden area of the room so that the beam cannot find me. The cloud then passes by, and a ghostly looking spaceship moves off into the distance. I remark that they were alien beings. I then wake up feeling very disturbed.

The round, dark cloud-cum-ghostly spaceship is a mandala of course, but we must not limit its meaning in any way because of that. As I said about the previous dream, a mandala is a chief symbol of the Higher Self, and when it has Christ in the center, for instance, surrounded by the symbols of the four Evangelists, it expresses nothing less than an immortal, a god. However, when we say "a god," we nevertheless think of a human shape because we would have difficulty imagining a god any other way. If we should actually experience a god in a dream or vision, we would indeed see a human shape, though it would be merely a pared-down, "human" *representation* of a phenomenon of inestimable nature.

The circle is a well-known symbol of God and spirit, so the cloud with the golden eye (flying saucer) is an equally valid representation of the eternal powers, or of God, as anything else. Elsewhere in this book, I mention the visions of Orfeo Angelucci in which "aliens" inform him that they only *appear* in those forms, and appear to come in flying saucers to manifest themselves to humans. If that is how humans expect to see them, then fair enough, that is how they will appear. But they are really immortals, gods to us, and we mortals live out our physical lives for them here on Earth. We are their agents, therefore, in material reality.

The round cloud in my dream would seem to express the spirit side of the Higher Self, or the Holy Spirit or the eye of God Himself. In any case, whether Self, Holy Spirit, or God, in the dream it is an extension of God come forth, to look at whoever has brought forth the divine child. However, it must be said that the whole situation seems to be more dangerous than that, and is certainly less personal than a humanized experience of the Higher Self. In fact, on reflection the dream image could actually represent pure spirit, which seems to be a force independent of Father and Son, and apparently more dangerous.

We are still strongly influenced more than we realize by the old traditional Church view of these things which sees God and the Holy Spirit, if they exist at all, as being only good. But this is far from being the case. God and spirit are eternal totalities that contain opposites within themselves, and like electricity, may bring light or destruction. We must also remember the saying of Christ that a sin against the Father and himself can be forgiven, but not one against the Holy Spirit, which seems to suggest that the Holy Spirit can be a dangerous and relentless force. Having said that, God and the Holy Spirit are nevertheless as wonderful as the mystics and visionaries have always insisted, and it is good, right, and excellent that such visions as those of St. Teresa of Avila, St. Bernadette of Lourdes, and the children of Fatima should fill us with awe and light. For make no mistake, these are genuine visions in accordance with the symbolism of the unconscious processes.

As for my mother and sister being with me in the dream, these are well known forms—that is, female family members sometimes taken by the anima, although it would not surprise me in the least if they really were my real life mother and sister as well, or at least their souls. Long experience of the unconscious processes has taught me that although people we know in dreams may represent parts of ourselves or parts of the unconscious realm itself, they frequently *also* represent the essence of those real people themselves, usually as they affect us. Whatever the case, the window through which we look in the dream represents the dividing line between our known world and the other realm of spirit and soul.

> An octopus has caught me in its tentacles under the sea. I fight my way up to the surface and fresh air, which is, of course, consciousness. As I awake, the octopus releases me and then sinks back to the depths, into the unconscious.

As I have said previously, whenever one side of the collective unconscious is experienced in the processes (or a content from it) you will then experience the other, reverse or opposite side of the content. In the last dream, I had to escape the golden beam of the round cloud from the higher spirit side, and now I escape the clutches of its counterpart, the octopus, which represents the lower, instinctual, or soul side. An octopus, with its eight arms or tentacles and central body, makes an excellent mandala symbol of the lower instinctual part of the Self.

This leads to the unmistakable conclusion that no matter how completely different and far apart the opposites of spirit and soul (matter) are, they are directly and inexorably connected, as if by a cable; to light up one side causes its opposite side to be lit up as well.

The whole of reality, which includes all universes, all dimensions, all of infinity and eternity, seems to be like a great sphere, (the mandala symbol again), with spokes going from one side, passing through the center point, and out to the far side. Perhaps the center point is the mind of God, and the linked contents of the sphere his parts, so that everything that exists, in all dimensions and all realities, is part of God. It may even be that God extends and fragments Himself—His parts—so that He may have a living and experiencing existence, which helps Him to develop or progress. Human beings—and life all over the universe— would therefore be extended parts of God, having a definite role to play in helping Him in that growth or evolution.

Man is a complexity of opposites that is a part of the Higher Self, which, or who, is in turn a complexity of opposites that is part of God.

Wheels within wheels, as it were, and there have been mystics and visionaries who have had visions of such wheels within wheels. (Perhaps "spheres within spheres" would be even better symbolism.)

The idea of Creation as a circle with God as the center point is an ancient one, and St. Bonaventure comments: "God is an intelligible sphere whose center is everywhere and whose circumference is nowhere" (1937). Orfeo Angelucci, whom I mentioned above, had UFO/spirit experiences that left him with the stigmata of a circle with a dot in the center on his chest. Jung comments that he had simply been touched by God. This symbol may be significant as the alchemists saw the *filius macrocosmi,* the lower Son, as a surrounding circle, and the *filius microcosmi,* the higher Son, as the central point. Orfeo has the symbol of the ancient philosophers and alchemists as his stigmata. This seems to have been an important symbol throughout the mysteries.

> I am in an old factory where I break through the floorboards to the cellars below. This is an ancient chamber in Egypt, full of fantastic, priceless treasures, and I have discovered it. Then two Egyptian policemen and an antiquities official come and tell me to clear off, but I now have some authority myself, and I answer, "Listen, you dumb-heads, there is a greater treasure under the ground of Egypt than has ever been discovered before, and I know where it is." My words are true, and the official knows it, and so is very apologetic towards me.

The treasure referred to in the dream is spiritual of course, and Egypt symbolizes the collective unconscious as the source of the spiritual treasures that were first known there. Christ, our Son of God symbol, has his roots in Egypt in the royal line that runs through the collective unconscious. I had another dream, which I give later, where Jung is overhead, spanning a stream of blue blood with his outstretched arms; this is the royal line which flows from the divine source in early Egypt. Horus and Set are based on experiences of the light and dark sides of the Higher Self, and Pharaoh as man and as god (Horus) represented ego-consciousness connected with and part of the Higher Self.

Horus as a god had his human aspect, namely, Pharaoh; so did Christ in the form of Jesus. Both gods symbolize the Higher Self, but whereas Christ has lost all traces of his dark side, Pharaoh was said to embody both Horus and Set, the hostile twin adversaries. It is also why the queen of Egypt, wife of Pharaoh, had the title, "She who sees Horus and Set."

The West, in accepting Christ, became heir to the royal line, but it never understood the full meaning and real significance of it all, projecting the mystery outwards into the sky. The West was oblivious to the inner man, to the "Christ within," as the Gnostics put it. The Church stamped out the Gnostics quite early, but on the other hand, without realizing it, still preserved much of their symbolism that had originally come through from the collective unconscious. Much has been discarded and lost over the centuries, though it is also true to say that the Church is still the caretaker of the eternal Mystery of Father, Son, Holy Spirit, and Great Mother (in the symbolic form of Mary).

Jung tells us that Ka-Mutef is responsible for the divine creation of Pharaoh through a symbolic human mother just as in the Christ myth, and that in both cases the human mother is left apart from the Trinity. Jung then says that God the Father speaks of the divine child. "He will exercise a kingship of grace in this land, for my soul is in him." Then, speaking to the child, God says: "You are the son of my body, begotten by me."

These ideas passed into Israel, Jung says, into Hellenistic syncretism, and eventually into Christianity, making Christ a phenomenon based on the Egyptian model that was by then thousands of years old. This was in terms of outer ideas and structures, but they were based on the divine incarnation of God as the Son through the unconscious, experienced and developed by the Old Testament prophets. We say Higher Self, following Jung who borrowed the term from the Far East, as did Blavatsky, but in my thousands of dreams the unconscious has never once referred to the "Higher Self," or indeed, to the "unconscious," or to the "individuation process." The collective unconscious is mythological by nature and is actually a great, eternal, religious complex. Even the word "complex" sounds like too scientific a term. Religious texts, myths, legends, fairy stories, and folklore are all in keeping with it and express its nature, and Jung says that religious dogma expresses the great truths of the unconscious far better than scientific theory could ever hope to do.

I am with screen hero Charlton Heston in the Napoleonic Wars, where we make ready to fight the French enemy. I say, "We must be brave and fight with all our might. We must overcome fear and fight to the death." Heston agrees, and when the French attack, we fight fero- ciously and recklessly, each killing many of the enemy. Then it is over and we have triumphed, at least for now. We see an old comrade, a vet- eran campaigner, and with him is his old horse pulling a cart. The old horse now has only three legs, one (a hind leg) having been shot off in battle. Suddenly, the remaining hind leg somehow gets caught in the wheel of the cart, causing the horse to scream horribly with pain. The driver, unfeelingly, merely hacks off the bottom half of the leg with an ax. Life has hardened the driver.

The scene then changes and I am in Sant Street, which I mistakenly took for Saint Street recently in real life, and a voice asks, "How can we believe in God when there is so much suffering in life? And God allows it." I then go to the end of the street, which seems to be at the end of the world, and I see a woman outside a door. I ask myself, "Could she be my true love?" She takes me into the building, which is a darkened stable inside, and she shows me a beautiful white horse that has just that instant been born, fully grown. It is a magnificent specimen, and although it does not seem to like me at first, it becomes friendlier and laughs. Not a horse laugh, but a fully human one. I am extremely impressed.

In the first part of the dream I am in the role of the hero, fighting the dark forces of the unconscious, here symbolized by the French. This is the meaning of the presence of film hero Charlton Heston, and he regu- larly appeared in my dreams during these years, and with the same meaning. I was frequently in wars and battles as the processes plowed onwards, fighting the French, Germans, Japanese, Mongols, Huron and Apache Indians—in fact, all kinds of foes that have appeared as such in movies, all representing hostile forces of the unconscious. This dream symbolizes the great war between the opposites that ensues in the unconscious when consciousness activates them. The "great war" is always blazing away in the depths during the quest.

The second part of the dream concerns rebirth. The suffering old horse is obviously reborn as the magnificent young but fully grown one. There is a similarity with the story of Osiris, who is dismembered and then resurrected; and also with Christ, who is crucified unto death and then resurrected into glory. There may also be an allusion to reincarna- tion in the dream, though it all depends on whether the horse is reborn in an afterlife or here again on Earth, and the one does not discount the other of course.

All of this occurs in answer to the question of why God allows such terrible suffering. The answer is obviously that suffering old life will be born anew, and this applies not only to humans, but to all forms of life. So although we may have to suffer greatly during our lifetime, we are all gloriously resurrected in the spirit when it is over. Christianity promises eternal life, as do all religions in one way or another, but the full truth seems to include reincarnation as part of the divine plan. I must say that all of my experiences in the unconscious over the years support this totally, as do experiences across thousands of years of so many people worldwide.

The street in the dream is at the end of the world, at death. For when we die, it is the end of the world for us. However, as I said earlier, "There is no such thing as death, only change," and it is the unconscious that has me state that.

Modern man possesses a tremendous amount of knowledge concerning the material universe, but knows nothing of spirit and believes even less. I speak mainly of the world of scholarship, and in particular, of science, whose pronouncements are taken to be ultimate truths, and whose word is law. But the eternal truths of the unconscious, which are irrational facts, merely laugh at the stunted thinking of modern man. The unconscious, or perhaps I should say God, is not against science, and indeed, welcomes the growth of knowledge, just not when it is limited only to matter. The greatest and most important truths are the religious ones that connect us to eternity, and these involve the Higher Self and God.

At some point spirit and soul enter a new life on Earth, though the process in its fullness remains a mystery to even the greatest initiates of the unconscious processes. Jung believed that reincarnation is probable, and saw the necessity of it from the view of evolving spirit through matter. In fact, a patient of his had a series of dreams which seemed to prove the truth of reincarnation, but they were of so personal a nature that Jung refused to publish them. As my later dreams will show, I have been informed of my own past lives several times by the unconscious, the last two being lived in America. But it is a complex subject and we cannot know the full truth of these things while on Earth. Certain evidence suggests that the afterlife is only one step up from our worldly life, so that true immortality and the heavenly state are really the province of the saintly.

When it comes to the death and resurrection symbolism of the Self, that of Osiris in ancient Egypt is well known. Even the Catholic Church admits that Osiris' is a kind of prefiguration of Christ's, though in the Annu cult of Egypt, Atum also dies and has his rebirth in Iusa, the "ever-coming son." But the original resurrection mysteries are apparently even older than these and involved Ptah, the "grandfather of the gods." Here divine birth, death, and resurrection were commemorated at the same time, and not on separate occasions as in Christianity.

The dismemberment of Osiris is matched by that of the serpent, but the former refers to the breaking up of the fuller Self into its constituent, conflicting parts. This also means bringing them to consciousness, which must occur in the unconscious processes for them to be reassembled in a harmonious way. This is the dangerous and heroic "night sea journey" that leads to the death, dismemberment, and rebirth that we find frequently in the esoteric mysteries, particularly alchemy.

However, as Jung tells us, though ego-consciousness must be involved in this, the dismemberment journey primarily concerns the hidden spirit in nature the alchemists called Mercurius which is freed by the quest. This involves death and rebirth, but as the Higher Self is immortal and cannot die, the image has to refer to the mortal man resurrecting into the Higher Self, equated with the resurrection of Jesus into Christ. The Catholic Mass is based on this same death and resurrection mystery. Jung, with his usual, careful understatement, calls this immortal figure "a consciousness-transcending content." Looked at from the point of view of man and his science of psychology, the Higher Self may be so evaluated, but from the view of the "other reality," he is nothing less than a god.

> I walk around the city where I live, though it could be any modern city in the Western world. All the buildings are made of stone and rise very high above the ground; they are supported by thin stone pillars. These are so weak and dilapidated that they are about to collapse at any moment, which means that the houses (buildings) will all come crashing down. Now, in the elevation gap between the houses and the ground, all sorts of vermin and disease have rushed in, and this, so the unconscious states through the dream, is the state of modern Western civilization: it's on the brink of total collapse.
>
> I carry on walking and come to a part of the city where all of the buildings have collapsed into piles of rubble, and on the rubble sit gangs

of lost and disoriented teenagers. A voice from the sky declares: "This has not happened because the young have no jobs or are underprivileged, but because man has lost his soul and God."

The dream is a dire warning. Western civilization is existing up in the air, supported only by weak and rotten values, away from the deep roots in the collective unconscious, where soul, living spirit, and God are to be found. The gap is a mass dissociation into which sickness and disease have flooded, and everything is on the verge of crashing down into chaos. Christ tells the parable of the man who built his house on unstable ground, and how the storms came and the house was washed away; but in this story there was also a man who built his house on solid foundations, and the storms came and the house stood firm.

Our culture has no solid foundations anymore, which means catastrophe unless we can build new associations with spirit reality through the collective unconscious, ones that are solid as rock. These can only be religious (mythological) associations, for as Jung stated, man must live within the myth.

The dream says that the collapse has already happened with the young, who are sitting on the rubble. This causes us to ask forlornly what hope there can be for the future. The only answer is that a fundamental change in our values, in our whole way of thinking, must occur, so that we form new associations with the unconscious powers, with God, or perhaps better still, so that we renew and further develop the old existing associations. This would involve the deeper understanding of the Higher Self, of the collective unconscious and its processes, and of the royal line of blue blood through the unconscious that began in, or which possibly even predates, ancient Egypt.

Jung pointed out that where the rational ends, there the irrational begins, the latter being just as important for psychic health as the former, even more so, perhaps. In rejecting the irrational we have thrown out the baby with the bath water, and as the phenomenon of the Higher Self as a psychic-religious process involves the appearance of the divine child, this is to be taken literally. It is true that many people today have become deeply interested in the paranormal or are seeking some form of spiritual meaning and enlightenment, but much of it has no deeper roots or more solid foundations than the precariously situated houses in my dream.

I recently saw a woman on TV who has written a book about angels. She claims that if we are in a troublesome situation—say we fail to find a parking space—then all we need do is pray to our angel and he will immediately find us a space. This kind of airy nonsense is like a feather tossed about by the wind, totally lacking weight to pull it down to reality. Angels have a somewhat deeper significance than as parking attendants. They are part of an eternal complexity of opposites that is intensely religious in nature. Ezekiel's vision, mentioned earlier, shows an example. Part of the complexity is the instinctual depths of the abyss, and experience of this on the quest causes extreme suffering. This occurs on the "night sea journey," and so forth.

It is then that the toad, reptiles, and other loathsome creatures—even the Devil—come to plague. But all of this is necessary to the processes as counterbalance to the spirit. Everything will float away with the angels without the heavy, obnoxious weight of the depths. Only when the terrible depths of the unconscious are suffered is the true meaning, holiness, and spiritual numinosity of the angels understood and felt.

If you experience these things then you may cry out to God or to Christ in your agony, and you may well invoke the appearance of a compensating angel to come in response to bring comfort to your tortured state. But you will have already drawn nearer to knowing the real nature of reality and religion, and the real needs of your soul.

> I am at the entrance of a cave, which is a stone room on the inside. This place was apparently sealed in the early centuries A.D. , then discovered and reopened in the latter part of the nineteenth century, then resealed and forgotten. It has now been reopened again, and a man leads me through the arched opening to the stone chamber inside.
>
> The chamber has shelves all around carved out of the solid rock, and on these are many books written by the ancients; they are piled up, though surprisingly, they are very clean. They have clear white covers with black titles, and inside the pages are also white with clear black print. They are spotless. These are works of the ancient philosophers and mystics, and when I look into a couple of them I reflect that they are consistent with what we know in depth psychology today. Then I may come across one of Jung's works, and then I find some books on ancient Egypt, and these too are all white with distinct black script, including the

covers, though they are like large paperbacks with soft covers. These were written around the 1890s, and I reflect with great enthusiasm that I might find something of worth here.

Here again is my rediscovery of the ancient mysteries in a cave, which I was fated to do, both in the unconscious and the outer world. The cave being sealed in the first centuries A.D. alludes to the Christian Mysteries and the early writers, including the Gnostics, for the original meaning of the Mysteries was lost at that time. These works are consistent with the findings of depth psychology, including my own experiences.

The Victorian books on Egypt I find in the cave describe Gerald Massey's works exactly—I have them in front of me at this moment—and which are large white paperbacks with distinct black script. They were written around the 1890s, and though Massey found the direct links between Christianity, the Old Testament, and ancient Egypt, his works were rejected and soon forgotten. With Jung's discoveries however, we can look at all of these works anew. But one very important point here is that I did not discover the Massey books in real life until some years after this dream. Black on white may also allude to the marriage of opposites, and it is said that God gave the Torah, the Law, to man as black fire on white fire.

> I am in the Houses of Parliament where a wedding ceremony is taking place between right wing politician Margaret Thatcher who was Prime Minister at the time and miners' leader Arthur Scargill. Both sign a marriage pact. As they do this, angels sing, rejoicing above. I stand up and make a speech, and I begin, "Man has suffered a fall so that he is now living at a lower level, a lower state of being. Therefore, such sacred marriages are no longer possible for him." I continue the speech, which is about spiritual truths and the marriage of opposites, and Mrs. Thatcher in particular is mesmerized by my words, but she then has to leave to appear on television.

In this dream, Margaret Thatcher and Arthur Scargill represent the opposites that separate into conflict when the higher, religious state of wholeness is lost, as happened when the West split into capitalism-fascism, on the one hand, and socialism-communism on the other. Yet here in the dream, these opposites sign a marriage pact, and angels sing because the transcendental religious state of wholeness has been reached, able to combine the lower opposites together in its higher One-ness, rendering them at the same time unnecessary.

This is the transcendental function, as Jung termed it, in which opposites are combined at a higher level in the unconscious and at the highest level of meaning. This is also why religion has always brought man a feeling of wholeness. As well as the unification of political opposites, the unconscious produces symbols in which both itself and consciousness can share, thus resulting in the unification of the two realities.

There is no doubt that modern man, particularly in the West, has suffered a fall into a lower state of being. Nineteenth century material-ism, with Darwin's theory of natural selection and other discoveries of science seeming to disprove the existence of God and spiritual reality, caused man to think, and therefore exist, in a lower, matter-bound way, resulting in a dissociation from the unconscious and its truths. Political materialism split into "left" and "right" views and the answers to the ills of life (and the search for its meaning) were no longer sought in religion, but in what remained, i.e., all the forms of materialism. Nietzsche declared "God is dead," and the world was desouled.

Freud then compounded the fact, stating that God and the human soul were indeed neurotic delusions, and that the basis of every psyche is a sewer. Then big business, using the discoveries of science to gain ever more wealth and power, gobbled up the Earth, polluting it probably beyond recovery in its infantile greed. The idea of a benign Father being responsible for creation had suffered its deathblow, and therefore the only law of existence was seen to be the survival of the fittest.

But the human spirit and soul are connected to the divine, eternal structures through the unconscious, and cannot suffer so diabolic a state of meaninglessness for too long. It is imperative that spiritual meaning is found which can result in the transcendental position being attained— rising above the lower opposites in a state of wholeness and true being. We are part of the Higher Self, and the Higher Self is part of God, and though we must fulfill our karma in our worldly lives, we must never forget our ultimate meaning in eternity.

Something very strange and magical happens to me concerning Christ and God, though I cannot recall any specific details. I then see the

clouds roll by very rapidly in a strange way, and I realize that I have received visionary gifts and special powers. This causes me to feel a little afraid, in case these powers are dangerous for me to possess, but this fear soon passes.

I then go to an upstairs office where I find a beautifully illustrated book, like a Bible or some other holy book of ancient wisdom, and my newly acquired powers enable me to see right through the cover to the writing inside. Some of it is in reverse, as it would be if I could see through the pages to what was on their other side.

Then someone asks me to forecast the winner of the next horse race and my powers quickly fade, but in any case, I say "These powers can only be used for the benefit of mankind or they do not work." I normally feel a lot of tension in my eyes due to nervousness and shyness, but the powers are such that they have taken this away.

This dream speaks for itself. As I was to learn, the rolling clouds are a sign of God's coming forth, His movement into time, just as is the symbol of the burning bush. It is then that I realize I have received visionary gifts. I hesitate to try and explain exactly what these gifts are, because in all honesty, it is difficult to say. I came away with greater insight certainly, and the power to experience the deepest and highest things of the unconscious. I was to experience the Higher Self and God directly later, and I received the four gold keys of authority from Jung.

I also found that I possessed the insight to discern and understand the secret wisdom of the unconscious when I come across it in the myths of the world. That is why I can see right through the holy book in the dream. The initiate who is partly defeated by the unconscious loses one eye, while the one who is totally defeated is blinded in both. However, he who masters the unconscious becomes far-sighted, and a "seer" of truths that others miss.

However, it is imperative that the adept should not become inflated by all of the highly numinous material that comes through. We must remain what we are, simple human souls before the immensity of God, realizing that the processes sometimes involve God. It is God and the things of God that are great and wondrous, not we ourselves, and whatever else the gifts may involve, they must all be used for the good of mankind. When the Persian prophet Zarathustra experienced his god, Ahura Mazda, he was told that the thing most pleasing to God is a husband and wife and their children living together with their animals on their farm. In other words, the warm, human, loving things are the greatest treasures to God. So although we may gain in wisdom and strength by means of the unconscious, it must ultimately make us more humbly human.

> I am in a church that has many symbolic paintings, and as the high priest, I talk to a barbarian king who has dark, shoulder-length hair and a drooping mustache. He has just conquered his foes and has made himself ruler of earthly kingdoms, and he has done this with my help. Now, like the early pagan kings who came to embrace Christianity, and who were then recognized by the Church, he must swear his allegiance to God. I say, "You receive your power and right to rule only from God, so you must acknowledge Him as master." The king bows his head and agrees.
>
> Then I am alone in the church where I try to balance a large, oblong stone on something, so that it goes up and down like a see-saw, first one side and then the other. On the center of the stone is a golden bowl which contains water, and colors that have to mix with the water. I have to balance the stone so as to keep the bowl still in the center so the water will not spill out.

In the last couple of dreams I have received visionary powers from above which apparently now qualify me to be a true priest, and even high priest. Originally, a true priest had to receive his authority directly from God (or the gods) which would have meant that he obtained it through processes of the unconscious. It was said of the man Jesus, when he had brought forth the Christ as the Higher Self from the unconscious, "Thou art a priest for ever after the order of Melchizedek," Melchizedek being the Higher Self to the man Abraham, and the first Messiah figure of Israel. Just as Melchizedek, who has no earthly parents nor beginning of days or end of life, brings bread and wine to Abraham, so Christ offers these to the disciples at the Last Supper. Abraham and Jesus, therefore, are a couple of examples of mortals who become true priests through the unconscious processes.

I must point out that I in no way regard myself as belonging to the illustrious company of Jesus and Abraham, only that they must have undergone similar journeys through the unconscious to what I am now experiencing. In fact, all the Old Testament prophets, and indeed, genuine initiates of the religious mysteries around the world, including shamans and medicine men must have undergone this.

As to the dream, the unconscious is stating that all worldly power must be subservient to the will of God. It is historical fact that cultures from the most primitive to the highly civilized have required the worldly ruler to be answerable to the authority of the priesthood to some degree, and through the priesthood to God, or the gods. Very strangely, certain political leaders and royal figures have conferred with me in dreams over the years, though I never intended this nor even thought about these figures in waking life.

The golden bowl, which must be balanced perfectly so as not to spill the water and the colors, is similar to the hermetic *vas* of the alchemists, which contained the divine "waters," the *aqua divina* or *aqua permanens*. It is also similar to the Holy Grail which contained Christ's blood, the Host. All must be perfectly balanced, and their essence is the divine spirit or soul. In keeping with this, it should be noted that the Gnostic text, *Poimandres,* tells us that God sent down a vessel of spiritual renewal from above, in which all can be baptized who wish for spiritual renewal.

> I watch a scene that is taking place in the hills, but in some other dimension or reality. A crowd of people is assembled for what appears to be a pagan rite, and a blond-haired barbarian, a wild man who carries a club, takes hold of a young boy and begins to torture him with the club, which by now has become a flaming torch.
>
> The boy, who is white at first, is burnt so black that he becomes a black boy, and the torture is so severe that he dies. Then the wild man gives the boy a drink of special liquid from a bottle, and miraculously the boy comes to life again. This is a very sacred rite and I reflect that it must be the answer to immortal life. Then I become amazed when I realize that the boy has been reborn as an old man.

In most religious mysteries and esoteric rites, torture, at least, symbolical, brings about transformation and rebirth. Osiris is dismembered and reborn again, and Christ is crucified and resurrected into glory. We find it throughout alchemy, and the *Turba Philosophorum* states, "Take the old black spirit and destroy and torture with it the bodies, until they are changed." It also states: "The tortured thing, when it is immersed in the body, changes it into an unalterable and indestructible nature" (Zosimos 1593). In the *Theatrum Chemicum*, Sir George Ripley (1602) says, "The unnatural fire must torment the bodies, for it is the dragon violently burning, like the fire of hell."

In the visions of Zosimos, the third-century A.D. century Gnostic alchemist, an old white man is tortured and burnt, but when put into a spring of the purest water, becomes first a silver, then a golden man. In another text, an old man is tortured to death, and then is reborn as a boy, the opposite of what occurs in my dream. But reversals and numerous variations frequently happen in the unconscious processes. The "old man and boy" symbol is well known in alchemy, and Metatron, as the Higher Self of Enoch, is both old man and youth. Many cultures of the world put these processes into practice; shamans, for example, being mentally and physically tortured into a spiritualized state. Even the transformation symbolism of the Mass is based on these same processes.

What they all boil down to is, on the one hand, the suffering and torment endured by ego-consciousness when undergoing the unconscious processes. On the other hand, and more importantly, they are about the "inner man," the Higher Self, who as his parts are assembled, reassembled, and made conscious, becomes fully aware of his own conflicting opposites and is crucified between them as the "god of the four quarters" as all of these parts pull him opposite ways. Here, the torture seems to be the scorching heat of the conflict, corresponding to the intense heat in the retort of the alchemists, and the scorching off of all of the hair in the processes, from which the baldness or tonsure of priesthood derives. So my dream has the same meaning as these examples.

Zosimos tells in one of his dream visions of the appearance of a priest, and Jung quotes part of it in his *Transformation Symbolism in the Mass*. I will cite part of this myself to demonstrate how the tortures of the unconscious may appear to us. The priest in Zosimos' dream says that his name is Ion and that he undergoes tortuous agonies as priest of the hidden mysteries. He has been pierced with a sword (reminding us of Mercurius as piercing sword and as he who is pierced) and though cut up in bits, his limbs are nevertheless still where they should be. He has been scalped and all of his "bones and flesh" burnt in a fire. This has caused his transformation into a spiritualized state. Now, in appearance before Zosimos, he spews out all of his torn parts as his eyes become bloody. Yet he is able to tear at himself with his teeth, until finally disappearing into his own self.

> I put a round, green fruit pastille into my mouth. I then think of its color, emerald green, and the pastille becomes a green emerald. Then I say, "The Roman Empire was dominated by a power-mad principle and so caused Christianity as a reaction." Then I awake and immediately think, "St. Bernard has just been in this room."

We know that perhaps the highest treasure of the alchemists was their Philosopher's Stone, "the stone that hath a spirit," according to the legendary Ostanes, and "the symbol of the immortal Self," according to Jung. The pastille in my dream is green, the traditional color of the Holy Spirit, and so becomes the emerald. As I have taken it into my mouth it is obviously to be digested, and therefore assimilated, meaning the assimilation of the Higher Self.

Since this dream, I have learned that in the Aztec legend, Quetzalcoatl's mother becomes pregnant by swallowing a green stone, and indeed, her name, Halca Huitzli, means "precious stone of sacrifice." Quetzalcoatl himself wears a turquoise mask, and is called "priest of the precious stone." Furthermore, when an Aztec person died, a green stone would be put in the mouth of the deceased, presumably to ensure future spiritual life. This has a similar meaning to the partaking of the bread and wine as the integration of the god; similarly, "god-eating" is widely known in ritual. When the Spanish conquered Mexico, the Catholic priests were amazed to find that the Aztecs had a ritual in which they made a little figure of the god from maize, pierced it with a weapon, and then broke it up and ate it—a ritual that is also part of the Mass. But as these rituals are based on symbolic processes of the collective unconscious, which is shared by all peoples, it should come as no surprise to find comparable ones the world over.

As I mention elsewhere, Blavatsky tells us that many centuries before Christ, a green stone talisman was well known to the Jews, and that this symbolized the Messiah, and therefore the Higher Self.

In the dream, I also speak of the Roman Empire being dominated by a power-mad principle that was slowly destroying it, thus causing Christianity as an antidote to the poison. Actually, the advent of Christ had been on the spiritual agenda for centuries, but it took the sickness of Rome to make its birth and fruition absolutely essential. That is why Rome was to accept Christ, partly at first, and then fully, while the Jews rejected him. The dire necessity existed far more with Rome than with the Jews, who already had Yahweh and the prophets. (Though it also true that the Jews, by and large, could not comprehend the Messiah as a gentle lamb. Furthermore, they had actually had Messiah figures throughout their history, brought forth by certain prophets, but never realized it.) The same dire necessity for further spiritual development exists today in our modern world, and it must be on the same spiritual line that reaches back to the distant past.

On waking from the dream, I say that St. Bernard has just been in the room, and this may allude to the Higher Self, symbolized as a saint, as Bernard of Clairvaux, for instance. But as a St. Bernard *dog*, it is also a symbol of the Higher Self as *guide*, and fits the meaning very aptly. The dream caused me to me to reflect on it so much that I came to study the life of St. Bernard of Clairvaux himself, which I found a worthwhile venture.

> I am in a strange, dark land, where I see many weird, frightening black reptiles of all descriptions. I am terrified and shivers of fear run through my body.

This is the realm of the serpent-dragon again in its darkest and basest instinctual aspect. If I experience the spiritual heights in these processes, then I am also required to experience the opposite side of the World Soul in both its light and dark aspects. As I commented earlier on a similar dream, St. Teresa of Avila had similar visions of the horrible depths, which contrasted with her higher ones of spirit.

> I go into a building where I put on a space suit similar to the one worn by Flash Gordon in the old serials of the 1930s. Climbing through a window, I float up to a higher reality, eventually finding myself on top of a hill on a pagan island, where a wedding is taking place between a gray-bearded old man and a slim young girl. The girl, who is on the old man's arm, must be his second wife because on his left is another, older woman who is his wife already. The latter is more well made than the girl and is heavy breasted—she is really very beautiful, in fact.
>
> The old, gray-bearded groom is also myself in some strange way, and he makes a joke about his first wife's breasts, calling them "The

Mountains of Pharaoh." I then go to the edge of a cliff where I see serial hero of the 1930s, Bruce Bennett (originally Herman Brix), dive into a river that is very far below. I think of the sacred rivers, the Nile and Ganges. Yet although all of this is holy and sacred, it is, at the same time, Victorian. The scene then changes completely and I find myself at home with my parents where the three of us are reading film books of the 1930s and '40s. We are madly enthusiastic about the old films, and indeed, about everything from those times.

Putting on the space suit means that I am preparing to go up to higher, spirit reality. The skies and outer space always refer to the place of spirit in dreams, whereas the sea and subterranean caves mean the lower soul depths. A window represents the opening or passageway between material reality and the other world, and going through a window here, I pass from this reality to that other. I once read about a woman who was dying and she dreamt that she died in her room, but then found herself on the other side of the window, where she was now alive and healthy again in that other reality. So as in my dream, the window is the dividing line between the two realities. A number of other dreams have had a window to represent the dividing line or doorway to the world of spirit.

In this dream, I float up to higher reality and find myself on a hill on an island where a wedding is taking place. An island often appears in my dreams, reflecting the sacred Mound of ancient Egypt which rose up out of the waters, the primeval ocean, at the first creation. The Mound in Egypt was also the sacred Mount, and in fact there were two of these, one above in spirit, and one below in the Underworld. Ra the High God had his throne on top of the former, while Osiris had his on top of the latter. These higher and lower places which contain the sacred Mounts refer to spirit and soul realities found through the collective unconscious, also known as Amenta, the Underworld to the Egyptians.

The gray-bearded old man is the "wise old man," "the personification of spirit" as Jung puts it, while the young woman is the personification of soul. The marriage between them is the unification of spirit and soul in the individuation processes. We find this same unification in the myths and religious texts of the world, though usually it is the hero who marries the anima-soul rather than the old man. Moses marries Zipporah, daughter of the wise old priest Jethro, and Joseph marries

Asenath, daughter of Potipherah, the high priest of On. However, in the dream I feel identical with the old graybeard to a degree, so in a sense I also marry the young woman, the personification of the individual soul.

The more mature woman refers to the collective, the World Soul, and her ample breasts being called "the Mountains of Pharaoh" by the old man in all probability refers to the two sacred Mounds of Egypt mentioned above, unified now with the sacred marriage. This means, of course, the unification of the higher spirit and lower soul realms. The hero who dives into the sacred river, the Nile or the Ganges, reflects consciousness traveling to the unconscious depths, made sacred by spirit in the marriage between the eternal opposites.

The ending of the dream is heavy with nostalgia for the 1930s and '40s, and in the time this dream took place—the mid 1970s to mid 1980s—this nostalgia did completely sweep over the Western world. Yet there was a deeper significance to it than just a conscious revival of the past. With the 1960s came the reversal of the old values, exemplified by the 1930s and '40s, and now came the age of the "permissive society" and the anti-hero when the line between light and shade became ever more indistinguishable. In the 1980s a survey was made in British schools which revealed that young pupils could not distinguish between the good guys and bad guys in modern movies, and cared even less. That is a frightening condemnation of modern civilization, evidence of the fall into barbarism and chaos that Jung feared deeply.

The great wave of nostalgia that hit the West in the late 1970s was an attempt by the collective unconscious to restore order and bring about a return to healthier and more positive values, and I saw evidence of this in a number of other dreams. However, when the attempt failed, I saw it in yet other dreams, and I was warned that the West now faces a very dubious and uncertain future. Only last night I dreamt of the barbarism and chaos across the land, with groups of soulless savages roaming about menacingly, and these were the majority of the people, not just the criminal element.

There are three airplanes in the sky at the beginning of the dream, but only briefly. Then a boyhood friend is injecting a prostrate body with eggs, or seeds, from a hypodermic needle, which means either new or increased life. Then I am on a train, pulling into a station, and crowds of people are cheering loudly, giving a hero's welcome to either myself or the man I am with—or perhaps to both of us. Fascist guards are present, trying to prevent all of this, but they are powerless to do so.

I am then elsewhere, lying on an altar, where I seem to be dead. A sort of mold, like a death mask, but one which fits all over my body—like a sarcophagus lid that fits my shape—is on me. This (or a ladder close by, or both) moves of its own accord, a sign from Heaven. Then as I lie there, a beautiful goddess hovers over me. She is very holy in a Christian way, and she wears robes of perhaps blue, red and gold. A wonderful feeling comes over me, like a prolonged orgasm, but spiritual rather than physical. This is a great joy and has to do with the immortal and the divine.

The three airplanes at the beginning of the dream signify spirit, or perhaps even the Holy Trinity—I know this from many other experiences. The body that is injected with the seeds of new life must be connected with myself because of what happens in the second part of the dream. The train pulling into the station after a journey refers to my own journey through the unconscious processes, which has been successful. The man with me, with whom I apparently share the hero's welcome, represents my help from the Higher Self. The fascists, the opposing negative forces, are unable to do anything about it and are therefore defeated.

Then I am lying on an altar, apparently dead. This means my old self is dead, and what follows is my rebirth into a more spiritual state of being. There is a sign from the heavens when the lid (and ladder probably) moves, and the goddess gives of herself to me in a spiritual way. The Egyptian sky goddess, Nut, was connected with coffins and rebirth, and her image was painted inside coffin lids so that she was lying, or hovering, directly over the deceased. One depiction shows Nut as an arc over the Earth god, Seb, with his erect phallus pointed at her navel, to show that the union is spiritual and not physically sexual.

Gerald Massey says that both Nut and Hathor had sacred trees in Egypt, and that the coffin was seen as a sacred tree. Massey says: "Hathor as a form of mother-earth, the tree-form, is portrayed inside the coffin on the board upon which the mummy rested, taking the dead to her embrace as the mother of life. Nut, the mother-Heaven, was represented on the inner part of the coffin-lid arching over the mummy as bringer of the manes to new life above" (1890). As I said above, this was all in connection with rebirth and resurrection.

The goddess in my dream seems to be a Christian version of the goddess Nut, despite the fact that there are no goddesses in Christianity, but the eternal feminine spirit can appear in any form, depending on the religious notions of the dreamer and his culture. In Egypt, though Nut was one form of the feminine spirit, others were Isis, Hathor, Neith, and Iusaas. In China, she is Kwan Yin, and in India, Kali and Shakti, to name just two aspects; to the Jews, she is *Ruach Elohim,* and to the later Greeks she was Sophia. As Jung points out, *Ruach Elohim,* the "Spirit of God," exists as a relatively independent being at God's side.

One final point is that in the dream the goddess has three colors in her robes: red, blue and gold. The first two, red and blue, are higher and lower feminine colors, which is why the Virgin Mary was for centuries portrayed with blue mantel over a red dress; the third color, gold, is the color of God, and of the gods mythologically. The alchemists had four colors of wholeness—red, blue, yellow (yellow and gold were sometimes interchangeable), and green—the missing color in my dream, accordingly, is green. However, as the three planes at the beginning of the dream represent the spirit, the traditional color of which is green, it is accounted for in any case.

> An old classmate comes to see me and we sit on a bench outside. He despises me a little because I have not done anything useful with my life, so I tell him that, though my life has been outwardly useless, I have yet been able to do some successful work in the unconscious. It is required by life for certain individuals to experience the depths of the collective unconscious to bring its truths through to society. Such individuals, often despite themselves, may become the prophets, true priests, and religious leaders of mankind. Then I tell him that although I have no illusions about my own capabilities in the world, I may nevertheless be able to bring some of the truths of the unconscious to the notice of society. I add that a transformation has certainly occurred within myself, but my old classmate is hard to convince.
>
> Another man, maybe a Russian, comes along and sits down by us as I continue, "All that we love passes and dies. What hope have we? Yet there is an answer. It is the resurrection of the soul. I have been shown the way." At my words the Russian says, "You are not very old, but you are very wise."

There is not much I can add to this dream except to say that the one hope of the ancient Egyptians, and of other cultures, was the resurrection of the soul. Yet this hope was based on deep experience of the processes of the unconscious, and must have been, else the myths could not fit the processes known to depth psychology so well. As for the man in the dream being perhaps Russian, it could refer to the long-suffering Russian soul.

> My father takes me to ancient Palestine, where we wait by a roadside for a procession to come along which is being led by Christ. Crowds of other people have gathered and are also waiting, but we manage to get a place at the front where there are stone pillars so many feet apart along the road. As Christ comes into view, I wonder if he will notice me because of my sufferings, but when he reaches where I am standing, he becomes a golden cloud of light, which then comes and envelopes me.
>
> I have to cover my eyes with my hands because the cloud is so bright and radiant, and an angelic choir sings from above. Then Christ, who has a human form again, holds my hand and takes me flying through the air to the town which is just south of where I live. Here, from above, we watch a Salvation Army procession as it marches through the streets, and Christ seems to be showing me that I must bring salvation to this place.

The personal father in these processes represents the male line of spirit, whereas the personal mother represents the soul line of the feminine depths. This is why in older societies boys were taken from their mothers at puberty to be instructed in the spiritual mysteries, not being allowed to see their mothers, and sometimes all females, for the time of the initiation period. It is also why Jesus, as a boy of twelve, rejects his mother in the temple.

As with other dreams involving the Christ figure, I must ask if this is the original Christ, or the Holy Spirit taking his form, or the Higher Self as a Christ parallel. In answer I must state I am not sure. To St. Teresa and other saints, the figure they saw was simply Christ and they were blissfully untroubled by the questions we must ask today. Yet in trying to ascertain the truth, perhaps we are in that sense lessening the mystery and its meaning. Perhaps I should just accept the figure as

Christ and not spoil the impact with too many questions that are futile in any case.

However, I must say that the radiance of Christ in the dream is such that I have to cover my eyes, and this makes me wonder more seriously if it actually was the original Christ, who will have become an eternal form of the Son of God in spirit reality. Furthermore, he instructs me to bring salvation to the town a couple of miles south of where I live—where Julie, the woman who is my anima figure, lives in real life—the soul depths not yet being part of the totality of the Higher Self in my processes. The Self is a *complexio oppositorum*, a complexity of opposites, which has parts reaching down to the animal and insect levels as well as up to God Himself: He is literally part of God come forth, like a son. Christ in my dream is apparently pure spirit, representing only that side of the Self, the higher, spiritual side, and yet complete in spirit reality. So this is not the lower Self, the Osiris of the lower unconscious; this is the higher, divine Son and part of God.

Jung says the divine figure experienced within the human soul is able to manifest and become amenable to understanding due to the presence of the psychic archetype. Thus the basic truth of Christianity, expressed partly in Church dogma, has its foundations in the unconscious, and is not something merely invented by conscious thought (1959a, 1963b).

> **A great treasure is hidden in Egypt, and I hold up a rod, or staff, which then becomes a snake. This is a clue to the treasure. Then in my mind's eye I see a cave halfway down a cliff face, and that is where the treasure lies. I must take an expedition to recover the treasure, which, while it is has to do with the unconscious, is also a real life treasure.**

When God calls Moses, he, Moses, is full of doubts: "And Moses answered and said, but behold, they will not believe me, nor hearken unto my voice: for they will say, the Lord hath not appeared unto thee" (Exodus 4:1). God then shows signs to Moses, including the rod changing into the serpent and back again. This clearly shows that Moses has God's authority, and as I know from my other dream-visions, it is the authority of the Higher Self. The latter is the great treasure alluded to in the dream, though there is also said to be a real-life treasure to be found. A cave is, symbolically, the "Earth womb" where saviors are born sometimes, and where dragons lurk to threaten them.

Now, do I take it that I too have God's authority since I have received the rod which turns into a snake; or at least, that I had it at the time of the dream? Well, I am a very cautious person by nature, particularly when it comes to these processes, so I must be careful not to read meanings into the dreams that are not there. However, on the other hand I must try to come up to what is required of me and not fail through too small a vision and understanding.

The rod-serpent was an Egyptian symbol originally, as there are depictions that clearly show figures carrying rods that are also serpents. The rod in Egypt was, in fact, "the *Matta*, Matteh to the Jews" and signified the divine power of the priest. However, another form was apparently the *Amsu* rod that was the support of Osiris in both life and in the afterlife. In the early period in Egypt such a rod would be interred with the deceased, to help him on his journey through the Underworld to the fields of Heaven.

The caduceus of classical antiquity was a central rod with two serpents entwined around it—originally three serpents, signifying the lower trinity—and was the staff of Hermes as messenger of the gods. Blavatsky says that the caduceus, of Mercury (Hermes) with which he directed the souls of the dead to Hades, and even raising them to life again, "shows the dual power of the Secret Wisdom" (1888). This came from the earlier Egyptian symbol, and when Moses receives the rod-serpent it is the sign that he is now the prophet and "mouthpiece" of God. In fact, Massey says:

"Here then we identify the serpent-rod of the Egyptian priests that was known by name as the great magical power, and it was sometimes a rod, at others a serpent. This we take to be the original of that rod with which the tricks are played in the Hebrew marched by the lord God of Israel for the purpose of frightening Pharaoh" (1907). He then quotes Exodus 4:2-5, "And the Lord said unto him (Moses), What is that in thine hand? And he said, A rod. And he said, Cast it on the ground. And he cast it on the ground, and it became a serpent: And Moses fled before it. And the Lord said unto Moses, Put forth thine hand and take it by the tail. And he put forth his hand and laid hold of it, and it became a rod in his hand."

It is interesting to note that Shu-Anhur, the Egyptian god upon whom Moses may partly be based, carries a rod with which to divide the waters of Amenta, the Underworld, in order to lead the saved souls to the "Promised Land," the heavenly fields of Aarru. Shu-Anhur also smites the rock with his rod and water gushes forth, just as Moses does the rock Seba. This refers to the sevenfold waters of the unconscious, comparable to Beersheba at the Well of Seven of Abraham. Seba and Sheba both mean "seven" and both incidents are about water, symbolizing the feminine unconscious. The Queen of Sheba has the same meaning basically, though not attached to water specifically in the texts.

> I see an old couple in a stable. The woman is pregnant and is lying on straw in a stall. Also on the straw there is a jelly-like substance which shakes and wobbles with new life yet to be born. This will be twins.

Earlier in these processes a voice from the skies said that an old woman would give birth to twins, which I now know meant the light and dark sides of the Higher Self. The dream prior to this one spoke of the great treasure to be found in the cave, the "Earth-womb," and now that womb is about to give birth.

> It is a cold, dark night, and snow is on the ground. Two little feather-less chicks have been born, and while one of them is friendly towards me, the other one hates me, spitting at and biting me. Its attack is so vehement that I try to squash the chick, though I find it cannot be killed. However, I manage to throw it over by a wall where it lies in the snow, sunk into it. The trouble is, I am loath to let it freeze, and so I dig it out—though it would not have died, apparently, as it cannot be killed.
>
> Later, the chicks have grown to become teenage boys; again, one mild and gentle-natured, and the other bold, arrogant, and shady. The mild one puts on a pair of trousers that are much too big for him, so he asks his twin to join him in them. The shady one neither accepts nor declines the offer, but stands there grinning defiantly. I am sort of an old uncle, guide, teacher, servant, and even father to them.

The life in the "spawn" of the previous dream has now been born as twins. These are chicks, first of all, reminiscent of the "philosophical egg" of the alchemists. From this egg was born the Anthropos, who is always twins, and called by the Chinese alchemists the *Chen-yen*, the "perfect man," the Higher Self, who is twins. Certain gods of Egypt were connected with the egg, and Osiris-Keb produced the cosmic egg, that is,

Osiris as the goose-god. In myths across the world we find examples of this phenomenon of a god or super-hero born as twins or hostile brothers, one good, one not so good, or downright evil. Consider Horus and Set, Cain and Abel, Romulus and Remus, Jacob and Esau, Krishna and Balarama, plus the American Indian twins produced when a star falls to Earth, which repeats, almost, the Dogon twins of Sirius. Blavatsky says that such twins in mythology are called "Egg-born," and she mentions an Egyptian myth called the "Hostile Brothers," based apparently on this same archetypal situation.

In my dream, the light twin asks the dark one to join him in the trousers, which would mean the unification of the two in one, but as we know from the above-mentioned myths, it is not the nature of the dark twin to be so obliging; it is rather the opposite. One final point is that the mother in certain biblical accounts is either too old to bear children or is otherwise barren, necessitating divine intervention for the pregnancy. But this means that the birth is a spiritual one, and that of the divine child.

> I am told a story which I see happening as it is related. When the Caliph wishes to breed a champion horse, he fetches a magical stallion, and then uses the body of a human being to carry its seed until the super young foal is born. This is the same as God begetting a son through a human being. When it is done, the human being may then die or be killed by the Caliph.

The story speaks for itself. The human individual is the vessel in which God begets his Son, the Higher Self. The human being counts for very little, if anything at all, and being merely human, will have a very limited life span. The Higher Self, on the other hand, is eternal, being part of God incarnated. However, I must add that all my experiences in the unconscious point to the probability that the human individual survives death as part of the total Self. Whether this is conscious survival or otherwise it is impossible to say, though certain other of my dream-visions have indicated it to be conscious survival. Still others have intimated reincarnation also to be fact.

In the above dream, we can say that the Caliph represents God; the magical stallion represents the Holy Spirit; and the young foal the Son of God, or Higher Self. We can also say that, in the Christian myth, Jesus the man is the human being used by God, through whom He may beget his divine Son, Christ.

> A black snake vomits up black bile and rises up to strike at me. There is great conflict between the snake and myself and I float up to the ceiling to try to escape, feeling very afraid.

As said previously, the snake often represents the dark side of the Self, and being black here means the very worst aspect, so naturally, I am very afraid. However, as we know, the blackest evil, the devil, is "that old serpent," so perhaps this is his representation, or an image of the Antichrist. For some Gnostics, the serpent, sometimes called Satanael, was the counterpart of the Anthropos, the Higher Self. This is repeated in my own dream processes.

> This dream was about the Devil and evil, though all the details have faded. I wake petrified with fear.

My fear was such that I forgot all the details of the dream, but the black snake in the previous dream has obviously now developed into the Devil. This means the dark side of the Higher Self, for if the light side parallels Christ, which it has done and will do in some of my dreams, then the dark side must equal Satan (or Satanael, or at least the Antichrist).

> My dog is going to eat a rasher of bacon out of a waste-bin, but I warn him not to do this as it will poison him. Then a strange thing happens. A ghost or spirit of a dog comes out of my dog, and where my dog has a white patch on his forehead, this spirit dog has a halo just above his head. I think what a lovely dog it is—the dog-spirit—and I say to my mother, who is present, "I know what it is. It is the Self. But it is too low as a dog. It must become Jesus Christ." I then look up and strain, as if trying to reach a higher moral state of being. I try to touch the dog-spirit, but my hand goes right through it.

Not only is the rasher of bacon possibly contaminated, being out of the waste-bin, it is also off a pig, and a pig is a highly dangerous creature in processes of the unconscious. This dates back to ancient Egypt, where we find the evil Set taking the form of a pig to blind Horus in one eye. It was taken so seriously by all Egyptians that if one accidentally touched a pig, one should immediately wash or jump into the river, whichever was the quicker. Many gods and heroes are menaced or killed by pigs or wild boars in mythology, and in the esoteric version of his death, the Buddha dies from eating a meal of pork.

In my dream, the dog-spirit comes out of my dog to demonstrate that when I dream of the latter, it is the Higher Self as dog-spirit that is meant. The dog-spirit appears often in myths and folklore, and my dog even appeared as the Egyptian dog-jackal god Anubis in one dream. I have given details of this phenomenon elsewhere in the book, but it is worth mentioning again that Mephistopheles, the dark Self of Faust, first appears as a black poodle, and that a black dog is also connected with the Teutonic god, Wotan.

The dream also says that I must strive hard to develop the dog-spirit, the Higher Self, into a Christ figure. This is to be my task, apparently, though it is not my own idea consciously; it is the way the unconscious processes are leading me. It has not been achieved in the West before, as far as I know, although the alchemists replaced the man Jesus in the unconscious processes, as Jung says; however, their goal remained too limited to matter.

But as many of my dreams show, I have become involved with the higher powers through the unconscious myself, and it has become my fate to try to accomplish certain things that the alchemists could not. Furthermore, I long felt compelled to search for the lost half of reality that modern man has become dangerously dissociated from, to transform a cold, meaningless universe into a positive, meaningful one again. I had to find an answer to Darwin, Freud, Einstein, and especially Nietzsche, and to all the materialistic-rationalistic minds of the nineteenth and twentieth centuries. Their ideas and discoveries, most of them perfectly valid, nevertheless have had a devastating effect on the psychic and spiritual health of modern man, making reality seem solely a material phenomenon. I had to find the antidote to the poison that has desouled Western culture, and that is gradually poisoning the whole world.

The ancient Egyptians symbolized many forces and facets of the collective unconscious—their "other world"—by animals, and used practically every animal known to them for the purpose. Nevertheless, it was long believed by modern scholars that they did not utilize the dog symbolically. A. E. Wallis Budge states that the dog never seems to have been a god to the Egyptians, though they were very fond of it as a pet (1904). He further states that Diodorus informs us that dogs accompanied and guarded Osiris and Isis, but that he was mistaking the dog for the jackal. Yet I personally could never credit the Egyptians with not making a god of the dog as it did not seem plausible. They made a god of practically every other animal, including the cat, so why not the most familiar one of all, the one closest to man, the dog?

However, there has now been a change of opinion and it is believed that Anubis, long thought to have been jackal-headed, may indeed have been a type of dog—or perhaps the jackal was regarded as a dog type by the Egyptians. Apuat (or Wepwuat) was another dog-jackal god of the Egyptians, sometimes confused with Anubis despite the fact that both appear on the sarcophagus of Ramses III, one on either side. Nevertheless, Apuat is probably an aspect of Anubis, and both were the "Opener of the Way" in the Underworld; Anubis was also guardian, guide, and companion of Osiris and other gods.

It was Anubis in the Underworld who weighed the dark deeds of the dead against a feather, so that only the truly righteous would pass over to the fields of Aarru. According to some legends, Anubis was the son of Osiris, and indeed, was Horus in a certain aspect; both Anubis and Horus were sons of Ra, the Great God, though they were also aspects of the same being. I mention all of this because Osiris and Horus, who represent the Higher Self, were closely associated with these dogs, especially Anubis, and in my dream processes my own dog appears as a lower form of the Higher Self. He is even my companion in the Underworld following the role of Anubis.

With this and other instances it becomes clear that Egyptian mythology must be based on processes of the unconscious, as must all mythologies. We find that a dog is the companion, guide, or follower of the hero or god in many myths across the world. We must also remember the white dog, the gift of Merlin's daughter, that accompanied Perceval on his quest to find the Holy Grail and the dog that led Gawain to the Grail Castle.

In the Greek myth, the great hunter Orion is transformed into the constellation that bears his name, while his dog companion becomes Sirius, the Dog Star, at his heel. In Egypt, the morning star was the herald of the coming of day, and Anubis was the announcer and "Opener of the Way" for the coming of Horus. Anubis was identified with Sirius originally, and in my own processes my dog is connected with a star and the Higher Self. In one dream I saw a shooting star and then my dog immediately appeared. Sirius was the morning star of the coming year, which meant a new birth of Horus; Thoth had a form of the Golden Dog, which was a form of Anubis symbolizing the light. In Central America Quetzalcoatl is accompanied by the dog-headed Xlolotl as he journeys to the Underworld, and in the Irish legend of Finn MacCool, the white dog Bran, the companion of Finn, fights and kills the evil black dog.

> I am followed by a black bear which intends to harm me, but as it comes near, a great gust of wind like a whirlwind scoops up the bear and takes it into the sky and into the distance.

The bear is one of the main animal symbols of the lower, feminine unconscious, and as it is black in this dream, it is in its most negative and dangerous form. Mythologically, earlier in Egypt the Great Mother was the Great Bear constellation originally; this would seem to fit, except for the fact the constellation we call Ursa Major (the Great Bear) was actually a hippopotamus to the Egyptians, and not a bear as such. Bears did exist in Egypt many thousands of years ago, but may have become extinct there by the time of the first human cultures.

Jung tells of a dream of one of his patients in which a bear with four differently colored eyes appears in the depths of a cave, i.e., the womb of Mother Earth. The bear represents the dangerous aspect of the *prima materia*, but at times may point to a further stage of the work.

The whirlwind that saves me in the dream symbolizes spirit, and throughout mythology, winds and storms have always represented the gods, their force and effects for good or ill. Wotan is a wind and storm god, and the Devil is said to be "the wind from the north." Certain scholars claim that the origin of the name Yahweh, the Jewish name of God, is derived from a word for wind. We can say, therefore, that, as the bear is highly dangerous here, I have been saved from the very dangerous side of the Great Mother, by the Great Father here represented as a wind god.

> Jung appears hovering over me as I sleep in my bed. He speaks of my going to university: "Of course, Basle isn't Heidelberg or Paris," he says, "but we must make the most of what circumstances are open to us."

This must remind him of his own education because he continues, "That
was when I was really able to break with my parents."

Jung has often appeared hovering over me as I sleep, although I am
awake in the dream of course. Now, if a dream reproduces the circumstances of outer reality exactly as they actually are, then we must take
the dream contents literally, and that is how it is here. For a long time I
interpreted these visitations to be of the "wise old man," the higher
spirit-wisdom figure, the "personification of spirit," but now I am partly
of the opinion that it is Jung himself, though merged with the Holy
Spirit. I have taken up and am trying to continue Jung's work, as far as
I am able. From what I now know of the collective unconscious, I would
say that it would be quite possible for Jung himself to pay me a visit,
though at the same time being part of the spirit itself. As for Jung speaking of my going to Basle University, he may well be talking about my
"education" in the unconscious processes, and perhaps he is also alluding to my own break with my parents.

> I am with two men, a noble, superior type, and an ugly, inferior type,
> and we put a new roof onto the stone ruins of an old Catholic church. I
> have to help the inferior man up on the roof because he is very afraid of
> the height. We have journeyed through a wood where we experienced
> many gods and goddesses, and this has deeply spiritualized me. An old
> priest appears with a young woman, and he says "This was another Song
> of Bernadette." The old priest does, in fact, closely resemble the one in
> the film of that title played by Charles Bickford. Then the superior type
> man, who is perhaps part of myself, looks through a window of the
> church at the sky, as if peering at God, and the old priest says of me, "No,
> he has not seen gods and goddesses; he has seen God."

The superior and inferior men are parts of the total psyche, the highest and lowest aspects of man, and we have put a new roof on the old
ruins of a church. In other words, we have renewed it, at least partly.
This could allude to my own spiritual renewal, though probably much
more is involved, perhaps an association with God that I have forged
through these processes of the unconscious, as this is indicated by the
old priest. It may also mean the possibility of a renewal of the Church
itself, for though I was not raised as a Catholic, that form of religion

seems to appear throughout my many thousands of dreams, pointing to the further development of Christianity.

This would mean that the central aim of the collective unconscious is the continuation of the royal line of blue blood that stretches back to ancient Egypt, of which the Church is still an expression, though much in need of further development. The church could also allude to the structure of the Self, so to put a new roof on it may mean to unite its opposites.

In the dream, I have come through a wood (the unconscious) with the noble and inferior men (the higher and lower psyches) and the spiritualizing experience is compared to the visions of St. Bernadette. I had watched the film *The Song of Bernadette* recently. The old priest, who resembles the one from the film, says that I have seen God, and this probably means that the gods and goddesses spoken of are his theophany, the signs and effects of God's coming forth. Later I was fated to experience God directly through the unconscious, as future dreams will reveal.

The old priest and the girl form the well-known archetype of the combination of higher spirit (meaning) and lower soul (life) in the processes experienced when the higher levels are reached, as in Jethro with Zipporah; Lao Tse and the dancing girl; and Elijah and Salome in Jung's own processes.

> I am in America in the 1890s where I am accused of murder, though I am innocent. I escape to the hills but am followed and shot dead by my pursuers. I am then reborn in an English village around 1900. In the dream, I am vaguely aware of a large Ferris wheel, which represents the wheel of rebirths.

A few years after this dream I had another in which I was taken up to the afterlife, to the place where we return when we leave earthly life. There I was informed that reincarnation is a fact, and that my past two lives were lived in America. In the first one, I died in the 1890s, and in the second in the late 1930s. I had entirely forgotten about the above dream, and only came across it again recently.

The later dream repeated what this earlier one had stated, and reincarnation is intimated by both. The only discrepancy is that in the dream above I am reborn into an English village at the turn of the last century, whereas the later dream states that my two previous lives were lived in

America. However, it is quite possible that in the second life I was taken from the village to America after the turn of the century to grow up there, dying in the late 1930s. As we know, a lot of people emigrated to America from Britain earlier in that century, so it is possible for it all to fit in.

The full truth of the mystery of life is far more complex than we limited human souls imagine, though it most certainly seems to involve reincarnation. I have seen the large Ferris wheel in a number of other dreams and it always seems to allude to the Higher Self, in higher reality, containing many lives past and future.

I had another dream in which I found myself in higher reality where I was informed that I have now done sufficient work in the unconscious processes to have won freedom from further rebirths. I hope that this is so, but I must say that I had the dream at the height of my success in the unconscious, and since that time I have lost some ground. I may well, therefore, be required to come again after all.

> I am on the banks of a small lake with a friend where we are trying to catch fish. We catch a number of round white ones, which we chuck onto the bank where they become fossilized. Suddenly, a hare comes out of the water and sits on the bank in front of us. Using the fishing rod as a lance, I spear the hare in the chest, severely wounding it. However, it manages to make its way back into the lake, where it disappears in the depths of the water out of which it came. I am then filled with deep remorse, and I keep repeating, "I shouldn't have harmed it. I shouldn't have harmed it."

Fish symbolism is well known in mythology and religions and, as said earlier in this book, it symbolizes the Higher Self as savior and culture-hero. St. Augustine called Christ "the fish drawn from the deep," and the fish almost became the main symbol of Christianity rather than the cross. To fish in a lake is to delve for contents of the unconscious as the Fisher King does in the Grail legends. The white round fish caught in this dream is reminiscent of ones mentioned in alchemy; those had to be round and edible, meaning psychologically that such a content was whole and could be assimilated, and in fact referred to the Self. The ones here become fossilized when thrown onto the bank, which means their state becomes altered, as if changed to stone, but the precise meaning of this must remain a mystery for the moment.

163

The lake itself refers to the largely feminine lower depths of the unconscious. The hare which comes out of the lake is not only a symbol for Mercurius as guide through the unconscious, but was also, as Unnefer, a form of Osiris in Egypt, with a similar meaning. The hare is therefore a symbol of the lower Self, or Osiris/Mercurius as guide, that is part of the Higher Self—the Osiris to the Horus. My spearing of the hare is a bad sign, of course, meaning that I have injured the content in some way, and perhaps severely. But I must wonder if this may not have a symbolic meaning, like Christ being wounded by the lance in both the Bible and the Grail legends. However, this may not be so, and the wounding probably refers to damage done by a wrong action of mine.

> There is a large Catholic church where, though I feel highly nervous, I nevertheless preach a fiery sermon on how the modern Mass has lost its original meaning. Later, and I am near a wood with my dog when four wild animals fall from the back of a lorry. There are three lions—possibly lionesses—and a baboon. None of these show me any hostility, but the baboon snarls and bares its teeth at my dog, so I quickly hurry him away. Coming to a building, I go inside, probably without my dog, where some Spanish youths menace me, but I talk to them in Spanish, though not understanding a word of what I am saying myself. However, I do somehow understand that I speak about God and Christ, and the building becomes a Spanish church.
>
> A black-bearded, black-robed priest, resembling a medieval monk, comes up, and he also listens to my words, and he and the youths are awestruck by what I am saying. I then notice some fancy, black, wrought iron work that is patterned in circles and squares, and suddenly, in the center circle, Christ appears crucified. He's wearing his purple robe rather than the usual sort of loincloth that he is depicted wearing in paintings. Furthermore, he has short hair and is beardless, and as I look up at him, an angelic choir sings heavenly music.

Though I was raised very loosely as a Protestant, the Catholic Church—and its churches—always seemed more magically alive to me than the somber Protestant ones. However, I lost all belief in Christianity when quite young, like millions of other people in the West who could no longer accept its teachings as being literally and physically true.

But I have by now been experiencing the unconscious processes for some time, and not only have they spiritualized me, they have done so in a Christian way. This is because the line of religious experience through the unconscious has become constellated in the collective Western unconscious in that particular form. Christ, as the Higher Self, was the Son of God, and the archetypal phenomenon reaches back to early Egypt. The Mass was originally based on the processes of the Higher Self, as was Osirification in Egypt and transformation symbolism in alchemy. The meaning of this has been entirely lost in the modern world, which is why I preach the fiery sermon.

The formulation of three lions (lionesses?) and baboon expresses the four emanations of the Self, which are of a 3 + 1 nature. These correspond to the prophet Daniel's four beasts rising from the sea, the fourth one of which was "dreadful and terrible"—recalcitrant, like the baboon. Just as in the dream I then see the crucified Christ figure, so Daniel sees "one like the Son of man" coming with the clouds of Heaven. As I say elsewhere, other examples of the fourfold structure of the Higher Self are Horus with his four sons, Marduk with his four dogs, Christ at the center of the four symbols of the evangelists, Ezekiel's wheels with their four faces, Enoch's four hollow places, and even the four Nommo gods of the Dogon people of Mali. All of these are examples of a 3 + 1 nature.

Earlier in Egypt, the Great Mother as goddess of the Seven Stars in the Great Bear Circle on the Four Quarters of the Horizon represented the wholeness of the feminine worship, as both sevenfold and fourfold, but this changed to the masculine worship of the Father and Son cults. The Great Mother was divided into two sister goddesses, one of the realm above, and one of the realm below, or sometimes of the North and South. These were also divided into the four rivers of the four quarters in the firmament, but below, the fourfold totality was symbolized as the hippopotamus with the nose of the Kaf-Ape, the feet of the lion, and the hind quarters of the crocodile. These also represented the four elements. This is a quaternity, though feminine, and the three lions in my dream may be lionesses, while the baboon is the Kaf-Ape. However, Christ on the cross here is masculine.

As to the other details of the dream, the circles and squares on the iron trellis mean the unification of the opposites of matter and spirit contained in the Higher Self. Here it is a sort of modern Gnostic Christ. He is beardless and has short hair, and so is certainly not the accepted image of the original Christ, but his parallel or equivalent. Jung says that it is God's intention to incarnate in man, and each development of the Higher Self to its ultimate form is precisely that, God's incarnation and nothing less.

As to the strong Spanish influence, the youths, the priest, the church, it is difficult to say, though Spain is a very Catholic country and the unconscious obviously sees the Catholic Church and its symbolism as better representatives of the Higher Self phenomenon in my processes than any other, probably because it has retained more of the original symbolism than other creeds.

The cross is a symbol of the unification of all opposites contained in the crucified figure, and the unification of these opposites is a veritable condition of crucifixion. The opposites cannot be unified at the level of man, only at the level of the Higher Self, though the individual may share in the state of wholeness. This is why the angels sing in the dream; it is seen as a holy event involving a unification of God with the World Soul. Though the cross with Christ is the "Tree of Death," it also has deeper symbolism as the Tree of Life known to many religions. This symbolizes both the inner transformation processes and also the processes of life itself which is why it is sometimes associated with the spirit Mercurius. From another aspect, the tree is a feminine symbol, so that with the god-man crucified upon it a unification of opposites is again indicated.

Jung does not give too much information about crucifixion throughout his works, and this is because there is not a great lot that one can say. He does tell us in *Symbols of Transformation* that the early Aztecs would nail either a young man or woman to a tree and shoot arrows into the victim to ensure a healthy and plentiful grain crop. In Peru, two ropes would be tied across a pool, forming a cross, and precious stones and fruit would then be tossed into the pool as sacrifices. Jung also equates crucifixion with self-sacrifice, and with the ultimate self-sacrifice in the case of Christ. But even without death itself, to renounce by free choice all of the worldly pleasures, appetites, and instincts, in order to serve God and mankind, does involve total self-sacrifice.

Crucifixion symbolism must have so much meaning for the higher and deeper levels of reality through the unconscious, that is to say, with God, that the angels sing when it occurs. Jung comments that "even for the knower of divine secrets" crucifixion remains unknowable, a great mystery, expressing, in part, the nature of God that is ultimately unknowable. Jung saw a vision of the crucified Christ, gold and green, concluding that it signified the unification of the "spirit gold" and the verdant green of alchemy. In my dream, the quaternity formed by the three lions and the baboon form the lower chthonic, or material counterpart to the crucified figure, the Christ parallel above.

The baboon, the "recalcitrant fourth" symbolizing the subhuman, is very hostile to my dog, who represents the higher spirit, the superhuman, though at animal level. This is why the baboon is hostile. The baboon was the "ape of God" to the Gnostics, because he represented the "recalcitrant fourth," the Devil to the Holy Trinity. However, in Egypt the god of wisdom, Thoth, was on the one hand the ibis bird, but on the other was the baboon, or Kaf-Ape, these representing the higher spirit and lower soul aspects. So the baboon was obviously not negative in that form. This was as Thoth-Aan, the saluter to the light of Horus, who held the Eye of Horus, the "eye of light," in his hands. It is Thoth-Aan who records all the words of truth in the wisdom texts, which would be the individuation processes involving the Higher Self or Horus/Osiris. These represent the two aspects, the higher and lower Selves. Horus means "he who is above" while Osiris is "lord of the Underworld"—thus the higher and lower spirits of the unconscious that the alchemists were to discover. In a later dream I saw the baboon wearing glasses and looking like a lovable old scholar, but someone warns me not to trust this creature.

> My dog, who is all black here, coughs up a black stone which is magical and which jumps about like a Mexican jumping bean. I must swallow this, though it is very difficult as it can appear and disappear at will. However, I finally manage to grab it and gulp it down.

My dog, as I have said earlier, represents a lower form of the Higher Self in the processes, and he is all black here, which means the dark, sinister side. The magical stone that is alive in some way is the equivalent of the alchemists' Philosopher's Stone but it's the shadow side as it is black. To swallow it means to take it in to be assimilated, a task I must accomplish for wholeness. If you experience one side of the unconsciousness then you must experience the opposite side for completeness.

The dream caused me a lot of worry at the time because both my dog and the magical stone are black, meaning the sinister and downright evil side, and I wondered if I was bringing forth a Mephistopheles as my bosom companion. I also dreamt of a dark magician right after this and knowing that this is usually a bad sign, it caused me some sweat and disturbance. However, I eventually came to realize that I was required to experience and assimilate the dark side for wholeness.

Most of my dreams in the processes seem to be a mixture of Christian/Gnostic and alchemical contents, the latter representing mostly the lower spirit of the unconscious, the Mercurial side. The unification of these opposite spirits has been the dire need of Western culture for two thousand years, and my processes seem to be accomplishing this. The alchemists came close to accomplishing the unification, but their aims were too matter-bound, and too much was unconscious projection. With the discoveries of Jung, however, and with the great foundations that he laid, we can now make attempts to further the work with full conscious awareness.

> I am at a meeting of psychologists, all old European men. Their leader is small and resembles Freud, but mentally he is like Jung. I have accomplished something special and am therefore welcome in the company of these distinguished men, as a guest of the leader. I begin to sing the old song, "The White Dove," and all the old psychologists join in. The lines we sing are: "In your heart, my sweet white dove, let me build my only throne."

The white dove refers to the Holy Spirit, and it is significant that of all the thousands of songs that I know, we sing that particular one. Birds mean spirit in dreams, and can we imagine any symbol more apt for the Holy Spirit than the white dove? When it descends on the man Jesus in the Gospels, God proclaims: "This is my beloved Son, in whom I am well pleased." The dream seems to be saying, therefore, that the Holy Spirit is ready to descend.

The Christian Holy Spirit is masculine, and the white dove is its symbol, but the dove was originally a feminine symbol, connected with Venus, Diana, and Sophia. There was much controversy among the ancients as to whether the Holy Spirit was masculine or feminine. Some Gnostics equated it with the feminine Sophia, and some even proclaimed

Sophia in authority over Christ, but St. Paul states emphatically that the Holy Spirit is masculine. Strictly speaking, as birds represent male spirit, the dove should be masculine. The dark side is usually symbolized by the black raven, as early as Noah, and we find the white dove and black raven as light and dark sides of the Holy Spirit in alchemy.

In Semitic tradition, it is the dove by day and the raven by night, which corresponds closely to the hawks of Isis and Nepthys in Egypt, one of the light, one of the dark. Massey says the dove was an earlier symbol of Father and Son (Ra and Horus) but later became the hawk, despite the fact that the dove was also the mother-bird of Hathor. This would be because of its softness and gentleness. Nevertheless, Ramses IX has a dove on the prow of his solar boat rather than a hawk. The dove of Hathor was placed on the mummy of the deceased, wings extended, "as quickener of the spirit for a future life."

Massey says in furtherance of this insight: "The divine Horus, or a form of him, rises again in the form of a dove, as well as in the shape of a hawk. 'I am the dove: I am the dove,' exclaims the risen spirit, as he soars up from Amenta, where the egg of his future being was hatched by the divine incubator." Iusaas, a form of Hathor, is the mother, and Atum the father, as "holy" spirit, who produce the divine Son, Iusa, as a dove. So there is much symbolism connected with the dove, but here in the dream it can only refer to the Holy Spirit.

> There is a large fire in my home and a lot of my clothes are burnt, in particular, my green jacket. My football coupon has also been burnt, and I cry, "How can I win the jackpot now?" This problem seems to be due mainly to a friend of mine, W, a slight shadow figure.
>
> Then I see an eagle tearing flesh to pieces, either in or just above the sea. I go to a house, and going upstairs, as I stand on the landing I can see a black dog in a bedroom thrusting as if in copulation. A naked woman then closes the door of the room in my face, saying, "You are not coming in here."

I must have done something very wrong in terms of the processes to bring about their collapse, though this seems to be partly due to the influence of my shadow side, represented by W. That is what the fire in my house (my psyche) alludes to. The green jacket and the jackpot that I have missed winning refer to the attainment of the Higher Self and Holy Spirit, the color of which is traditionally green, and which I have now forfeited and lost. In previous dreams I saw the crucified Christ figure, and sang of the white dove, which referred to the Holy Spirit, with the elders, but the collapse has meant that they have now faded, and the flesh-tearing eagle, perhaps the dark side of the Holy Spirit, has replaced the gentle dove. So rather than the unification of the opposites, one side savagely tears at the other.

The black dog, always a sign of danger as it represents the dark side of the Self, is copulating in lust, and the naked woman, the anima, is also involved in the lust. "Lust" and "copulation" may be enjoyable and necessary to normal life, but the bringing forth of the Higher Self may ultimately involve the incarnation of God as the Son. As the dreams show, this involves the Holy Spirit, and as this is obviously a special event of light and spirit, the lower instinctual powers must be kept out of it. It is the higher union of male and female that must be accomplished. Luckily, perhaps, I am not allowed into the room, (into the situation), which means I am not part of the corruption. But it is dark and foreboding. Again, under normal circumstances lust would not necessarily mean corruption as such, but in this special situation, it leads to the dark, evil side of the Self.

The collapse almost always happens in these processes, as we know from mythology and alchemy. The alchemists would work for weeks and months on a process, only to have the temptations of the world break in and bring it to ruin. Then they would have to begin all over again. The same happens with myself in my own processes. I was only reading recently where the Aztec culture-hero, Quetzalcoatl, after defeating the dark forces and bringing light and culture to his people, finally succumbs to drunkenness and commits rape, thus losing his powers. All such myths are based on the processes of the unconscious, and ultimate failure is almost always the rule—probably always, in fact. The pig or boar is often the killer of the hero in mythology. Set takes the form of a pig to blind Horus in one eye. Pigs cause fear in dreams for the same reason. The Buddha was supposedly vegetarian, yet not only does he eat flesh, it is pork off a pig. Of all the things he could choke on, it is pork. This is highly symbolical of his fall to the dark side.

A woman throws a purple pad to me from some distance away. On it I find illustrated some brightly colored fishes, which remind me of cockroaches a bit, but as I look closer, I just see the sign of the fish. Then it is pointed out somehow that the world of dry land is the offspring of, and grew out of, the depths of the ocean. It even seems that fresh air itself was constructed from water, and is merely one of the latter's forms.

The woman is the anima, of course, the "lady of the unconscious," and though she has many functions, perhaps the chief one is that she is able, as psychopomp, to lead consciousness to the realm of the archetypal contents of the unconscious. The little colored fishes are such contents and perhaps remind me of cockroaches because the latter are an extremely old and unaltered form of life. These could be connected with the white round fishes that became fossilized on dry land a few dreams ago. The pad the woman throws, and on which the fishes are depicted, is purple, the color of royalty, and true royalty is the Higher Self. This is exactly what I see next: the sign of the fish on the pad, which as I said earlier, almost became the symbol of Christianity rather than the cross.

It is then pointed out in the dream that the world of dry land, i.e., of conscious reality, grew out of the depths of the ocean, the eternal unconscious; even the air did, which could mean the spirit. The ancient Egyptians believed that all of reality, including the spirit world and the gods, came originally from the great primordial waters, by which they meant the other reality through the unconscious, and the dream seems to be saying the same; in fact, many mythologies claim something similar. The great truths of the unconscious to be found in these myths— which, we must never forget, represent religion in its truest sense—can only astonish those of us who have directly experienced the depths and heights of the unconscious.

As I stand by my bed I seem to feel that God is present in my mind, or at least, affects from Him are. This causes me to swoon with the heaviness of it all, and I fall onto the bed.

Somewhere in the Bible, God says: "Who is near unto me is near unto the fire," and Deuteronomy 4:24. says: "For the Lord thy God is a consuming fire," and it seems that I personally have come too near, too soon. This was a terrible and very dangerous time for me. For about a month I felt that my head, particularly the back of my head was made of lead. I felt hot needles jabbing into my brain, and I could not raise my eyes to look at anything for fear of swooning. I had dreams in which things became reversed and confused, north becoming south, and in fact, all four directions becoming jumbled up.

In one dream, a ghost was clinging to my back and I could not shake it off, and in another, the notes coming out of a nickelodeon were little blue angels, which floated up to Heaven, seeming to take me floating up with them. I would suddenly become tremendously elated with the most wonderful feelings, only to be cast down again seconds later to the most tortuous despair. I finally had a dream that informed me that my mind was almost sure to break, and that I would become a mindless vegetable; even unable to watch television, so the dream said.

I believed that my mind was going to break, so one day I went out for a walk to look for the last time at the streets and fields where I have lived all my life. I realized how much I love this homely place, and the people I have known here. I remember that tears rolled down my cheeks and onto the grass, and I had the strangest feeling they were fertilizing the earth.

This lasted for about a month, and I sadly awaited my fate, unable to raise my lead-heavy head and fearful of the crazy, confused dreams that kept coming. But it did not happen; I did not go mad and become a mindless vegetable. I had come close to it, but somehow I had scraped through, as if by a miracle.

I had a dream in which I just managed to get back across a bridge safely. On the far side of the bridge lay madness and destruction, and I had almost crossed it, teetering on the edge of madness, as it were. I knew that shamans have been severely mentally damaged due to experiences of the unconscious, and as the alchemists stated, "Not a few have perished in our work." I had vowed that if by a miracle I did survive, I would leave dreams and the unconscious alone.

Yet, though I had approached mental catastrophe, I could not keep my vow. I told myself that this work is far too important and must be done by someone, and in any case, I truly loved it. I remembered the time before I had discovered Jung and the unconscious, before I started my quest, when I was lost and afraid in a meaningless universe of mere matter, which I only wished to escape. No, I decided, it is better to go mad on the quest, journeying through the unconscious, than to live an existence of mere matter. It is better to go mad *with* God, than for there to be no God, I told myself. But henceforth I would have to be *extremely* careful.

> I have a vision of a stream of blue blood which starts at the unrecorded beginnings of ancient Egypt, in a sort of lake and runs through the Egypt of the Pharaohs, through the Israel of the prophets, and to Christ. However, it becomes stuck there and does not develop further as it is meant to do.
>
> A giant-size Jung is overhead, but just from the waist up, and his mighty arms are outstretched to span the stream of blue blood, which is a royal line from Egypt to the present. Jung says, "The royal line unites," but must, I gather, be brought up to the present. Where the stream becomes stuck two thousand years ago, I see Christ crucified. It is not on a hill, as always depicted, but in a small public square, surrounded by buildings.

The stream of blue blood is the royal line of spiritual kings, not kings of this world, but successive developments of the Higher Self as Son of God, through the collective unconscious. Egyptian kingship was based on the phenomenon of the Higher Self, or rather on the divine Father and Son ("out of the father comes the son"), as were many gods and culture-heroes around the world. Abraham, Moses, Joseph, David, Solomon, Enoch, Ezekiel, and Daniel, the latter three with their Son of Man figures, were of this line, and Jesus with the Son of Man, or the Christ, was possibly the highest development of it ever.

The Pharaohs were worldly kings, of course, but each of them was said to be Horus in human form, with the High God, Ra, as Father. At Annu, Iu-em-hetep was divine Son of Atum, and at Memphis he was Son of Ptah (also son of Atum-Ra). Iu-em-hetep has since been demoted to the merely human Imhotep, whom we can now take as the human initiate, corresponding to the man Jesus. So Pharaoh/Horus/Ra, Imhotep/Iu-em-hetep/Atum, Daniel/Son of Man/Ancient of Days, and Jesus/Christ/God are all based on the same developing model. Melchizedek, the mysterious priest-king from whom Abraham receives bread and wine, who has "neither beginning of days, nor end of life; but made like unto the Son of God," is certainly the Higher Self of Abraham. Samson with his great strength, which is actually the power of the Higher Self, is another version, while the story of Moses is full of symbolism of processes that can only involve the Higher Self and God.

The roots of Christianity, therefore, as well as lying far back in the ancient past, also, and primarily, lie rooted deeply in the collective unconscious, and ultimately involve God literally and directly, but must undergo further development. This, if it occurs at all, will be a great leap forward and will bring the royal line up to date. The effects of this will continue the relationship, the covenant, of man with God which began so many thousands of years ago. This must involve the Higher Self in all of his aspects, including the divine Father/Son incarnation, as well as the recognition of the lower depths of the unconscious, the lower Self, the World Soul, and so forth, whether as the Virgin Mary as goddess or otherwise. It must also involve the dark underside of the unconscious that alchemy revealed to us.

But the development must also include such things as reincarnation and Jungian depth psychology. In fact, it is with the knowledge and understanding of depth psychology that we can now understand all that has gone before. We must also include the valuable experiences of not only the alchemists, but of all the other esoteric mysteries based on the unconscious processes, while keeping to the central royal line that is our heritage.

Other royal lines are just as valid. Hinduism and Buddhism are, for instance, but they do not speak the language of the Western collective unconscious, just as ours does not speak theirs, even if the symbolism is similar, expressing the same archetypal truths. No matter what our conscious attitudes and beliefs may be, Vishnu, Krishna, and the Buddha do not speak to the depths of the Western collective unconscious, for it thinks in terms of Christ and the lower spirit of Mercurius and their respective realms.

These are not just my own ideas, or even Jung's, but the facts as presented to me by the unconscious during my years undergoing the individuation processes. I was even instructed a couple of times in dreams to send all of this information to the Pope as evidence of these things, and of what must be done, but I never did. Perhaps I should have for the unconscious was quite adamant about this.

One further thing worth mentioning concerning the Higher Self as divine Son is pointed out by Gerald Massey. He says that the first divine Son in Egypt was Son of the Mother, but in the second phase, the divine Son was Son of the Father. The Egyptians termed the High God Ra the "male mother" because the second divine son issues from the Father alone. It is true that Hathor is mother of Horus when Ra is father, but this is in other myths. This is wise and fits in with the Higher Self's processes in the unconscious, who in the first phase is born of the feminine soul depths, but in the second phase is born of the higher spirit—Son of the Mother in lower form, but Son of the Father in higher form (or this may be reversed).

Both Horus and Christ are born of the Mother first, but are later claimed by the Father, who says in both cases, roughly speaking, "This is my beloved son." However, looked at from the view of the whole process, the divine inspiration from above comes first. In my case it involved the visitations of Christ who instructed me to spiritualize the lower depths which must be won over in the great task.

> I am standing by the sea with actor Burt Lancaster and I reflect that he once played Moses in a television series. Suddenly, a baby boy, wrapped in white linen, comes floating in across the waters, his smiling face the loveliest I have ever seen.

I will save my comments on this dream until after the next one, as it follows on from this.

> I sit on rocks by the sea and close by on the rocks there is a baby boy wrapped in white linen. Also present is a friend of mine, a slightly shadowy figure, though here he has a clean and gentle look. Suddenly, a strange reptile appears, shaped like a stick insect, but much larger; it is a type of lizard perhaps. It walks over the child, filling me with fear. It then goes to the shallows at the sea's edge and joins other reptiles of various sorts that are in a pool of green slime.

The story of Moses in the bulrushes is suggested here with the infant child floating on the waters, and with my companion being Burt Lancaster, who once played Moses in a TV series. The sea, the waters, represents the depths of the collective unconscious, and the lovely boy-child is the divine child, the infant Higher Self. The symbolism is archetypal and widely known in mythology. Earlier today I was reading of how King Arthur comes floating across the waters as a baby boy, to be found by Merlin the magician, who then rears him. This obviously was based on the same archetypal situation. Sometimes the child grows up to be a hero or a god because of the immortal nature of the Higher Self, whose birth this ultimately is. Sometimes the myth or legend tells the mortal side of the story, sometimes the immortal side, and sometimes both.

But it frequently happens that the divine birth of the Higher Self becomes that of the human individual, as with Moses, and although the later Christ child is a god, it is taken to be also that of the human Jesus. A similar story of the birth of Moses can be seen in the much earlier birth of Sargon of Akkad, whose mother places him in an ark of rushes, setting him afloat in the river, where he is found by the water carrier, Akki. The story, being archetypal, is based on facts of the unconscious.

The child in my dream is wrapped in white linen, cloth sacred to the ancient Egyptians and other cultures, and said to be worn by the gods. The child's face is the loveliest I have ever seen because this is the light form of the Higher Self, Horus or Osiris rather than Set. In the second dream, the myth of the birth of Horus is partly suggested when the reptile crawls over the child, causing me much fear. The baby Horus was menaced by a serpent, and in one myth was bitten, though in others *he* stamped on *it*.

There is also a myth similar to the Moses story where Isis takes the baby Horus into the bulrushes to escape the wrath of Set. The place of the marshes was called Kheb, and the plants were so hidden and secret there that Set could not follow. The myth says that this area would be impenetrable to Set. Nevertheless, in some stories, as in the myth of the sorrows of Isis, Horus is bitten by the serpent, while in others he stamps on it, or escapes it. Pyramid Text 681 relates that Horus needed to jump up quickly to escape a dangerous serpent, and that there was no one else there to help him. Horus then trod on the mouth of the snake, the "vile miscreant" (1959).

The god-hero and serpent belong together in the same myths because they represent the contending opposite sides of the Self and of full reality itself. In the Hindu myths, always so wise with experience of the unconscious processes, the god Vishnu and the serpent Ananta are but different aspects of the same divine nature, which is why Ananta is never totally slain.

In Egypt, Horus does slay his uncle, Set, who takes the form of a serpent or dragon-monster. Set has murdered his own brother, Osiris, the father of Horus (though Osiris and Horus are also really different aspects of the Higher Self, and Set is their dark side). However, in one early myth, Set is a positive figure and slays the serpent Apep (or Apophis) on behalf of Ra, the High God.

These myths represent instances of actual unconscious conflicts and processes as experienced by living human beings, involving the Higher Self and the serpent and its realms. This must be so, for how else could they have been known and recorded to match what we know today, to match my own processes? Modern depth psychology has only recently discovered the fundamental truth of myths as symbolism of unconscious processes. Basically, when the hero, who is largely ego-consciousness aided by the Self, has slain the serpent-dragon, which means the defeat and chaining up of the dark instinctual depths, the Higher Self may then reign in its positive aspect and society can grow and flourish. Sometimes it is the child who slays the serpent, as with the Horus text and with the baby Herakles who strangles the two serpents, although both heroes have to slay the serpents again when they are adults.

In my second dream, the fact that the child is on the rocks means that he has become real and concrete to worldly reality, though is still in the unconscious. My companion, who is usually a little shady, but who is clean and gentle here, represents my own *purified* shadow, a necessary preliminary for the birth of the child.

This dream symbolizes the birth of the Higher Self as the divine child. An earlier dream (I trapped the boy with a square to bring him to Earth, and God said, "This is indeed my beloved Son") also symbolized the coming of the divine child. So why are there two symbolic births of the Higher Self in my processes?

The answer is supplied by Gerald Massey. He states there must be two births of the divine Son, one from the sky (the spirit, the realm of the Father) and one from the waters (the sea, realm of the Great Mother, the World Soul). These are the two eternal sides of full reality, and both must be represented in the coming of the Son. This is why the star and the fish are always found together in the myths of divine Sons across the world. Even the Dogon of Mali say that when their savior, Nommo, comes again as a fish, it will be the "Day of the Star." The full Higher Self must be Son of the Father as well as Son of the Mother, for if he is merely Son of the Mother he will be the alchemical Mercurius. Mercurius, though having both light and dark sides, will not be the ultimate, full Self, and indeed, may well be the crocodile Sevekh of the Egyptians, or serve as serpent or Mephistopheles. Jung tells us of the alchemical *filius macrocosmi*, the lower Mercurial son, and the *filius microcosmi*, the higher son of spirit, stating that these sons and their respective realms must be united in the processes, adding that the lower Self is really a part of the Higher Self.

Jesus himself comments on this (John 3:4) when Nicodemus asks, "How can a man be born when he is old? Can he enter a second time into his mother's womb, and be born?"

Jesus answered, "Verily, verily, I say unto thee, Except a man be born of water, and of the Spirit, he cannot enter into the kingdom of God."

Jesus would appear to be saying the same thing as myself above: the higher personality must be born of both the water, the lower feminine or soul depths of the unconscious, *and* the higher Spirit side of the unconscious.

Isaiah 11:8 says, "The suckling child shall play on the hole of the asp, and the weaned child shall put his hand on the adder's den." The connection is that the child is together with the reptile, as in my dream and the Horus and other myths. These are the two sides of the Self, though with Isaiah there is no danger as unification is implied. This is an allusion to the two sides of the Higher Self, divine child and serpent.

> I am in a small, old castle where I nurse C. G. Jung, who is very old and ailing. Suddenly, a hazy vision appears before me, coming from out of another hazy reality. I see four gold petals form, like a cross with arms of equal length. Jung, who is unable to see himself because his sight is fading badly, asks, "What do you see before you?" When I reply, "Four gold petals, forming a cross," he says, "That is it. It is done" (or "It is finished").
>
> I then help him up a flight of stairs, but at the top, he dies, his blue eyes staring blankly. His body falls over the rail to the ground floor below, where it splatters. At first I am very concerned that his body will be something of a mess at his funeral, but then I think, "What does it matter what his body looks like? His spirit is intact and is now floating upwards."
>
> I then realize that I have received four gold keys on a gold key ring from Jung. I say, or the dream causes me to say, "How strange that I am Jung's follower and successor, considering our very different lives and backgrounds."

The small old castle resembled Jung's medieval-style house at Bollingen, Switzerland, which Jung had built in a 3 + 1 structure to symbolize the nature of the Higher Self. My vision of the four gold petals forming a flower-cross is reminiscent of the Golden Flower of Chinese Taoism and alchemy, one of the main Eastern symbols of the Higher Self. As Jung states, the inner immortal in Western man must be developed in a similar way to the Golden Flower, though through a Christ-parallel to fit both our Western traditions and the needs of the developing religious spirit in the West.

Gold has always symbolized the things most precious to man since ancient times, and it will be recalled that in an earlier dream, Christ became a golden cloud that enveloped me. The four gold keys on the gold key ring have the same meaning as the four gold petals forming a cross: the Higher Self with his four emanations, its fourfold structure, which is also the squaring of the circle. The cross within the circle was perhaps the main symbol of the Gnostics, but it is actually much older and we find it in certain forms at the very beginnings of ancient Egypt and other early cultures. Matriarchal worship preceded the patriarchal in these cultures, and so the first form of the symbol in Egypt was the Great Mother of the Great Bear Circle with the Heaven of the Four Quarters. In this symbol later, when Patriarchal, Heaven itself was a circle supported by the four pillars of Shu. Other versions are Ezekiel's Wheel with the four faces; the Buddha sitting on his circular podium with a pillar at each corner; the Four Sons of Horus rising from the waters on a lotus. The symbol is universal, and I give various examples elsewhere.

The gold keys themselves have a specific meaning: they unlock doors that lead to the eternal reality of spirit and soul through the unconscious, to the reality of the Higher Self. I bought an old book after this dream about priesthood and prophetship in ancient Israel. A couple of sentences alluded to the receiving of four keys as the sign of receiving the office of high priest or prophet from the predecessor. St. Peter receiving the keys of the kingdom from Jesus must be based on that same tradition. Jung reports an alchemical text states that the door to the treasure is opened by four keys.

Jung himself received the gold keys from his winged "wise old man" figure, Philemon, "the personification of spirit," as Jung puts it. Jung as my spirit guru in the processes has the same significance for me. Massey gives a piece of information that is very relevant here: "In the coming forth to day from out the dark of death which is the resurrection in the Ritual, Atum-Iu, the closer and the opener of Amenta, carries in his hands the keys that close and open the Underworld. These are the Ankh key of life, and the Un-scepter, with which Amenta is closed and opened. These are repeated in Revelation as the keys of death and hell" (Massey 1907).

In other versions it is Shu-Anhur who provides the keys to unlock the gates, these keys again being in the form of the Ankh cross, which is actually the cross and circle combined, just as are the keys on the ring that I receive from Jung. Amenta, the Egyptian Underworld, was the lower realm of the unconscious, and just as the Egyptians stated that it was necessary to descend to the depths to reach Heaven, so in the unconscious processes it is experience of the lower depths that brings forth the spiritual heights.

Two types of keys are indicated in Massey's quote, and the meaning is the same as those which both Jung and myself receive in our dreams, though these latter have associated meanings. Christ's words in Revelation (1:18) are, "I have the keys of death and Hades," (in the modern world meaning the collective unconscious). However an old Jewish saying was ". . . the keys of four things are in the hands of God alone." This implies four keys and could refer to this very same process.

Jung recently visited me in a dream wearing a tam (a round hat) that had the edges folded over on four sides to form a square, thus the squaring of the circle, just as the four keys on the key ring denoted. As he left, Jung said, "I'm off to see the Holy Ghost." Now, it is the function of the Holy Ghost to spiritualize mankind—I am speaking of the actual psychological process, not just a belief that this may occur as an outer event—and this is, in fact, what Jung does, or what the unconscious processes do. Jung connects us to the immortal aspects of our nature and thereby spiritualizes us to varying degrees; how much depends upon each individual, but in this sense he is doing the work of the Holy Spirit. Jung in my dreams is "the personification of spirit," but sometimes I could swear that it is the representation of Jung himself, and perhaps he has become blended with that Holy Spirit in higher reality.

In *Psychology and Religion*, Jung states that for Christianity the Holy Ghost is the breath of God that brings healing. Yet this is not just a force, as the Holy Ghost is the Third Person of the divine Trinity that binds together Father and Son, so that these three are nevertheless one. But because this force can descend into the human psyche, Man shares in the Holy Ghost with Father and Son. This is the force that Christ said he was leaving as the Paraclete. Jung says the Cosmic Man, the ultimate

Higher Self, has been known for two thousand years, having merged with our concepts of God and Christ, and that the stigmata of the saints shows them to be carriers of the Christ or Anthropos-image. These, he says, are symbolical examples of the Holy Ghost at work among men.

The god Shu-Anhur provided the keys to the Underworld in ancient Egypt and was called "the breath of Ra." Shu-Anhur was identified as part of God even more so than the divine Son, Horus, and he merges with Ra "as a flame of fire merges with the sun." The Christian Holy Ghost, also called the "breath of God," seems to identify it with Shu-Anhur as being the same spirit force of God. And just as Shu-Anhur provided the keys to Amenta so it seems to be the Holy Ghost, in the form of Jung, from which I receive the four gold keys in my dream.

Jung mentions the alchemist Michael Maier, who says that God is the sun, and as it turns, it spins gold which falls to and affects the Earth. In this way God is the gold which becomes gold within man. This is the same as God being the fire of the Holy Ghost, which, Jung says, is sometimes represented as a winged old man or in alchemy Mercurius as the god of revelation. Together with the King and his Son, the three are the alchemical trinity.

Philemon was the winged old man who brought the four gold keys to Jung. Considering what he says above, Jung must have known that it was the Holy Ghost who had visited him, providing the keys that lead to the great mysteries of eternal spirit and soul, and ultimately to God. However, Jung was always very cautious about revealing his personal experiences, even in his autobiography, but he must have known the tremendous significance of it all. He must have known that the Holy Ghost had descended upon him. But as the world, and particularly his fellow psychologists, would not accept even the simpler things he had discovered concerning the psyche, they certainly would not accept the religious ravings of a maniac claiming he was working under the direct supervision of the Holy Ghost. Yet such indeed appears to have been the case!

It became Jung's task with this gift of the four gold keys to develop the Higher Self in Western man on the lines laid down by our religious past, which, as stated, reaches back to ancient Egypt, source of the royal line, or river, of true blue blood. Receiving the four gold keys myself from Jung, I can only conclude that I am meant to continue with the great task myself, to whatever extent I am able. When I look back now, I realize I too have been under the influence of a higher force. The divine child coming from across the waters in the previous dream is further proof that this is so, for it means the birth in time of the Higher Self. Later dream-visions reported in this book will reinforce this conclusion.

In the dream, when I help Jung up the stairs, he is beginning his ascent to that higher reality. Then comes the parting: when I speak of his spirit ascending, his material body goes in the other direction to the ground below. His body splattering alludes to its decomposition, but as I say in the dream, what does that matter now? It is his surviving spirit that is important, that is now ascending to higher spirit reality itself to merge with the Holy Ghost. So the Jung in my dream appears to be Jung as himself and as part of the Holy Ghost.

> I encounter a toad, a baboon, and a snake. The first two do not disturb me, but I am terrified of the snake. However, I steel myself, saying, "Oh well, I have to get used to it sometime." Putting my finger in the snake's mouth, I expect it to bite me. Surprisingly, it does not and becomes a white fish.

The toad is considered to be loathsome, its habitat being cold, dark, and damp. I speak further of the toad later, so I will just say here that it is often experienced in the processes because it represents that lower part of the unconscious, or Self, the basest level of Earth which cannot be sublimated. It has long been associated with evil.

The Devil was the "Ape of God" to the Gnostics, and the baboon here partly represents this, although Thoth, the Egyptian god of wisdom, was associated with the baboon, or Kaf-Ape. The snake has always represented the dark, instinctual forces of nature, and as we know, the Devil sometimes takes the form of the serpent. The snake is also associated with wisdom, and was even said to be the most spiritual creature by the Gnostics. But it is also the symbol of the dark side of the Self, and dangerous to the development of the light side. To the Egyptians the uraeus serpent was light and helpful, whereas the Apep form was dark and highly dangerous. So in the dream we have a sort of Devil's trinity: toad, baboon, and snake, though the latter two also have wisdom associations.

When I think the snake is going to bite me, it becomes the white fish, the Ichthys, symbol of Christ and other Higher Self/savior figures such as Vishnu, Oannes, Horus, Bacchus, and others that manifest as savior-fish. The three Devil's creatures with the white fish form the 3 + 1 nature of the Self; here these are opposite and counter-wise to the usual schema, which is three positive creatures or things, plus one shadowy, "recalcitrant fourth." Now the formation is reversed to three negative and one positive. This is to be expected as both sides, light and dark, must appear and be experienced for wholeness in the processes to form a counter-balancing mandala. The white fish and serpent are themselves representations of the higher spiritual and lower chthonic sides of the Self.

Four dark, menacing dreams now occur. I will comment on them after I have given all four briefly.

> A black bird sits on my shoulder.

> I find myself among some very primitive black people. A marriage is arranged for me with one of the naked black women.

> I see a black dog emerging from a thick black mass.

> In the dream I lie on my bed feeling ill. I am filled with fear and the deepest anxiety which I try to shrug off with a laugh, and an "Oh well, not to worry." But the processes have gone very wrong again.

The processes have become very negative, so perhaps I have done something to bring the dark side foreword, meaning at the same time the fading of the light side. It takes little to injure the light side and thus reverse the processes so that the negative side comes to the fore. A little bit of human greed, malice, envy, or animal lust can be all it takes. Fortunately, it is possible to try harder and get back on the right track again, but the nearer to the goal we get, the more the serpent-dragon pours on the pressure from the instinctual—and downright evil—side. Sexuality, for instance, will be felt far more powerfully, unbearably so, and to make matters worse, the opposite sex unconsciously responds accordingly, their own sexuality being strongly heightened by their contact with you.

This is because the pressure is poured on by the instincts from the collective levels, in the depths of the greater unconscious, which is shared by all. The same is true of the will to power, or whatever else your primary weakness happens to be. That will be your Achilles' heel. A hero on the quest who can withstand the almost unbearable pressures and conquer his strongest instinct or desire, truly is a slayer of dragons. Christ's temptation in the wilderness, where he defeats his own inner temptations to inflation and power-worship, defeats the power-devil that had possessed and poisoned the whole Roman Empire, is a prime example.

In the dream above, the black bird, black primitives, and black dog all represent the dark, sinister side of the unconscious and Self, as did the toad, baboon, and snake in the earlier dream. Naturally, this makes me feel ill, for you never know when you have reached a point where the processes are irreversible, which means that you are then stuck with a Mephistopheles on your shoulder. It is fine when these come as enemies, as opposing forces that you must fight, but the black bird sitting on my shoulder is tantamount to Old Nick sitting there.

Marriage with the black primitive woman would mean disaster, as she would then represent that state of my soul lost in dark primitivity. (This has nothing to do with black people themselves, being merely the way the unconscious symbolizes things. We must remember that even in early Zulu myths, black means sinister and white good.) The black dog is known throughout mythology and folklore to have evil connotations, and it does, in fact, represent the dark Self.

> Socrates takes me to meet his son, a youth of about eighteen, who is "wisdom" manifested. The son is a transparent spirit who merges with me so that I grow twice as big and strong—not physically so, but mentally, spiritually, and in wisdom. I am now two-in-one. Even the nervous tension that I always feel completely goes as I feel myself grow and widen inwardly.

After the near catastrophe of the last few dreams, I have managed to rise above the mire and reach a higher state. I would say that to merge with "wisdom," here the son of Socrates, would mean precisely that: to grow in wisdom and as a personality. A transformation certainly did take place within me during these processes, and the Higher Self was also developing in its highest form. Though immortal, the Self has to have its many opposite parts brought together by ego-consciousness if a full incarnation is to be brought about. Incidentally, in my years of depression, and even when I had my breakdown, just thinking of the word "wisdom" always caused a warm glow inside, bringing me comfort.

St. Paul, who knew the hidden wisdom in the mysteries of the soul and spirit, said:

> ... That your faith should not stand in the wisdom of men, but in the power of God. Howbeit we speak wisdom among them that are perfect: yet not the wisdom of this world, nor of the princes of this world, that come to naught: but we speak the wisdom of God in a mystery, even the hidden wisdom, which God ordained before the world unto our glory. which none of the princes of this world know: for had they known it, they would not have crucified the Lord of glory (1 Cor. 2:5-8).

> My dog goes into a pool, though I warn him that this is dangerous. Sure enough, a she-bear appears in the water and takes a swipe at my dog with her paw, injuring him. I manage to pull him away so that his injury is not too serious, and then I take him home. He becomes a young boy, wearing two sets of identical clothes, one on top of the other.

The pool represents the feminine collective depths of the unconscious. We find examples of this throughout mythology, and especially in the Bible. Abraham, Jacob, Moses, and Jesus all meet feminine representations of the unconscious at wells or pools. The she-bear is one of the main animal symbols of the feminine unconscious, while my dog represents the spiritual Self in a lower aspect, these—the bear and the dog—being opposites. As spirit the dog had better keep clear of the lower depths, which is why I warn him, but the she-bear takes a swipe at him. Once at home my dog becomes a boy who wears two sets of identical clothing. In other words, he is the twins of the Self become one, or, conversely, the one with two aspects.

There is an old Celtic myth which is based on the same archetypes of the feminine pool and the dog-spirit. Finn MacCool's dog, Bran, was leader of the hounds, but Bran's death came about precisely because he was the strongest and fleetest of them all. One day, he was leading the pack chasing a white hart that had golden hooves. Eventually all the hounds tired and stopped, but not the stout-hearted Bran. Reaching a cliff with a lake below, the white hart plunged down into it, with Bran following close behind. But then the white hart became a beautiful woman who swam on the surface of the lake. Taking hold of Bran, she dragged him to the depths and he was seen no more. Though very beautiful, the woman was known as the Hag of the Water. This is precisely the theme of my dream.

The dog-spirit is exactly what the term says: a representation of spirit taking the form of a dog. As such, the feminine soul depths may be very dangerous for him, being his diametrical opposite. The feminine soul force takes the form of a bear in my dream while in the Celtic myth it is a white hart first then a beautiful woman, but the meaning is the same. It is a wise man—and dog-spirit—who realizes that a beautiful woman is just as dangerous as a wild bear.

I recently looked at an old Walt Disney book of fairy tales. Thumbing through it, I came to an illustration of the ghostly shape of a woman rising up out of a pool, and the story turned out to be one about a nixie in the pool. Fairy tales, like myths, are expressions of the processes of the unconscious, and as such are truer representatives of reality than very limited scientific treatises on physics.

> I am in underground caverns with some companions when a black crocodile appears in front of us. It is after food—a human being—and naturally, we are all terrified. But there are some bleeding dead bodies close by, so the crocodile grabs one of these, and then goes over the side of a bridge, where it falls with its meal to the depths below. I say, "I am going to kill that crocodile before it has me for a meal," but the trouble is I don't have a weapon to fight it with. So I go to a certain man and ask him for a weapon. He gives me an electrical fuse.

The black crocodile is the terrible dragon at its worst and it apparently needs human beings as its victims. I must kill it before it gets me, though having no weapon I am given the electric fuse, though why is unclear. Electricity is a symbol of spirit, but why the fuse?

In ancient Egypt the crocodile was the terrible dragon. Sevekh was the seven-headed dragon, son of the Earth Mother, but he sometimes has a solar aspect, or had one in early times and then later went over to the depths. But there were also crocodiles from the depths who took away and devoured the corpses and souls of the dead who had failed to live a righteous life on Earth. The heart of the deceased would be weighed against a feather and any who had a heavier heart were not fit to undergo resurrection, and so would become crocodile meat. My dream seems to reflect some of this as we are in underground caverns, possibly in Amenta, the Underworld, and the black crocodile is searching for food. Perhaps the bleeding corpses are those of wicked people who will not now be resurrected.

> A mentally ill person I know is with me, and I say to him, "Listen very closely to what I am going to say. These are not naïve, pie-in-the-sky words, but the truest ones that can ever be spoken. The only real defense against mental illness, the only real answer, is Christian love." At my words, which I mean from the depths of my being, a pale green snake coils itself around my neck and rubs its face against mine. Then it is gone.

Mental illness is the breakdown or malfunctioning of the psyche, and usually means the break up of its parts into a painful disharmony. Christian love can conquer this state if it is genuine, and it can bring healing. Think about it. If you could replace, or even accompany, that state of inner chaos with Christian love, then a unifying light would shine within your being to counteract the disintegration.

The Higher Self is the unification of all opposites, and its highest state of wholeness is symbolized by Christ with his love, as an everlasting canopy spanning all the opposites, an eternal mandala integrating all the fragments of the Higher Self, psyche, and personality. This is so despite the fact that the dark side of the Self is regarded as the eternal opposite and antagonist of the Christ figure.

If the conflicting parts of the psyche can all share in the light above, and within, then inner peace can reign. But even if this state cannot be achieved, if consciousness, by sheer will, can impose Christian love, refusing to feel enmity and bitterness, then, though the suffering will still have to be borne, it will be accompanied by grace. As I say in the dream, these are not pie-in-the-sky words based on wishful thinking, but definite facts of depth psychology. Love can conquer all, and if it is genuinely Christian (or of any other true religion), it reaches non-personal levels which prove to be the most solid foundations possible for a personality.

Christian love is not just an ideal but a definite transcendental state that is attached to God through the Higher Self. The lower depths of the psyche, and of the collective unconscious itself, must be won over in the processes, but the imperative principle is all-embracing love. Love unites and brings harmony, whereas dislikes, hatred, and hostility divide. If a mentally ill person could fill himself with "Christian love," as the dream puts it, it is difficult to see how he could remain mentally ill—unless the illness is a type of insanity such that the Christian love state could not be imposed as a matter of will. The kabbalist text, the *Zohar,* says; "In love is found the secret of divine unity; It is love that unites higher and lower stages, and that lifts every thing to that stage where all must be one."

> In the dream it is the middle of the night when I am awakened from my sleep by a white spirit that comes out of my body. This is very eerie and it creates vibrations all over the house, which brings a couple of male relatives to my room to investigate. However, by then the spirit, which is very large and powerful, has come back into my body again.
>
> The scene changes and I am on a beach where I throw some heavy dumbbells high into the air. I am able to do this because of the enormously powerful spirit inside me. Then I am with a group of townspeople with shotguns, led by the sheriff; they are trying to hunt down the powerful spirit. The spirit has now become a solid being and it is rather like in the old Frankenstein films, where the townsfolk hunt down the monster because it is different and they fail to understand it.
>
> I try to explain the situation to the sheriff and a young woman, beginning, "You know how the Frankenstein monster was put together with different parts?" However, I get no further because the strange spirit suddenly appears before us, though now he is a very large American teenager, wearing a white T-shirt and a black baseball cap. As he smiles at us, the sheriff says, "Oh, is that who it is? I remember him when he was a small boy. He is all right." Yet I am quite worried myself because, by his look, the youth seems to lack a sense of morality. But then he winks and smiles at me; he was only teasing. He does have a high moral sense, which is of paramount importance to the process. The sheriff says, "Yes, we will recruit him to fight for law and order."

The white spirit is of course the Higher Self (or its representation) of the unconscious/spirit realm, yet comes forth into worldly reality through the processes. He first appears in the bedroom, and then on the beach, taking the form of an American teenager. A beach symbolizes the meeting place of the two realities, the conscious and collective unconscious. I now have the added strength of the Self, which is why I can throw the heavy dumbbells so high, these symbolizing the unification of consciousness with the unconscious in the Self, the two opposite spheres (bells) being united by the bar.

The townsfolk (the contents of the psyche) try to hunt down the spirit, and are led by the sheriff, who represents the ordering power of the psyche. There is a valid comparison between the Frankenstein monster and the Higher Self, because both are assembled from different parts, but there are enormous differences. The monster is merely an assemblage of physical parts, taken from different bodies, whereas the Self consists of parts from the spirit and soul realms, which are its own. The Frankenstein monster is so much less than human, possessing no immortal soul and spirit. The Self is so much more; it is superhuman, essentially immortal soul and spirit, and ultimately the Son of God.

In the dream I am very worried in case the Self, as the American youth, has no moral sense. In these circumstances it would not be a force for good, and might equal Mephistopheles or Nietzsche's Zarathustra, which could mean catastrophe. The moral sense is of paramount importance. A force for good helps consciousness and the world, bringing light, truth and health. The opposite would be a superpsychopath, a Mephistopheles or a Set, and all would be lost in darkness. This is why I am greatly relieved to find that the youth has a high moral sense, and as the sheriff says, can fight to bring law and order to the unconscious realm. The sheriff apparently remembers the birth of the (divine) child earlier in my processes.

I sit back on a chair, which then swivels backwards, swinging me up in a huge arc. I lose consciousness and when I awake, I am in a higher reality, lying on a bed like an operating table. I seem to be in a spaceship, which is also higher reality, and a Mongoloid looking young woman is at my feet holding a knife. She makes as if to cut off my right foot, but does not, and then I realize that two primitive-looking men are also standing at my side, rather like ancient Egyptians, but with the blood of very archaic primitives in them.

> When they speak, I realize they are actually highly educated superiors, and they are peeved I took them to be inferior. Then I see that I have a large growth coming out of my chest, perhaps signifying a malignant psychic growth. One of the "men" puts a bow (a weapon) over my head as if to show how superior they are, although it may also be a clue to their identity.

Being taken up into a spaceship, to higher reality, has happened to me several times in the unconscious processes. The dream corresponds to what many other people have experienced in outer reality, alien abduction, and so forth. However, dreams involving the collective unconscious are not just fantasies but events in another reality. It is my strong belief that alien abductions, in either inner or outer realities, involve forces of spirit. That is why aliens are seen in so many different shapes and forms; being spirit they have no actual physical forms and so can manifest as anything. Furthermore, many abductees claim that no earthly time passed during the period of the abduction; if they have been "abducted" to the collective unconscious, which is a timeless reality, then no worldly time would have passed.

I know that in my abduction (in another dream) I was taken up through the unconscious to a higher, spirit reality, though I eventually learned how to escape the aliens when they came for me. It was not a religious experience in any way, and this kind of spirit is not holy and numinous, it is just a powerful force. This seems to correspond to the watchers, instructors, builders, architects, and so forth, known to the ancients. These seven, elemental, creative powers often appear in the myths of the ancient world. In Egypt, Ptah, "the grandfather of the gods," was said to have employed them to create both the world and the Underworld. These are really his Seven Souls, or Seven Spirits. We see this idea repeated in the Bible as "Elohim," said there to be singular for "God," is actually plural, "El," for the seven Elohim. The Shebtiu gods of Egypt are the same creators, and Blavatsky says that the "Seven Angels of the Presence" in the Kaballah are similar beings. She points out, however, that these seven elemental powers who create the world and man are not God Himself, and are therefore imperfect.

It seems to me that these powers may be connected with certain UFO sightings in the modern world. Seven lights were seen over New Zealand twenty or so years ago, and those seen more recently over Phoenix, Arizona, were seven in front, with two behind. The Seven Khuti in ancient Egypt meant the "Seven Lights," and the seven Lumazi of Assyria/Babylonia meant the same. Perhaps the modern sightings are these creative forces projecting themselves through to material reality.

Returning to the Elohim, the Western Kabalist, Macgregor Mathers, stated that they were a combination of male and female powers. This could be correct as the seven powers of the higher Self are a combination of masculine spirit and feminine soul, of three and four. Creative forces would have to be a mixture of both, which is why the Holy Spirit has been both male and female historically. Noah, as a higher self figure, has three males and four females with him in the ark. As Egyptian these are celestial powers, and correspond to the higher seven powers of other myths.

I cannot explain what the details of the dream signify, but I would say that as well as being "superior" in some way, the aliens also have their dark, primitive aspect. Everything that exists has its shadow side— even spirit, even God. The aliens are probably pure spirit, but just not the highest form. The bow possibly alludes to Sirius, the "Bow Star" or to the god Shu, the "breath of Ra."

In *Alien Dawn*, Colin Wilson relates a version of the visions of a certain Orfeo Angelucci, which were examined earlier in Jung's book, *Flying Saucers: A Modern Myth of Things Seen in the Skies*, and which Jung took to be genuine. These visions are of some importance as they demonstrate perfectly the symbolic processes that are occurring in the collective unconscious, coming through to many people, often unknowingly so in sleeping or waking states, in other words, coming through in dreams or visions.

Some of Angelucci's experiences are similar to my own, the difference being that his apparently occurred in the waking state, while mine did so in dream processes while I was asleep. Angelucci's visions and my dreams, though products essentially of another reality, are nevertheless real, for the collective unconscious is timeless, eternal, and unchanging, it can therefore more justifiably be regarded as real than our own material world, which is ephemeral and in a constant state of change.

In 1952, Angelucci was driving home one night when he saw two balls of green fire coming out of a red oval object. A voice told him not to be afraid, that he was being contacted by another world, and that he must drink from a crystal cup. Two beings male and female, of supernatural beauty appeared on a huge, luminous screen.

The voice spoke again and told him that man has been watched for centuries, and that each individual is more important to the aliens than they are to one another because man is unaware of the true meaning of his existence (Wilson 1998). It was then explained that these beings were "etheric entities" who only use space ships in order to become manifest to man. All through the experience Angelucci was in a dream-like state, "the dulling of consciousness," as he put it. This was a state of lowered consciousness, although he felt he had transcended mortality, a sure sign of a Higher-Self experience.

In a later vision, Angelucci was told that human beings are human extensions of immortal beings who can only develop spiritually through earthly man (Wilson 1998). According to Colin Wilson, Angelucci next "seemed to see all his previous incarnations and understood the mystery of life. He thought he was about to die." Compare this with a quotation from Blavatsky's *The Secret Doctrine:* "Thus every mortal has his immortal counterpart, or rather his Archetype, in Heaven. This means that the former is indissolubly united to the latter, in each incarnation, and for the duration of the cycles of births." She also says that the human individual is the agent of the Higher Self on Earth.

This has exactly the same basic meaning as the information given to Angelucci by the aliens, that divine beings are working out their salvation through their "mortal shadows," i.e. their agents, through incarnations on Earth. Jung stated that man is part of the immortal Higher Self in, or through, the collective unconscious, and he took reincarnation to be very probable. In fact, Jung quotes Angelucci, who says that all human beings have a "spiritual, unknown self" that is above worldly reality, and which is eternal. This being exists in perfect union with the oversoul, beyond what we know as the time dimension. This seems to be describing man's connection with the Higher Self, first of all, and then the Higher Self as part of God. On the lower level, it would be the Lower Self, the Osiris, in connection with the World Soul (Wilson 1998).

You can find evidence of this immortal figure in the myths of mankind across the world, and in all of the esoteric mysteries. In fact, it can be found wherever and whenever the mind of man has gone deeply within itself to experience inner reality, even if that inner reality expands to apparent infinity and timeless eternity. Usually it is the nervous, sensitive types who make the inner journeys—Moses stammered so badly that his brother Aaron had to speak for him, and Angelucci admitted that he was nervous by nature and felt inadequate.

After traveling on a UFO and seeing others, Angelucci returned to his bed where he found a stigma (a circle with a dot in the center) on the left side of his chest. This would have been the final evidence to convince him that he had been singled out—"chosen"—to receive divine revelation, for he says that his experiences were extremely religious in nature. All of this inspired him to become an evangelist, for he surely had a new gospel to spread, but he was ridiculed in the usual tradition of prophets of new truths, particularly religious ones. This shows once again the enormous powers of influence and transformation that these experiences have, for Angelucci was not religious before his experiences, and was, Jung says, knowledgeable about science to a far higher degree than you would expect from his position and education. We must remember the immense religious transformations of personality brought about in such figures as St. Paul and St. Francis of Assisi, who were not, it seems, overly religious personalities prior to their visions.

Later, Angelucci fell into a sleeping state that lasted a week, and he afterwards recalled that he had been with his otherworldly friends, called now Orion and Lyra, on a planetoid. Angelucci had believed for a time that Lyra wished to have physical sex with him, though when he mentioned this, it horrified the two celestial beings. However, when Angelucci had conquered his physical arousal, mystical union took place between Lyra and himself.

As Colin Wilson says, Jung believed that Angelucci was telling the truth, but that it was all due to dreams and fantasy images; Jung also thought it a somewhat naïve version of the archetypal experience. Jung believed that the "fragmentation, confusion, and perplexity" of our age is causing all of these contents to appear in the psyches of individuals, as he had witnessed in his patients for over forty years.

Although it would be naïve not to question these episodes as literally happening in the outer, physical world, it is not naïve to see the contents themselves as symbolical events of the collective unconscious. I have experienced similar material in my dreams, although my visions were usually in the traditional religious forms. However, some of the material does involve aliens, as in this dream. I learned long ago not to limit these experiences to my own personal unconscious, as contents of dreams at the personal level. They exist outside and beyond it, just as

Angelucci's visions do. If taken out of traditional religious context, Angelucci's "fantasies" are how they would have to appear to us, as UFOs and aliens. That is how modern man interprets all of these phenomena. One difference between Angelucci's alien experiences and my own is that while his seem to have been quite pleasant, mine were not so—though they were not too bad.

Angelucci first sees two balls of green fire coming out of the oval red object. This is the whole dividing into its two opposite sides, male and female, which then appear on the television screen as beings of supernatural beauty. Green is the age-old color of spirit, and in my dream processes, television sets pick up the "spirit signals" from the collective unconscious, just as real television sets pick up signals transmitted by the station. How else could it be better symbolized?

Orion and Lyra appear to be the male and female sides of the Higher Self, and in one vision, Angelucci is informed that mankind has to work for the "etheric entities" on Earth, returning in various incarnations to accomplish the tasks; Orfeo even sees his past incarnations. This is in keeping with thousands of years of Hindu and Buddhist experience, and also with that of many mystics the world over. A large number of normal and well-balanced people in the West have also experienced past lives through regression hypnosis.

The mystical union Angelucci experiences with Lyra is also well known in all religious and esoteric processes that involve the unconscious. I experienced it myself when the "goddess" hovered over me, just as in the depictions of Nut and Seb in ancient Egyptian depictions, and an "orgasmic" union took place. Although sexual in a sense, it was not physically so, rather being union of an emotional-spiritual nature, and apparently with the eternal feminine spirit. Angelucci's was the same sort of experience, it seems. (John Anthony West in *Serpent in the Sky* points out that when Nut leans over the prostrate form of the god Seb in an arc, in the ancient Egyptian painting, Seb's erect phallus points to Nut's navel to show that the union is spiritual, and not physical.)

Jung had no doubts, and neither have I, that Angelucci's experiences were of the Higher Self, and that he had, in that sense, been touched by God. Up to a point, we could say that Angelucci's visions are similar to those of Moses, though, as Jung says, in a more naïve way. Both Jung and Blavatsky see the experience of Moses on Mount Sinai, where he receives the name of God, as being one of the higher androgynous Self.

So a heavenly sphere—or oval here because the two sides are already expanding it—that divides itself into its male and female parts, is certainly a very apt symbol of the Higher Self.

Personally, I like these visions of Angelucci's because there is great meaning to them, and as the entities say of themselves, they are spirit beings and only appear in UFOs in order to manifest themselves to mankind. However, it must be remembered and taken with the utmost seriousness that Angelucci was warned that mankind is presently in a very negative and dangerous state. These concur with grave warnings that I have received myself. But all in all, from the point of view of depth psychology, which knows that the collective unconscious expands out into eternity and does sometimes affect people with strange and paranormal experiences, Angelucci's visions are tenable and valid.

After years of undergoing the unconscious processes myself, I understand why people who have these experiences are driven to become prophets and saviors. It is the old idea of being filled with the Holy Spirit, and some of these people actually have been "scorched" by experiences of spirit, whatever symbolic forms it has taken. They become literally inspired—"in-spirited"—and this is how it has always worked throughout the ages.

When contents of spirit and soul reality wish to come through to mankind, usually at times of disorientation and dissociation, they appear through the collective unconscious and affect certain individuals. Again, these are usually nervous and sensitive types. Many of these individuals will not be suitable "vehicles of the gods"; most will not be listened to in any case and will be ridiculed. Some of them have suffered horrible fates at the hands of blind mankind. But it must be remembered that the world's greatest religions and religious movements were begun by crazy people with "savior complexes," including Judaism, Christianity, Buddhism, and Islam.

When the right personality is found and so affected, mankind really is saved, the connection (the covenant) with the collective unconscious (with God) is maintained, or reestablished and further developed. It is the dissociation from the unconscious, from God ultimately, that causes man to sink into the bog of matter where he may well drown, and this fate sometimes befalls whole civilizations. However, as Jung said, Christ as symbol of the Higher Self and as mediator between the opposite realms of matter and spirit, prevents man from falling into dissociation—if he is accepted. Christ is the symbol of that higher immortal to whom we are all attached and for whom we are agents in matter. This is signified by Orion and Lyra to Angelucci, the male/female sides of the Higher Self.

In a disoriented age like our own the collective unconscious will be violently activated in the attempt to restore vision and balance. We can expect a spouting of individuals who have visions and paranormal experiences, which drive some of them to be prophets. Only, almost all will be inferior to the true task.

Both Colin Wilson and Jung see the leap forward for mankind as imminent. While Wilson thinks it will occur naturally, because man is ready for it, Jung and myself see it as a dire necessity that may yet not occur. It is up to man himself. The opportunity is there for us if only we can take it. History shows that cultures large and small eventually collapse when they become too dissociated from the primal foundations in the unconscious, and we today are dissociated as no other culture before us has been. If we are to transform ourselves, it must involve acceptance of the religious-mythological nature of the reality to which we belong, of the "other world" and our connection to it, and of the Higher Self as the immortal power of which we are part. Furthermore, just as Orfeo Angelucci saw all of his past incarnations, we must realize that we too have ours. That is why Orion and Lyra, when first encountered by Angelucci, seemed strangely familiar to him. As representatives of the Higher Self, they are eternally connected to him.

Jung says that the stigma that appeared on Angelucci's chest was the symbol of the Self and that he had been marked by God. Angelucci experienced something immortal of which he was the mortal part. That fits with Jung's discoveries concerning the Higher Self, and with all the religious, mythological, mystical, and esoteric experience of mankind. "Every mortal has his immortal counterpart in Heaven," as Blavatsky puts it. Once we can understand that, we are on the way to bringing about a transformation within ourselves.

> I am in a sort of studio where I pick up a round vessel about a foot in diameter. It has some clear, steaming liquid in it. This clears to reveal a painting of an old man and a young woman holding hands, wearing clothes that seem to belong to the ancient world. The old man is a prophet-philosopher, and at the bottom of the page is written his name: "Elijah."

The round vessel is similar to the hermetic *vas* of the alchemists, or even to the Holy Grail, and the "wise old man" with his young female companion is a well-known symbol for the unification of what we could call "spirit/meaning" and "soul/life," or "the personification of spirit" and "the personification of soul." But why is the old man Elijah? We saw similar figures in an earlier dream at a marriage on an island in higher reality, but that was supposedly a pagan one; now the Bible is implicated, and no less a figure than Elijah who ascended to Heaven. The first "wise old man" figure that appeared to Jung was called Elijah (with Salome as the anima), then later it was Philemon, another Biblical and mythological figure.

The round vessel represents the feminine earth, or soul, as a containing vessel, while the special liquid means masculine spirit. The two are unified here, as are the old Elijah and young woman. The higher Christian version of the vessel and the spirit liquid would be Mary containing Christ. It is probable that the vessel is more than a symbol of the feminine earth, representing, as the mandala does, the Higher Self, for it contains both spirit and soul contents. Also, Jung tells us that Elijah is not merely the mortal man, but also the Higher Self. However, the reason why the unconscious chooses Elijah specifically in the dream must remain a mystery, unless, as I suggest, he is connected with Jung's "wise old man" figure.

> The day before this dream I saw a television program about how the map of Europe has changed over the centuries. This was well illustrated with diagrams. Now, in the dream, I am with a youth who has been studying religions, the occult, alchemy, and so forth. He has not grasped the significance of them, so I try to advise him. "Look, I've been studying these things for years," I say, "so I can tell you it is no use looking for worldly gold. You have to have a real love for these things you have been studying." He then mentions reincarnation, so I continue, "Living people come and go, like the changing map of Europe. All that change takes place on dry land. But the other world is like the bottom of the ocean; it is unchanging."

Although I speak these words, it is the unconscious that puts them into my mouth. It is saying that the world changes, and different people come and go, living out their short lives in the flesh. But the world of spirit and of soul, from whence we come and to where we apparently return, is like the bottom of the sea, unchanging and eternal. The unconscious is alluding to ourselves more than to the mere change in our physical environment, although the world and its cultures change largely because of man. This dream shows how the unconscious is aware of all the things we see in our daily lives, and which it then sometimes uses to illustrate its messages to us.

All I remember of this dream is that I see a burning bush.

This was the first of God's theophanies to Moses—appearances to a human being, signs of God coming forth—and as my own processes and visions demonstrate, the meaning is similar for me. The burning bush is the sign of God's actual presence, His coming forth.

Gerald Massey gives some very interesting information of how the burning bush was known in ancient Egypt. In the vision of Moses (Exodus 3:2-6), the Bible reports:

> And the angel of the lord appeared unto him in a flame of fire out of the midst of a bush: and he looked, and, behold, the bush was burning, yet it was not consumed. And Moses said, I will now turn aside, and see this great sight, why the bush is not burnt. And when the Lord saw that he turned aside to see, God called unto him out of the midst of the bush, and said, Moses, Moses. And he said, Here am I. And he said, Draw not nigh hither: put off thy shoes off thy feet, for the place whereon thou standest is holy ground. Moreover he said, I am the God of thy Father, the God of Abraham, the God of Isaac, and the God of Jacob. And Moses hid his face, for he was afraid to look upon God.

That is what the Bible says. But Massey (1907) states:

> Now, this "burning bush" is to be seen full blaze in pictures to the [Egyptian] *Ritual*. There is a vignette to chapter 64 in which the burning bush is saluted. In the texts the golden unbu is a symbol of the solar god. It is a figure of the radiating disc which is depicted raying all aflame at the summit of a

sycamore-fig tree which thus appears to burn with fire, and the tree is not consumed. It images the lord of the resurrection going forth to give light. . . . This was the burning bush in which the Sun-god manifested as Tum, whose other name is Iu or Unbu, the burning bush being the solar unbu.

There are two corollaries following this identification: the one is that the god of the burning bush is the same as the god of the flaming thorn bush named the "Unbu," and the god being the same, the person addressed by the god is the same in both versions, and the lion-god who is Shu-Anhur in the *Ritual* is the prototype of Moses in the book of Exodus. Further, in the manifestation of the burning bush *duality of person is implied*. First it is "an angel of the Lord" that appears "in a flame of fire out of the midst of a bush." Then the Lord or Elohim speaks in person and calls on Moses by name. These two correspond to the divine duality of Ra and Unbu in the original representation, when Unbu (Horus or Iu) as the ever-coming son of the eternal father (Huhi), is the manifestor for Ra in the flowering thorn. The burning bush, then, is identical with the "golden Unbu" in the Book of the Dead. . . .

Massey thus posits the Hebrew and Egyptian versions of the "burning bush" as being the same. However, they may be independent experiences of the same archetype. The burning bush is a constellated symbol involving God's presence in the collective unconscious, so it could appear to both Moses and an Egyptian adept independently, just as it has appeared in my dream. What is most important, however, is that Massey states that the manifestation in the burning bush is a dual representation in the Biblical and Egyptian versions of God and the divine Son. This is of both the Higher Self as Son of God and of God Himself in both versions. This is the archetypal pattern for many of these divine manifestations: the prophet Daniel sees the Son of Man together with the Ancient of Days; St. Stephen sees Christ on the right-hand side of God.

A religious ceremony is taking place at a very bright and colorful Catholic church and a number of priests are present, all wearing brightly colored robes. The dominant color of the whole scene is gold, and there

199

is a lot of it all over. This could be taking place above in higher reality as well as below, on Earth. Christ is present himself, and although I do not see his face, I manage to touch the bottom of the purple robe he is wearing. This greatly uplifts me—a shot in the arm, so to speak.

Suddenly, the place becomes flooded with a couple of feet of water, and this has excrement in it. Then a naked girl is there and we start to make love. As she reaches orgasm she cries out, "Jesus Christ," but this angers me, so that I snap, "Don't use his name like that." I feel that it is blasphemy, and as this latter part occurs, and as the girl and I have sex, we are lying in water and excrement.

The first part of the dream is a marvelous vision of holiness, dominated by the gold, the symbolic metal of the gods, and it culminates in my touching Christ's purple robe, the "Robe of Glory." But then the filth comes pouring in from the dark, lower, instinctual depths, the realm of the serpent dragon; the girl as anima pulls me down from the holiness to the filth, sexuality being usually the strongest weapon that the serpent-dragon uses against spirit and holiness.

It is not that sexuality is wrong in itself, but it is out of place with the extreme holiness of this higher spiritual level. It is a well-known fact in the esoteric mysteries and secret wisdom religions around the world that sexual abstinence is a must to attain higher spirituality. This is why any idea that the man Jesus had a sex life with Mary Magdalene (who represents the feminine unconscious) or with anyone else, is entirely mistaken, although higher union between male spirit and female soul must occur.

As to Christ in the dream, this is apparently the Higher Self as a Christ equivalent, and the church with its gold and holiness represents his realm.

I have to fight off a black dog, which may savage me a little. Then I am indoors, full of fear, because I know that the Devil himself is close by outside. The black dog is the Devil, or Antichrist, in its first form.

In a recent dream I saw the burning bush as a sign of God's presence, and in the last dream the Higher Self appeared as a Christ parallel. As we know, both sides of the collective unconscious, must be experienced for wholeness, so I am now required to suffer the Devil's appearance. The black dog signifies the dark side of the Self, the Devil's parallel. Perhaps the sex with the girl in the water and filth brought forth the evil side, but the question then would be: Was this due to my weakness, to something negative I had done in real life, or are the higher forces behind the scenes responsible for it?

In other words, am I required to experience the dark side for wholeness, which would mean that it is not just something brought on by my negative actions? In truth, it is impossible to say now, but experience of the negative side always brings fear and dread. This is what the alchemists meant by the increase of heat in the retort to the highest intensity. It was not merely a physical action to them, but a state of psychological suffering.

In *Alien Dawn*, Colin Wilson tells a story in which I recognize classic material of the collective unconscious. It concerns a black dog and what appeared to be poltergeist activity at a farm near Quebec in 1899. Windows were smashed, water was poured over the floor, fires were started, stones were thrown. Then a spirit appeared in the woodshed. When asked, "Who are you?" it replied, "I am the Devil. I'll have you in my clutches. Get out or I'll break your neck."

Later, three children reported seeing the spirit, at separate times, as a "tall man with a cow's head, a cloven hoof [sic], and horns; as a big, black dog; and as an angel in white robes, wearing a starry crown." The spirit appeared again as a beautiful man in the white robes, and to prove he was an angel, floated up into the sky engulfed in a sort of fire. One child said, "He was all red." Wilson comments: "If the same spirit had appeared a century later, it would undoubtedly have claimed to be the inhabitants of a UFO, and the children would probably have seen it climb aboard one as it departed into the blue. As it is, its departure recalls Elijah and his chariot of fire."

A UFO and a chariot of fire may both be symbols of the Higher Self in a specific aspect, and the latter is especially a sign of God's authority to his prophet, for anyone who sees it has become chosen. The prophets of old really would have experienced this symbol (in dreams or as outer visions), for when consciousness is lowered somewhat, the collective unconscious can then break through. Many people in the modern world feel religious intensity when experiencing UFO phenomena, though this may be projected onto the objects which need not be of a religious nature in themselves. As Jung says, circular symbols, mandalas, have been known throughout history, and fiery chariots make perfect mandalas of wholeness, as they are four wheels on a four-sided frame, marking the unification of the circle and the square, or matter and spirit (the fieriness denotes spirit). It is also true that the overwhelming majority of UFO sightings are of circular shapes, or circular lights when seen at night.

But to return to the tale of the weird figures seen at the farm. We can see symbols of alchemy, mythology, Gnosticism, and folklore in them, although it all begins with poltergeist activity and the appearance of the unfriendly spirit who claims to be the Devil. Many years ago, in *The Idea of the Holy,* Rudolf Otto stated that certain religious experiences seem to drag up ghostly activity with them, particularly ghosts of the past, swirling spirits, and so forth, and I can verify this by my own experiences.

On one occasion, I awoke very suddenly—snapped awake—and the room was aswirl with spirit activity. I could *see* it. But quick as a flash it all vanished and the room was still. It could be claimed that it was merely the dream lingering on and that I was projecting the activity from the unconscious into the room. That would have been valid, as the collective unconscious is just as real as the outer world, and projection of its contents is a known fact. But that was not the case on this occasion.

The spirits existed *behind* the facade of outer reality, and for a brief instant I saw through to it. We can also approach this other world through the unconscious, once we go beyond the personal level. The personal unconscious is the doorway to what appears to be an infinity and eternity of spirit, which in ancient Egypt concerned the hidden doorway to Amenta, the Underworld of the unconscious depths.

The poltergeist activity at the farm seems to have been of the same nature as the swirling spirits I saw, and the ghostly form that claimed "I am the Devil" may have been a representation of the dark side of the Higher Self, particularly since a black dog was also seen, a definite symbol of the dark Self. There would have been no doubt had the figure with the cloven hooves and horns had a goat's head instead of a cow's. Even so, it is still a sinister representation.

Blavatsky makes a relevant observation in *The Secret Doctrine.* She says:

Oannes, or Dogon, the Chaldean "Man-fish," divides his Cosmogony and Genesis into two portions. First the abyss of waters and darkness, wherein resided most hideous beings—men with wings, four and two winged men, human beings with two heads, with the legs and horns of a goat—our goat men—hippocentaurs, bulls with heads of men, and dogs with tails of fishes. In short, combinations of various animals and men, of fishes, reptiles, and other monstrous animals, assuming each other's shapes and countenances. The feminine element they resided in is personified by Thalatth—the Sea, or "Water"—which was finally conquered by Belus, the male principle.

She is describing perfectly the lower depths of the collective unconscious, the feminine sea and the combinations of shapes that some of its contents take when consciousness—in this case Belus—experiences them. The hero, consciousness, goes down to experience and conquer the collective unconscious. But these forms often appear in our dreams, and sometimes even as outer visions. That is what was happening at the farm in Wilson's account. The soul depths of the unconscious had been activated and were rising up to conscious experience, and the strange forms were parts of the Self, the World Soul side.

A black dog was also experienced at the farm, and Colin Wilson points out that a black dog is associated with spirits in folklore. In mythology, a dog is often the companion of the hero or god on the way to the Underworld, i.e., the unconscious. Both the god and the dog represent the Higher Self in different aspects, the dog in lower and first form. As I said above, the hero is the human part (ego-consciousness) of the Higher Self in matter, and its agent. Thus Quetzalcoatl is accompanied by the dog-headed Xolotl in the Central American myth, and in Egypt, Apuat and Anup (Anubis), both dog-jackals and "Openers of the Way" accompany Osiris on his journey through the unconscious. In the Greek myth, Orion has his pet dog, which is transformed into Sirius, the Dog Star.

Graham Hancock, in *Fingerprints of the Gods*, again hypothesizes whether the myth-makers of long ago, in order to point the way to future initiates, did not construct their myths of dogs, jackals, and so forth, accordingly.

But the answer is not to be found in lost scientific knowledge. It lies in the processes of the collective unconscious, the "other reality" which lies behind the physical universe. The knowledge is not "scientific," but mythological, and ultimately religious. Only last week, after seeing a shooting star in a dream, which heralds the approach of the Higher Self from the spirit side, my own dog, long dead, then immediately appeared in a follow-up dream. He represents the spirit side of the Self, but at a lower level, and has appeared in my dreams as such for many years.

I have also seen a black dog on occasions, and this always causes fear as it portends that the dark, evil Self must also be near. In one dream, I saw the dark Self as the Antichrist, and have never been so petrified in my whole life. Yet I loved it. If there is an Antichrist who is so real, it means there is also a Christ; if there is the Devil, then there is also God. I can live happily in such a reality. What I cannot do is live in a reduced, stifling reality of matter-worship and scientific rationalism.

As I have mentioned previously, we find a fairly modern example of the dark Self in Goethe's *Faust*, where Mephistopheles first appears as a black poodle. When Mephistopheles does subsequently appear, Faust exclaims, "So that's what was in the poodle!" Thus a dog (white for good or black for evil) represents the first appearance of the Higher Self. So in the visions at the farm, the black dog, the cloven-hoofed, cow-headed, horned figure, and the malicious spirit, all represent the dark side of the Self. The Self, we should remember, is the totality of all unified opposites, high and low, animal and spiritual, and can and does appear in any number of the forms, or as a conglomeration of them.

Afterwards at the farm, the angelic figure in white robes and starry crown appeared, which represented, of course, the light side of the Higher Self, and in highly developed form. This is certainly a version of the Gnostic/alchemical Anthropos, the Christ parallel and Higher Self. A similar figure appears in a medieval alchemical text, the *Aurelia Occulta,* wearing a robe of white linen with flowers on it, a crown of stars on his head. Jung says that it is a parallel Christ figure, a "second Adam"; it corresponds to certain of my own experiences of the Self as a white-robed figure.

The individuation process that produces all these figures is not necessarily a conscious process, and Jung states that it often occurs in a person, or in a group of people, unconsciously. They will then have strange dreams, mood swings from one extreme to the other, strange feelings of uncanniness and disorientation, and irrational ones of fear and joy. Sometimes one or more other people may have visions caused by the phenomenon, and they too will be unconscious victims. The spread of effects through the unconscious is very common, especially in family groups.

We all sit on the same unconscious foundations, and not only small groups of people, but whole nations may be affected by the same phenomena occurring beneath the surface of life. Mass movements of both positive and negative types may spread like wildfire across a country or a continent due to unconscious possession.

One or more persons at the farm were presumably undergoing unconscious individuation processes, of which the visions were products. It is such classic material from unconscious processes that there can be no doubt as to its nature and origin. Not that the collective unconscious is limited to the Higher Self. It is an eternal, timeless, and other reality, which is mostly beyond our experience even though some of it filters through to us. Although the unconscious is mostly beyond us, Jung says we can nevertheless know God, and directly. By "directly" I mean that it is not just a matter of belief and conscious thinking, but of direct experience through the unconscious.

> As I lie in my bed I rattle with pain, but I know that this is necessary to bring about an effect. Then I am in the main street of our town, and although it is already bright daylight, I nevertheless see the sun rise up from behind the horizon, and I know that this means Jesus Christ is rising. Then I see a man I know who is suffering from schizophrenia, and I ask if it is possible to help him.

In ancient Egypt, Ra was the sun-god, but Horus was his son, known as the Rising Sun. Jung says that the early Christians symbolized Christ in the same way. Aten, god to Akhenaten, had been prefigured by Ra as the rising sun a thousand to two thousand years earlier than Akhenaten, suggesting the new-born, divine Son. Then much later, at the beginning of the Christian era, Eusabius witnessed Christian sun-worship, and St. Augustine felt compelled to argue, because of this, that God was not the sun, but the power that made the sun. I say in the dream that I know the rising sun is Jesus Christ, but is it the original Christ, or the Higher Self as his parallel?

If we mere mortals survive death, as seems certain, then Jesus the man, who brought forth and merged with the Christ, the divine Self, would now be One with Christ as an eternal part of God, although separate from him also, in a sense. It would therefore be possible for the original Christ himself to now appear to mortals in the form of Jesus.

I had this problem earlier in a number of dreams, being unable to decide which is meant, but here I would say that it must allude to the Christ parallel. Christ symbolizes the Higher Self, and the rising sun symbolizes both. As to the final point of the dream, where I ask if the man suffering from schizophrenia can be helped, the next dream comes in answer.

> I see two figures in the street merge and become one. Then the man who was mentally ill in the previous dream asks me to help him with his illness. I tell him that all split and divided things become united and healed in Jesus Christ.

Every psyche consists of conflicting opposite parts vying for supremacy. The Self is the unification of all these parts under a "psychic dominant," that is, a factor that dominates the organization of the psyche. In the West, the symbol of this dominant is Christ, while in the East it may be Purusha, Krishna, the Atman, or the Buddha. The Self is not just the dominant; it is the totality of all the parts, including the dominant, under the dominant. Anyone who undergoes the journey through the unconscious may, with the help of the Self, bring all of these parts together under that dominant, but it is a Herculean task, as these processes may show.

However, for man in general, it is enough to accept the symbol, as long as the belief is genuine and the religion followed conscientiously. The great problem now in the modern West is that the method of belief needs updating. We can no longer believe naïvely in the old way. We would not take the symbolic contents in any other mythology or religion to be literally true either. But I am trying to show in this book that Christianity, as well as other mythologies and religions, are based on *facts* of the unconscious, and that this is therefore the new way to believe and know. If the mentally ill man in this dream can genuinely take Christ and all that he represents as his dominant and center, and be ready to sacrifice everything, even life, in that cause, then healing can take place. The savior figure brings order to the psyche of individuals and to society, but when the savior figure is lost, not only individuals, but whole civilizations fall into chaos.

A deadly black mamba snake has bitten me on the foot, but has it gone through the thick leather of my shoe?

The black mamba is the deadliest of snakes and so symbolizes the serpent power of the unconscious at its very worst. In the dream the deadly snake bites me, but has it penetrated? As usual with dream processes, I shall have to wait and see. The serpent represents the darkest side of the Self of course, the opposite of the rising Sun, the Christ parallel of the previous dream. This is the law of the unconscious: if you experience one side of a content, then you must experience the opposite side for wholeness. It is seemingly the rule in my processes that when I experience the Higher Self, usually as Christ, in a following dream I am menaced by the serpent.

I look up at the night sky and see a round white star move slowly across the heavens from right to left. This seems to last for minutes. I realize that it is a very meaningful and important omen.

The star is a well known symbol the world over and goes back to primitive times to herald the birth of a god or special being, and his advent in worldly reality. Not only would early man witness such events in the outer heavens as real, he would also experience them as contents and omens in his dreams and visions, as I did in my latest dream.

The unconscious chooses signs and symbols that best fit the situation, and a shooting star portending the arrival of a special being is appropriate. Jung (1959a) says: "Always the hope of a Messiah is connected with the birth of a star," and he quotes Numbers 24:7: "A star shall come forth out of Jacob."

We find similar symbolism in certain world myths. For example, a Wichita Indian legend tells of a savior who was a star from the south, and as the "flint man," he brought salvation to the Earth. What real difference is there between this and Christ—Star of Bethlehem, Star from the East—bringing salvation to mankind?

In Egypt, Pharaoh, as a god, was a star; and in India, Vishnu has his six-pointed star, as two merged triangles signifying the unification of upper and lower trinities (Vishnu is the Second Person of the Hindu Trinity just as Christ is in the Western one). At the birth of the Persian Zarathustra, a star hovered over his village for three days and nights, illuminating it magically. Both Horus and Christ are connected with the Morning Star. In Assyria the divine son, Assur, and the goddess Ishtar were eight-rayed stars; Christ was the eight-rayed star for the Gnostics because he was manifestor of the seven stars, which culminated in him as the eighth. In Revelation, the sign of the birth of the son of the Sun Woman will be a star, which repeats the "Star of the Pleroma" of the Gnostics.

> A hero is looking for a magical stone. A fish appears in a river, but then a crocodile swallows it. The hero must fight the crocodile to free the fish.

Here again is the archetypal myth of the hero's quest for the Higher Self, of the great danger from the dark, chthonic, serpent or dragon, and of the great fight with the dragon that results. In the dream, this was now happening with myself. The crocodile was the dragon, Sevekh, in Egypt. The fish, as we know, is a symbol of the Higher Self as savior, and so too is the magic stone; ultimately, it is alchemical as the lapis, "rock," and Philosopher's Stone, "the stone that hath a spirit," according to Ostanes. One alchemical text, *Aurora Consurgens*, tells of Moses' rod smiting a rock three times "so that the waters flow forth freely," and it notes it is a "sacred rock" and has four parts. For the alchemists, the rock is obviously comparable to the circle that is quartered or squared, as my four gold keys on the key ring are.

The alchemists began with the goal of transmuting base metals into gold, but finished up with their magical stone which they were forced to posit as a parallel to Christ. This is what the processes of the unconscious led them to, and this is why Jung said they took the place of Jesus in the work. 1 Corinthians 10:4 says, "For they drank from that spiritual rock that did follow them; and that Rock was Christ." Further, the first Epistle of Peter (2:4-8) states of Christ and his priests: "To whom coming, as unto a living stone . . . chosen of God, and precious . . . Ye also, as lively stones, are built up a spiritual house . . . / Behold, I lay in Zion a chief corner stone, elect, precious . . . / the stone which the builders disallowed, / the same is made head of the corner / . . . (but to the disobedient) a stone of stumbling, / and a rock of offense."

As the alchemists said, their stone was "good with the good, and evil with the evil," which means that we develop the Self according to our conscious aims and values. But the magical stone is very ancient, pre-dating both alchemy and Christ; in ancient Palestine, for example, there was the messianic stone centuries before the advent of Christ himself. In Mexican myth, Quetzalcoatl was conceived when his mother swallowed a green stone.

Very early in Egypt, the White Stone lay on top of the sacred Mound, as did the White House and White Throne, and when he entered the religious mysteries of Amenta, the initiate was given a white stone, or "pillar of crystal." Similarly, Revelation (2:17) states of the triumphant initiate, "I will give him a white stone, and in the stone a new name written, which no one knoweth saving he that receiveth it." This is apparently derived from not only the Egyptian mysteries as outer teachings, but from the symbolism revealed by the unconscious processes themselves.

The fish, though coming from the Waters, is nevertheless ultimately celestial. As the crocodile swallows the fish in the dream, the hero must slay the dragon to "save" the savior (fish), as it were. In fact, in one Egyptian text, Horus rides a creature that is called both fish and crocodile, and he is also depicted standing on a crocodile while holding a fish above his head.

For the alchemists, Jung says, the parallel of the stone to Christ helped to reveal the meaning of the latter and in the same way, the fish had the deepest symbolic meaning for the ancient world (1959a). St. Augustine comments: "For the fish is drawn from the deep in order to nourish the needy ones of the earth" (1943).

> I am in a large hall of a medieval building in France or Italy, proba-bly a castle, and the people who are there wear clothes from the period. The building is perhaps a church or chapel within the castle, as I am standing on some steps by an altar. A sort of feast could be taking place, and a very dark, evil looking woman approaches, carrying a platter on which there are two small knives, apparently for a castration ceremony. This disturbs me as I could be the intended victim.
>
> Suddenly, a white dove falls behind one of the ornaments on the altar, a chalice or a cross, and someone says that the dove is wounded. The people then pair off and leave, and I notice one man in particular, who has a trimmed beard and looks like the portrait of King Francis I of France. Like the others, he goes off with a woman. The dream had a very intense and heavy religious atmosphere, which was quite unpleasant.

The evil-looking woman appears in the next dream, where she is plainly part serpent. In alchemy, and particularly with Paracelsus, we find the melusine, a type of mermaid, half woman, half fish or some other creature. The melusine is a personification of the depths of the unconscious. Here she is in evil aspect, as she serves and is part of the dark, evil side of the feminine unconscious, symbolized by reptiles. It is she, apparently, who is to carry out the castration, but this could perhaps be intended for the white dove, which symbolizes the Holy Spirit. It falls injured behind one of the ornaments, the chalice or cross, both of them very meaningful and powerful symbols themselves. The chalice reminds us also of the Holy Grail, and we find the two knives on a platter in the Grail story of Wolfram von Eschenbach's *Parzifal,* though no one apparently knows what this signifies.

The knives perhaps take the place of the lance, which wound not Christ, but the dove, symbol of the Holy Spirit. The dove in Wolfram's romance brings the Host to the stone altar, and the unconscious seems to be using the symbolism again here, though I did not know any of this at the time of the dream, not having studied the Grail stories at that time. Wolfram's *Parzifal* is a German tale, while I seem to think the castle is in France, but I could be mistaken. In any case, medieval Christendom seems very much the same to us now. Alchemically the dove equals the Queen of Sheba, who is "pure, chaste, and wise." The reptile woman could be the dark counterpart of this. However, the dove may be in its masculine aspect here, representing the third person of the Holy Trinity.

Castration in the unconscious is actually of two types. One involves consciousness losing potency, in which the individual would feel ill, weak, and at the mercy of the unconscious. The other type is voluntary, in which physical sexuality is sacrificed for a higher spiritual purpose. The more virile a person is, of course, the harder it will be to make the sacrifice, and sexual temptation would be greatly increased correspondingly. So it takes great strength of purpose and personality to voluntarily choose celibacy, but if successful, it means the defeat of lower instinctual power, the serpent-dragon, rather than being defeated by it. So only in one sense can this be called "castration," and the adept gains greatly in a spiritual way.

> I am with Saracen soldiers and we capture a castle from enemy
> forces. In one of the rooms I find a dark-haired, evil woman who has

been in charge of the castle until our liberation of it. She confronts me, saying, "You can't kill me because she (the queen of the castle) hasn't given you a sharp weapon to do it with." However, I am then joined by the queen who helps me to suspend the evil woman upside down from the balcony, with her legs apart. This reveals her womb, which is green and that of a reptile. Then the queen lifts her own leg and puts the stiletto heel of her shoe into the womb. Then all I will need to do is to press hard on the queen's foot to stab and kill the evil one with the stiletto heel. In this way the queen has given me a sharp weapon, but I have no wish to kill the evil woman because it seems too brutal. Now, there is much treasure in the castle, though I am not at all interested in it because it is only worldly gold.

The castle is a well-known symbol of the Higher Self, and the dark, evil woman, who had the knives for castration in the previous dream, seems to be the dark counterpart to the queen, the feminine part of the Self. The evil one has a reptilian womb, which shows that she belongs to the serpent-dragon and is either its agent, or the dragon itself. In any case, she has long been known in processes of the unconscious. She has been occupying the castle, which means that she has control of the Self; this is probably why she had the power to wound the white dove. Now the tables are turned and it is she who will lose her power, and by death possibly, according to my wish. As to the worldly treasure in the castle, the gold which I seek is of a higher and more lasting kind. As a medieval alchemist put it, "Our gold is not the common gold."

My dog, and my one-time she-cat, both of which died many years ago, fight ferociously.

These two pets often appear in my dreams as representations of the masculine spirit and the feminine soul parts of the unconscious, which must be brought to unification in the processes. Obviously, at the moment they are in the opposite state to this, which means that I must persevere even harder in my task to unite the opposites.

I explained earlier that in Egypt, the dog-jackal Anubis, or Anpu, was guide and weigher of hearts (souls) in the Underworld (the unconscious depths) but he was also identified and merged with Horus at times, merged with the light aspect of the Higher Self. However, Anubis was also identified in his dark aspect with the evil Set, the dark side of the Higher Self. Therefore, Anubis was both revered and greatly feared by the Egyptians. This corresponds to my own dream processes, in which the sight of my dog causes much joy, while the sight of his counterpart, the black dog, causes much fear. The dogs represent, as said, the light and dark aspects of the Higher Self,

On the other hand, my old she-cat represents the collective feminine soul in personal aspect, and the goddess who personified this in Egypt was Bast, an aspect of the Great Mother goddess Mut, and in another aspect, the soul of Isis. Bast was a goddess of the moon, and in later times was occasionally a lioness, but from very early times she was the cat. Merged with other goddesses she was sometimes the mother of the divine Son, such as Horus or Khonsu. My cat represents the light, positive side of the feminine soul. I have, however, experienced many negative, savage, and licentious cats in dreams, cats which try to draw and lure my cat away to their own degeneracy. A later dream will show that my dog and cat do finally unify as one and have four sons (a 3 + 1 formation) comprising the basis of the fourfold structure of the Higher Self.

> In the dream I lie in my bed dreaming, and a voice from above says, "You are Christ." Then a hand with extended finger points down from the clouds, and the voice continues. "It is you." I find this very worrying, but then, still in the dream, I wake up to see two tiny deer, only about four inches long, with lovely little faces smiling at me at about the level of my face. Then I see a cow of about the same size, and it too smiles at me. I pick this up and give it a drink of milk that is in a trough, but I dip the cow too deeply and its head is partly covered with milk. The little cow becomes a hen and in admonition it nips me on the finger with its beak. The cow/hen then becomes a little old lady sitting in a rocking chair, smoking a pipe, a sort of Granny from *The Beverly Hillbillies* television show. She tells me something, which I have forgotten, but I then put all of the little figures, including Granny, behind the head of my bed, for that will now be their little home.

I suppose most psychiatrists would go to town on this dream, convinced that I am crazy, or at least suffering from a savior complex. However, the contents are quite acceptable in terms of the individuation processes. Jung said that the alchemists took the place of Christ in their work, though he should have said the man Jesus, for any human individual who becomes involved in the processes may bring forth the Redeemer figure in a successful quest at highest level. So it would not be me who was Christ, or his equivalent, but the Higher Self to whom I, as mere mortal, am attached. Go to India and they will tell you that this is quite possible, and, in fact, they have been teaching the same phenomenon for thousands of years. In Western terms, however, it adds up to the continuance of Christ.

Christ was of the seed of King David, was Son of David, but not in the worldly sense, as it is usually taken to be. The real bloodline was through the unconscious. David himself was of the same line, carrying on the same line of spiritual blue blood—the Higher Self phenomenon—that began in Egypt. Later, alchemy and the Grail quests dipped into this river and went some way with the processes. Certain people today will be involved in this royal bloodline, as I am myself, or will become so, for the West is in dire need of respiritualization. We will all continue Christ to some degree, depending how far each initiate goes with the processes.

The little creatures including old Granny that then appear are corresponding contents from the lower, soul side of the unconscious, in feminine and positive form. It is a pity I could not remember what she said to me because it would have revealed more of her meaning. They now have a home behind my bed, which presumably means as part of the structure of the Higher Self. I have seen little twin creatures in many forms, twins of the Self at lower level. The cow was mother of the divine son in ancient Egypt, and the hen lays the egg out of which hatches the Anthropos. The cow and hen are thus symbols of the Great Mother, who then appears as Granny.

It is a bright, sunny day as I somehow focus on a crucifixion scene. I seem to see the unfortunate victim from the waist up. He is black-haired, clean-shaven, like the film figure Conan the Barbarian. He has a white bird perched on his head; maybe it is a large dove. It pecks at the bleeding wounds in his face and eyes, and may do this every day so that the victim is a sort of Prometheus.

The scene then changes to a lovely garden and I see a vision of a holy lady—a goddess—dressed in robes of gold and white, similar in style to those of the Middle Ages. Though the vision lasts only a few seconds and I do not see her face clearly, it seems that the goddess smiles tenderly. Then a voice says, "This is very important." Last of all, I see a sign which says "The End."

The first part of the dream is similar to the myth of Prometheus, who was condemned to be chained to a rock, and every morning an eagle would tear out his liver afresh. It is also similar to the crucifixion of Christ, and to the hanging on a tree, and impalement motifs that we find in other myths. It may signify the Higher Self caught between the opposites, as it must be when brought forth to the world (in the unconscious), for then it, and God, suddenly come to know what it is to be merely human and to suffer the fears and dangers of the mortal life. The Self is also "quartered," so to speak, pulled from four directions.

The vision of the holy lady in the lovely garden counterbalances the crucifixion scene. She is doubtless the eternal feminine spirit in highest aspect, the immortal counterpart to the masculine Higher Self, brought forth by the sufferings of the figure on the cross. The white and gold of her robes state that she is indeed divine. The suffering of her male "twin" causes the goddess (the feminine World Soul) to respond in her highest, most loving and compassionate form.

There is a story in the Old Testament where Joseph is in prison in Egypt and meets two fellow prisoners who were formerly butler and baker to Pharaoh. Both have had dreams which Joseph now interprets. The butler had dreamt of a vine with three branches upon which grew clusters of grapes, and the butler squeezed the grapes into a cup and gave it to Pharaoh to drink. Joseph then gives the interpretation of this dream, which is that the butler will be restored to his position within three days.

The baker then relates his dream, in which he had three white baskets of bakemeats (pastries) on his head, but the birds ate the bakemeats from out of the baskets. Joseph then gives the interpretation that within three days Pharaoh will have the baker hanged on a tree, and the birds will eat the flesh off him.

So here is reference similar to the one in my dream of being hanged on a tree and to birds eating the flesh. However, in the Joseph story, other deep symbolism is involved. The three branches with the grapes and the three baskets with the bakemeats seem to symbolize higher and lower trinities, since the first refers to wine, and therefore spirit, while the second refers to bread and therefore matter. The first has a good outcome, but the second has a bad one. Basically, it a story of bread, wine, and crucifixion.

Abraham is met by Melchizedek, the King of Salem (King of Peace) who offers him bread and wine, while Bera, the King of Sodom (the opposite of Salem: while Salem is "peace," Sodom is "chaos") offers worldly things, which Abraham refuses. In other words, the one offers the light side of the Higher Self, while the other offers the dark side and chaos. The same meaning is there in the dreams of Pharaoh's butler and baker. Nevertheless, the significant part of the story as regards my dream is the crucifixion on a tree with the birds pecking at the flesh. The symbolism must be very ancient, and concerns the Higher Self—such that a version apparently with the same meaning is reproduced again in my dream by the unconscious.

The Nordic/Germanic god Odin was hanged on a tree, as was Marsysus, while Mithras was hung in effigy. As mentioned earlier, the Aztecs would nail a boy or girl to a tree and shoot arrows at them in ritual. Yet Christ himself was not apparently depicted crucified on the cross until some centuries after the actual event; usually the lamb itself was portrayed on the cross, or even some other god, such as Horus, to represent Christ. You can see this with the carvings in the catacombs in Rome. Jung states that as the cross is a quaternity, the four parts of a divided totality, it is the symbol of the Self *par excellence*. But crucifixion itself has many meanings, some of them obscure even for the most experienced initiates, so it remains mostly a mystery. However, its main significance for us is perhaps that it symbolizes corresponding psychic events in our own inner depths (Jung 1958).

> It is night as I secretly watch a religious rite from a small cliff above as it takes place below. This is in ancient Egypt, perhaps at its remote beginnings. The participants are facing four huge statues of gods, which are in a line facing forward. One or more of the statues speak, and there is an eerie hum. The atmosphere is eerie and frightening, charged with intense, heavy spirit. I think, "This is where our religion comes from, but this was way back in the past. It is now much lighter and more up to date." I do seem to be in Egypt at its very beginnings.

I am always uncertain how to take this type of dream. What am I witnessing and where? I know that I am in the collective unconscious, in the other reality, which is a timeless reality beyond our notions of time and space, but am I actually watching a real event in ancient Egypt itself? Is it still "alive" in the other reality, or is it all symbolical, though having the same meaning? Some dreams are spun for us like plays or films in which we take part, while others are more like real events that we witness. This dream is of the latter type, a vision observed.

As to the contents, the four statues are not just totem poles, but more like statues of gods. We must think, perhaps, of the four sons of Horus who expressed the totality of the god. We are also reminded of the four pillars of Shu which supported the plate that was said to be the floor of Heaven by the Egyptians. The four pillars were alternatively the four gods, the four sons of Horus: Hapi, Tuamutef, Qebhsennuf, and Amset. These supported the Face of Heaven that was in one form Horus; the scepter held by each god was a supporting pillar. This was to establish the kingdom of god the father, and may even be the basis of the Israelite God, Yahweh, represented by the four letters YHVH (the Tetragrammaton).

Furthermore, the dream says that Christianity, through Judaism, comes from this ancient source. This would be the stream of blue blood, the royal line, of my earlier dream. Christianity is thus a resurrection mystery, and the earlier form of this was Osiris in the Underworld where the four gods were a quaternity. The fourfoldness of the human psyche, of the Higher Self, of God, all mean wholeness, totality, and completeness, and so the four totems in the dream symbolize and exemplify the "god of the four quarters." Jung has often been criticized for being obsessed by quaternity symbolism and by the number four generally, but the truth is it is alluded to throughout the unconscious processes.

> I lead a party of explorers first to New Guinea and then to Australia, where strange creatures come out of the ground to attack us. They are rather like octopus-spiders, but have only three legs, and are about six-feet high and jet-black in color. They shoot arrowlike spikes at us, and one of these sticks in my right hand. I am afraid and tell myself that I must stop invading the land of these creatures. As I think this, the spikes stop.

To go south in dreams is to travel to the instinctual depths, to the World Soul or the "Realm of the Mothers" as it has been called. You cannot go much further south from England than Australia, which means, therefore, that I am in the deepest depths of the unconscious. As we also "take in" New Guinea, which has been called the most primitive place on Earth, it is obviously an omen of what we are likely to encounter on our journey. Jung says that a dark, chthonic triad residing in the depths of matter was revealed by alchemy, the lower counterpart to the higher, divine Trinity. Though its symbolism shows that the lower triad has definite connections with evil, we must not hastily conclude that it is solely that (1959b).

The black three-legged creatures that come up from out of the ground can only mean the black, chthonic trinity spoken of by the alchemists and others investigating the depths of the collective unconscious. The black trinitarian creatures (expressions of the chthonic spirit) do not like this invasion of their domain and repel us, but my intention to leave this place alone in the future has a placating effect on them. Journeying to these depths means that a response will be invoked from the higher, spirit side of this other reality, as that is the law of the unconscious as the next dream demonstrates.

> I am in a space station in Australia and the country—the world—is about to be invaded by alien beings who arrive in round, tripod-like spaceships; flying saucers most probably. However, we do not actually see them at first, though we are aware of them, as rays from the saucers are zapping everybody. Then the flying saucers appear, and though I cannot see the aliens, I somehow know that their essence is Trinitarian. They continue zapping everybody, either paralyzing or killing them, but when it becomes my turn and I say, "We also have a holy trinity, consisting of Father, Son, and Holy Spirit," it causes the invaders to pass me over, though they continue zapping everyone else.

In the last dream I was in Australia where black, three-legged creatures, the chthonic trinity, came up out of the earth. Now in response, their opposite, the trinity of spirit arrives *over* Australia. The spirit, though trinitarian, is not necessarily Christian and not necessarily "good" or benign. In fact, as it zaps everybody, the opposite seems to be the case. The fact that when I mention the Christian trinity I am passed over, suggests it is *willing* to be Christian, as the Christian trinity expresses adequately the light side of its nature.

217

This image may fit with certain modern sightings of UFOs where a light, or disc, joins two others, yet seems partly independent of them, just as though the Holy Spirit were an independent entity from Father and Son. It may also fit the saying of Christ that a sin against Father and Son may be forgiven, but not one against the Holy Spirit.

Jung stated that the Christian trinity is based on the same model as that of ancient Egypt, and that this was based on long and deep experience of their "other world." Jung points out that the structure of Father, Son, and Ka-Mutef found in ancient Egyptian mythology, was produced by the same archetype through the unconscious that was responsible for the Christian Trinity (1958).

Wallis Budge was of the opinion that the Egyptians arranged their gods in trinities after the human models of man, wife, and child, for example. In other words, the god triads were projections of the human state. However, with experience of the unconscious processes we now know this is not so. Trinities are the natural order of the unconscious forces and eternal powers as are quaternities. Atum as father, Iusaas as mother, and Iusa (or Nefer-Tem) as divine son were the trinity at Annu; Amun-Ra/Mut/Khonsu at Thebes; Ptah/Sekhet/Iu-em-hetep at Memphis. Other triads were Osiris, Isis, and Horus; Set, Nepthys, and Anubis; and the exclusively male trinity of Ra, Atum, and Horus.

Though the original gods of Egypt were triads, later, Budge says, there were nine gods, and the High God ruled over four male/female pairs of deities. The nine were also seen as three trinities. However, Massey says that the true situation is that there were first seven gods, who became 1 + 7, known as the Ogdoad; Thoth with the seven powers or their equivalents is an example of this. But when Ra as Father-god was put over these, there were thus nine gods.

> There is a square on the wall and in it there forms the shape of a circle with wings, a winged sun-disc. Then there is something about sexuality, but a voice says of this, "To be taken symbolically."

The winged sun-disc is an ancient Egyptian symbol of divinity, particularly of Horus, and therefore is an appropriate one for the Higher Self (as the Son). This also fits with the rising sun I saw a few dreams ago that was Christ (or so I believed in the dream). As for the mention of sexuality taken symbolically, this is as it should almost always be in the unconscious processes. It is amusing to think of how shocking alchemical symbolism was generally regarded in the past, with it incestuous marriages and illustrations of naked copulation, when all it referred to was the *symbolic* unification of opposites in the unconscious.

In one Egyptian myth, when Horus cuts off the head of the serpent fiend, Apep, Isis asks Ra to give Horus the winged sun-disc. Then Horus instructs Thoth to bring the winged sun-disc with two guardian serpents, one either side, into every temple and sanctuary of all the gods to drive away evil. Wallis Budge says that this is why the winged sun-disc is found carved over the court entrances of the temples of the gods all over Egypt. After all these events Thoth decreed that Horus should be called "Light-giver, who cometh forth from the horizon." This again is the Higher Self as Son of God coming forth in the Egyptian Mysteries, as based on processes of the unconscious.

> Circles of gold—golden spheres—rain down from the sky. I have half of one in my hands; it is about a foot in diameter and filled with fire. Then, still in the dream, I awake, and I have a snakeskin belt in my hand, but instead of this one, I put on a purple one. I own both belts.

Golden fireballs are, of course, symbols of spirit coming to Earth, while the snake-belt symbolizes the corresponding position from lower soul reality. Being a belt, a circle that surrounds, it has the same significance as the cobra, the uraeus serpent that surrounds Pharaoh's crown, and the uroboros serpent that swallows its own tail. As the golden fireballs bring eternal spirit, so the uroboros serpent is the "deadly, but life-bringing water."

The purple belt that I put on reminds me of an alchemical statement I once came across: "Come hither, ye sons of wisdom, and rejoice, for death is over, and the son reigns; he wears the red garment, and the purple is put on." Purple was the color of royalty, and, as the color of Christ's crucifixion robe, marked him as spiritual royalty. One further point is that the two belts allude to the higher light and lower dark sides of the Self.

> I am at a place a few miles north of where I live, at a site similar to Stonehenge with huge stones. Archaeological excavations are taking place, and as I look at one of the large stones at eye level, I see the name

"SOKRATES" chiseled on it, spelled with a "K" instead of the usual "C" in English. In fact, it seems to be in Old Celtic. Next to this are chiseled a circle that depicts a stone, and a cross. So that, while it is a circle, it is also a stone. "Not just a circular stone," this is how the dream expresses it. The circle and stone, though being one here, express different, though connected symbols. Then I hear the words "The stone and the cross."

To go north in dreams is to travel to the spirit side of unconscious reality, and indeed, the place I go to is ancient and holy. The name of the wise, old philosopher, Socrates, is chiseled in what I take to be old Celtic, though it is possibly in Greek. Socrates was the "father of wisdom" in the earlier dream, and it seems that the hidden wisdom is the meaning here. As a circular stone and cross are in evidence, I am reminded of the Celtic cross, though the site itself is like Stonehenge. The cross within a circle was also the chief symbol of the Gnostics, a mandala that was the symbol of the Higher Self, and there is some likelihood that the Celtic cross came from the Gnostic symbol, as monks from Cornwall and South Wales are known to have made many journeys across the Mediterranean to Alexandria and other places where Gnosticism flourished at that time. Indeed, Celtic Christianity itself does not have its roots in Rome, but North Africa.

On this matter, Gerald Massey writes:

> The cross of symbolism has no significance without the circle; both go together and are indivisible . . . The circle and four corners are also depicted as a circle and a square . . . The circle and square constituted the "Quadrangular Caer" of the Druids, as the circle of the four quarters . . . The square was held by the Pythagoreans and Neo-Platonists to be the symbol of earth, and inferior to the circle, the symbol of Heaven (1880).

The dream is making a connection between the ancient cultures of Britain and Greece, some of whom were the same Celtic peoples. Sokrates with a "K" is an allusion to the Celtic peoples that flooded many European countries. Such words as Macedonia—Makedhonia in Greek and Makedonija in Yugoslav—being spelled in those countries with a "k" rather than a "c." When the Romans invaded Britain, they were very surprised that they understood certain native words. Many people of Celtic origin in Britain look Italian or Greek (singer Tom Jones, for example). A further point is that the Greeks, Scots, and Irish all wear kilts and play bagpipes.

Taking all of my processes as a whole, one of the aims seems to be to extract all of the religious threads from the roots, to make them all conscious and to bring them all under one framework of understanding. Yet this extends beyond the West, for I have found myself in lands all over the globe, covering it from the Far East westwards to the Americas, so that all peoples, from the Japanese to the Apache Indians, are involved. This is uniting the four corners of the World Soul, as Enoch does in his journeys.

The Philosopher's Stone is perhaps the main symbol of the alchemists, but they also used the circle and cross to signify the unification of opposites, as the Gnostics had.

It is a simple symbol and yet covers so much. Christ on the cross means basically the same, and I had a dream where the divine child was at the center of the cross, though not crucified. Jung also speaks of the circle divided into four, found the world over, that always has magical connotations (1958). Jung further states that the inner Great Man is projected onto the outer stone, and that the totality of this stone expresses the individuation process whereby wholeness may be attained (1959a).

So my dream speaks of both the stone and the cross. The unification of the two would mean the further development of Christianity, to include all of the processes of the vast unconscious, of which alchemy was a product.

> I am sitting on the front step of a cottage with a lovely little girl who has golden curls and who laughs happily. The girl's mother puts a woolen, fishnet blanket around the child. It is a sunny day, but somehow we see beyond the clouds to where the sky is dark, or perhaps it has become night. Suddenly, we see a shooting star travel across the heavens from left to right, but then I tell the girl to look to the right where a second star moves across from right to left, though this second one is partly covered by a dark cloud and is somewhat hazy. They meet in the center of the sky and unite, and pulsate and flash like a neon light.

The lovely little girl with golden curls is the female side of the divine child. Jung saw this very same child at the beginning of his own processes just before World War I. The child here is brought a woolen, fishnet blanket, which alludes to the lamb and the fish, symbols of aspects of the Self as savior (i.e., Christ) by her mother, who represents the Great Mother (the World Soul).

As I said with my earlier dream of a star, it heralds the approach or coming forth of the Higher Self, but as there are two stars in the present dream, coming from either side of the sky, it means the Self comes in both light and dark aspects. This is further intimated by the second star being partly obscured by the dark, hazy cloud. The stars meeting and pulsating signifies their unification into the One, into wholeness.

In *The Sirius Mystery*, author Robert Temple cites a dark, hazy star in the ancient Egyptian texts and concludes that it alludes to the star Sirius B. But as the above dream indicates, it is all symbolism of the unconscious processes, or, from the spirit aspect, events of the "other reality" involving the two sides of the Higher Self. The ancient Egyptians could not have known about Sirius B in any case, and it is only coincidence. As Robert Temple points out himself, though not realizing the true and full significance of what he is saying, Set, or Typhon, the evil twin of Osiris/Horus, is said to be a dark, hazy, moving star in the myth. Again, this means the dark underside of the Self. The contents of this dream demonstrate excellently how the mythology of Egypt was based on the unconscious processes, and this is true of myths worldwide.

This dream in my view is the answer to the modern mystery of how the Egyptians knew of Sirius B. The claims of Temple's book are not just that the Dogon myths—originally Egyptian, etc.—are the account of amphibious Sirians coming to Earth, but that the myths also contain material that proves the Egyptians must have known of Sirius B. This is because the mythic accounts tell of a dark twin of the god associated with Sirius. In other words, the Dogon say that Sirius has a dark twin—and, Temple concludes this is hence Sirius B. (It is actually Isis who is Sirius, but she gives birth to Horus out of the star.)

However, as the myths of Sirius originally involved Horus, the dark twin is obviously Set, not Sirius B. The Higher Self is always connected with a star mythologically, and as in my dream, the dark side is sometimes symbolized by a dark, clouded star. The ancient Egyptians did not know of Sirius B, their initiates experienced these things through the unconscious, and if Sirius alluded to the birth of the divine child, he would have had a dark twin; again as the symbolism in my dream.

So both my dream and the Egyptian/Dogon myths say that a star and dark star represent the twins of the Self, and Sirius is an example. It is pure coincidence that thousands of years later science discovered that Sirius has an unseen twin star, Sirius B.

> Evil forces invade the city and one poor man is impaled on a stake. This seems to be the work of Vlad the Impaler, who seems to be quite near.

This could mean the "crucified" Higher Self again, caught between the opposites in a state of crucifixion. He is pulled in, and from, all directions, and perhaps in particular between his own extremes of good and evil. Count Dracula was partly based on Vlad the Impaler, the mad medieval tyrant of Eastern Europe who would impale his many victims on stakes. Vlad makes a very apt representation of the shadow side of the Self, as does Dracula, who, draining his victims of blood, symbolically drains them of spirit. Blood has been a symbol of spirit since ancient times.

> I am in a church when a plague of locusts invade; these then become wasps. Suddenly, a flock of white birds appear and swallow the wasps.

The locusts and wasps indicate negative spirit, the wasps being particularly dangerous. The white birds represent positive spirit, and this side is the stronger as they swallow the wasps. The evil was close on the heels of Vlad the Impaler in the previous dream, and the locusts/wasps continue this, invading the church, which means the religious or spiritual side of the Higher Self. There is a similar story concerning Brigham Young and the Mormons in mid-nineteenth century Utah: flocks of seagulls suddenly appeared to eat up the plague of locusts that were destroying all their crops.

> I walk down the street with a girl and a chimpanzee, and I am stronger than the latter. Holding hands with the monkey, I say "My friend."

The girl is the anima, my feminine unconscious, and the chimp represents the subhuman part of the psyche. I have "made friends" with them, unifying the three of us. In the individuation process, the reconstruction of the psyche begins at the lower level of the ape.

> I find an old piece of rag, which is actually a great treasure, and I remind myself that the greatest treasure may be that which everybody scorns, such as an old piece of rag. A poor old woman comes up to me and says she will help me if she can, and then a young Asian man appears, who has been searching for the rag. He demands that I hand it over to him, though we apparently had agreed beforehand that whoever found it would keep it. I tell him that it is rightfully mine, but not for myself, for my team; still he demands it from me.
>
> He is a great karate expert and is very tough, and though I hit him a number of times as hard as I can, it has no affect, and he goes to attack me in return. So I say to him, "You have no honor," which seems to awaken him from a trance, and he stops the attack. An evil magician appears, who is possibly Ainu (of the oldest ethnic group in Japan), because, though he looks somewhat Mongoloid, he has a thick, black beard. He wears long robes which have stars, crescent moons, and the like on them, and he is obviously the young karate expert's master.
>
> The sorcerer conjures up dark powers to attack me, but I compose and speak a simple little rhyme, which ends with something like, "Make his powers as harmless as spit." The old woman who has come to help me is actually a very humble witch, and because she stands with me, the magic forces which leave the magician's hands like lightning coming at us become spittle, which falls harmlessly to the ground in front of him.

The old rag that is a treasure is a symbol which appears in alchemy, though I did not know this at the time. The young Asian seems to have been entranced by the magician, his master, though my words about honor snap him out of it. The magician in the dream processes is the opposite of the priest; the latter wants nothing for himself, whereas the magician wants everything. The priest wishes to serve God and mankind with wisdom and truth, whereas the magician craves power for his own evil ends and wants others to serve him. The contest between Simon Peter and Simon Magus (the magician) in the New Testament illustrates this difference.

I am very relieved that the magician has come as an enemy, because for him to come as a friend could mean having a devil on my shoulder which I might not be able to shake off. If he comes as an adversary then at least I am on the right side and can fight him. It is not fighting evil in dreams that is to be feared; it is being influenced by evil or being on the side of evil. If you are a bit too lustful, avaricious, or otherwise too worldly in everyday life, for too long a spell, then you may have to suffer the consequences permanently.

The old woman in the dream is poor and humble, in direct contrast to the magician, and though she has magical powers herself, she obviously does not use them for selfish purposes. Otherwise she would not be "poor" and "humble." It is with her help that I am able to withstand the magician's evil powers. She is representative of the collective anima, or World Soul, as a humble, but powerful, crone.

> As I lie in my bed I see the smiling face of Jung beaming down on me from just above.

This has happened to me many times in the processes. Jung sometimes speaks, but sometimes he just smiles. Whether this is the "wise old man," the "personification of spirit" as my guru or as Jung himself it is impossible to say. But whichever, this is a visitation in spirit from the other side of the curtain that divides the worlds of the conscious and the unconscious.

> I am attacked by a very large, brown-black bull, and am almost savagely gored. However, I find myself doing a karate leap, and kicking the bull in the head, which sends it reeling. This hurts the bull a lot and it is neither as strong nor as menacing afterwards.

This is a recurring theme in my dreams over the years and usually I leap over the bull's head and horns as it charges. However, I do much better this time, injuring and weakening it. The bull as a symbol and bull worship reach back to ancient times, and we still see surviving remnants of it today in Spanish-speaking countries. There are ancient depictions of leaping over the bull, and "braving the bull." Today, these are connected with virility in defeating it in some way, originally meaning a higher stage of virility, the defeat of sexuality itself. It is a fact that the more a person tries to diminish one's own sexuality the more it attacks like a raging bull. The defeat of this, therefore, is a heroic feat.

Bull symbolism seems to have been almost the foundation of mythology in ancient Crete with the Minoans, and was also very pronounced in Greece and Egypt. In the latter, Horus was "the Bull of his Mother," and Osiris was "Bull of the West," and the Apis-bull, a very powerful and massive beast, contained the soul of Osiris. Horus actually slays the bull in the star Sirius, the latter being the symbol of Horus' mother, Isis, as Sept (or Sothis). During the astrological age of the bull (Taurus), the bull naturally featured very prominently in Egypt, but as can be expected, it declined with the coming of the age of the ram (Aries).

In real life there is a brass bell at the side of our living-room window. I have attached a cord to it, and at night I hook the cord, stretched across the curtains, onto the other side. So if unwelcome intruders enter during the night, the bell will ring loudly.

I was deep in sleep, not dreaming, when suddenly I sat bolt upright in my bed, suddenly awake, and declared, "The bell has rung. Someone has entered this house. It is God." I say I was suddenly awake, but I was actually still partly asleep, and the overwhelming feeling that came over me was unpleasant. It was, in fact, extremely heavy and stark. Then I fell back onto my pillow again, falling asleep immediately, and had the following dream.

Superman, as played by actor Christopher Reeve, is standing by me as I lie in my bed, and I ask him, somewhat anxiously, "Are you good or evil?" I am very relieved when he laughs and replies, "Oh, I am good."

I have always believed that it was God who entered the house that night; have always known it. Superman is a representation of the Higher Self, the latter being part of God come forth. But, as Superman, it is not high enough and must be developed into more of a religious figure, a true savior, a god, a Christ parallel. Superman may have super strength but he is still a physical hero, a Samson or Herakles, rather than a Moses or Jesus, or even a Horus or a Christ. It is true, though, that Samson and Herakles do reflect Higher Self experiences and their births are divine ones if understood correctly. However, Superman laughs and says he is good, and this is of paramount importance as the phenomenon of his appearance means either the coming forth of the light side of the Higher Self or the dark side. Which one comes forth makes all the difference.

There are important differences here with Nietzsche's Superman. The Superman in my dream is from another reality, and God has been in the house. So while the figure is not high enough yet, is not a religious savior, he is nevertheless otherworldly and good. Nietzsche's Superman by contrast is the conscious personality blown up like a balloon, so that it finally bursts. It is definitely not otherworldly, for as Nietzsche warns, "Believe not in otherworldly realities. There is only the earth." Furthermore, Nietzsche's Superman is neither moral nor good.

However, it is true that the Self must have been building up in Nietzsche's unconscious. For, denying any other realities, he identified everything with consciousness. For Nietzsche, the Superman was the ego-personality, or what it can become—and was beyond good, evil, and compassion. Christ, by contrast, is essentially spirit, highly moral, and full of compassion. He is definitely not human consciousness, but Son of God. Nietzsche unconsciously experienced the Self, but because he denied what Christ represents, he himself became "the Crucified."

I am holding the tail of a black dragon and I beat the dragon on the head with its own tail.

This dream involves the defeat of the dragon, the dark, instinctual powers of the unconscious. It is similar in meaning to the uroboros serpent that swallows its own tail, and forms the main mandala of alchemy. When this tail swallowing occurs, a higher stage is reached in the processes. In alchemy, the dragon's head is sometimes identified with Christ and the tail with Antichrist, or the Devil, thus the dragon eats its own tail, and even devours itself. The oroboros is also Mercurius, "the beginning and end of the work," who devours himself and dies but is then born again as the magical stone which possesses the masculine spiritual and feminine material (or soul) aspects.

In the *Theatrum Chemicum* text of 1622 (vol. II) it says of the dragon: "The whole body obeys the head, and the head hates the body, and slays it beginning with the tail, gnawing it with its teeth, until the whole body enters into the head and remains there for ever." My dream is the opposite of this, the tail beating the head, so it would seem that the dark side dominates. But not necessarily so: Alchemical processes wind in and out and around with thousands of variations and meanings, and what was so for one alchemist was the reverse for another.

> I am in an old frontier outpost in North America, where there are a lot of trappers and Indians. The ground is muddy in places and the woman who is with me finds a chunk of crystal in the mud. This sort of thing has been rejected by the white man (non-Indians here) as worthless, but when the woman hands the crystal to me and I hold it high, to inspect it, I say, "This is what the Indians worship, but the white man has pulled down all of his temples and statues to it."
>
> I see some white men pushing over a temple to demolish it a little way off. The woman then finds another piece of the crystal—the mud could be full of it—and when she again hands it to me and I hold it up to the light, I see that it is a large, white diamond.

The dream itself says "the white man," but is very critical of him. By contrast, the Indians are wise and spiritual, and are praised. If any ethnic group could complain here it is the "white man" because he is made inferior to the Indians—with much justification; in losing spirit, the "white man" has become slave to the dark side of Mercurius, who is "prince of this world."

The "white diamond" is a symbol of alchemy, and all over the world, including African myths, white is good and black sinister. It would not be natural for the black magician to be good, and the white magician to be evil. The Egyptians said that the gods wore white linen. This has nothing whatsoever to do with ethnic type.

The "white man" is not white, of course, but ranges from pink to brown. My father, who was Welsh, had a very brown skin. However, the dream says "white man," but as I say, is very critical of him because all of his values have become material ones.

This theme is found in many myths worldwide: the thing of highest value, the real treasure, is only to be found in the lowly and the simple, in the mud. But the crystal turns out to be a diamond, no less, and there could be more lying around in the mud, which would add up to an exceedingly rich treasure. The Indians who appear in the dream worship the crystal found in the mud (or the precious stone that the crystal becomes), which is not surprising since the sacredness of such a stone has been known worldwide.

The mother of the Aztec god Quetzalcoatl becomes pregnant with him after swallowing a green stone, for example. However, the sacred stone is often the simplest of stones and not what we would call precious.

Massey tells us that, "The stone, or knife of flint, that fell or was flung from Heaven, is the opener in many Aztec, Mexican, and other myths" (1880). Here it was "flung from Heaven" and that is precisely the meaning given to the sacred stone, though it may still be picked up from the common mud. Massey also says that the Oneida, Ojibwa, and Dakota Indians all claim to derive (as a people) from a sacred stone. The Dakotas painted the stone with red paint to signify blood, or used blood itself, and the stone was then called the "grandfather," the original creative power.

Further, the sacred "white stone" was known in very early Egypt, to the Maori of New Zealand, the Aborigines of Australia, as well as in the Mithraic and Masonic mysteries. Revelation speaks of a white stone being given to a new initiate, and the Foundation Stone which God cast into the abyss to form the world. It was on this stone that Jacob lay his head to rest. These are just a few examples of how a sacred stone has been known to cultures around the world from early times.

Western man, as my dream says, has pulled down all of his temples over such wonders because he has come to believe that all values, all reality, are solely concerned with matter, whereas for all cultures of the past, plus perhaps a few today who have not yet been corrupted by modern values, a stone (or a diamond) is a sacred symbol. Diamonds, rubies, and other precious stones are of the highest value to us because they mean money in the bank, and so are only precious in a worldly way. But a stone that means a higher immortal, a god, a son of the high God who comes as a savior and redeemer to bring the spiritual gold to even the poorest and most lowly man—that is the real meaning of "precious"; that is the real gold.

The gospels tell us, "The stone which the builders rejected, the same is become the head of the corner" (Ps 118:22, Mark 12:10, Luke 20:17. See also Peter 2:7). To the alchemists, the Philosopher's Stone, the magical lapis, and the "diamond body" came to mean far more than just the common gold—"our gold is not the common gold," they said. So the real treasure is to be found in the simple and lowly, in the mud which is where the alchemists swore their Philosopher's Stone lay. Or the treasure may be found in a stable where humble shepherds visit, and to which wise men, possessing true wisdom, bring their gifts.

Primitive man existed nearer to nature and the unconscious, and lived his life *within* the myth. He was, therefore, in harmony with the eternal powers and structures, and though he could break out into savagery for any number of reasons, the harmony was always restored because religion was the foundation and mainstay of his culture. With modern man, savagery is gradually becoming the norm, as there is now no myth to live within. We are so fundamentally dissociated that the result will almost inevitably be catastrophic, and for the whole world, unless we can take the leap forward to a respiritualization of Western civilization, based on Jung's discoveries of the unconscious. This would change our dissociation into association, our disorientation into reorientation. We must relearn how a stone may be sacred and how the unconscious has reproduced this symbol for thousands of years.

The precious stone in the dream actually has the same basic meaning as the Philosopher's Stone, which, though having spirit and posited as a parallel to Christ, was originally a lump of matter thereby capable of uniting the spirit with matter or the soul depths.

> I see a voluptuous woman I know and she looks at me desirously. Then I become aware of God, and reflect that what I am thinking of concerning the woman is not at all to do with the things of God.

Jung speaks of the ferocious conflict between the sex instinct and the love of God. You cannot go to the extreme with the unconscious processes and have a vigorous sex life at the same time. Sacrifices have to be made. There are people who believe that Jesus had a physical sex life with Mary Magdalene, but it could not have been so. The primary prerequisite of the processes at such a level is that the union of male and female is, and must be, at a higher and spiritual level.

To go that far is not the lot of most people, but for the initiates whose fate it is to serve the higher powers, questions must be asked and decisions made. How far do you want to go with the processes? How far are you capable of going? Can you fight your own worldly and instinctual drives and hope to win? Do you want to? Can you suffer the lack of understanding, and even the persecution, of others? And even if you believe you can do all of these, do you know that it almost always ends in failure? Do you have the makings of a mythical hero? Do you know that even Moses and the Buddha failed in the end, and they were very special personalities? To be honest, I could not answer any of these questions correctly, so I told myself that I would travel as far as I could with the processes and that would have to be far enough.

A young woman asked me in a dream once if we all must give up sex. Words were put into my mouth which answered, "No, but you must only make love with the one you love." This was the answer from the higher powers themselves, and a lot of people would perhaps be willing to go along with that, and indeed, may already do so. But the person who wishes to go all the way with the processes must go one step further. I have always liked and admired women tremendously, finding them immensely attractive, so I always avoided making any decisions regarding them. I just kept out of situations where there was a chance I might become involved, because then I knew I would not be strong. In a word, I always loved women, but God (and wisdom and truth) must come first.

A horned toad is on a table and it suddenly attacks my dog, biting him savagely on the side of his body.

As I have said before, my dog in these processes means the dog-spirit, symbolizing the Higher Self at a lower level. As we well know, the horned toad is traditionally a creature of the Devil. It seems that my temptation, my weakness, over the voluptuous woman in the last dream has created an opening for the dark side of the Self to jump in. If the Self is ultimately a Christ parallel, then the dark twin will equal an Antichrist parallel, if not the Devil himself.

The toad is a symbol of solid earth which cannot be sublimated, and is actually necessary to the processes as an anchor so that everything does not fly away upward to become lost and dissociated in sublimity. St. Teresa of Avila and Nietzsche experienced the toad as a content of their dreams and visions, yet had completely different fates because their conscious attitudes and values were totally opposite. St. Teresa accepted God and Christianity, and filling herself with the power of love, achieved a state of holiness in a universal reality belonging to God. Nietzsche, on the other hand, rejected God and Christian values, preaching the Superman and the Will to Power, an inflated idea of how the physical man can become godlike. Inhabiting a cold, soulless universe bereft of spiritual meaning and promulgating mental abandonment to extreme and overwhelming sensation, he went insane. As Jung says, Nietzsche was basically a deeply religious personality, but his God was dead and he had lost his way.

> I am outside our garden gate at night when I am whisked off my feet
> and taken up into the sky fifty miles above the Earth. As I look down, I
> reflect on what a long way back it is to Earth. A strange man, who proba-
> bly brought me up here, shows me the sun, which I can look at directly
> because it is also the moon, and is therefore not so bright. I see conti-
> nents on it, as though I were looking at the Earth. I say, "Well, it looks a
> lot different from up here." Then I see the twelve signs of the zodiac cir-
> cling it.

The cosmic aspect of the work was well known to the alchemists
and astrology has been central to many religions from the earliest times.
In the dream, the sun, moon, and Earth are combined into one, meaning the unification of spirit, soul, and body, not only at my own, personal level, but at the collective and cosmic level. We find this goal of
unification not only in alchemy but also in the religious mysteries worldwide. In alchemy, the "Three Words" refer to the body, soul, and spirit
unified in "imperishable union." In my dream, the sun, moon, and Earth
combined as one refer to the same union at a cosmic level. It ultimately
means the opposites are brought together in the Higher Self.

The unified sphere with the twelve zodiac signs encircling it has the
same meaning as Christ surrounded by the twelve disciples, the twelve
chapters of the Egyptian Amenta, the twelve alchemical stages, twelve
tribes of Israel, the twelve labors of Herakles, and so on, all signifying
totality. The twelve buckets of the Manichean cosmic wheel have the
same symbolic meaning as the twelve zodiac signs in my dream. The
three of spirit and four of matter (soul) when unified give the seven powers, expressed in numerous forms in the world's myths and religions.
This adding is easy enough to understand, but more difficult is the fact
that the unconscious processes also multiply the three and four to make
twelve. We frequently find seven together with twelve in mythology and
the Bible. The pyramid unifies the three and four and expresses them as
both seven and twelve.

> I see an insect which at first I think is a spider, but then I realize it
> has wings and is strangely colored. One wing is green, but I am uncertain
> what the other is. The first is initially like a bird's wing, and yet also a
> dragon's, while the other is difficult to determine. The fluffy white head
> is like a bird's, but then it becomes that of a lovely little snowy white

bear cub. The creature gently licks the back of my hand with affection and gratitude, and then flies away. I ask a woman who is now present, "What color were its wings?" to which she replies, "One was green and the other was pale brown."

I have given this dream because it demonstrates the unification of the opposites of the Self at a lower-animal level. I first see a spider, an earthy creature, its eight legs emanating from the center forming a mandala, and it then flies, suggesting the spirit. The bird connotations represent masculine spirit, whereas the bear cub means feminine matter, a bear being one of the main symbols of the lower feminine unconscious.

The green wing again refers to spirit, green being the traditional color of spirit, while the dragon's wing is that of an earthbound creature. The snowy white color of the heads, the bird's and the bear's, refer to purity, the best possible aspect; the pale brown wing suggests the best possible aspect of the chthonic earth. All in all, these creatures form a totality of opposites that could have been a horrible conglomeration, but this is not the case. All the best possible aspects are to the fore. These are the unified opposites at the lower animal level of the Self, corresponding, up to a point, to the unification of the sun, moon, and Earth at the cosmic level in the previous dream.

The chick and bear cub as one symbolize the opposites of spirit and matter. When I say "matter," I do not mean the solid, physical shell, but the soul that inhabits the shell. Soul in this sense is a kind of lower spirit that is the opposite of higher pure spirit. This is why the alchemists said there were two spirits, the higher and the lower, involved in their opus.

The world of science, which is regarded as the authority, sees only the physical shell and makes everything of it, but while the shell may be of much importance, and only a fool would deny it, spirit and soul are the true life which permeate the shell. That is why esoteric teachings all the way back to ancient Egypt speak of "body, soul, and spirit." It is also why the religious person is in harmony with the true nature of reality, even though his creed may be in a naïve form, while the person who holds a scientific or atheistic view and sees only the shell misses everything of ultimate significance.

I am in the grounds of a church, where everything is light and vague. A voice says, "One day you will wear the purple."

Purple is the color of royalty, worn to show high rank and authority. It is also the color of Christ's robe, known as the Robe of Glory. This is the true royalty, and purple is said to express the mystery of the Lord's Passion. Purple represents the esoteric mantle of the true priest in the same way that the true priest is "after the order of Melchizedek." There was a Gnostic robe of initiation called the wedding garment, or the robe of power that reflected the highest stage of the individuation process, the *principium individuationis,* which was said to allow man to experience the divine nature of the Higher Self. However, I always had serious doubts—indeed, disbelief—about my own capabilities in this area as I know my faults and weaknesses only too well.

> I have a blister on my right index finger, and pulling the top off it, I put the finger under a tap out of which runs pure, clear water. This causes the blister to swell up like an egg, and it grows to quite a large size. Then the head and neck of a reptile emerges from the egg on my finger, resembling the film creature, E. T., which I have always considered to be a symbol of the Higher Self. There is a threeness about this creature at first, but it then becomes a castle with four turrets.

The creature in the dream is not a reptile as such, but an extraterrestrial. This is reinforced by its threeness, which denotes spirit. Triadic aliens often represent spirit in dreams, and sometimes in outer experiences as well. However, the creature in the dream then becomes a castle with four turrets, four being a symbol of matter, on the one hand; but a castle is also a symbol of the Higher Self, who is fourfold, and so the four turrets confirm this. This makes the creature of a mixed three and four nature; that is, a mixture of spirit and matter (soul) in the Self. This has the same meaning as Christ, who is trinitarian, on the four-armed Cross, making him the "god of the four quarters." In support of this observation is the fact that the Gnostics called one of their gods Barbelo, which means "God is four."

I have pointed out earlier that the Babylonian god Marduk is accompanied by four dogs, and that the Egyptian god Horus has four sons (of a 3 + 1 structure) and we could add the Buddha on his podium with a pillar at each corner. The Gnostic Anthropos rested on a four-legged table, and, along with the Cross, Christ has the four gospels, which also happen to be of a 3 + 1 formulation.

Matthew, Mark, and Luke, are known as the Synoptic Gospels because the material and basic attitudes are in harmony to some extent. Matthew and Luke are thought to have taken a fair amount of their material from Mark, though they probably used another source, known as "Q" for *Quelle* ("source") for other material that does not appear in Mark.

The Gospel of John, however, is in a different vein, being more highly spiritual—it has even been called the Gnostic Gospel. It has also been said that it has the eagle as its symbol because it soars up to the spirit. So many scholars have said that the Gospels are of a 3 + 1 nature, including Jung.

As for the egg, it is a well known symbol of the alchemists, out of which rises the Anthropos, or Self. In Egypt there was the primeval egg, out of which the primeval bird burst forth. In other versions, the egg was filled with the air which separates Earth and sky. When Isis is pregnant with Horus she says: "I have formed the body of a god as an egg." In one of the Egyptian Coffin texts, the High God states: "I was also he who came into existence as a circle. He who was the dweller in his egg." Blavatsky tells us that many gods and heroes were "egg-born," and Brahma, Vishnu, and Ra are associated with the egg, which is, in fact, mentioned throughout the Book of the Dead. The finger is the easiest and most familiar way to make contact with water, which the alien must do—the contact of spirit with soul. Earlier today I put my finger under the tap to see if my bath water had heated up; this is where the egg is born from, the point of contact with the water.

> There is a holy man dressed in white who seems to be a pope, and he is trying to explain something to another man. As I approach them, the pope asks me to speak on the matter, putting an arm around the shoulders of the other man and myself. I begin, "I have a shadow side; if I die, then so does he. The opposite is also true; if he dies, then so do I." Then I continue, "The Christian Church (or Christianity) must develop by accepting the shadow side of Christ." The scene then changes and I am walking along the street with my mother. I say to her, "Christianity is not just a faith and a creed, it actually heals the sickness in us." In other words, it is also a healing process.

Just as the individual must accept his own shadow side (while not succumbing to it) for wholeness, so too must Christianity as a whole.

This means accepting the unconscious in all its aspects, which is where religion springs from in the first place. This would mean what Jung calls the evolution of the religious spirit. Christianity is an inner healing process because it brings the conflicting contents of the psyche together, united under the psychic dominant of the Higher Self in his light aspect, which in the West is symbolized by Christ. An example of this is the way that Mary Magdalene is won over to God after first being lost to the dragon. As a prostitute, she is lost to the instinctual depths, symbolized by the dragon.

So the acceptance of the dark side of Christ will mean a broadening and a deepening which the Church sadly lacks at present. As Jung commented, Christianity meant a tremendous leap forward in consciousness for mankind, yet it was never fully developed. Christ said, "I came not to send peace, but a sword" (Mat 10:34), which means that he brings inner division at first. This is a higher state of consciousness, to separate our good from our evil, for we then no longer automatically project our own evil onto others. We carry it as our own burden, but it is this which helps us reach a higher state as human beings. It brings humility and inner suffering, which in turn can bring Christ as Comforter.

Christ as an inner reality causes us to distinguish between our own good and evil and to make the moral choice between them. This is naturally felt as a state of inner division and conflict, for we must fight, and defeat our selfishness, our shadow. At the same time, we feel a new optimism and hope, light and illumination, and there is a broadening of the personality. Nevertheless, there is much suffering and this may lead to a direct experience of Christ.

Christ has his dark, opposite side in the Antichrist, but to the Church these are separate. In other traditions such as Gnosticism and world mythology, they are the hostile twins, like Osiris and Set, Cain and Abel, two sides of the same coin. This is the true nature of the Higher Self, yet as man experiences them they are as separate as God and the Devil are to us.

The Gnostic Valentinus said that Christ was born with a shadow, but later cast if off. And Epiphanius wrote: "On this account they say that Jesus was begotten of the seed of man, and was chosen; and so by the choice of God he was called the Son of God from the Christ that came into him from above in the likeness of a dove" (1868). Epiphanius is speaking of the beliefs and teachings of the Ebionite sect. He also commented that, according to the Ebionites, "Two were begotten by God, one of them Christ, the other the Devil." These are the light and dark sides of the Higher Self.

> I briefly visit the stars and planets and travel through them. I know that we are going to be invaded by those planets, but though I should tell the world about it, particularly the world leaders, I feel that no one will take the slightest notice of me.

This dream means that alien spirit is going to invade the world, though perhaps in a way that will not be obvious. It is a certain fact that since the time of the dream—some years ago—there has been a proliferation of both UFO sightings and alien abductions. They existed before, but the number of abductions reported has soared especially since then. There is no doubt that a spirit is watching us and that it is not necessarily benign. The attitude of the spirit towards man depends on our conscious attitudes and values, which concerning the spirit are not at the moment in a healthy state. Man has to learn to humble himself before the eternal powers, and before the Higher Self and God. He must learn to be responsible or there will be an end of him, for these higher powers will not tolerate greed and Godlessness indefinitely. Nor is it merely man's obvious failings that put us at such great risk. Intellectualism, the belief that man's intellect, science, technology, reason, and intelligence, emanate a sufficiently radiant light for him to rule not only the Earth but the whole universe, is an immense error which may well lead us to destruction. The light of man is in reality not so bright a light; neither is our reason so reasonable or our intelligence so intelligent. It is only by the light of higher spirit that man has made any real and lasting advancements. Ironically, this is the very thing that man has rejected and dissociated himself from in the modern world.

The eternal powers—God—will not tolerate a dangerous mankind for too long, and may well decide that it is time for man to go, unless man can be altered fundamentally, and quickly. I once had a dream which said that God can utterly destroy man without compunction, and then had another in which an alien (representing spirit) informed me that man has a very dangerous gene that must be removed. This means a psychic gene, rather than a physical one, though just how the necessary change can be brought about was not made clear. I had yet another

237

dream, given later in this series, in which I saw a row of animals lined up, waiting to be developed in turn, until a suitable one may be found that can fulfill God's purpose.

> I am in Occupied France where I watch Nazi troops in the streets, and close by me is a young man, a freedom fighter and lover of truth and light. With him is a young woman who is either his sister or his sweetheart. Suddenly, the Nazis arrest the young man, taking him away to be tortured and questioned, before suffering the horrible death which has been planned for him. Then, as I and the townspeople watch, a large slab is brought and put down; a greasy, oil-like substance coats this which will burn human flesh off the bone, like napalm.
>
> The young man is then brought forth, obviously having been tortured already, and he is to be spread-eagled on the slab by his tormentors. However, before they can do this I jump onto the slab myself to take the young man's place and suffer the death myself. I make my last speech, "Good people," I begin, "evil is very strong in the world, but this is how we can defeat it. Yet evil must always be beyond God's control for life to be possible."
>
> One of the Nazi leaders, who has set up this death by torture, suddenly understands by this sacrifice the real meaning of Christianity. Then fleetingly, I see two images; the first is of a Concord plane in the sky; the second, of Jung as a white-haired old man without his mustache, and looking like a saint as he plays with a young boy, maybe his grandchild.

This was not my conscious mind and attitudes imposing the Christian "way" upon the unconscious, but was rather the position taken by the higher powers themselves. Christ is still the symbol of the Higher-Self phenomenon for Western man, and Christianity still the form in which we experience God and the Holy Spirit through the unconscious, whether we know it or not. The essence of Christianity in action is self-sacrifice, denying ourselves the fulfillment of our own worldly desires, selfish or otherwise so as to put others, and God Himself, before us. This is something Nietzsche could never grasp, and it shows the inferiority and error of his philosophy as he tried to develop a way for man to live that reverses these highest of values, attainments, and achievements. For no matter how much clever intellectualism deludes itself that there is a wisdom in Nietzsche that ordinary mortals fail to see, Nietzsche's philosophy is merely a surrender to the earth and animal selfishness.

The dreams show how we may defeat evil in the world by self-sacrifice, though I do not delude myself that I could be as brave in real life as I am in the dream. Nevertheless, I see the wisdom of the message and of the fact that no matter how terrible evil may be, we must admit that life would be impossible without evil.

The ancients, going back to the beginnings of Egyptian high civilization, realized this and strove to construct their religious systems to accommodate evil, though still fully rejecting it. Evil, as the dream says, must be beyond God's control; otherwise the valid eternal system could not be moral and religious. Only when they involve free choice do these things rate substantiality and significance.

The details of the self-sacrifice in the dream are not so important, although it is significant that one of the Nazi leaders (the opposing forces of the unconscious) comes to understand what it all means. The Concord plane alludes to the higher spirit, perhaps to God Himself, and the young boy with Jung, who in all probability represents the Holy Spirit here, is the divine child. The "wise old man" with the young boy, the *puer aeternus*, is a well-known archetype in the esoteric mysteries.

I am somehow told that this association with the Higher Self, this journeying through the unconscious processes in Jungian depth psychology, is to be the new religion for modern man. I am also informed that the psyches of certain individuals, are at this moment, being affected to that end.

The unconscious in Western man has had up to two thousand years of Christianization, so that when the unconscious produces symbols in dreams, if they are from a deep enough level, they will usually be in Christian/Gnostic forms or of alchemical and ancient Egyptian motifs. The roots of Christianity through the unconscious lie in Egypt, via the Old Testament experiences, and these forms and symbols have become constellated in the unconscious and will keep appearing in our dreams.

Journeying through the processes with depth psychology allows us to tap into the *original* divine source, to experience the eternal archetypes anew, though this can be extremely dangerous and most people should perhaps leave the collective depths alone. Nevertheless, the clear message here is that Jung and depth psychology are to be the new religion for us, although it is important to understand that it is not depth psychology itself that is meant, but the great and *deep* spiritual truths it leads to. In other words, depth psychology is the means to an end that is breathtaking in its implications.

> I have a lovely little lamb in my hands which I start to squeeze hard, hurting it, causing it much pain. So it asks me, "Why do you hurt me like this?" It is such a lovely little lamb and I am amazed it can talk.

This is the Higher Self as the Lamb, such a gentle little creature that it is always at the mercy of the wolves. It is the most appropriate of symbols for the Self in its highest form, which is always in so much danger in its early stages of development from the serpent-dragon and from the foolishness and ineptitude of consciousness.

In the dream I hurt the lamb, which means that I must have been doing something in real life that was causing harm to the Higher Self, although I probably would not have known exactly what this was. Ultimately, in higher reality, the Self cannot be harmed, being immortal, and can only be hurt when brought forth and partly developed in worldly reality, though this is still in the unconscious. That is why, in all the myths of the divine child, it is always threatened by a Herod or a serpent. (As King Herod was a real person, the fact that Herod, or *herrut*, means "snake" must be coincidence.)

It is interesting to note that one of the names for the Higher Self in Sanskrit, *Aja,* also means "lamb," and that Horus was "the Lamb, Son of a Sheep" when it became the astrological age of the Ram (Aries). He had been the calf in the age of the Bull (Taurus). On this point, the Victorian mythologist Gerald Massey tells us: "As Egyptian, the lamb, 'son of a sheep,' had been a type of Horus called the child. This was Har-Ur, the first or elder Horus, 'born but not begotten' of the virgin mother. The seven powers, or spirits, that were unified in Horus who became the all-one as the 'eighth to the seven' are now represented by the seven horns and seven eyes of the lamb, which are correctly described as the seven powers or 'seven spirits of God'" (1907).

This dream also refers to Revelation, where Christ is symbolically the Lamb, and as the horn in Biblical times referred to power, seven horns of the lamb probably means the Higher Self with the seven powers. The seven eyes have a similar meaning "the seven spirits of God sent out into all the Earth." We find the parallel to these two sets of seven with the Babylonian seven Anunnaki and seven Igigi, and in India with the seven Brahmas of above and below. The Lamb in Revelation is the only one worthy to open the book of destiny, to take charge of the book of life, and this "Lamb" is the risen Christ. God sits upon His throne surrounded by twenty-four elders wearing golden crowns, and by four beasts, three animal-headed and one man-headed who hold seven lamps of fire that are the Seven Spirits of God. It is then that the Lamb comes forward to open the book to let loose the seven seals.

Returning to Egypt, it was when the vernal equinox was moving out of Taurus and into Aries that Horus the calf became Horus the lamb. This was around 2,410 B.C. when Horus became the "lamb on the mount," just as we find the Lamb on Mount Zion in Revelation. There were four rivers flowing from the mountain making Horus the "god of the four quarters." This type of manifestation of the Father was continued so that Christ was also the Lamb; the earliest forms of depictions of Christ's crucifixion are of the Lamb on the cross, found in the catacombs of Rome. This has exactly the same meaning as the lamb with the four rivers. In the eighth century A.D., the Council of Truro decreed that the Lamb must no longer be depicted on the Cross, but rather the human Jesus, though the Lamb could still appear on the rear of the cross.

So the new Messiah at his coming, according to Revelation, will be the Lamb who alone can open the Book of Seven Seals. This reminds us of the Box of Thoth though these were actually seven boxes, one within the next, that contained the seven potent metals guarded by a serpent; this idea was repeated later as the seven metals of alchemy.

We also find the marriage of the Lamb in Revelation, which, we are told, will occur at the end of time. Jung says that this Lamb is more like a wrathful ram and will rule with "a rod of iron." This may be due to a certain wrathfulness in John the Divine, the author of Revelation, for we develop the Higher Self according to our own conscious attitudes, and John himself seems very wrathful towards certain other churches.

However, the wrathful Lamb may be due to the wickedness of man himself. We cannot help but feel that we are approaching the "end of days" ourselves, considering how we are destroying the Earth in our greed and disrespect for its well-being. As Jung says, materialism and atheism, coupled with man's frightening scientific powers and his large shadow side (of which he is criminally unaware) are more than enough to accomplish the Earth's destruction.

However, the Lamb may be wrathful due to resentment felt by the Jews for their Roman conquerors, so that a vengeful, warlike Messiah was longed for to destroy the hated conquerors. Though somewhat negative from that angle, the "seven-horned lamb" is not the Antichrist, Jung concludes, and so is not altogether irreconcilable with Christ, as the Antichrist would be. The "Second Coming" will not, by the way, be Christ himself, but his equivalent, and will be the Son of the Sun-Woman, the Virgin in Heaven clothed with the sun, and with the moon at her feet. Something is going to happen, so my latest dreams say, though we may not recognize it and miss the opportunity.

> I see a super-human figure, surrounded by sunlight, float into a bedroom and merge with a man who is asleep there, probably connected with myself. A voice from above says, "This is what you missed."

This is what the Christian myth is all about. The super-human figure, the Higher Self, merges with the mortal man. The Christ or Son of Man merges with the man Jesus. I appear to have been near to this myself but my harming of the lamb probably has ruined the processes for the present. Blavatsky says of this phenomenon:

> For it is not only the presence of a God, but an actual—howbeit temporary—incarnation, the blending, so to say, of the personal Deity, the Higher Self, with man—its representative or agent on earth. As a general law, the Highest God, the Oversoul of the human being (Atma-Buddhi), only overshadows the individual during his life, for purposes of instruction and revelation; or as Roman Catholics—who erroneously call that Oversoul "Guardian Angel" would say, "it stands outside and watches." But in cases of the theophonic mystery, it incarnates itself in the Theurgist for purposes of revelation. . . . In exceptional cases, however, the mystery becomes complete; the Word is made Flesh in real fact, the individual becoming divine in the full sense of the term, since his personal God has made of him his permanent lifelong tabernacle—"the temple of God," as Paul says. . . . In perfect unity with its [seventh]

Principle, the Spirit unalloyed, it is the divine Higher Self. . . . After every new incarnation Buddhi-Manas culls, so to say, the aroma of the flower called personality, the purely earthly residue of which—its dregs—is left to fade out as a shadow. This is the most difficult—because so transcendentally metaphysical—portion of the doctrine (1888).

Naturally I must question whether I have come so close to achieving this phenomenon, but all of the other dreams of the processes seem to substantiate it. At this time I had been enmeshed in the processes for a period of some years, perhaps about seven or eight, turned away from the world and devoted to the work. As it turned out, I missed the unification with the Self, as I was not quite adequate, it appears, and because I had too many faults. Who knows, perhaps it was for the best, but nevertheless, I have failed the Higher Self, and therefore God also; or had done so at the time of the dream, for future events will show that I am able to develop things successfully again. These higher powers are real, as my processes show, and we must bow very low before them. The world does not belong to humans; it is not ours but God's and the great feminine Spirit's. We are their mortal agents and as such must be responsible caretakers of the Earth. As Jung says, we must not shirk this task if fate places it upon us, for it is the goal and intention of evolution, of the life process itself and it is the will and intention of God.

It is perhaps important to note that the super-human figure comes from outside of the room, meaning that it is separate from me—or from the human figure that lies in the bed. We must never identify with the Higher Self and must realize that we remain what we are, simple mortal human beings. There is a tendency in both Eastern philosophy and Western depth psychology to speak of the Self as being what we truly are, but this kind of thinking is dangerous for man, as we possess a strong tendency toward inflation.

Hippolytus says, "And if thou shouldst closely investigate these things, thou wilt find Him in thyself, the One and the many, like to that little point, for it is in thee that he hath his origin and his deliverance" (1921). Now while this may be true in one sense, from the view of the unconscious processes, when we look "within," it is nevertheless truer to say that we are within Him, the Higher Self, though separated, and that He is ultimately within both God and the World Soul.

> I see a scene that is taking place in a city to the south, where there is
> a foreign young woman with large breasts; she is quite a woman in a sen-
> sual way. Then I witness another scene which is taking place to the north,
> and here there is a green mountain with religious symbols on it, with a
> spiral road winding up it. Then a voice says of the scene to the south,
> "Not for those on the spiritual path."

This dream displays what is meant by being caught between the opposites. It is torture. Both sides pull, the spirit and the flesh, but it is not possible to go both ways, not if you wish to go the whole way with the processes. It would only be easy for a one-sided personality, who does not have a choice to make. A lot of men are all sexuality with little or no spiritual sense; far fewer are those of only spiritual desires, though such men do exist. For those like myself, who are pulled both ways, it is agony. North in dreams symbolizes the spiritual, whereas the south alludes to the soul/instinctual. Man is forever between these opposites, though there is a powerful tendency in modern man to believe that only the south exists.

On the one hand, I must have meaning in the life process, with spirit, and soul, and God; otherwise all creatures are just physical "things" devouring one another in a reality that is ugly, cruel, and meaningless. Holiness and divine purpose transform it all and we are all redeemed. On the other hand, I was always romantically inclined and a lover of women, and as the old song says, "Without romance this world would be a world without any charm."

While we can admire those who sacrifice lower pleasures for the sake of higher truth—and this is a heroic feat that most people could not accomplish—we would not admire those who sacrifice higher truth just for the sake of lower sexuality, though we would perhaps understand and identify with them. Further, those who can live a life of holiness are regarded by both God and man as the highest products of the life process, whereas those who are consumed by only animal passions are lost in the depths. These are the extremes, of course.

For myself, I am a man who tries to reach higher wisdom and wider reality, and not just for myself; I try to bring that meaning to the world. Then I shall have accomplished something with my life, and at its end I can be satisfied. Relevant to this is the fact that the ancient Egyptians believed in a decent society under a noble God, whose Son came forth in wisdom and truth to bring light and justice to the world. I go along with that all the way. I am apparently not a large enough personality to achieve this divine incarnation myself, but I may at least work towards the spiritual enrichment of society and the increase of man's knowledge of such things.

> I see a brown bear, and then a white rhinoceros.

All I can say about this dream is that a bear is one of the main symbols of Mother Earth, the lower collective unconscious in a dangerous aspect usually, though perhaps not so here. A rhinoceros is an old symbol for God, so this dream would seem to allude to the World Soul and Divine Spirit, the eternal opposites that must be united in the processes.

Both the bear and the rhinoceros are somewhat bad-tempered, and certainly highly dangerous, which is why they make such apt symbols for the dark side of the World Soul and God. But they do not seem to be bad-tempered here, and the rhinoceros is white, indicating the good and light aspect. Incidentally it was on the rhinoceros, in fact, that the legends of the unicorn were based, and the monoceros, the single-horned creature, was known to both alchemy and medieval mysticism.

> As I lie on my bed at night a yellow snake slithers under the sheets and entwines itself around my body. I try to wrestle with it but it just carries on, coiling itself around me several times in an upward movement, and even going into and through my body. I go into a darkened room where I see four men from India, one of them an archaeologist. I ask them the meaning of the yellow serpent and the archaeologist answers, "It is your gift." Then the four of them surround me and, looking upward, chant, "Kundalini, Kundalini, Kundalini." However, I know that the snake which they refer to is yellow on top and black underneath, whereas the snake that visited me was all yellow. This takes place in a town to the north of where I live, further north than the town usually referred to in my dreams.

The kundalini serpent refers to the ascending feminine power of the lower unconscious, the goddess who brings renewal and transformation. However, according to my thoughts in the dream, that would have its light and dark aspects, yellow and black, a balance of opposites. But, the snake I experience is all yellow, which means that it is all light. This is in keeping with Christianity because Christ is all light, having lost all darkness in the mythos and in Western thought. The East understands more about the psychological truth that light always has its shadow.

The Self, a term of Eastern philosophy itself, is a complexity of opposites, and Christ is a symbol of only the light side, corresponding to Horus, "He who is Above." This is perhaps why the snake in the dream is all yellow, in keeping with Western Christianity, rather than with Eastern, kundalini yoga. One further point is that Christ is the God from above, while the kundalini serpent represents the goddess from below, from the lower unconscious.

Kundalini has its effect on the human body, and Blavatsky connects it with "electric fluid and nerve-force." There are forty-nine fires that are states of kundalini, and I did dream of shooting an arrow that became seven, each one of the seven then becoming seven, making forty-nine in all. Blavatsky's "seven sons of Fohat" are also connected with kundalini, their female aspects being the seven Shakti, and in a dream I met a young Indian woman in a dense jungle around this time who called herself Shakti, but I had no understanding of these Eastern forms at that time. The processes in the West take mostly a Christian/alchemical form, but if there are sometimes parts of a process that cannot be symbolized in these terms, symbolism from elsewhere will be used by the unconscious.

> I go into an old library where I find some heavy, ancient volumes about religion. Looking inside one of them, I find that it is illustrated with paintings from the Italian Renaissance, one of which contains four large figures. As I put the book back I hear a strange voice say, "Mary Soul," as if from the past.

"Mary Soul" possibly refers to the collective anima as virginal, that is, pure and suitable to receive the divine child. This is only conjecture on my part and the meaning may well be otherwise. However, Mary Soul here may be the Western form of Shakti, discussed in the previous dream. The voice that speaks the name seems to be from the past, so I assume that the words refer to something from the past. As to the four figures in the painting, four is the number of wholeness, and the meaning may be similar to the four sons of Horus in ancient Egypt and the four apostles in medieval mysticism.

Mary Soul implies the World Soul, the Great Mother, the total, universal soul, and Jung equates Mary with Sophia, Gnostic goddess of Wisdom, Sophia of course has many equivalents: the Shekinah of the Kabbalah; the Queen of Sheba; Bathsheba; Beersheba; and Zipporah, wife of Moses, and her six sisters. All of these refer to the same collective feminine spirit. The voice from the past in my dream is from the Renaissance, so perhaps there is a need to connect the anima force with the conceptions (or with the reality, through the unconscious) of the Virgin Mary at that time. Blavatsky says, "Thus does the Church drag down the noble spiritual ideal of the Virgin Mary to the earth, and, making her 'of the earth earthy' degrades the ideal she portrays . . ." (1888).

Just as Christ corresponds to Horus as the son of Ra, so Mary corresponds to Hathor, mother of Horus, as Hathor means "abode of Horus," i.e., the heavenly womb from which he comes forth. One form of Hathor is *Meri*, symbolically the cow who gives birth to Horus the calf, and it is quite possible that the name Mary derives from *Meri*. Though she is from the past in the dream, she must have some relevance for us now, or why would she appear? In a later dream she does appear as a goddess in the sky. So Mary, the eternal feminine Spirit, is coming close, to correspond with the Higher Self and God, who are also approaching, as again, future dreams will show.

> I see a very ugly woman who has a young son, likewise ugly and thuglike. I then go into my house through the front door, but as I do, a green toad belonging to the boy manages to run in also.

As I have said elsewhere, both St. Teresa of Avila and the philosopher Nietzsche had visions of the toad. The toad inhabits dark, damp, hidden places, and has long been considered a creature of the devil in Western folklore. In ancient Egypt the frog and toad were not so negative, being connected with creation. The toad is green in the dream, which traditionally is the color of spirit, and also of the *"viradescence,"* *"viriditas,"* *"verdigris,"* which refer to green which has a special meaning in alchemy. The green toad would mean, therefore, a symbol of devilish or evil spirit, connected as it is with the ugly, thuglike son. Together with the equally ugly mother, this couple represents the lower, negative side of the processes, counterparts to the Virgin Mother and the divine child from the previous dream of Mary Soul.

> I am on a hilltop where my nose and throat keep filling with green mucus, so that I have to keep blowing my nose, filling three handkerchiefs which were not clean to begin with. I even see the green mucus as the vegetation around me, and I hear the words "fatal son."

I am on a hilltop, which means I am close to the spiritual in unconscious processes. That is why in so many Biblical stories and myths worldwide, the prophets, shamans, and heroes, go up a mountain to experience God or the gods. The Mount, or Mound, in ancient Egypt was where Atum or Ra sat on his throne, and there was a corresponding Mount in the Underworld where Osiris sat upon his throne. The green toad in the last dream managed to run into my house (representing the psyche) before I could close the door, and now I am feeling the negative effects (the nasal discharge).

The traditional color of spirit is green, particularly so for the Holy Spirit, but the green mucus, as well as the toad, alludes to the dark side of it. In alchemy there is the *viriditas gloriosa*, the "glorious green," but green mucus is the opposite of this. The "blessed greenness" *(benedicta viriditas)* is the hidden, divine life-spirit that permeates all nature, but again the dark side is the "leprosy of the metals." Green signified the perfection that would turn to "truest gold" in the opus for the alchemist.

Alchemists equated greenness with the Soul of the World and the Holy Spirit, which in a sense matches ancient Egyptian concepts. Shu, or Shu-Anhur, was the "breath of Ra," a sort of higher form of the Holy Spirit who merges with the high God; Kneph, who was perhaps a lower form, was said to "rest upon the waters" i. e; the lower depths of the unconscious. Interestingly, Osiris, who was lord of so many things, was also lord of green vegetation, linking him again with the spirit Mercurius.

In the dream, I hear the words "fatal son," and this refers not only to the ugly son of the last dream, but to what follows on in a couple of later dreams. A "fatal son" means the dark son, which would be fatal to myself and perhaps to the unconscious and conscious collective realms.

> My dog is very ill. His whole body is steaming as if being boiled.

My dog is a dog-spirit in these processes and as such represents the Higher Self in its lower or first form. Here he is very sick, and this is due to the dark side of the Holy Spirit, or the *viriditas*, which is obviously having a very harmful affect on him. If we recall, a number of dreams ago my dog was bitten on the side of his body by a green toad, and in the last dream but one, the toad ran into my house (into my total psyche) not only gaining a foothold, but setting up permanent residence. Then, in the last dream, there appeared the green mucus and the "fatal son." The plot thickens.

> Film actor Boris Karloff is present in character as one of his horror roles, and there is a great atmosphere of evil everywhere because of him.

The evil green spirit has now taken on human form, as a personification, though "human" he is not. Perhaps monster or demon would be more apt, and he appears again in the next dream.

> Although the scene is at a seaside resort and takes place during the day, it is more like the night because of the evil that is about. A maniacal killer of tremendous strength is butchering people with a large knife as he roams around the town. He is in the form of actor Boris Karloff in one of his horror roles, as in the last dream. He murders a priest and a nun, though it is not certain if they are dead. This is a tremendously strong force that may be too strong for anyone to destroy, even the light form of the Higher Self. A voice calls out from above, "The green man must be killed."

It seems that this is the dark side of the Holy Spirit on the rampage. This brings to mind the *verdigris*, the greenness of the alchemists, but again in its shadow form. This is almost certainly the origin of the story of the Green Knight whom Gawain has to defeat in the Arthurian legends; this knight acts like an uncontrollable force of spirit.

There has been some argument over the centuries as to whether the Holy Spirit is a force or a person, as well as much disagreement in the ancient world as to whether it is male or female. Christ refers to it as "he" a number of times in the Gospels, indicating that it is both a person and male. The answer is that it is both force and person.

It is a force that can appear in humanized form, or any other shape, come to that. In fact, Jung called the "wise old man" figure who appeared in his dreams "the personification of spirit." As the man (Philemon) presented the four keys to open the gates to the unconscious to Jung, Philemon repeats the gesture of Shu-Anhur, the "breath" or spirit force of Ra, who presented the keys to Amenta to the initiate in Egypt. Whether the green force who becomes the green man in this dream is the Holy Spirit, or the *verdigris* in demonic form (a force of Mercurius) is a moot point. It certainly appears in negative form as the ferociously strong and evil Boris Karloff. Whichever it is, the voice of authority from above says that it, or he, must be killed.

The Green Man was the green spirit of nature, and the Celtic stag god Kerunnus Kernunnos, Mercurius, the Green Knight, and so on, are all expressions of him. The stag is his chief animal form, and not far from where I live in the middle of England, at a town called Abbots Bromley, they still do "the dance of the Green Man" wearing stags' antlers.

So as we can see, the Green Man has been known through history in various forms, and has been plaguing me in my processes. I said that the spirit Mercurius is an expression of him, but it is really truer to say that he is one of the expressions of Mercurius.

It is very significant that the Green Man cuts off his own head, or that Perceval does it, because the decapitating of the lower-earth spirit runs right through the Western Mysteries. It was the severed head of Osiris that was all important to the early alchemists, the "Sons of the Golden Head." Osiris is Lord of the Waters, and John the Baptist says that he baptizes with water, i.e., the lower spirit, or soul, while Christ will baptize with the higher spirit of God. John is decapitated, just as Osiris and the Green Man are. John represents the same lower spirit. It was the head of Jung that first led me into the Mysteries, of course.

> I am full of fear because I know that a tremendously powerful, demonic force is loose among the people, the whole atmosphere being a heavy gloom of evil. So I go to a certain public house (pub), which is situated near where I live, to warn the customers of the great danger from this evil. It is night as I stand outside the front door, and the pub regulars, all men it seems, come out to hear what I have to say. But when I tell them of the demonic force and the great danger, they refuse to believe me and laugh.

> Just then, I feel an intensely evil presence behind me, and I turn to see a handsome, somewhat presentable young man dressed in a frock coat, cape, and top hat, all jet black. The figure says to me, "I am the Antichrist." This fills me with absolute terror; full of fear but wishing to warn them, I turn to the men and point to the figure and cry, "That is him. That is the Antichrist." No one seems to take my warnings seriously.
>
> Things are then somewhat hazy and the next thing I know is that the black figure has caught me by the genitals and is torturing me savagely, trying to force me to follow him. The other men are gone now. Yet I defy the Antichrist, crying out "Jesus Christ." Still, I wonder how much of all this I can take.

On waking from this dream I was so petrified and full of fear that my lower jaw kept snapping open and shut of its own accord. I have never been so starkly terrified in my whole life before. Yet afterwards, I loved it. Not the Antichrist and the suffering but the enormous *meaning* that lies behind it all.

In the modern world, good and evil have become blurred, especially in their eternal aspects and implications. Evil is rationalized and has lost its utter terribleness, so that no one seems to be seen as evil anymore. It is no longer believed that an individual can be born with a truly evil soul; consequently, any vicious killer can be "rehabilitated" and made into a respectable part of society. At the same time, we now have children killing other children, but there seems to be no awareness of just how stark evil can be and how it possesses certain individuals.

A dream-vision can wake us up with a jolt. When we stare it in the face, we realize that stark evil does exist, and that it is as eternally real as good. Other dreams, following later, demonstrate how certain evil lives, which exist within the Higher Self in higher reality, must continually be born through history to bring evil to the world. These personalities are unfortunately always amongst us, and must be so, as evil is necessary to the full reality of life. However, we are meant to recognize it as such, to give the Devil his due, but then to fight against him with all our strength. This is one of the things our higher consciousness allows us, or requires us, to do.

The Antichrist figure in the dream, the dark Self, has obviously built up over the past few dreams, so that now he comes forth. There has been a succession of figures: the ugly, thugish boy, the "fatal son," the green toad and mucus, the maniacal Boris Karloff figure, and now the

Antichrist. Just as the Holy Spirit accompanied Christ's coming forth in the Gospels, so the dark side of it, the green mucus/Green Man, accompanies the dark side of the Self coming forth here.

Jung says that when seen from the view of psychology, though Christ is the personification of the Self, this is nevertheless only the light side of the phenomenon. This is why the Antichrist appeared almost immediately in Christian traditions to make up and complete the full archetype (1959a). Or as a Gnostic saying had it, *daemon est deus inversus*, "the Devil is the reverse side of God."

> As I walk along the street wearing the dark red robe of a priest, my eyes have the gaze of the religious seer and mystic. I meet a man and say to him, "It has been after me since I first saw it in the shop years ago."

In one of my first dreams, I was in the shop where I once worked, and on the wall I saw the face of Christ. Since that time, all the processes in the unconscious in which I have been involved have been heading in one direction; that is, to make of me a priest of the unconscious. A priest of the world, of the Church, may dedicate his life to God and to goodness, but if he has not experienced religion directly, at the divine source (which is both so wondrous and terrible that a transformation of personality takes place) then it is all only a matter of faith and belief with him. It is exceedingly admirable and praiseworthy, but it must entail a certain amount of secret uncertainty and doubt. But a priest who has been to the depths and experienced divine spirit directly does not believe; he *knows*. He has gnosis and certainty; he is made a priest not by man, but by the eternal powers themselves.

> I am sitting at home when a strange looking creature comes into the room. At first it is a lizard, but then it becomes a dog that has flippers. These flippers become like the wings of an airplane, with rockets at the tips, though the rockets are really fish with lovely little faces. Then the fish become gray birds. At first I am afraid and try to escape, but then I calm down.

Here, in this strange creature, we have a conglomeration of opposites which symbolically make up the Self at animal level. The lizard represents the lowest level, the dragon in positive form, but then it changes into a dog which is its opposite. The lizard means the instinctual side, while the dog represents the spirit side. The latter has flippers, which makes it partly aquatic and partly of the lower unconscious. But the flippers become like the wings of a plane, suggesting spirit again.

However, the rocketlike tips become lovely little fish which become birds. These creatures keep changing into their opposites, matter to spirit, and vice versa, though they are all of the positive, light side. Even the lizard signifies the light side of the lowest instincts, in contradistinction to the crocodile, which represents their terrible side. Such conglomerate creatures are depicted in ancient Egypt, and we now know the source—the unconscious processes.

> I am quite ill, my body twisted up, due perhaps to my contact with cosmic forces. However, I manage to laugh and say, "The most important thing for us is our humanity. However awesome, terrible, and overwhelming cosmic forces may be, our simple humanity keeps us small, humble, and warm-hearted, and therefore safe."

I remember this dream well and recall what a very heavy weight I was carrying with all of the material coming through from the non-personal levels. Visions from the spirit side can wear you down just as much as fearful contents that come through from the depths. Visions of spirit are not always pleasant and are like having a deeply disturbing electric current running through your body. It's not dangerous if you keep and have the best motives at heart, but it can be rather unpleasant at times.

No matter what we experience, including great or dangerous things, we must remember that our simple humanity is our greatest gift. Then no matter what assails us from the unconscious, we will remain safe, though somewhat screwed up at times, as the dream states. In contrast with this, Nietzsche went beyond himself with inflated consciousness so that we are forced to ask not where his greatness is, but where his smallness, his humility, his humanness are. Jung says we must shrink to the size of a pea before the eternal powers of the unconscious, before God, and he is so right.

> There is a dark, heavy, evil atmosphere over everything as an evil shape roams about. I don't see who or what it is, but when I awaken, my body is as heavy as lead and aches all over.

Back to the evil again, it seems, and the next dream follows on and develops directly from this one.

> Jack the Ripper is about. I don't see him, but I know that it is he, and I am filled with great fear.

This is the evil figure which caused me so much stress in the previous dream. Its image is clearer now as I know who it is. This often happens, on both the light and dark sides: we feel the approach of a content first and then it arrives in a follow-up dream. Here, the content is much too evil and devastating, much too powerful, to be my own shadow. Yet I have a friend who is something of a "light" shadow figure, and he appears in dreams sometimes in an integrated way. So Jack the Ripper here is the dark side of the lower Self, a Set or Mephistopheles, roaming about.

We are still involved in the series of dreams concerning the negative green force and the Antichrist, as the following dreams show, and that reinforces the conclusion that Jack the Ripper is the dark Self here. He traditionally wears black top hat and cape as did the Antichrist figure. The Ripper slashes women—the anima in the unconscious—but why? To lure the anima to evil should be his business.

> There is still the heavy atmosphere of evil about and I hear and perhaps see, the words, "black magic." This frightens me, so I mentally impose the sign of the Gnostic cross symbol (the cross within the circle) over the words and my fear then goes.

The evil of the last two dreams is still present and I have to impose the Gnostic symbol over the words, "black magic," to diminish the evil's power. The symbol means the union of spirit and soul into a whole, and therefore represents the Higher Self, who, in positive and ultimate form, is nothing less than the Son of God.

It seems that I was right that Jack the Ripper represents the dark side of the Self. The evil is continued with the black magic in this dream, because only its counterpart, the Gnostic sign of the Anthropos (as union of opposites in the god-man) can diminish the evil. This symbol, as said earlier, was known in earliest Egypt with the circle of Heaven on the four quarters of the horizon. The ankh cross unites the circle and the cross, and in one meaning is the key to Amenta (the Underworld that is the collective unconscious). This is also part of the meaning of the four gold keys on the key ring that I received from Jung.

> A hero—a young, blond-haired god, so it seems—is gravely ill, lying flat out on my living room floor. An angel comes. It is as a being of the light, but he is also villainous and wears black armor (in contrast to the hero's white suit). The angel sends beams of light from his hands, which are covered by black, metal gloves, and these beams revive the hero, who stands up, no longer ill. Then the dark angel turns the beam of light into his own mouth, destroying himself, as though he had to die to give the hero life. There is something highly unusual about this; a black angel destroying himself for the sake of a white, "good" hero.

Sometimes the workings of the unconscious baffle us. Why should this mostly dark angel make the ultimate self-sacrifice on behalf of the forces of the light side? It should be helping the forces of darkness to win. All I can say is that this sort of thing happens sometimes, for reasons unseen by consciousness.

However, the dark angel does have some light within, which suggests a unification of the opposite sides. If the dark side wins the war between the opposites, it can only lead to lasting conflict and dissociation, and I, as consciousness, will split away from the unconscious, as it would be the evil side in power and dominating the Self. It will all mean catastrophe if evil wins, and so perhaps the dark side is willing to give way somewhat in the interests of the wholeness of the total Self.

> A large black dog comes up to me and while it is quite friendly, I know that it is very dangerous for me. So, picking up two old pieces of wood, I make a cross with them and hold them up as protection. I feel tremendous power in this cross; it is not light and joyous, but full of suffering and heart-rending anguish. Yet even these words cannot convey what the feeling is like.

The black dog denotes the dark, shadow side of the Self in lower form. In the Teutonic Wotan myths, when Wotan the wild huntsman rides across the skies leading the eerie hunters, the black dog leads his pack of hounds, and is sometimes left behind to the horror of the

255

countryfolk. We can see how this myth is based on actual experiences of the unconscious processes.

The poodle was originally a hunting dog, so it becomes clear why Goethe's dream processes, on which he based *Faust*, came up with the black poodle as the first form of Mephistopheles. Although the black dog in my dream wishes to be friendly, the last thing I want is the dark Self as a friend, so I make a cross out of the pieces of wood to drive the dog away.

The most potent symbol of Western civilization is the cross, and here it is full of great power, suffering, and anguish. However, this is not the Gnostic cross within the circle from a couple of dreams ago, which likewise diminished the power of evil. It seems as though my individuation processes, the unconscious processes, are uniting the different Gnostic, orthodox Christian traditions, and the alchemical underside.

> I am with my dog in the Greenwood in Scotland where a green stag attacks us. Between us, my dog and I manage to fight the stag off, and I then pull yards and yards of a green elastic-like mucus from out of my chest. Finally, it is all expunged, and I feel much better and laugh heartily. All the vegetation has now become a beautiful, healthy green, and I see a lake that has a burning bush by the side of it. I then join a group of people who are journeying to a Promised Land.

This is a very significant dream. Here, I finally manage to overcome the negative force of green spirit that has been causing so much havoc, causing all of the dark contents to come forth in the processes. The nose seems to have been the way in for the mucus and the chest the way out. There is so much of it now because the force has grown to dangerous proportions. This was all begun by the ugly, thuglike boy and the green toad. Here the stag is obviously associated with these and with the green mucus. The spirit Mercurius sometimes appears as a stag in alchemy, and indeed, the stag also represents soul in general, but here it is obviously the dark side. Mercurius is the product of the soul depths, or rather *is* the soul depths, whereas Christ is the product of spirit. Osiris and Horus are based on the same archetypes—the higher and lower forms of the Self. In fact, there is an alchemical engraving of a stag as soul standing face-to-face with a unicorn as spirit, representing the unification of both.

My dog in the dream represents the Higher Self in first form on the spirit side, which is why he helps me fight the Mercurial stag. In the Holy Grail material, Perceval fights a stag with the help of a white dog accompanying him on his quest, exactly as in my dream. A Star Woman—that is, a woman wearing a red dress covered in stars—ascends from a pool and sets Perceval off to find a stag, and to bring its head to her. To help him in this task, she gives him the white hound as guide and companion.

As to the stag, representing the nature spirit Mercurius, we find that Cernunnos, a type of Mercurius or Green Man, took the form of a stag in Celtic mythology; Merlin is also associated with these. It may seem strange that the stag is also a symbol of Christ, but this signifies that very aspect of the Higher Self below in the soul depths—the lower soul of Christ, so to speak. Perceval must cut off the stag's head, just as the alchemists had to cut off the lion's paws, and I too must defeat the stag with the help of my dog, though it is sufficient for me to drive it away.

The Star Woman requires Perceval to nail the stag's head to a tree, as a sort of crucifixion of the lower Self; this has been interpreted as a complete cutting off of the instinctual depths. However, I must question this, because the crucifixion of Christ does not mean the cutting off from the higher spirit, rather the opposite, in fact. Cernunnos, the stag god, suffers death and resurrection himself, and so is obviously based upon the same archetype as Osiris and Christ, though in a more primitive form.

The lake and the burning bush then appear together in my dream. While the lake signifies the feminine depths, as in many myths, in Biblical texts, and the Arthurian and Grail legends, the burning bush being a sign of God's theophany, represents the spirit. The lake and the burning bush appearing together means their unification; the Promised Land to which the people and myself journey refers to the wholeness and fulfillment of the Higher Self, which can now occur. This could be called the Paradise of Peace, instances of which we find in the myths and sacred texts.

As said elsewhere, Moses first sits by the well at Midian and the seven sisters appear, and then he goes up the mountain to experience the burning bush, from the water to the fire, from soul to spirit, and the unification of both. Moses first sees a young "angel" in the bush, and then God speaks from it, signifying first the Higher Self comes forth as manifestor of his Father, and then the Father himself. These formed the divine pair we find together right through the Egyptian myths and the Bible. The "god with two faces" in Egypt did not refer to the two sides of the divine son, the light and dark of the Higher Self, but to the divine Father and Son together in one being (One Being was an actual title of the High God).

> I am fishing with a friend and remark that we may catch a very big fish. Suddenly, a large fish does appear and it starts to grow larger and larger until it is about six or eight feet long. It then swims upstream, diving and resurfacing like a dolphin as it goes. It must then go onto dry land because it changes into a stag.

I have just given some details of the symbolism of the stag as a nature spirit, (as the spirit of the unconscious), and earlier I explained the fish symbol. So I will just say here that this dream demonstrates how these very old symbols are still alive in the collective unconscious, and how they may merge one into another simply because they are all representations and aspects of the Higher Self.

> Everywhere there is lovely green vegetation and close by there is a lake. There are crowds of people all rushing to see a burning bush led by a film hero, and I go with them. I say, "We can either go by way of the vegetation or the lake; both lead to where we are going."

With the defeat of the stag in its negative aspect—which then appeared in the last dream, apparently in a more positive aspect—the healthy side of the greenness is now to the fore, that is, it signifies the light side of the spirit of nature. The burning bush is also still evident, signifying God's theophany. The lake is similarly evident as the feminine depths, meaning unification is continuing.

I say that we can go to the burning bush by way of the green vegetation or by way of the lake, but this must mean to the Promised Land, as intimated in a previous dream. There is always confusion as to exactly what the Holy Spirit is. As part of the Trinity it is exclusively male, and yet in certain religious systems it is feminine. In ancient Egypt, Ka-Mutef was a creative force of spirit, "Mutef" being a form of "mother," but it was as a *male* mother. In the same way, the god Ptah was said to have a womb because he gave birth to all of creation. I doubt if anyone has ever solved the mystery of the male and female Holy Spirit, and it may well be that it is a complexity of opposites—spirit and soul, male and female, light and dark—just as is the Higher Self.

> Jesus Christ appears seated on this throne just above me, wearing his red-purple robe, while I kneel before him. Taking his phallus into my mouth, I thus receive Christ's seed into myself. However, this is implied rather than happening as a physical act.

What does it mean to receive the seed of Christ? What is involved? What is given? What is required? To be honest, I confess that I cannot answer these questions very well. All I can say is that I have become involved in processes of the collective unconscious, the "other reality," in which the divine drama is being enacted, stretching over thousands of years, involving man and the world of consciousness, matter and soul on the one hand, and God, Christ (Higher Self), and the realm of spirit on the other.

Having become involved, I now have a role to play on behalf of Christ (of the Higher Self as a Christ parallel) and God. That is the only way I can interpret it, although more may be involved. I can only continue with the processes in the same way as I have proceeded from the beginning. Much of the symbolism found in my processes is Biblical, though some is Gnostic, alchemical, or ancient Egyptian. What is intended, it seems, is the further development of the religious spirit, and literally so, involving the world of matter, the lower soul depths, and the higher spirit. One thing is sure, the depth psychology of Jung is involved, and this is because depth psychology is the new way of understanding what were once the very ancient mysteries of the Underworld of Egypt.

One further point is that this is the real meaning to Christ being of the seed of David. This is not of a human line in the outer world, but of the spiritual seed, the blue blood through the unconscious.

> I hear the words "The Holy Spirit" and I become aware of the light fixture in the room which has three arms, each with a bulb on it. It is night and the room is in darkness, but as the words are spoken, the bulbs light up and the room becomes bright.
>
> I am then walking in the street with three strange men, and one of them, the spokesman, wears a rough animal skin and has long, unkempt, mousy colored hair. He carries a staff and is obviously a prophet and

soothsayer, a sort of Elijah or John the Baptist. He is expected to prophesy about the Higher Self and myself. He stares at me intently then raises his arms and declares, "One shall become three; then three shall become six."

As he speaks with raised arms his stomach is bare, and a small round lump appears on it. This becomes three vertically lined lumps, and then three more appear by their sides so that there are now six. I make a comment about the soil of the Earth being ready to take seed.

Suddenly, actor Spencer Tracy, in his role of the tyrannical father in the film "Broken Lance," comes charging up in a horse-drawn carriage (or a buckboard) coming dangerously close. The prophet figure takes a swing at him with a three-pronged trident, though he misses and Tracy just laughs spitefully. (The "three shall become six," spoken by the prophet, probably refers to empires.)

The Holy Trinity is three in one, as Father, Son and Holy Spirit. But the Holy Spirit itself is also three in one, and is experienced as threefold in dreams and visions. This may be as tripodic spaceships, three lights, three-eyed aliens, the Three Wise Men, and so on. As other of my dreams reveal, there is also the chthonic trinity which is of the lower Earth, or soul depths. The three-headed devil of Dante, the black trinity of the alchemists, and my own dream-visions of a lower, Earth trinity, are examples of the latter.

In the dream, I hear the words "Holy Spirit" and the three lightbulbs light up, and then the three men arrive. The John the Baptist figure may be significant because when Jesus the man is baptized by John, he immediately receives the Holy Spirit in the form of the descending dove. So in both my dream and the gospel account this rough, hairy, animal-skinned figure is associated with the Holy Spirit.

As for the prophecy of "one shall become three, and three shall become six," it could mean that the Higher Self, the one, will be part of the three, the Holy Trinity. My following dreams support this interpretation. It may also be the case that the lower trinity will be united with the higher one, so that "three become six." The Devil's number is six, and as a lower trinity the number of the beast is 666. However, the realm of the lower unconscious is only evil in its dark aspect, for the light aspect is the realm of Osiris, or the light side of Mercurius, and so the two trinities would be in positive unification.

I realize that my interpretation of this and other dreams might seem incredible in the original sense of the word: not to be credited with validity. But I also realized a long time ago that I am involved in the unfolding divine drama with these processes and that we live in an age when there will be fundamental change, for good or ill, and that it will involve man, the eternal powers of spirit and soul, and ultimately, God. All this is difficult for me to believe myself—in fact, it is incredible still to me; but I know that it is all absolutely genuine and meaningful, though of the dark, as well as the light, and all of the evidence shows that it is so.

Many people think we are at the beginning of a new age of progress, a leap forward, but the wiser ones realize that we may well be nearer to the end of things, the "end of days." If we are to survive to the new age, which will mean either a further spiritual development or nothing, then we have to realize that such things as appear in my processes are real, that they constitute the real and true nature of reality itself.

As for the appearance of actor Spencer Tracy as the tyrannical father riding the buckboard and with the wheels forming a fourfold mandala symbol, I wonder if this could be a reference to the dark side of the Father himself? The four-wheeled chariot is known as the Merkabah in esoteric Jewish literature, and Jung says, referring to this, that God's vehicle means the quaternity of the Higher Self. The alchemists had a serpent riding on the fourfold chariot as a symbol of the lower wholeness. In Zechariah, we find that four chariots and the horses represent the "four spirits of Heaven."

Since Tracy in the dream is a negative father figure, and since the buckboard or chariot is either the vehicle of God or the Higher Self, we can only conclude that this represents either a negative side of either God or the Higher Self, though from a certain angle they both amount to the same thing.

> I see a message in white letters on a red background, and there is an intense, numinous atmosphere of wholeness, as though all is golden. The message is the line, "Hail to the Lord's anointed."

In ancient Egypt red and white symbolized the eternal opposites, as they did later with the alchemists, and the union of them was said to produce, symbolically, the gold. The red drops of blood from a wounded bird on the white snow, found in a Grail legend, means the same basically.

Perceval, wearing the red armor taken from the slain Red Knight, together with the maiden Blancheflor (white flower), repeat the motif of the Red Slave and White Queen of alchemy—the opposites to be united.

"The Lord's anointed" means "God's chosen," and although this referred to the Messiah, it nevertheless predates Jesus and meant the royal line of "kings" even before there were kings in Israel. The line of Psalm 23, "Thou anointest my head with oil" refers to the same thing, to the anointed ones who were spiritual kings, initiates, prophets, and so forth, who had experienced God directly and brought forth the Higher Self.

The prophet Isaiah refers to the "Lord's anointed" who will raise up the dead from the depths of Sheol at the end of days. In Egypt, Horus was the "anointed, only begotten Son of God the Father; that is . . . Horus glorified, who followed the human Horus," which of course refers to the Higher Self as Son of God, who is the anointed. The same applies to Christ, the anointed. The anointing of kings may reach back to early Egypt to the covering of the mummy with oil in the process of embalming, which was the beginning of the Osirification of the deceased. This symbolically linked the Osirified with his eternal aspect. Though Osiris is mainly the resurrected one, Horus too in one form is resurrected after being anointed, as Massey puts it, "the anointed Son of God the Father."

> I am on a hillside near a beach when a goat runs up the hill and bites my right hand, though not hard. My dog is with me so I have to pick him up to protect him from the goat. But then the latter goes down the hill again. The dream somehow points out that I am "with the lambs," and that the goat is opposite to these. Also, I think a shepherd is mentioned.

The goat is associated with unbridled lust and earthiness—with the world, the flesh, and the Devil. As we know, the Devil's form is traditionally that of a goat while Christ is the Lamb. I am on a hill in the dream, which means I am close to the spirit, the religious, where the goat bites my hand. This could mean temptation, and worse, great danger, so I have to lift up my dog—the representative of the Higher Self—out of harm's way. The dream points out that I belong with the lambs, which means I belong with the higher religious, the spiritual, the Christian. This distinction between the symbolic goat and lamb is very ancient, and led to Pan being depicted as goatlike and Satan goat-headed.

The hill reminds us of the Egyptian Mount and the Hebrew Mount Zion of Revelation, on which Christ is the Lamb. The child Horus was the calf earlier, but when the astrological age changed to the Ram, he became the lamb. However, the nearest reference seems to be Matthew 25; 31-34.

> When the Son of Man shall come in his glory, and all the holy angels with him, then shall he sit upon the throne of his glory: And before him shall be gathered all nations: and he shall separate them from one another, as a shepherd divideth his sheep from the goats: And he shall set the sheep on his right hand, but the goats on the left. Then shall the King say to them on his right hand, Come, ye blessed of my Father, inherit the kingdom prepared for you from the foundations of the world. . . .

I awaken in the dream, though I am still asleep, and I have a severe headache and am heavy with worry. "The trouble is, it is the Old Testament God," I sigh. This is causing me some anguish.

The God of the Old Testament can be bad tempered and quite destructive when humans, true to form, display our many failings and destructiveness. It would be fine if God were all-loving and full of forgiveness, as in the New Testament, but such is not the case. God is a *complexio oppositorum,* the ultimate complexity of opposites, and all opposites are contained in Him and are of Him. This means the dark side as well as the light. God would prefer to be in His light form, but man's powerful inclination to selfishness, dissociation, and downright wickedness are not conducive to bringing forth that good side.

I have been warned in many dreams that man's continual failure could bring about his destruction once and for all. This is the cause of my bad headache in the dream. I know that the true nature of God is the Old Testament one—that is, not merely good. Jung tells us that all opposites are of God, but that we must bend to this burden, though it means that God may even incarnate Himself within us, filling us with divine conflict. Jung asks what does a mere human do with such intolerable a burden? He answers by saying that we must wait and see what solution our dreams come up with. The tyrannical father, actor Spencer Tracy in the earlier dream, could represent this negative situation.

> I see three white cords plaited to make one single rope.

This must be an allusion to the Holy Trinity, the three-in-one deity, or at least, its symbol, considering all that has gone before in my dreams, and it is the positive side, as the three cords, the one rope, are white. Jung says that as an archetype, the Trinity may force spiritual development upon us, not merely suggest it, but if there is any danger of it being detrimental to health, the archetype will fade. Jung also says that the Trinity represents the three-part process that is taking place within us, but that it is not just a symbolic representation of the three persons in one nature; it actually *is* them.

The Holy Trinity is exclusively male, and would have to be in the circumstances, as the Son comes forth from the Father, and the Holy Spirit is the force that binds them, but this cannot be the whole picture; there must be more to the Holy Spirit. In fact, Jung says that it is unfathomable, but is sure that it is dual-natured, light and dark, just as the Father and Son are. The feminine element, being missing from the Trinity, must be unified with it in the interests of wholeness and totality, making the quaternity, and the accomplishment of this is what these processes have been about from the most ancient times.

> I am in the street where dark yellow clouds come rolling over. They become lighter and brighter with more colors, and then take the shape of the Virgin Mary, who wears a red dress and blue mantle. I become overjoyed as I point upwards and cry, "Look, it's Holy Mary. She has seen the state we are in and has come to help us."

Holy Mary represents the eternal feminine spirit in Christian form, the mother goddess who in her light form comes to help suffering mankind. In the visions of St. Bernadette at Lourdes, and of the children of Fatima in Portugal, it was Holy Mary who appeared to offer help to the people of the world. From the view of depth psychology and its unlimited possibilities, we know that the visions were genuine because of the archetypal symbolism involved: the Great Mother coming through to us. Unfortunately, we seem to have learned nothing from those appearances and the situation grows steadily worse. Can you imagine a group of politicians, or of high-powered businessmen, listening to the message from Fatima? Yet it is these people who rule (or misrule) the world.

As mentioned elsewhere, Jung sees the Assumption of the Virgin into Heaven, proclaimed by the Catholic Church in 1950, as a very important step in the evolution of the religious spirit. It restores the Old Testament Sophia, who was with God from the beginning, to Heaven where she becomes Queen of Heaven. This will ultimately lead, so Jung believes, to the *hieros gamos*, the sacred marriage, leading in turn to the prophesied incarnation of a savior, a new Christ. Sophia was always known for her love of mankind, and so in my dream she has come, as Mary, to help us.

The red dress and blue mantle are traditional, and can be found in the majority of depictions of the Virgin Mary from early centuries, particularly during the Renaissance. They refer to the lower and higher feminine colors, red for the Earth, and blue for the celestial. In alchemy, the four colors of totality are red, blue, yellow, and green, and if the first two are feminine we can expect the latter two to be masculine. This is indeed the case, and in dreams and visions Christ, or what he represents, is yellow, while green is the color of the Holy Ghost.

There is a variation to this, for in Pontmain, France, in 1871, a group of children saw a vision where Christ was colored red. This was known to ancient Egypt where Horus in one form was the Red God. Mary actually appeared before Christ at Pontmain, wearing a blue dress covered in stars, linking her with the sky/mother goddess Nut, who was usually depicted as covered in stars. Nut/Hathor and Horus are prefigurations of Mary and Christ.

My old she-cat, which died over twenty years ago, comes in the night and speaks to me, though the words have now faded.

The she-cat represents my anima-soul at animal level, just as my dog takes the part of a dog-spirit. It is no coincidence that in Egypt the cat goddess, Bast was the "Lady of Life," life being an apt term to describe the essential function of the anima. Bast was not connected with water, however, but with "mild fire," therefore having a solar and warming significance. She was mother of Nefer-Tem, a form of Iu-em-hetep in one cult; Iu-em-hetep was a Higher Self figure and a sort of forerunner of Christ. Unfortunately, the words my cat spoke have now faded, but whatever they were, they would have been of much interest.

> There are two bishops wearing golden robes and with them are two nuns (though it is not specified what they wear). With them are two baby boys, twins, and it is all a sort of Nativity scene.

This imagery again alludes to the birth of the Higher Self, which is truly twins, being the totality *par excellence*. This divine birth can continue to occur through history because it is an eternal occurrence. The Higher Self as Sun-god and savior is always dual, although it is not so obvious at times because the figures are so separate, the dark one sometimes being a serpent. A lower example, in animal form, is my dog and the black, evil dog representing the light and dark sides.

> My sister has a large, heavy Bible and she reads a quotation from it, though exactly what is not clear. I say, "It all started going wrong thirty to forty years ago," meaning that society has been tumbling slowly into chaos since that time.
> I then see a large sack on the floor filled with something heavy and I say, "If I can lift it, I can do it." By this I mean that I will be able to fight against the chaos with the religious processes from the unconscious, and I do, in fact, lift up the heavy sack quite easily. Later a woman I know who is a Jehovah's Witness gives me a fish.

My sister represents my anima in this dream, as the sister and mother are quite common representations of the anima in a man's unconscious. As she quotes from the Bible, it causes me to comment on the sickness of modern society. The answer and the antidote to this is religion from the divine source, from the depths of the unconscious itself, but to take up the fight will be a very heavy task and burden for any person. However, by lifting the sack easily I am shown that I can undertake this responsibility. Then a woman I know, a Jehovah's Witness, appropriately gives me the fish. Symbolically, this is the antidote to the poison that is afflicting the modern world. As Jung writes about the similar situation two thousand years ago (and speaking of the Gnostic Hymn to the Soul): "Mankind looked and waited, and it was a fish—*levatus de profundo* [drawn from the deep]—that became the symbol of the savior, the bringer of healing" (1959b).

The fish, as I said elsewhere, though being the symbol of the savior, represents the son of the Great Mother, sometimes the Fish-Mother, the collective soul side of the unconscious. The son as savior historically has at times been depicted coming from out of the Fish-Mother's mouth. This is the origin of the *vesica piscis* of the Church, which is an oval shape, either horizontal or upright. Some churches were built to this shape, and the Virgin and Child, or the adult Christ, are sometimes portrayed in the upright form of the fish's mouth. But much earlier in the ancient world we find the symbol of the mouth of the fish. There are depictions of Oannes, the man-fish, with a star above, and the fish's mouth below. This latter was on the one hand the *entrance* to the watery depths, but on the other, the exit, or what Massey calls the *outrance*, out of which the god came.

In the constellation of the Southern Fish we find the royal star, Fomalhaut, which means "mouth of the fish." Massey says that the coming of Horus was associated to this star of the south, also called the "eye of the southern fish." The fish, the water-cow, and the crocodile were all stated mythically to "bring forth words from the mouth." This is the Word, the Logos. As stated, Christ, Horus, Oannes, Bacchus, Vishnu, are all the Fish, and Vishnu carries the Word in his hand as he comes out the mouth of the Fish-Mother.

Oannes is really Ea, the Sublime Fish that has seven fins, corresponding to the seven Annedoti of Oannes. Although the abode of Ea, Apsu, was said to be in the waters, these were *celestial* waters, as distinct from the waters of the deep. This connects Ea with the higher side of the unconscious, the Spirit, and with the High God, as with Christ. So though we may experience the fish in the watery depths in the processes, it is still ultimately the symbol of the full Higher Self.

> This was a heavy dream, causing me stress by the heavy atmosphere, and it involves God in none too pleasant a mood. I find myself in a city inhabited by savage, warlike Apache Indians. I am taken to a great palace where in a large dark hall I have to crawl on my stomach to the Apache "emperor" seated on his throne.
>
> I have a message to give to this emperor, and though I am severely warned against it, I rise to my feet and say, "The Great Spirit is very angry." By this I mean that God is showing His anger at the evil ways of not only the Apaches, but of mankind as a whole, for they have not accepted the divine child, the Higher Self symbolized by the fish in the previous dream, and are behaving in a barbarous, degenerate manner.

The world has rejected the divine child and all he involves, and therefore it has rejected God. Out of the Father comes the Son, though it also comes out of the Fish-Mother's mouth, symbolically. This means it comes out at the level of collective soul, in and through the unconscious, the basis and foundations of reality that exist behind and below the facade of conscious reality. The collective soul of man in the modern world, particularly in the West, has become exceedingly materialistic and atheistic, and is gradually slipping into barbarism, symbolized by the savage Apaches. Naturally, God is angry.

All of this is happening at the collective levels of Western culture at this moment, and we are deeply affecting the rest of the world. Our conscious lives are only the small tip of a vast iceberg that stretches out, through the unconscious, to infinity and eternity, with God at one extreme and the World Soul at the other. Soul must permeate matter all over the universe, and spirit is its divine opposite, though they ultimately must unite. The Apache emperor represents Christ's opposite in the lower realm of the unconscious, the spirit Mercurius to the alchemists. This situation is exemplified extremely well by Egyptian mythology, where Osiris is Lord of the Underworld, though he is the positive form, whereas the Apache emperor is not so positive, though perhaps he is not altogether evil.

> There are great storms, with thunder and lightning, and earthquakes and floods are deluging the world because of God's anger with mankind. All the houses of the city where I live have been swept away, though the house in which I live is still standing. I have just minutes to grab a few things before the house goes too.

As I remarked on the last dream, all of this upheaval takes place in the collective unconscious, but society is not aware of it consciously. This may cause the reader to ask just what effects it has on society in everyday life. The answer is that the *gap* between consciousness and the unconscious gradually becomes a neurotic dissociation, even a mass psychosis.

Society loses its foundations and all sorts of sickness flows in to fill the gap, the ultimate result of which is the fall into chaos. Political correctness and idiotic, over-intellectualized thinking replace wisdom and common sense. Moral corruption, and greedy commercial and political opportunism come to be admired, as long as they show success. With the general malaise, cruelty becomes more pronounced, sickening violence becomes exciting, and sadistic sensationalism and rabid pleasure-seeking take the place of beauty and spiritual meaning. The warm, homely values of decent family life are no longer the high ideals to be lived and fought for. Society succumbs to the shadow, or the serpent-dragon, and all sorts of evils take hold. In the end chaos comes to reign, and destructive floods from the unconscious deluge the culture, which has lost all semblance of real "culture" long ago.

All of this happens *gradually,* so that few people realize the ship is sinking. But it is the age-old fate of societies that lose their religious foundations which exist through the unconscious.

When the Persian prophet Zarathustra experiences his God, Ahura Mazda, the latter states that one thing most pleasing to God is a man and wife with their children, together with their animals, at home together on their farm. It is my experience during these processes that God does indeed love such things in man as decency, humility, modesty, and the love that exists in a family group, though it should not be limited to that. These are not just sentimental words, for we bring out of God a response according to our values and the way we live. God can be utterly terrible if that is the response we invoke, which is why Jung often quoted the old saying: "We can love God, but we must also fear Him."

> There is still the terrible heaviness as I take passage on a ship which I think is going to Africa (this is in the 1930s). However, we pass that continent and go on to an island somewhere in Indonesia. As we arrive, I see a youth on the beach dive into the sea and swim down under water. Then I have disembarked and stand in front of a cave, which has a large, eerie looking skull as an entrance, the open jaws and teeth being the opening. There is still the terrible, foreboding atmosphere hanging over everything, and I see a fire-god with fire belching from its mouth. This reminds me of the Goya painting where the god Saturn devours his children. The place is probably called "Skull Island."

To the ancient Egyptians, the first act of creation was the manifestation of the Mound arising from the out of the Primordial Waters of Nun, and this was associated with Ptah, the "grandfather of the gods." The island with the fire-god seems to have the same archaic meaning, and

269

the youth diving into the watery depths could be the divine son. Not the higher form of the Son, such as Horus, but the lower son of the depths. I have found myself at islands in a number of my dreams, situated all over the world, and all no doubt with a similar meaning. However, the precise meaning of the details is difficult to figure. A cave is generally the Earth-womb, the entrance to the Underworld, the collective unconscious, but it must all remain a mystery for now.

Skull worship is very ancient and the skull was considered the vessel of transformation, and indeed, was a sacred relic associated with ancestor worship. The terrible, foreboding atmosphere goes with the terrible nature of the god, which seems to be the lower counterpart to the higher God of Spirit. This and other dreams of the Mound, or island, rising from the waters, shows that the Egyptian initiates must have experienced this themselves in the Mysteries. Thus they did not *invent* the Mound, they *experienced* it in the processes.

> I go to my doctor and try to explain the sickness of modern man to him with the following words: "When the unconscious functions in a religious way, but consciousness, being unaware of this, functions in a different way, this results in a split in the total psyche, causing illness."

Let me say first of all how succinctly the unconscious has expressed the situation. This sums up the basis of the sickness of modern man, whose dissociation has now become so chronic that it has developed into mass psychosis. The only cure possible is to heal the dissociation; but this is such a nigh-impossible task because most people are so far away from true reality that it would take a fundamental alteration of their basic thinking to do any good.

Yet this kind of alteration was forced upon St. Paul, who, though a persecutor of Christians (as Saul), was nevertheless not drowning in the scientific materialism and rationalism which have become the whirlpool of our modern world. The tragedy is that many people have no inkling that they are drowning in it, and that the true meaning of their lives lies in precisely the opposite direction to the way they live them.

Paul, as Saul, was very diligent in his persecution of Christians, male and female alike, and says that he was responsible for many of their deaths. In fact, he seems to have been pursuing a private crusade to obliterate all Christians from the face of the Earth. He was almost certainly involved in the martyrdom of St. Stephen, as Acts 8:1 says, "And Saul was consenting to his death." According to Paul, "I persecuted the church of God violently and tried to destroy it" (Galatians 1:13).

Then came the trip to Damascus to fetch bound Christians back to Jerusalem, where they were to be punished. At midday, as he and officials traveled the road, a light brighter than the sun suddenly shone all around, and Paul (and his companions as well, according to one version) fell to earth. Then the voice of Christ spoke out, saying, "Saul, Saul, why persecutest thou me?" (Acts 9:4). He was then told that he must go to Damascus to become witness and minister of the things he had seen. However, Paul was now blind and so had to be led to that place by his companions. Once there, he lay ill for three days, neither eating or drinking. Then, as the account goes, one Ananias had a vision in which "the Lord" instructed him to go to Paul and lay his hands upon him, to restore sight and health, and to confer upon him the Holy Ghost.

Seen from the view of depth psychology, Paul was living contrary to his true nature, which as we know, was that of a religious visionary and reformer. But the more he experienced strange stirrings within—the workings of the unconscious—which must have disturbed him greatly, the more he projected them onto the Christians as the source. There was, of course, close correspondence between the Christian teachings and the powerful unconscious stirrings within himself. Furthermore, because powerful unconscious contents can become contaminated with our own repressed shadow, the receptacle of the projection may be felt to be the very Devil himself.

With such a visionary personality as Paul, this situation cannot continue indefinitely, and steps are taken by the unconscious to force us to see the light. This may be forced upon us violently, as in the case of Paul. But if it is not, we will spend the rest of our days in a state of neurotic depression, or worse. Jung found such was the case with many of his patients. One, an intelligent, beautiful, and rich Jewish girl, was shot through with neurosis until Jung revealed her true nature to her. Jung says she had the soul of a saint and was meant, like Paul, for holiness, but was living completely contrary to her true self.

There was much conflict in the early church between Paul, on the one side, and Peter and James, the brother of Jesus, on the other. This was because Paul was a man who had powerful visions, and to him Christ was literally the Son of God in spirit, whereas for Peter and James,

Jesus had been in the flesh. They had known him personally—James, as his brother, had grown up with Jesus. Paul said his visions must make him seem mad, but it did not worry him because it was all in the service of God.

> I am with a group of people, all male except for one female, and there are either seven or eight of us, probably eight. We are stars in the universe, and we must now fall back to Earth. What amazes me—and I express this to my companions—is that we will fall back to our own planet and no other. I find this incredible because there is so far to fall, billions of miles, yet this is nevertheless what we do, all falling to America. Excepting one who falls to Russia, and who, it is said, drinks like a fish.

In ancient Egypt it was said that the souls of the dead must ascend through the seven planets; the number eight was the "Ogdoad," the number of totality. Later, the alchemists repeated this belief concerning the ascent to the seven planets believing that it meant freedom from the shackles of unconsciousness and the widening of consciousness in spiritual realities. After the ascent must follow the descent back to Earth, so perhaps my dream has a similar meaning.

On the other hand, the seven stars of Revelation may be alluded to, eight with Christ, who holds up the seven. The seven stars referred originally to Egyptian and Babylonian gods, and later, in the Book of Enoch, the prophet has a vision of seven stars. Meister Eckhart, the medieval mystic, writes of seven planets, "seven noble stars," that are nearer to us than all the rest, but he is speaking of our solar system. The seven stars of mythology were not these (Eckhart 1924). An alchemical text, the *Rosarium Philosophorum* (1593), says of Wisdom, "she wears the royal crown of seven glittering stars." Perhaps the mention in Revelation is the most apt meaning, as it refers to the Son of Man, the Higher Self in that form, "and he had in his right hand seven stars."

In Egypt, the seven stars were sometimes sons of the mother star (and mother dragon), Kefa, Sefekh, Hathor, and later the Gnostic Sophia with her seven sons; the Queen of Sheba was also sevenfold, as was Aditi in India with her seven sons. All are expressions of the same archetype. (On the male side, most of the gods of Egypt and other mythologies were sevenfold, plus certain figures of the Bible, as I demonstrate elsewhere.)

In the dream, when we, as stars, fall to Earth, one of us lands in Russia and drinks like a fish. I wonder if this could be a reference to the Higher Self as the savior-fish, especially since not only was Christ the Fish, but also the Babylonian Oannes, the Man-Fish, of the Seven Annedoti, the seven powers. Christ the Anthropos, with the Seven Archons, that we find in certain Gnostic doctrines, is of the same formation. Earlier, we saw where Christ joins seven disciples who are fishing in a boat, and onshore he feeds them with a cooked fish. These are the same expressions as the Anunnaki, Igigi, Kabiri, and so forth, which, as seven stars, descend in a *solar* boat. Noah, with seven companions in the Ark, means precisely the same, for in the Egyptian original, these are in the *solar* ark. However, the eighth one here in the dream is female, as in the mentioned formulations. The seven stars of the dream, of which I am one, with the eighth—or first—female, seems to imply the 1 + 7 structure of the Egyptian and Gnostic Ogdoad, of which the eighth was sometimes female.

We find a similar formulation with Bran the Blessed in Celtic myth, where he instructs his seven male companions to cut off his head because he is poisoned. Bran's sister is also present, so she and the seven then take the head to the White Mountain, in London. This is the lower counterpart to the higher formulation of the 1 + 7. The seven powers appear in various forms throughout mythology and the Bible, sometimes as 1 + 7, and in both cosmic and earthly aspects. Snow White and the seven dwarfs are the same archetype; the dwarfs are miners, and when the Anunnaki descend they too go underground as miners.

I mentioned Christ with the seven stars in Revelation, but in the Gnostic myths the seven stars fall to earth first to prepare the way for Christ. He was the eight-rayed star because he was the star accompanied by seven others. The seven stars appear very early in the Book of the Dead, where they are called "the seven glorious ones," "the seven spirits of fire," and "the lords of eternity." The concept was also referred to as "the mystery of the seven stars."

A star, often a shooting star, is the symbol of the Higher Self in mythologies worldwide, sometimes seen as a special human personality. But as the Higher Self comprises the three of spirit and the four of matter (soul) within its full nature, it is sevenfold, and these become its seven powers; or, as it is a star, its seven stars. In this dream I have found myself as part of this archetype, as part of the higher cosmic seven, or eight.

The alchemists spoke of the cosmic aspect of the work because when the lower four corners of the World Soul have been covered, the corresponding higher cosmic aspect must also be experienced.

> I am possibly in Crete where a local fisherman warns me of danger from villains who are out to get me. He is very serious and worried over this. However, I resolve to fight without fear and for all I am worth. As I walk down a dark lane, there is something about treasure in the air, but I must be ready to meet my attackers at any time. Suddenly, three old hags come out of the darkness to attack me, flailing their arms about wildly, so I fly at them with swinging punches. The trouble is, they turn out to be witch-spirits and my fists go right through them.

The three witch-spirits seem to be a dark, feminine trinity from the lower depths, the counterpart to the exclusively male, higher trinity. It is a fisherman who warns me of the danger, and he spends a large part of his life drawing up contents from the depths of the sea, i.e., the unconscious, so he is qualified to know. But why does it take place on the island of Crete?

Many of my journeys in the unconscious are to islands, dark mysterious ones, and Crete has always seemed dark and mysterious to me, a land of hidden secrets. Islands are also surrounded by the sea and look as though they have just popped their heads up from out of the depths, and this is what happens with contents of the collective unconscious, which "pop through" during the process.

> I see troops of the first World War moving to the front, and there is going to be total war again, the worst ever. My right foot throbs with pain, and as I look at it, I see a ghostly face in it. I say, "I am going to suffer more than ever before."

The warring opposites are now at a fevered pitch. As we know, the Great War was the worst and most terrible ever, and this new one in the depths of the unconscious is going to be the same. I am about to suffer much because of it. What the ghostly face, which appears in my right foot, represents it is difficult to say as the dream is not specific, but it is apparently that which is causing the pain.

The total war is on and I am in the trenches, trying to get through to someplace. Death and destruction are everywhere, and dead, uniformed bodies are piled high on either side. The stench of death is so great that I can hardly breathe.

Now I am really in the thick of it, and I am feeling the great strain. To be caught up between the warring opposites of the unconscious is a terrible position to be in, and the only real hope is that the opposites can be united. However, at the same time I have a feeling of satisfaction because of being involved in something important and worthwhile. These things just have to be suffered as part of the quest.

There are a little kitten, a baby rhinoceros—these seem to be sister and brother—and a lioness, who is their mother. The lioness is very greedy over food.

As I have said earlier, a cat symbolizes the lower, feminine side of the psyche, the soul as part of matter. The rhinoceros, on the other hand, is a symbol for the god of the Old Testament because both are said to be short-tempered. Here it represents the spirit side of the Self, which is ultimately the divine Son, and it seems to be integrated with its opposite, the kitten. As for the lioness, it must represent the unconscious as bearer and mother of the Self in animal aspect. Only, it is too greedy for food, and therefore too worldly and materialistic. The Self here would be the lower Osiris type, Lord of the Underworld, though ultimately part of the Higher Self. This dream returns to the lower, soul side, after the cosmic aspect of a few dreams ago. All sides must be included for wholeness, like the numbers around the central point on the face of a clock. If any part is missing then the wholeness is lost.

I go to the ruins of a very old Catholic Church, and some of the stones are built up to form a circle. I then find, within the stone circle, an old cross, and then a very old Bible, which is illustrated with paintings from very early Christianity. As I look at this, a Protestant vicar arrogantly pushes me out of the way as he passes, dismissing me and what I have found as worthless.

An elderly woman and her daughter are then sitting by me, Italian Catholics—I think I may be in Rome—and the mother says something to me which is not clear now, but I reply, "I am not a Catholic myself. I was brought up a Protestant," but when I kiss the ancient Bible and place it on my heart with great love, the old woman and I smile at each other knowingly, as though to say, "We know where the great truth lies."

I show her the first illustration in the Bible, which is a very early painting of St. Peter. I then show her the second illustration, which is possibly one of the streets of Jerusalem in Christ's time, and yet it is of a later date than the first one. I think of how the Arabs conquered Jerusalem, and that they include Jesus in the Koran, though not as Son of God.

I must stress first of all that all of the items and atmosphere of a religious nature are produced spontaneously by the unconscious and are not due to the influence of conscious thinking. Now, as to the details of the above dream, the old stones forming a circle, plus the cross, make a mandala, and also the Gnostic symbol that means the unification of spirit and matter, Heaven and Earth, though "Earth" must be understood as "soul." This is perhaps the main symbol of the Higher Self as Anthropos and Son of God. The very old Bible with its first illustration of St. Peter alludes to the beginnings of the Church, and also therefore, to the original Christ Himself.

It all comes together here, just as it must have originally been: Christ as Anthropos, early Church, and Gnosticism, all springing from the phenomenon of the Higher Self as Son of Man/Son of God, the "manifestor for the Father." The first Christians, with St. Peter as leader, were the carriers and caretakers of the incarnation phenomenon that grew into the Church, although it had all sprung from the divine source through the collective unconscious.

The Protestant vicar is oblivious to all of this, and it reflects, for the most part, the attitude of the Protestant Church, where everything is externalized and intellectualized, being split off from the inner source and fragmented. Many, if not all, Protestant worshippers may be genuinely religious people, and even fine human beings, but the Protestant faith lacks the old symbolism and magic of the Catholic, and I say this having been raised a Protestant myself. A religion must be alive with visions and experiences of spirit reality, rather than just a matter of abstract beliefs and ideas, no mater how intelligently structured the latter may be.

276

The Catholic Church, on the other hand, has feminine feeling highly developed, and though largely ignorant of the fact that the original source of its dogma is the unconscious itself, nevertheless has kept some of the original symbolism that came through the unconscious. The old woman and her daughter represent both the feminine nature of the Church and the feminine depths of the unconscious.

The early Church stamped out Gnosticism, but as Jung points out, this was both necessary and desirable, for although much of the original understanding and experience was thereby lost, there was also much that was quite dangerous which needed to be curtailed. We have the examples of Simon Magus, Faust, and Nietzsche as evidence of the catastrophic consequences of dabbling in the powers of the unconscious when not done within the protective framework of a religious tradition. Even the alchemists held up all of the Christian virtues as guides in their work, and used much Biblical symbolism.

As to the Islamic inference in the dream, this seems to mean that the Islamic experience is on the same developing tree as the Egyptian, Judaic, and Christian, though it is an offshoot that is not as highly developed as the others. However, Sufism is certainly based on direct experience of the processes of the collective unconscious, and Islam itself was founded on the religious dream-visions of Mohammed.

> I am taking my dog for a walk on his lead, only he is also my old she-cat. Both are now combined into one creature. He is somewhat dirty because I have allowed him a lot of freedom of late, but he had to be allowed some freedom. Still, I will have to bath him later. Then I see his four sons, all pups, though one is somewhat different from the rest, and stands out as the angel "Zephael, son of the Dark Angel" so the dream says.

My dog-spirit and cat-soul have become unified, which means that the spirit and soul parts of the Higher Self are now united at the lower level. Throughout the unconscious processes it has been necessary to keep my dog tightly on his lead, which means that I protect the developing Self from the dirt, desires, and dangers of the world, though of late I seem to have been somewhat lax. Bathing means to wash off the dirt, and therefore the crass worldliness, and we find a comparison in alchemy with the alchemical bath, the *Ablutio*, which produced the one white color that contained all other colors and was sometimes called the "peacock's tail." This basically means the unification of all the opposites in the one, which ultimately is the Higher Self.

The four emanations of the Self are often symbolized by animals, sometimes 3 + 1 in some way, as with the four sons of Horus, the vision of the wheel of Ezekiel with the four faces, and the medieval mandalas of Christ, all of the 3 + 1 nature. In the last example, the structure is three animals and one angel, as in my dream, and though my fourth may be "son of the Dark Angel," this may allude to man as representative of dark matter. However, the "Dark Angel" that is "prince of this world," is the very Devil himself.

As has been said, the totality of the Higher Self is 3 + 1 in nature, and this is represented from various angles and levels in the processes. At the fullest and highest level, it appears usually as three males and a female; that is, the Trinity of spirit plus the female as representative of matter, or soul. This is sometimes symbolized by three animals and a man, and the latter represents all mankind. (The "fourth" with Horus, a man, was originally a woman.)

The fourth is always somewhat recalcitrant, and as "the Devil is prince of this world," the fourth appears as the Dark Angel. In the eyes of the Spirit, man must appear to be connected with the Devil, or the Dark Angel. In the dream, the spirit and soul sides of the Self in unification are represented by my dog and cat, and the fourth one of the quaternity produced is naturally associated with the Dark Angel.

Jung says that the wheel of Ezekiel, expressing a quaternity of 3 + 1, is the symbol of the Higher Self, and that the "axiom of Maria" in alchemy is related to this. He also comments that the quaternity that expresses Yahweh consists of three animal symbols and one human, the latter representing Satan as "godfather" to man in spiritual aspect. The four sons of Horus exemplify this quaternity, probably the earliest example we know (1958, 1963b).

Many psychiatrists have been of the opinion that Ezekiel's visions were the products of a severely disturbed mind. The truth is, Ezekiel must have possessed a highly developed and extensively broadened consciousness, which enabled him to successfully assimilate such complex symbolic contents from the unconscious. Make no mistake, he did experience the Higher Self as Son of Man, and through him, God. But it is quite in keeping with the dissociated, over-rationalized thinking of modern psychiatry that a prophet of God and leader of his people should be so misunderstood as to be classified insane.

> I see a number of stars fall from the sky towards Russia, and I get the feeling that they are falling from God. There are probably seven of them, and as they land, they explode like bombs.

In an earlier dream I was one of seven stars that fell from up in the universe down to Earth, six landing safely in America, but one landed and exploded in Russia. Here, six or seven fall and explode in Russia. The seven stars or seven powers accompany the incarnation of the Higher Self, much evidence of which you will find in other parts of this book. But let me add this: The dream came some time before the collapse of communism in Russia and the subsequent rise of the Church. Were these seven stars the power of spirit that unseeingly brought about the change, working through the collective unconscious? It is quite possible.

> I dig up a very ancient statuette of the Earth Mother, the type with very heavy breasts and buttocks that are the first depictions known to us. The scene changes and a man mentions a certain film about Devil's Island.

The Earth-Mother in this form represents sexuality, fecundity, and also the heaviness of matter, as opposed to the Spirit-Father, whose qualities are directly opposite, of course. It must be remembered, however, that if the Earth-Mother has her light and dark aspects, so too does the Spirit-Father. As to the reference to Devil's Island, I have pointed out earlier that, during these unconscious processes I often go to an island, usually where it is eerie, supernatural and dangerous. These have included Crete, Ceylon, and "Skull Island." In the present dream there is now a Devil's Island, and if the name is anything to go by, it should be interesting.

If the sea is the unconscious, then the Mound or island would be conscious creation rising out of it. But it is much more than animal life, as a god is involved. This could be the lower, chthonic aspect of God, in contrast to his higher spirit aspect.

The most relevant myths say that the High God, Atum, as pure spirit, had nowhere to stand, and so he created the Mound in the Primordial Waters, Nun, as a place on which he could stand. From another aspect, he could only become active in physical reality when the Mound appeared. The ancient capital, Memphis, was called "Divine Emerging

Primeval Island." As I said earlier, the Egyptian initiates must have experienced this symbolism in their processes. So while the statuette of the Earth Mother alludes to man's first experience of the feminine spirit, the Mother Goddess, the island (the Mound or "Risen Land" to the Egyptians) represents the Father God in first form.

> I am with an older man and we visit a learned professor at his home in Vienna. We wait in his study, and when the professor joins us he turns out to be a priest of high authority, wearing cream-colored robes.
>
> There are many books on shelves, and all seem to be religious works. One is a work by St. John of the Cross, perhaps *The Long Night of the Soul*. I ask the priest about this book. Suddenly, a hazy vision appears on the wall of the head of Christ. However, the face does not completely form, or only faintly does so, as if seen through a veil, and it is obviously coming through from another reality. Then water pours forth from the obscure face, and it too is flowing through from another reality. It is a highly numinous and holy vision, with an extremely intense atmosphere pouring out as if with the water.
>
> I bow my head to this head of Christ, but this is not enough, so the priest and my companion force me to my knees, and perhaps even lower, before the holy vision. Then suddenly, my companion and I are leaving the city, and as we go along I look at all the tall, old buildings in Vienna.

This dream contains an extremely holy vision, coming through from that other, spirit reality. The "spiritual water" is referred to several times in the scriptures; for instance, Christ, in John 7:37-39 says; "If any man thirst, let him come unto me and drink. He that believeth on me, as the scriptures hath said, out of his belly flow rivers of running water." While in John 4:14. he states: "But whosoever drinketh of the water I shall give him shall never thirst; but the water that I shall give him shall be in him a well of water springing up into everlasting life."

Water is an allegory for Holy Spirit, and it was said that "Water is the living grace of the Holy Spirit." It was for a time generally used in the Mass instead of wine, because it is not the symbolic substance itself that matters, but what it symbolizes (though wine is more suitable than water because it is more like blood). Jung comments that the savior himself is the River of Water. For the alchemists the *Aqua permanens* was a symbol of the Holy Spirit assimilated to matter, which transformed body into spirit.

In dreams, water usually represents the lower unconscious, and at the marriage at Cana, it is this that Christ changes into wine, i.e., spirit. In Numbers 20:11. Moses strikes the rock with his rod, "and the waters came out abundantly"; the Egyptian god, Shu-Anhur also does this. For both the alchemists and the early Christians, spirit and water were often synonymous, however, and for the latter, water was *spiritus veritatus*. Several times in the Bible feminine spirit (sometimes sevenfold) is connected with water, wells especially, and we find this generally in myths, but the water in the dream flows from Christ, and would not allude to the feminine here.

In the earlier dreams of this present work Christ came as a real figure, laying his hands on my head, taking me flying through the air to the soul depths. This dream is different, as though it is not the same Christ, or as though the first Christ was the historical one, and this is a new Christ breaking through the veil.

This may be significant because Jung says that Mercurius is the "water" and that he is so very often compared to water by the alchemists. Jung adds that the many symbols of Mercurius mark him out as the Self, and he quotes the alchemical phrase "age-old son of the Mother." This again equates Mercurius with Osiris, who was himself so often associated with water; Osiris is sometimes depicted sitting on his throne resting on the water, as "Lord of the Waters." This means the Underworld, the soul depths of the unconscious, of which Mercurius is also lord.

Furthermore, Gerald Massey tells us that in mythology, and even with Christ, the god or savior is in first phase "son of the Mother" and then becomes also "son of the Father." Jesus is in this sense son of Mary the Mother and foster father Joseph. This was until God proclaims "This is my beloved Son" at the baptism, when Jesus is submerged in the Jordan to signify the unconscious depths, and then the higher Spirit descends in the form of the dove. There is thus the Higher Self as Son of God, but also his parallel, the lower Self, the "age-old son of the Mother." Yet both are part of the total Self.

Could Christ in my dream vision be the lower form of the Self, the god Mercurius or Osiris equaling Christ? I am not sure about this because the vision is holy and the water seems to refer to the Holy Spirit. Would this pour forth from the "other reality," from Mercurius?

Another thing that puzzles me is that the dream takes place in Vienna. Why not Rome, still the center of the Christian faith (though certain other creeds may not agree), especially since a number of my religious dreams have concerned Rome. It may have to do with the fact that the Church still projects religion outside, whereas it actually involves inner psychic processes and the "Christ within," and that the beginnings of modern psychology are thought to be in Vienna with Freud and Jung. Or it may be that while Rome symbolizes the higher Spirit, Vienna represents the lower spirit of the unconscious depths, brought to highest form here, paralleling or taking Christian form. Rome would be the Christian, and Vienna Gnostic, so to speak, with Christ above in the first instance and Christ below in the second as his own parallel.

> The woman I love, my anima-figure, has gone away with her lover, leaving me distressed. I go to a public house, where I am told from above that God has visited this place and that henceforth it must be a shrine of Christianity as God has made it holy with his presence.

Julie, my anima-figure, appeared in many dreams at this time, all concerning my yearning for her, and therefore for my missing unconscious counterpart. I had no way of knowing whether the real Julie had gone away, and whether the outer event matched the inner one. However, God is said to make the pub holy with His presence, but as it is a real life place, am I to take this literally?

I would say so, for the dream has no other reason for making the statement, though I would not contemplate for a moment trying to convince the landlord of this pub of the fact. However, I must say that on the few occasions that I visited the actual place since the dream, the landlord always seemed to be oddly affected by my presence, as though he were experiencing something that was unknowingly affecting him consciously.

> I am the captive of singer Frank Sinatra, who wears an Abe Lincoln type beard, and two of his henchmen. I am bound with my arms and legs outstretched, facing the wall, and my captors intend to molest me. This is to befoul and insult me, and I am filled with horror and disgust by it. I say, "I am a Christian, and as such I call on Christ to be with me in my suffering." This gives me courage and I say to my persecutors, "Do your worst."

(The processes have changed me, making of me a Christian, especially in the esoteric sense.)

The scene then immediately changes to a place called Goldenhill, which is being invaded by Turkish-Mongol horsemen clad in black. Falling to the ground, I lie still and play dead, but this does not fool one of the Mongols—the only one who is clad in white, actually—and he shoots an arrow straight at me. Whether it hits me or not is unclear, but I know that I must suffer it, for the sake of the unconscious processes and for Christianity.

An old woman aged about sixty comes along, and she leads me to a Catholic church, which we enter. The old woman bows and crosses herself, but I do not follow suit because I am not a Catholic. Two young men are also there and they are called to a room behind the altar to see the priest, as they are new initiates. I look up and see faded crimson robes, obviously very old, stacked high above the room's entrance. The priest and the youths then come out of the room and the four of us go to a large passage, where, on a large wall, are ancient writings and symbols.

I say to the priest, "It looks as if these symbols were carved by the Gnostics," and he agrees. I continue, "They were inspired, and 'inspired' means filled with and moved by spirit." Then, after a short pause, I begin again, "This is from the old Celtic Church, which was here some time before the Church of Rome came. The Celtic Church had a cross with a circle, which is a Gnostic symbol." The priest again agrees and is surprised at my knowledge. Then I notice that I am at least as tall as the priest.

I cannot say why Frank Sinatra is the leader of the villainous trinity, unless it is because he was said to have connections with gangsters in real life. In certain other of my dreams he appears in not so dark a role, so he must represent a force that flits between the lighter and darker sides as the spirit Mercurius does. The intention to assault me is probably to humiliate and insult me, though this may well be a necessary part of the processes. We have to be prepared to suffer in the processes, and also to make sacrifices, otherwise we achieve nothing.

The scene then changes in the dream and the Turkish-Mongol horsemen, representing the wild, anti-Christian forces of the unconscious, invade, though why the one who shoots me with an arrow wears white, while the others wear black, is unclear. White normally symbolizes the light, positive side, so why should the white-clad warrior shoot the arrow at me? Earlier, the black-clad angel saved the life of the blond hero at the cost of his own. It all takes place at Goldenhill, which actually exists in real life, directly to the north of where I live. Since going north in dreams means going to the spirit side, this is very appropriate to the events that occur.

There is also a corresponding real place called Silverdale just to the south of Goldenhill, but surprisingly, I do not recall ever having found myself there in a dream.

The rest of the dream is about the Gnostic roots of Christianity, or at least, how Christianity and Gnosticism are close to each other and from the same origins. Both have their sources in the Judaic and Egyptian mysteries, and Christ was in the tradition of Horus and Iu-em-hetep, as well as the Son of Man figures and other Higher Self instances of the Old Testament. The Celtic Church seems to have had strong Gnostic influences, and we know that Celtic priests from ancient Britain made many journeys to North Africa, where Gnosticism flourished, long before the Church of Rome came to Britain. In real life, as well as in the dream, I find this deeply interesting, and there are perhaps some answers to many puzzling questions regarding Christianity to be found in this area.

I see Jung with a young woman, going across a plank from a yacht that is moored by a bank. Suddenly, a great ugly fish comes out of the water, similar to the archaic coelacanth fish, and this is very dangerous. Then everywhere is filled with evil spirits and creatures, like those you find in sickening horror films. These merge into one super-evil spirit, which then chases me, causing me to run to my bed, trying to awaken myself in order to escape.

The evil spirit then becomes a ghostly hand which starts to strangle me, and though I fight hard to wake up, I cannot do so. I seem to see Christianity above me, simple, humble, and warm, in direct contrast to the evil that is choking me. So in a final effort I say, "The blessings of the Father, and of the Son, and of the Holy Spirit, be with me and remain with me always."

I stress the word "remain" and repeat it, and then I am finally able to wake up, though I feel heavy as lead and ache all over. But the evil spirit is still present, trying to pull me down into sleep again, so I still have to fight to stay awake. After about half an hour, the evil spirit fades, and I am able to go back to sleep again peacefully.

Christ is the Ichthys, the good savior-fish, so this ugly fish in the dream obviously represents the dark opposite, the Antichrist, or something similar. The evil spirits which follow are those that are taking possession of modern man, for when the light side is lost, the dark side moves in from the depths of the unconsciousness. Modern man thinks that he can live by his reason and his intellect alone, believing that everything has to do with just the physical world and consciousness. But as this and my other dreams reveal, we are but tiny, ephemeral specks in between mighty, eternal forces of light and darkness, eternal spirit and soul.

The only possible way to exist with these forces, and to approach them, is through religion, as only that can allow us to comprehend and express their true and full nature. It is not necessary to go to church (although it certainly does no harm to do so), so long as we think and function in a mental framework of religious orientation. Denial of God and religion means the fall into chaos, where floods of the dark side of the unconscious then deluge society, as in the Biblical story of Noah and so many other legends around the world. As to Jung and the young woman in the dream, they represent spirit-meaning, and soul-life, the two necessary opposite forces of full reality, united here.

> In real life, I have concentrated too much of late on the things of the
> world, thereby neglecting my work on the unconscious. So in this dream,
> a frail old woman of much authority comes to me and says that I have
> killed a boy and am therefore a murderer. This causes me much distress.

Worldly pleasures belong to the realm of matter, whereas the divine child is of spirit reality. The instinctual side always tries to destroy the divine child because it curbs and chains up its own power, replacing the authority and influence over the individual which the instincts crave. This, of course, is the basis of the story of Herod trying to kill the baby Jesus, and of all the myths of the menacing serpent-dragon trying to destroy the special child. As for myself, the instinctual side has been successful enough, apparently, in influencing me so that the upshot is the death of the divine child.

> A lovely boy child hovers over my bed and smiles at me as I sleep.
> He has come to comfort me in my distress.

The divine child is an "in-time" representation of something immense and essentially out of time, the product of the unification of consciousness with the unconscious, stretching out to eternity and to God. This boy was really lovely, with golden curls, the immortal product of the inner processes. The last dream stated that the child is dead, but as this dream shows, it cannot be so. He is here, more radiant than ever. Perhaps only an aspect of him had died, or maybe the dream was waking me up, snapping me to.

> I am a shepherd with a crook and I take a few sheep down a hill road. One of the sheep eats a thin sheaf of wheat.

The divine shepherd in ancient Egypt signified the relationship between God and man. Osiris was the Good Shepherd, as were Horus, Krishna, Tammuz, King David, and Christ, and we find that in his guise as Hermes Kriophorus ("Lamb Bearer"), Hermes was closely connected with the Good Shepherd. The shepherd's crook itself is symbolic, on the one hand meaning authority, and on the other the instrument by which the flock are pulled in. Pharaoh carried a small version, called the *hek*, which ceremonially had the same meaning.

Osiris was also the wheat, the "Bread of Eternity" and his son Horus ate of this. Christ was the "Bread of Heaven." All of the symbolism of this dream is connected with the Higher Self as a savior figure, and specifically to do with the lamb and the wheat. I must be developing the Self—helping him to develop—in the form of the symbolic lamb. Further dreams will substantiate this. Neither the problem of the Lamb nor the Grail was solved in the Middle Ages, though these symbols came to great prominence then. It has become the responsibility of our own age to solve these problems, which we now may through depth psychology.

> I see former Prime Minister Margaret Thatcher in front of a small cave mouth which looks something like a womb. She goes inside but I am afraid to follow, although my fear is founded partly in wisdom. However, I do follow, and I find myself in a very primitive land, perhaps a swamp. Suddenly, coming towards me, I see a python chasing a man, intending to devour him. This horrifies me, though I am somehow told that a pig will be swallowed in place of the man. I see this happen and it causes me to kick and shake with horror and disgust as I lie in my bed.

> In my revulsion, I blame God for it all, for creating a sickening life process where life devours life.

A cave in mythology is the Earth-womb, and the entrance here in the dream is so shaped. Margaret Thatcher represents the Great Mother and she leads to the maternal depths, the very primitive land of the dream. The lower feminine unconscious, the World Soul, in its devouring aspect, is symbolized by the python, which swallows up its prey, and here it is about to swallow a man.

However, a pig is substituted, and though I did not realize it for some time, this was actually a very positive action. Mythologically, pigs are always a great danger to the hero or god. The evil Set takes the form of a pig to blind Horus in one eye, and a number of gods are menaced or killed by wild boars. Even the Buddha dies from a meal of pork in an esoteric version of his story. So the pig being devoured in my dream means that the danger is killed, or at least curtailed, by the instinctual depths themselves, and the light, higher side, is therefore allowed to flourish. But I had no knowledge of this meaning, either consciously or unconsciously at the time of the dream. I took the symbolism literally, which causes me to blame God for the sickening cruelty of nature.

> This was a very religious dream, holy and numinous, involving Jesus Christ, perhaps on an island or more probably on a cloud. However, it was also very brief and remote.

From dreams that follow this would seem to be the first appearance of the Higher Self as the Son, corresponding to the Gnostic Anthropos and the Biblical Son of Man figures. I could say it even corresponds to Horus, whose name means "he who is above." The island and the cloud mean the same as the island (the Mound or Risen Land of ancient Egypt), both celestial in one form and of the Underworld in the other.

My father actually died a few days before I had this dream, which occurred in the early hours before he was to be buried the next morning.

> I awake—in the dream—to find my father sitting at the bottom of my bed, looking down on me. He wears his glasses on the end of his nose, as he did in life, and he carries a pound of bacon wrapped up in paper under his arm. He died aged seventy-six, but here he is younger

287

and has all of his hair, which is dark again. I would say that he is perhaps approaching fifty here.

I say, "What are you doing here? You are dead now." He answers, "They couldn't save me," meaning the doctors. "Are you in Heaven then?" I continue. "Nah," he snorts, "they won't let you go there. Only the saints go there. The rest of us go to a different place."

As he says this, I seem to see a very busy place, like outside an outpatient hospital or an airport, and the many people going into the building are dead, returning to a large common pool, so to speak. But the saints would not go there, having won through to a higher place. As I look at my father, I realize that, though he was a fairly decent man, he just was not saintly enough to go to the higher place where the saints go.

Because of this and many other similar dreams I have no doubt that there is continued life after death on Earth. I have seen the spirits in dreams of people who have recently died and who are about to "go over"; I have seen the spirits of people who had already gone over but who returned to tell me something; and I even saw the spirit of one man who refused to go over until I convinced him that he must do so. The unconscious insists that not only is there life after death, but that reincarnation is also true.

The visitation by the spirit of my father in the dream contradicts the zombielike view of man held by modern science, that we are merely the living dead because we have no real spirit life within us. My father tells me, in fact, that the spirits of most dead people go to the common pool— to be reincarnated, the evidence shows—and that only the saints win through to Heaven. This is in keeping with the Eastern view which states that only the holy few manage to win freedom from the chain of rebirths on the wheel of life.

I have a staff which I cast to the ground, where it becomes a snake. This coils and then, raising itself up, prepares to strike at me. But when I say, "In the name of Jesus Christ," and somehow mention "wisdom," the snake is pacified and becomes a staff again.

We know this symbol from episodes in the story of Moses; when he is first called by God, it appears as one of the signs to convince him (and the Israelites) that he is so chosen; and later at the court of Pharaoh, where it is the brother of Moses, Aaron, who casts down the rod. However, Aaron may refer to the Higher Self of Moses here, as Jung states.

This symbol of rod and serpent means God's authority through the Higher Self, the rod/serpent representing the latter's spirit and chthonic sides. Anyone who is able to bring forth the Higher Self automatically becomes God's prophet and agent. As I said earlier, the symbol was originally Egyptian, and there are depictions of such rod/serpents being held by priests. Furthermore, Shu-Anhur parts the waters of Amenta (the collective unconscious) with his rod and brings forth water from a rock with it, just as Moses is said to have done.

The rod/serpent in the above dream, being a symbol of the Higher Self, is connected with Christ. Although the serpent represents the dark chthonic side of the Self, this too has a light, "wisdom" side, and it is this that can identify with Christ, in the sense of sharing in his wholeness.

> I see a black dinosaur with two black pigs, and the vision terrifies me.

The black dinosaur is the terrible dragon in its worst aspect, and the black pigs seem to be twins of the dragon, just as there are the twins of the Self. As I have mentioned before, though the dragon is usually slain by the hero, the hero is sometimes killed by the pigs (or by wild boars, or the dragon).

> In this dream I have the staring eyes of a seer and prophet, and I am compared to Moses. More happens concerning this but it has faded.

I must point out again that none of my dreams are due to conscious imaginings which I then dream. All are products of the unconscious processes, sometimes surprising, and even amazing—to myself as much as to anyone else. It is always wise not to become carried away by dreams like this, though there must be some truth in it, as it is impossible to get very far in the work unless you gain in special knowledge and acquire a little wisdom—"Gnosis" and "Sapienta," as the Gnostics called them.

However, no matter what grandiose truths we may experience in the unconscious, we nevertheless remain what we basically are. There is always the danger of inflation at this stage in the work, which could ruin the processes, and may even end in catastrophe. If a man is meant to be another Moses, he will grow into it naturally, without imagining himself to be such, though he may conversely not take the message seriously enough and thereby miss his life's greatest chance.

I personally tread very cautiously and just carry on with my everyday life as normally as possible, though, of course, the processes must work on us and alter our attitudes, and drastically so, to bring about a transformation in our being. It is difficult keeping the right balance, but the processes must be taken very seriously indeed, and the truths experienced must override those of consciousness. There are even indications in the Biblical texts that Moses himself had the same problems, the same doubts.

However, looked at it from view of unconscious reality, it is true to say that I may be too cautious. The story of Moses is full of archetypal material of the unconscious processes, and he eventually experiences the Higher Self and God directly. I have experienced some of the same symbolism myself, the burning bush, the rod that changes into a serpent, and so forth. Future dreams will show that I too experience the Higher Self and God. Earlier I dreamt of the birth of the divine child, and God spoke from above to claim the child as his own. In another dream, a finger pointed from out of the clouds and a voice proclaimed, "You are Christ." So with all of this I could ask, "Just who and what am I?"

But again, I know that I am only as good as my latest dream. It may all collapse and I am then back to square one, though I will have gained much in knowledge and experience. Yet this itself is of great importance to the world, for it is knowledge of God of which modern man is largely unaware. Moses took his processes to his society and changed it; Jesus went even further. I too, therefore, have to take my experiences of the spirit to the world, to try to reorient it in the spiritual direction. It is not a matter of copying these traditional figures, but of following the pattern that is meant to happen. If we do not act in accordance with experiences of God, then He was wasting His time with us in the first place.

My aim is to add my experiences to our religious traditions, which in the widest sense includes the unification of the Church with the findings of depth psychology. It also means adding the traditions of the Holy Grail, of alchemy, and of Gnosticism to the full picture, although the higher Spirit must always reign. The material experienced in my own individuation process is very important to all of this, because it proves the solid foundations upon which they are all based, most importantly, upon which Christianity itself is based.

It is all within the scope of the individuation process, and anyone else who goes a long way with it will experience similar material. But it is above all a moral quest, otherwise the process becomes very dangerous. Jung said that he was and remained a psychologist; that was his job. I suppose I am the same, a sort of psychologist, or a philosopher, in the original meaning of the word. But, like Jung, I simply do a job.

> There are four creatures born of the same mother. One is a little ginger-colored fox cub, but the others are not so pleasant. One may be a crab, while the other two are reptiles, a crocodile and something else, all young ones. They are perhaps captive at first, but they then escape to the four directions. This is frightening. Then, going into a field, I find the fox cub, which pleases me, though I am worried about the other three, wondering if I should phone the police.

The number four, being a quaternity, symbolizes wholeness in the Self, usually of a 3 + 1 structure, as the four creatures are here. It is so with Ezekiel's vision of the wheel with the four heads, three animal and one human. It was also the case with the medieval symbol of Christ with the four evangelists, where again, three are symbolized by animal heads while one is human. However, the quaternity in this dream is a lower one, three of the creatures being reptilian/crustacean, while the highest is the fox cub. These represent the wholeness of the Self at lower level, and perhaps in complement to the higher quaternity structure. However, the fact that I may send for the police, the forces of order in the Self, may mean that this breaking-through of the lower quaternity could be dangerous.

> I am half drawing, half doodling with a pencil and a piece of paper, and what begins to take shape is a head with pointed ears like that of the Devil.

It is the rule of the unconscious that if you experience one side of anything, you will be sure to experience its opposite side. Therefore, if you come close to God, you will find that you are also close to the Devil. The quaternity in the last dream seems to be the first form and structure of the Devil now taking more developed shape, and this continues to develop in the next dream. The lower Self in negative form equals Set, dark twin of Osiris, and Set as good equals the Devil. There is no Devil as such in ancient Egypt; Set (and the Apep serpent) fills that role. The name Satan may well derive from Set, as certain scholars have pointed out. If the Higher Self at highest level is God Himself manifested, then the lower Self in darkest form is the Devil manifested. All are parts of the great mandala that is the total God.

> I am in the pub where the woman who is my anima figure used to work in real life—and still does in this dream—only here it is a Victorian music hall. She has just gone outside and I am filled with terror as I know that Jack the Ripper is lying in wait for her in the darkness. I go outside myself and shout her name as loudly as I can, and continue to do so, trying to warn her.

In the last dream, the face of the Devil started to take shape. Now he is about as Jack the Ripper, and as such is a great danger to my anima (and to myself, come to that). If we experience the light side of the processes, the Self, then we are compelled to experience the dark side. There is no way around it; it just has to be suffered.

> I am approached by three strange men, and one asks me about my religious values. "Why Christianity?" he asks. "Why cling to such an out-moded, archaic form?" I reply, "Because we have nothing else with which to express our religious values, to symbolize them." This answer is satisfactory to the three figures, who, I have realized by now, represent the Holy Trinity (or Holy Spirit, which is also often represented as threefold), and they accept Christianity as a valid form of religion which expresses their own eternal truth.
>
> The three figures merge into one and become the vertical bar of the cross. I then say, somewhat fearfully, that it is not the spiritual Trinity that is the problem, but the lower one, "the world, the flesh, and the Devil," which is symbolized by the horizontal bar of the cross.

This dream demonstrates that the Trinity is not necessarily Christian, but that it is willing to be so because Christianity is able to express its nature, validity, and truth. Indeed, it was originally founded on experience of it. In fact, many cultures have felt the need to arrange their gods in triads, due to the unconscious influence of the Trinity, the most notable example being ancient Egypt, which had the structure of Ra, Horus, and Ka-Mutef.

The three figures in the dream merge to become the vertical bar of the cross, which connects the lower with the higher and vice versa, man with God and God with man. However, the horizontal bar does not reach upwards but across, and therefore is not spiritual but worldly and chthonic. It does not, of course, connect man with God. The horizontal bar is on the flat plane of the Earth and is therefore entirely worldly and chthonic. Furthermore, the dream itself connects the horizontal bar with the world, flesh, and the Devil.

The Holy Trinity does not express the whole of reality but one half of it, namely the spirit side, though each side is whole according to its own nature. The spiritual Trinity is fine as long as it remains unto itself, and the same is true of the lower trinity found in the depths of matter, yet they are not in the most complete state, just as human nature can only be expressed by the male and the female together, though each can exist without the other. It seems to be God's intention and need to unite the opposites in His total self to gain an integrated state of completeness. This is why man was developed in the first place, to help God to fulfill this task; but if man comes to deny God and spirit reality, it means that he, man, has malfunctioned, and is therefore of no further use to his Creator. This dream is stating that the horizontal bar of the cross, the lower trinity, must be united with the vertical bar, the higher Trinity.

> The figure of a woman appears in my room before me and is so ill that she looks as though she has been crucified, her suffering being so great. She wears a dark green cassock that has some red on it, and her face is thin and pale. She could be anywhere from thirty to fifty years of age, and she is a little like a queen from a pack of playing cards, perhaps because of her cassock, though it is much darker than a card. She asks me what I care about and I reply, "the poor, the sick, and the suffering." She then changes rapidly into a number of ghostly figures, finally becoming a malicious skull.
>
> She now means to do me harm, but before she can, I grab the skull. With one hand over her mouth, and the other at the back, I squeeze it, containing and compressing it. I am now angry as I demand, "Now bring me some proper dreams."

This figure has long been known to the Hindus as Maya, spinner of dreams. She is the feminine unconscious, more in her collective aspect here, who has many roles, including the spinning of dreams. We have no way of knowing just who, or what, composes dreams—though they are nevertheless "real" events—but mythologically they are assigned to such as Maya, who personifies the feminine unconscious in a certain aspect. She, the anima, can appear as very human, but is actually connected to the collective unconscious and recedes into feminine spirit, even ghost-liness and timelessness. Here, she has suffered greatly though I cannot say why, unless it is because she has been caught between the opposites, a state symbolized by crucifixion.

Further, the higher Trinity of the last dream would be an assault on her independence and freedom, because now she has to control her tendency to break out into waywardness, and even evil, of all sorts—of course, this is only the negative side. She can be malicious and danger-ous, as this dream shows, but I am able to contain her and her bad effects.

> As I lie in my bed the spirit of Jung hovers above me, coming through from the "other reality." His life's work is symbolized by a folk song here, and Jung, his face beaming, says that I have written a line of that folk song. He then reaches down and touches my private parts, which has a symbolic meaning to do with the procreative life force.

In this work that I do in the unconscious processes I am helping to continue Jung's life work. It is possibly the most important work that anyone can do in the modern world, simply because man has become so dissociated from the irrational, spiritual truths. These processes can primarily bring the antidote to the poison of dissociation of the individ-ual, but what cures one person can potentially cure a whole culture.

I have long suspected that Jung in my dreams represents the Holy Spirit, whose function it is to spiritualize mankind. Jung calls the "wise old man" figure the "personification of spirit," and this is precisely what he is. Jung provided me with the keys to the unconscious. The Holy Spirit is a procreative force, and although this obviously covers the spir-itual aspect, it may also include the generative force of life itself within its scope. Though we naturally see physical sexuality as coming from the lower, animal side, the creative force behind it is a type of spirit. The

Egyptians had two forces of Holy Spirit: Shu, who was the "breath of Ra," and Kneph, who "rested upon the waters," probably two aspects of the one total force.

> I am in a large underground court where a king sits on his throne surrounded by his subjects. I personally seem to be safe and well, but walking through the court in single file is a long line of people who look ill and drawn, and who are dirty and shabbily dressed, like the extremely poor in Victorian illustrations. These wretches appear to be lost souls, the condemned, who are being led to somewhere below to be punished for their many sins.
>
> Suddenly, I am shocked to see the woman I love, my anima figure, Julie, among their number. Going up to her, I see that she is ill and dirty like the others. She is also very worn and looks older than when I last saw her. When she sees me she just shrugs, as if to say, "so what?" not concerned for herself at all. Then with tears falling down my cheeks, I sink to my knees and kiss her hand. I try to speak but I am so full of emotion that I falter and choke, so that the only words that I manage to utter are "my lady." She is not concerned in any way, either about herself or me, and she turns and carries on walking in file with the rest.

This dream begins, "I am in a large underground court where a king sits on his throne," and this corresponds to Osiris, Lord of Amenta, the Underworld, sitting upon his throne. It is the lower Self, the spirit Mercurius, and the "king" of medieval alchemy and mysticism. This is where the souls of the dead are judged and separated, to go above or below, as the case may be.

I had projected my feminine soul onto this woman for some years, my yearning for her being also the yearning for the feminine part of myself. Yet as this dream and others seem to indicate, it is not just my own anima that is involved, but the soul of the woman herself. When I had almost won the ultimate treasure in the processes, I suddenly fell for another woman in waking life, whom I will call Jane. This caused me to fail in my quest at the very end (or at least, up to that time). This second woman was my Achilles' heel, and I had a dream which told me as much. My weakness for her was due largely to the machinations of the serpent-dragon, searching for a weak spot in me in order to ruin the processes. In this other woman, that weak spot was found.

I transferred the yearning to the second woman, thus neglecting my anima, which I had to win over and unite with in the unconscious to bring wholeness to the Higher Self. This neglect allowed my anima to sink back into the unredeemed state, which is tantamount to being condemned to the depths. Fortunately, as later dreams were to show, it need not be permanent, depending on whether I could get back on the right track again.

> I see some wallpaper that has a pattern of green and gold in three sections. However, this is only so on the surface, as underneath the three sections are one.

Gold (or sometimes yellow) is the symbolic color of God and of the Self, while the color of the Holy Spirit is green. Christ is sometimes experienced in visions as gold-green, and Jung himself had such a vision, waking one night to see the crucified Christ in those colors at the foot of the bed. These are the colors in the wallpaper in my dream, and though the wallpaper seems to be in three sections, it is really three in one, which, of course, alludes to the Holy Trinity.

I now have had four dreams that are heavy with Holy Spirit, though I cannot give any proper interpretations to them. They just "are" and certainly were not highly pleasurable as religious visions are usually imagined to be. Perhaps the term "a terrible beauty" would apply, signifying they were highly meaningful but intensely heavy.

> I see a holy procession being led by priests who wear cassocks of the Middle Ages and carry crosses upright before them. The procession consists of Catholic worshippers and goes to the Catholic church situated up the road from where I live. The religious atmosphere is intense—not light or joyful, but heavy and severe with spiritual presence.
>
> I go into the church where I see a boy in a side room carrying a bucket of excrement which he intends to pour down a deep shaft. Then I go into another side room where I see a number of books on a shelf, but surprisingly, a cross is nowhere to be seen. I then go outside where I say to a man standing there, "Phew, that was heavy, was it not?" I wipe the sweat off my brow.

The experience of spirit in such a vision is not always pleasant. As a matter of fact, it is often the visions of the higher feminine side which have a very pleasant feeling to them; for instance, the dream where I saw the goddess/holy lady in the garden, and the one where, as I lay on my bed, the goddess appeared hovering over me and then merged with me spiritually. Jung reports that to the Chinese the spirit is not usually so pleasant, being fiery and dangerous.

The atmosphere that emanates from the priests leading the procession in this dream is so intense that they can only represent pure Holy Spirit. The boy in the side room must be the divine child, and his pouring the bucket of filth down a deep shaft could possibly mean that the filth of the world is being sent far below to render it harmless. As to why the cross was absent, however, it is difficult to say. I was in the actual church a week ago, and it is beautiful, expressing the spirit side of the unconscious perfectly. There is a Byzantine-style painting of Christ in the dome above the altar, and when I look up, it is like the Higher Self above. But then, this is what Christ represents, the Higher Self in ultimate form. But why the absence of the cross in the church in the dream, though the priests carry them high in the procession? It must have specific meaning for the dream to have me notice this. I should add that the priests carrying the crosses are not real-life priests of the church, but are part of the vision, sort of spirit themselves—they are very "unearthly." In other words, if priests appear in a vision, though they have human form, they are nevertheless not of this reality.

It is a Sunday morning when I find myself in an old air-raid shelter (an actual place which existed until a few years ago) next to the Catholic church of the previous dream. Two boys are with me, and as the Mass is being conducted, the boys and I have our own ceremony in front of a makeshift altar, complete with cross, candlesticks, and bread and wine.

We have sung a couple of hymns and we now cross ourselves in front of the altar. The boys and I do a round dance, making circles with our bodies, and it is somehow pointed out that we should hold this little ritual every Sunday morning.

The scene changes to my bedroom where I awaken in the dream. The room is intensely heavy with the presence of spirit, so much so that my dog, who sleeps in his basket by my bed, is very frightened. So I show him some overalls, crumpled on the floor, which the spirit has apparently just vacated. In other words, it has now left the room.

The Catholic Church has, for most of its many centuries of existence, projected religion outside, into the outer heavens, not realizing that the roots of Christianity lie within or through man, through the unconscious. As Christ said, "The kingdom of Heaven is within you." In the Apocryphal Acts of John, there appears the round dance, where Christ stands in the center of a circle of the Apostles, who hold hands and move around him in a circular movement. This is a ritual apparently connected with the unconscious processes, which work in a circular, or spiral path around a central point, which is the Self. This also mirrors the mandala symbol, the holy wheel.

Here in the dream, the boys—the twins of the Self—and I do a similar dance, having first crossed ourselves. This symbolizes the squaring of the circle, the unification of spirit and matter in a state wholeness. Everything takes place underground in the shelter next to the church, rather than above ground in the church, which means that it takes place in the unconscious, where religion originates and where it can be experienced directly. I have attended ceremonies within the church itself in certain dreams, which must allude to the higher spirit side, the counterpart to what is here a sort of Gnostic Mass.

The ending of the dream demonstrates that the main part of the dream concerned events of the collective unconscious, or spirit reality, and that I then awake in the personal unconscious, in my bedroom, which the spirit has just left. My dog seems to be himself for once, rather than representing the Higher Self at a lower level.

> I face an old teacher of mine and I can read his true character, which is not pleasant. I say, "You are really just scum. You haven't a clue what wisdom and truth are." At my words he faints to the floor. Bending over him, I make the sign of the cross and say, "In the name of the Lord Jesus Christ." As I do so I can feel God—or at least, spirit—above me, watching, and the atmosphere becomes so heavy and intense that I become afraid and stop.

The next dream is similar so I will relate it and then attempt the explanations of both afterwards.

> A young man standing next to me in a crowd mentions a strange occurrence which happened to him as a boy, but I say under my breath,

"If I told you of the things which I have experienced you would be truly amazed." As I say this, a glowing red patch hovers above us, though I realize that I am the only one who can see it. This is spirit; holy spirit, and wild spirit; both the positive and negative sides of it, together.

In both this and the previous dream, there is the heavy force of spirit from above. This can be highly dangerous, for just as being near unto God is being "near unto the fire," so is being close to raw spirit. I am worried that I may have gone too far and may suffer for it. However, I have always managed to keep a level head and carry on with my life in a fairly normal way. I know that if you have the right mental attitude in the work, though it may cause stress at times, you will not be harmed. The spirit in these four dreams has not been as we imagine spirit to be, light and joyous, though it can be experienced as such. This heavy, "terrible" type of spirit is nevertheless intensely holy. We must remember that the main symbol of Christianity, the cross, is full of agony and suffering, and that Christ was said to sweat drops of blood in his torment.

When I was a boy at school and we sang Easter hymns of Christ on the cross, I would get a similar feeling of religious heaviness caused by the agony and holiness combined in the crucifixion. In the film, *The Robe,* at Christ's crucifixion, the heavens darken, lightning flashes, and a powerful wind soars through everywhere. Actor Victor Mature, as Demetrius, has an agonized look on his face as he cries out that his Lord has been crucified. Nothing light and joyous here; but instead the powerful, agonized holiness. These dreams are the same, and so too are later ones where I hold up the cross to fight evil.

The teacher in the first dream was about the only one I did not like at school. He belonged to a religious group, but was somewhat sadistic in his punishments, and he must represent a similar content in the unconscious, a sadistic hypocrite and bigot.

I help Jung build a time machine which lights up as he pedals away at it. It is similar to the one in the 1960 film of the H. G. Wells story. Yet it is I who find myself in the future, walking along a street, where all the residents are running about. They believe that something good and wonderful is in store for them, but I know differently, for I know they are going to be murdered and devoured by aliens, as others have been. Then one of the aliens, who looks like an ordinary man, comes up to

> murder me too, but when I say, "I helped the Professor [Jung] build the time machine," the alien leaves me alone.

Building the time machine has to do with the development of the Higher Self, which is outside of time, and which is, therefore, timeless, and capable of traveling through time. I, as agent of the Self in earthly reality, am inside time. The Self could know what is going to happen in the future because, being outside of time and in timeless reality, it can see past, present, and future all at once. The Higher Self possesses all of the facts that are behind worldly reality and knows where all situations are leading.

Aliens in dreams mean raw spirit, though why they are killing everybody, and why the people think something wonderful is going to happen when the opposite seems to be the case is unclear. This is to happen in the future, perhaps brought about by the negative state of modern man, with his intense greed and materialistic view of reality that will almost certainly bring about his destruction. Spirit may finish man off, and rightly so from the view of the overall good, unless a fundamental change can be brought about in man himself.

It occurs to me that when Orfeo Angelucci had his visions of aliens in America in the early 1950s, the aliens informed him that they do not actually come in UFO's, but only manifest themselves to humans in that way because that is how we now expect to see them. It would seem that I am seeing the aliens prior to their outer manifestations, i.e. as spirit through the unconscious, but nevertheless taking the form of aliens, as spirit is "alien" to the world of matter and soul. Spirit has no definite form of its own.

This next dream was horrible; it upset me a lot and I shall never forget it.

> There is a large wooden tub of hot water with washing in it. Among the clothing is a young woman with a white poodle, but also two young, small crocodiles. Suddenly, the young woman screams and cries out because the crocodiles have started to devour her and the poodle. Her cries and screams are terrible to hear as the water is splashed about frantically. I get a stick and try to help stop the horror, but to no avail. Then I ask with anguish, "Surely this can't be happening for real?" But then the water is very still, and in a way this is worse than the splashing

because now it is all over and the young woman and the poodle have
been eaten alive.

The young crocodiles are the dark, instinctual counterparts in negative form to the twin boys of the Self, often found in mythology and
sometimes appearing in my dreams. Where the boys reflect the light
side, the young crocodiles belong to the serpent-dragon, that is, matter
in its worst aspect. The white poodle means the dog-spirit in its most
positive form, representative of the Self at animal level, similar to the
companion of Perceval in his quest for the Holy Grail, a white hound.
The poodle was once a hunting dog also, and the one in my dream is
likewise white. The young woman must be the collective anima, and in
fact, it is the Star Woman who comes from a pool of water and gives the
dog to Perceval.

The tub of hot water containing the washing seems to be the equivalent of the alchemical bath, in which all the filth had to be washed off
to reach the higher stage of the work. Here it is the filth that devours the
light, good side. For some time after this dream I was filled with fear and
despair, believing that the dark side of the Self had won, and that my
future lay with evil. But it did not turn out that way.

> This dream came after a number of very bad ones which intensified
> the fear that I felt after the one just related. I am in a stream and up to my
> knees in water when I am attacked by three ferocious Apaches. I have to
> fight harder than ever before in the unconscious, as one of the Apaches
> tries to kill and scalp me. I am pushed to the limits, but I manage to beat
> my attacker off, at least temporarily. Then I realize that I have a compan-
> ion with me who turns out to be Jung, and I say, "Come on, Jung, let us get
> out of here while we can."

The fight in the stream had an air of final decision about it, and is
why I have to fight as never before. We see such fights in old movies,
where Buffalo Bill defeats Yellow Hand in a river and then things turn
out okay. The three Apaches represent the lower, chthonic trinity in wild,
negative aspect. The lower spirit Mercurius, whom the three Apaches
represent, is a three-headed serpent in one form. My fight is not only on
my own behalf but also for Jung's sake, to get him safely across the
stream, as he represents the higher spirit here, "the personification of

spirit," as Jung himself termed the "wise old man." Even so, it appears that the Apaches could soon return.

> God is in the clouds above me and is very angry with mankind, particularly with Western civilization. I am very much afraid of God's wrath, but then I see a rainbow, which gives me hope. God speaks of His anger, but I was so amazed by it that when I awoke I completely forgot God's words.

I have no doubt it was God speaking to me from the clouds, and that is how it has been symbolized from the earliest times. God took "human" shape in the dream, but not very clearly or specifically so, and it seemed to be just the top half of God coming through from spirit reality. Clouds and their movement are signs of God's movement, His approach to man. God in my vision is angry with mankind because we have more or less rejected Him, worshipping all the forms of matter, from science and technology to big business and sex satiation.

The human species was developed specially out of the rest of nature to be nearer to the spirit so that God can communicate with the physical world. As Jung pointed out, God desires to *incarnate* into the world. Orfeo Angelucci, in his visionary experiences, was informed that Man was developed on Earth to live human life on behalf of the gods, but if Man denies the existence of God and spirit reality, Angelucci said, then Man has malfunctioned and is not fulfilling the purpose for which he was created. No wonder God is angry. We must understand that we are always watched by the "Watchers," and by God, as the ancients well knew.

However, in the dream I see a rainbow, the meaning of which was unknown to me at the time. I later discovered that God tells Noah that if ever the covenant with Him is broken, He will use the sign of the rainbow to remind Himself and mankind of the covenant. Jung comments on this: "In order to strengthen this contract and keep it fresh in the memory, he instituted the rainbow as a token of the covenant. If, in the future, he summoned the thunder clouds which hide within them floods of water and lightning, then the rainbow would appear reminding him and his people of the contract" (1958).

Such a deluge would not be one that takes place as an outer, meteorological event, but one in the collective unconscious which causes civilizations to collapse. If I speak of this vision of God in something of a matter-of-fact way here, it is because I am so used to it now, after all these years undergoing the processes. God is as natural and normal to me as anything in the material world, but much more permanent of course and far more real.

Christ said, "No man cometh unto the Father but by me," and he is speaking as the Higher Self. I personally have now developed the Self to the degree that Christ is the intermediary to God, as he has always been historically.

> I am told from above that this work I do in the unconscious is very important pioneer work, especially the religious part. I am further told that Man has been exploring the material world for so long that he no longer believes in the spiritual religious reality.

This dream speaks clearly enough and has no need of further interpretation. I will just say that Jung, and Blavatsky up to a point, began something with their discoveries in the unconscious that may bring about the necessary fundamental change in modern man, and be our saving grace. This is what has driven me on through the unconscious processes over the years, for we must all play our part as we may.

> I am somehow informed by the higher reality that animals did not appear on Earth through evolution; they appeared too quickly for that. This causes me to ask myself, in the dream, just how did they appear? The answer, no matter what it is, can only be startling to us now, as we are so very used to the theory of evolution.

Like most others today, I have always assumed that evolution is a fact and that science has proved it. I further assumed that evolution is God's and Mother Nature's method of putting life on the planet. However, the dream states that this is not so as regards animals. This possibly means the higher animals especially—not as we imagine them to be, at any rate. In the dream, I have the strong feeling it was all due to God's direct intervention, at least man's sudden appearance and rapid development. A type of evolution may be the general rule, but the intervention of spirit makes special and rapid changes.

> As I lie on my bed, a spiritual power, dark red in color, comes down
> into my hand. This could be dangerous, but I am able to assimilate it.

Normally, spirit is green in the processes, but the spiritual power here
is dark red, and reminds me, in fact, of blood, though it acts more like electricity. It is somehow more intense and unearthly than spirit green, and I
wonder: was this the spirit power that the Apostles and the first Christians
experienced, the "tongues of fire," so to speak? It is possible as this power
in the dream is certainly of God, and very dangerous unless all circumstances are right. Furthermore, red and green are paired opposites as colors,
so that red and green spirit would be two aspects of spirit, higher and lower.

I mentioned previously that in Pontmain, France, in 1871, a group of
children saw the vision of the Virgin, covered in stars. Then Christ
appeared on the cross, and His skin was dark red in color. Horus, Osiris,
and Atum have all been portrayed as red gods in ancient Egypt. Earlier
dreams have connected the color red with this same intensity of spirit,
and again we must think of Christ sweating blood in his agony upon the
cross. This is also why he wears the red robe; it is as if only the bloody
agony of the cross can express this sort of holiness of spirit.

> I go to the future again in the time machine and everything is in a
> state of collapse. Earthquakes are upturning everything, so that as I go
> down the street, I have to avoid the upheavals. I manage to reach a
> church, and I seem to be safe there. I reflect that all this has happened
> because of God's wrath, and I comment, "Well, society would have its
> sex and violence and the rest of it, and this is the outcome." But I am safe
> in the church, as are my family, plus a congregation of other people who
> have also found shelter and safety.

Again I am shown the future, which I reach with the time machine,
and everywhere is in chaos and upheaval due to the loss of God and the
ensuing flood from the negative side of the collective unconscious.
However, as with so many other dream-visions in these processes, safety
is to be found in religion, if it is genuinely felt and not just a façade, for
it has to reach down into the soul and be a living reality. The church may
quite possibly be, symbolically, the Higher Self, as is Solomon's Temple,
though this includes the collective substratum of the culture. But the
future for man, generally speaking, looks bleak.

> I am somehow told from above, from the higher reality, that "time is
> a con-trick," set up for us to live our earthly lives within.

The world of conscious reality is a world "in time," and we are con-ditioned to it. Yet we know that even in this physical universe time is rel-ative. We could, so the scientists tell us, travel in space and age at a different rate from the people on Earth. So how incomprehensibly dif-ferent time must be in that "other reality," the realm of the eternal unconscious. It is as good as certain, in fact, that our concept of time does not apply there at all. That is why time travel in the collective unconscious seems to be possible.

When I am told that "time is a con-trick," and that it has been set up to deceive us, I understand this means for the best possible reasons. Jung states: "whereas we think in periods of years, the unconscious thinks and lives in terms of millennia" (1959b).

> I am high above in the sky, beyond the light, but still in the clouds.
> On one of the clouds I see a figure wearing long, white robes; he is obvi-
> ously a Christ equivalent, though he is clean-shaven. He is looking
> upwards, addressing God, and says about me, "Father, I am stopping
> this. You can see from his dispatches that he has a broken heart."

The figure on the clouds is the Higher Self, developed and brought forth in his highest and ultimate form, as a Son-of-Man and Son-of-God phenomenon. He is a Christ equivalent, corresponding to not only the Christ of the Gospels, but also to all other Sons of the Father. This is not the lower form of the Self, from the Mercurial depths, for he addresses God as "Father." He is a *cosmic* figure, a god, to whom we are all con-nected and of the tradition of the Son of Man figures of the Old Testament prophets and the Pharaoh/Horus experience of Egypt.

But in this dream the Higher Self tells God, his Father, that he is stop-ping the processes because I have a broken heart. At this time I had fallen heavily for a young woman, and she felt the same way about me, and although a relationship was not possible for a number of reasons, it was chiefly because I knew that I had to continue with this important work involving the Higher Self. You cannot serve the processes to this extreme and live a normal life, unfortunately, for the two will not mix, and the work demands total dedication.

After what I had experienced in the processes for all those years, my path could now only lie one way. My bed was made, and the young woman could not be in it. Or rather she could, but then the processes at the highest level would fade, and the work would not then be what it could have otherwise been. But the instinctual depths, the serpent-dragon, spied their chance and turned on the pressure full blast. The conflict was unbearable, just as bad as the suffering I endured years earlier over my anima figure, Julie. Julie basically represented the anima and unification with the unconscious, whereas this other woman represented the outer world and marriage. I could not have both and I knew it, and I also knew basically that I had to go the way of the unconscious. But it was breaking my heart, and the Higher Self knew it, and so informed God of the situation accordingly.

Until this dream, I had not fully realized that I was fated to experience the Higher Self in ultimate form, even though God had spoken to me in a dream, so I was amazed by it all. I never imagined that I would go so far, but that is where the processes led me.

> Julie sits as my helper, taking notes. I hear the word "Zeitgeist," and am filled with a wonderful feeling which is not only in myself, but which also seems to be permeating the whole world. I seem to see an elderly woman who symbolizes the Earth and the whole of nature—the World Soul, in fact.

This feeling within me was something that I have never felt before or since. Even my dog, who lay in his basket close by, was moaning with pleasure, as he too was affected. At the time, I thought "Zeitgeist" meant "World Soul," so that is what the dream used it to mean, and that is what the old woman represented, the Soul of the World. The unconscious sometimes uses our mistaken conceptions to mean what we think they do, when the real meaning is unimportant at the time. Zeitgeist really means something like the current cultural climate or spirit of the times. Julie, my anima figure, was finally won over as she had become my helper in the processes. Obviously, her sickness and condemned state in the underworld in the earlier dream had been only a possibility—unless it foretold the ultimate and future outcome. Be that as it may, the Self had come forth as a Son-of-Man figure in the processes, and the World Soul was now responding.

But then it all turned sour as I lay there. I suddenly felt an intense yearning for "Jane" (my other anima woman), who represented the outer, material world, and who was taking the place of my anima figure in my heart. This ruined everything and the wonderful feeling changed to a terrible, bitter one, which was painful to endure.

> A voice from the clouds offers me a choice: "You can either be a prophet-philosopher or a fool."

The message means that I have accomplished something special for the modern world. I have brought forth the Higher Self as a Son-of-Man figure, for I saw him on the clouds in a dream recently, looking up and addressing God as Father. Now I should serve this higher wisdom, and indeed, God. But I have fallen for Jane, and this will ruin the process if I keep hankering for her, for she will take me the way of the world, away from spirituality.

For most human beings, to live life together with another person is natural and good, but fate has placed me in a different set of circumstances. I can perhaps achieve something beyond the normal—on behalf of God and man, on behalf of the realms of the unconscious and the conscious—while at the same time, perhaps reach a state of "peace." Consequently, I would be a fool to throw away what I have been able to achieve, and what I may further achieve. As I said above, in these processes, at this stage you cannot lead a normal life, so a choice has to be made.

> I am fishing by the seashore (or it may be a lake) and soon catch a large fish. This is one of seven fish, so I say I will try to catch at least one more. Suddenly, a larger creature, a mixture of a hammerhead shark, dolphin, and human, swims across the water. My dog is with me, and he goes off in the water. I worry whether he will return safely.

At the time, I had not heard of the Assyrian/Babylonian Fish-Man, Oannes, and the Seven Annedoti. Nor had I studied the symbolism of the Higher Self with the seven powers, which is what the dream above concerns. There is the dream where I am one of seven stars in the universe (with an eighth feminine one). This dream is the counterpart from below, so it seems, moving from the heights of spirit to the depths of soul. I go into this symbolism in other parts of this book, so let me just say here that ancient mythology is full of symbolism of the Higher Self and the seven powers, including Horus with the Seven Lights, Vishnu with seven rishis, and Christ with the Seven Stars. In fact, Oannes is really the god Ea, two of whose titles were "The Sublime Fish" and "The Fish with the Seven Fins."

The fish, as also said earlier, is a symbol of the Higher Self as savior (Christ as the Ichthys), though the waters are the soul depths primarily. My dog, representing the dog-spirit, is also the spirit side of the Self. Going off in the waters (the soul depths) may be highly dangerous for him, and is therefore worrying for me. One final point is that the creature is composed of fish, dolphin, and man; the dolphin, belonging to the water like a fish, yet a mammal like a man, is a unifying symbol, uniting the unconscious with consciousness, but even more so: spirit with soul.

> I see an alien from outer space which has a completely nonhuman head. It is a bit like an insect's, but has three vertical eyes in the center. These eyes then merge into one and emit a beam.

The alien represents Trinitarian spirit, and such experiences may account for the sightings of spacemen and aliens that people believe they have seen in the outer world. These "spirit beings" are apparently able to manifest themselves in the material world, as they also can and do in unconscious reality. The unconscious is a real "place," not just an unreal fantasy, a "place" that extends to infinity and eternity, it seems. Likewise, the alien is also real, and the threeness of its eyes is of the nature of spirit, as we know from examples going back to the most ancient times. But the three eyes merge into one showing that the alien is a representative of the three-in-one deity.

> The flags of all nations of the world are flying high in the breeze, but suddenly, a holy golden cross appears in the sky above them all. Then a pope speaks from a high pulpit in the open air saying that we must look above the many flags to the one cross, which is above all of this.

It is often said that religion has been the cause of many wars. Only in those cases it was not true religion but greed, hatred, cruelty, stupidity.

True religion unites, produces oneness and wholeness. The dream illustrates how separated people are by their nationalism, but shows how religion and the holiness of God can unite them under one banner, or symbol: the cross. It is good and necessary to accept and honor our own cultural traditions, but we must also accept and honor the validity of others. Yet the cross unites all at a higher level.

On the personal level, the Higher Self is the unification of all opposites, from the higher spiritual to the lower material, including consciousness. As such it is the entity of wholeness *par excellence*. Christ symbolizes the Self for Western man, and the cross is also a powerful symbol of unification, the four directions of total reality meeting at its center. Christ on the cross is a "god of the four quarters" in unification.

I am with Jane, and her friend Mary is with us. The two of them are becoming part of the unconscious processes, for they keep appearing in my dreams, though they are, as far as I know, completely unaware of it in real life. This should not happen, and it angers God, who appears in the sky and says "I will teach you some humility," addressing the three of us.

This was an appearance by God Himself and it was not the Higher Self, who, in highest form, is a part of God come forth. In fact, it is through the latter, who has always been an intermediary between mankind and God, that I have come to experience God Himself. Jung, speaking of Christ, says that man and God, though extremes and hard to unite, nevertheless are united by Christ, who is nothing less than the Higher Self in ultimate form.

However, it is God Himself who is above here in the dream, and he is displeased because my involvement with Jane is causing not only her, but also her friend, who at this time was her constant companion, to become involved in the processes. They do not belong there, for God has other plans for me. It is only Julie, my anima figure, who belongs in the processes.

As said above, it is not wrong for a man and a woman to fall for each other and to be together—in normal circumstances. But that is the whole point; the circumstances here are not normal. They are as abnormal—supernormal—as could be, and great and tremendous things are involved, as the next dream demonstrates.

> Two figures come through in the clouds above, though just from
> the waist up; they come from the spirit reality into this one. They are
> vague, and I do not see their faces, but I am aware that one figure is God,
> and to His right—on the left as I look—is his Son, who seems to be a
> Christ equivalent. God speaks to me saying, "The West needs cleaning
> up."

At the time of this dream I was not aware that Christ had foretold
that he would return, seated on the right-hand side of God ". . . and ye
shall see the Son of man sitting on the right hand of power, and coming
in the clouds of Heaven" (Mark 14:62). "Hereafter, shall the Son of man
sit on the right hand of the power of God" (Luke 22:69).

Neither was I aware that St. Stephen, in Acts, had experienced a
vision of Christ *standing* on the right hand of God. "But he, being full of
the Holy Ghost, looked up steadfastly into Heaven, and saw the glory of
God, and Jesus standing on the right hand of God. And said, Behold, I
see the heavens opened, and the Son of man standing on the right hand
of God" (Acts 7:55-56). So while the Gospels tell of the coming Christ *sitting* on the right side of God, my vision is of a Son of Man figure *standing* on the right hand of God. This follows Stephen's vision, though it is
actually the Higher Self as a Christ equivalent that I see.

God then speaks in my dream, saying, "The West needs cleaning
up." Surely we can only agree with this statement. (Who could disagree
with God, in any case?) It is gradually falling into chaos, inch by inch,
as one of my dreams put it, due to the loss of its mythic/religious foundations, upon which all cultures rest.

We can see it in so many ways, and scholarship itself has used its
knowledge to dissect and destroy the Christian myth with rationalistic
and materialistic misunderstanding that Freud himself would have been
proud of. Few, if any, scholars have realized that Christianity, and
indeed, all genuine myths and religions, are based on experiences of the
"other world," through the collective unconscious, where, as my own
processes have revealed, the Higher Self, God, and the World Soul are
the greatest *facts*. Sometimes the two realities merge, and so visions are
seen as outer events, but it is the same other reality coming through
whether seen in dreams or otherwise.

This dream vision is a direct experience of God and the Son, of the
royal line reaching back through Biblical examples to early Egypt. I have

experienced the phenomenon a number of other times. Atum-Iu, Ra-Horus, Amun-Khonsu, the Ancient of Days with the Son of Man, and other similar experiences of the Old Testament prophets (Ezekiel, Daniel, and the Apocryphal Enoch, with their Son of Man together with the Ancient of Days) reveal experiences of the divine Son with his Father. My dream repeats the phenomenon.

Moses first sees an angel in the burning bush and then God speaks, and this too can have the same meaning. If you take the unconscious processes far enough, this is what occurs: a part of God becomes the Son who is manifestor for the Father. In another dream, which I will relate shortly, I was on top of a hill where I was struck by lightning—touched by God, as the dream said. I knew this meant I could never be the same again, never be my old self. I knew that God and the Son are certainties, as much as I know any other fact of reality.

The roots of Western culture lie in Christian soil with beginnings in ancient Egypt, but while other ethnic and cultural groups search out and proclaim their cultural roots, we of European descent deny ours. We either exist superficially in over-intellectualized psychic dissociation or try to find religious meaning in Far-Eastern forms that are foreign to the Western collective unconscious. But our own Western "soil" is extremely rich in religious contents, and as Blavatsky states, while the Buddha is the penultimate stage of the inner processes, Christ is the ultimate, which is why Christ is the Son of God, and the Buddha is not. We in the West must discover our roots again and develop them further.

> A man of extreme holiness, dressed in red- and white-striped robes
> and a turban, takes me by the hand and points to a silvery blob of liquid
> metal that falls from Heaven to Earth.

Red and white have symbolized the opposites of spirit and matter (soul) since ancient Egypt, and they still do in our dreams today. The silvery, liquid metal reminds me of quicksilver, or mercury, one of the favorite symbols of the alchemists for the unification of the opposites. For the alchemists, Mercurius was the creative spirit contained in matter, and revealed and released out of it by the work. However, the silvery blob in this dream falls from Heaven, which suggests that it is spirit from God. It would seem to allude to the coming forth of the Higher Self as an emanation and incarnation of God. But then quicksilver always alludes to Mercurius, the spirit of the Earth, so that cannot be the explanation here. We would expect the metal from Heaven to be gold, but that is not the case. I have long puzzled over this dream, but all I can say is that it is not given to us to fully understand all of the Mysteries of God and the unconscious.

> I am a lowly Catholic priest on a visit to Rome with three other priests who are higher up in the Church than me. We are taken to a garden in the Vatican where my companions are invited one by one to meet the Pope. I am considered to be of no consequence and there is no intention of taking me for an audience. Then circumstances are altered by fate, and the Pope and I come face-to-face accidentally in the garden. He immediately recognizes that I have had religious experiences in dreams and so invites me indoors, where we sit facing each other. Incidentally, I wear a dark gray cassock while the Pope wears a light cream or white robe.
>
> I am very shy and nervous as I say, "You know, I am very nervous when I speak to people, but it is often my type who are chosen." Then I continue, "You know that I have dream-visions because just as you appear in my dreams, I appear in yours," to which the Pope replies, "Yes, that is true." As we speak, I gaze into his eyes, my own eyes being those of seer and prophet, and the Pope almost wavers and turns away. Then I am in the garden again, where I say to a cardinal, "You see, the Pope did want an audience with me."

Let me say first of all that I am not Catholic in conscious life, though the unconscious usually makes one of me in dreams, and a priest to boot. However, I am a lowly priest of no consequence to anyone, though the Pope himself recognizes that there is something deeper in me. This causes him to stop and talk with me; and we have apparently appeared in each other's dreams. Nevertheless, I am shy and nervous, though as I say, it is usually my type of extremely sensitive personality who have become shamans and prophets since the earliest times.

But then I gaze into the Pope's eyes with my own eyes, seer's eyes, and the Pope almost turns away, but does not quite. This shows that whatever authority I may have in the unconscious, the Pope also has it. A couple of dreams ago, God, accompanied by the Son, spoke to me from the clouds, so this perhaps gives me the right to see the Pope and talk with him about religious matters.

In the dream I am a priest, nominated as such by the unconscious, not by the worldly Church. Originally, a true priest had to suffer the fires of the unconscious, the dragon depths, to experience the spiritual heights; if he survived, he had the authority to speak on behalf of the gods. The dream seems to say that I have earned that right and I should act on it in the world. If the figures of the past who had religious experiences had not acted on them, the world would not have had its many religions nor would it have had its many cultures and civilizations.

Just as the Pope occasionally appears in my dreams, I apparently also appear in his. Whether this is actually so is another matter, of course, but anything is possible. Jung had a number of dreams during the first World War in which he visited and spoke with the German Kaiser, and he wondered, years later and half humorously, if the Kaiser himself had dreams in which he was aware of this. I know that this sort of thing is possible because I have had dreams in which I conversed with certain famous people and afterwards they made public statements concerning the things we discussed. We all share the collective unconscious so there is good reason to think we should meet there.

> Nazi soldiers are after me so I run into a cellar to escape and hide. A Nazi officer follows me there and points his pistol at me, but then a magical cross appears just above us and the Nazi gazes at it with great fear, his face looking as if it is starting to disintegrate. I think I can use this cross to fight the enemy.

The Nazi soldiers are the dark opposition forces of the unconscious, of course, but the magical cross is the symbol of Christ and therefore of the Higher Self as divine Son. The cross is therefore the most powerful of symbols. No matter what modern man thinks consciously about the cross and similar symbols, in that reality through the unconscious, which extends to infinity and eternity, these things have tremendous power and meaning. (Just a couple of nights ago I defeated an alien in negative form with a cross.)

> I have a vision in which I am shown all the creatures, wild and hard, of the forest. They are not at all the soft, cuddly animals we usually see them as. This is nature in the raw. I see the immense, stark power of physical life working through its creatures.

313

> I then see a line of different animal species, with different types of
> apes at the end. They are all waiting to be evolved, to take the place of
> man as God's chosen creature if man should fail. I am informed that this
> will almost certainly happen, as man is indeed failing badly.

It is not very pleasant to be shown these things in dreams, but the
truth is the truth, and if we would all listen to what the unconscious tells
us, perhaps we could plan things differently. If we humans are the cause
of the great problem, which we are, we can also be the solution.

> I am in a pub with a number of people where a golden vessel, a sort
> of goblet, appears in the air before us, coming through from spirit reality.
> I try to explain to the others that it is from the spirit dimension, but I am
> jeered at in disbelief. A man tries to touch the vessel but his hand goes
> through it, though it is actually filled with a special, and even magical,
> liquid. I try to explain again that it is from another dimension, but still no
> one listens.

The golden vessel is of course a sort of Holy Grail, and symbolism
connected with this has figured in a number of my dreams. The Grail has
its counterparts in other creative vessel symbolism: the alchemical *vas*,
the Hermetic vessel, the uterus out of which the lapis is born; the Celtic
Cauldron of Dagda; and so on. All are vessels out of which the Higher
Self, in one form or another, may be born.

However, certain authorities believe the Grail is a spontaneous product of solely Christian foundations, not being based on earlier or other
traditions, and I believe this is probably so. It would be foolish to believe
that pagan and alchemical sources could spontaneously produce such
symbolism as a holy containing vessel, but that Christian sources could
not. It is also a fact that the pagan vessels are not so purely and spot-
lessly holy as the Grail.

However, the Grail was not a product of consciousness or conscious
invention, being rather a spontaneous symbol of spirit experienced
through the unconscious. The Grail as a containing vessel may represent
feminine soul partly, but the special liquid, Christ's blood, or the Host,
means the divine spirit of Christ present in the vessel. In fact, the real
meaning of the Grail may be that it is a mandala expressing the Higher
Self, which contains all opposites within its nature. In some versions of

the Grail legend, a fish is placed on the table next to the Grail, and so the fish (the soul depths) and the Host (or Christ's blood, meaning divine spirit) are united in the mandala symbol of the Grail.

The Middle Ages were given a task concerning the Holy Grail and the Lamb, a problem which they failed to solve; meanwhile alchemy was more concerned with the lower, Mercurial side of the unconscious. It looks as though it has become our task in the modern world, through Jungian depth psychology, to try to solve the mysteries of the Grail and the Lamb, and this can only be done through the unconscious.

Jung says, "The vas is often synonymous with the lapis, so there is no difference between the vessel and its content: in other words it is the same arcanum. According to the old view the soul is round and the vessel must be round too, like the heavens or the world. The form of the original man is round" (1959a). However, this statement concerns alchemy and the situation is higher and somewhat different with the Grail, for it is Christ's blood, the very essence of God, that is contained in it. The stone or lapis also contains a spirit, but it is the lower spirit. It is true that in Wolfram's von Eschenbach's version the Grail is a stone, but this was imagined as an altar on which the Host, brought by a dove, was laid.

> There are a lot of vicious youths about and an atmosphere of evil hangs over everything. The world has gone crazy and I am much afraid. Then I am in the Far East, or perhaps the South Seas, where a man speaks of black magic and points to an island a few miles away. This island is dark and is shaped like a table mountain, or maybe a whale lying on the water. It is very sinister.

As I have said previously, sooner or later, I always go to a sinister island where eerie, supernatural things occur. An island is surrounded by water, i.e., by the unconscious, and looks as though it has just risen up from the depths, like the Egyptian Mound from the Primordial Waters. However, the island in the dream above is very sinister and black magic is mentioned, so I shall have to wait and see what develops. As for the world having gone crazy, it really has, although a lot of people are just carried along by the chaos.

> I am near a hilltop church where I am told from above that the divine child is actually pre-Christian and has been known all over the

world since the very earliest times. I then see a sort of Aztec or Inca scene, as if to say that it (the appearance of the divine child) has happened there also. Therefore, the divine child is universal and for all times, including the Christian, but not exclusive to it.

Before giving the interpretation here I will first present the next dream, as they are related.

I am near a Catholic church where a beautiful baby boy appears to me dressed in white linen. I cannot so much see his face as feel it inside of me. Though pink, it is golden and magical as he glows with religious power and light. I am filled with great strength, though spiritual and not physical. It is truly holy. Then the lovely child rises up and disappears.

The myths of the world are rich with the stories of the divine child and many individuals must have experienced them in processes of the unconscious in order to record the myths. We should not find this at all surprising, as ancient cultures, and recent simpler ones, were nearer to the unconscious and its influences, whereas modern man has grown further away, becoming dissociated finally. The Aztec experience mentioned in the first dream would involve Quetzalcoatl, but there are other examples in original American cultures.

In the second dream the lovely child appears to me. It is difficult to describe his numinous beauty. This is the Higher Self as the divine child in his highest and lightest aspect, of course, and as a Catholic church is involved, it is in specifically Christian form.

One further point is that although Christ is one of many divine Sons, he is nevertheless special because he is the highest development. As Jung says, human consciousness takes a leap forward with the phenomenon. Horus was a very high development in Egypt, as was Iu-em-hetep, the latter being Prince of Peace, and both were divine Sons of the Father, but for Western culture the divine Son is Christ. The Son of God comes forth in wisdom and truth and with heavenly light as manifestor for the Father. This was so for a number of divine Sons, producing high culture, but if Western civilization should totally lose Christ, as it may well do, then it will sink into a chaos that will destroy it.

I receive a letter from my old teacher, Mr. J., which tells me that my true "career" is a religious one, "To transform the Church," the letter says.

I have tried to show earlier that the Church must open its arms to embrace the truths of the unconscious which is where Christianity sprang from in the first place. It must recognize what the East has known for thousands of years, that true religion lies within the individual. Christ himself said, "The kingdom of Heaven is within you." If the Church fails to realize this, it will fail both itself and mankind. However, it is also true that spiritual reality is outside, and even in the skies, as it were, as it surrounds, and is behind, and permeates, the whole physical universe. The message from my old teacher is from that other reality itself, of course.

Jung visits me and we are in the front parlor of my house. I go to the door to call my dog in from outside, and as he comes in, Jung pats him on the head. Then Jung and I sit in armchairs in front of the fire, facing each other, and we realize that it is now early dawn. All the while Jung has been beaming that bright smile of his.

I want to discuss with him the deep issues of psychology and religion, but as my family are in the adjoining room and would hear us, it would be somewhat embarrassing to have the discussion. Just then, a small ape wearing clothes sits with Jung, and with it is its young offspring, so it is a sort of animal mother-and-child combination, though the adult one is also a male.

It has waited for Jung to come, and it now sits with him as a pet sits with its master; yet it is not just a matter of master and pet somehow. I say to myself, "Jung and the ape belong together, being representatives of the opposite extremes of man; the ape as the early stage, and Jung as the latest and highest development of man."

An ape featured in a couple of dreams early on in my processes when I pointed out that it is the foundation on which the Higher Self has to be built. The process then builds up from the sub-human symbolized by the ape. Jung, with his high intelligence, knowledge, and wisdom, apparently symbolizes the highest level which has been attained. It seems that all the levels are still there in the unconscious, including the higher spiritual level, which consciousness very rarely attains.

In Jung and the chimp are the two extremes of what we call "the human." However, there is much more involved. As I know from many dreams, Jung not only represents himself, but is the "personification of spirit." If this association is as part of the Holy Spirit, as the dreams suggest, then Jung would ultimately be part of the higher Trinity.

The lower extreme of the human could have been represented by a single chimp, as the other extreme was by Jung, but instead we have the three chimps. Therefore the chimpanzee family represents a lower trinity, but actually the lower counterpart to the higher Gnostic trinity of Father, Mother, and Son. Obviously, more is represented here than merely the two extremes of man.

> I am in the town just to the north of where I live, and it is alive and very heavy with spiritual forces, and with possible danger from them. These forces are partly ancient Egyptian, though, I hear the name "Melchizedek," the mysterious, Biblical priest-king. I am warned not to become involved with this at this time as it would be too dangerous.

In these processes I have become involved with the forces of God, and these can be beneficial or dangerous, usually depending on consciousness and its attitudes. Normally, these forces would have meant no danger for me, but as I had recently become emotionally entangled with Jane, which was pulling me away from the processes just when they were being most fruitful, the outcome could have been a negative one.

The first savior/Higher Self figure of Jewish religious history is Melchizedek, who offers bread and wine to Abraham. As I say elsewhere, this figure is probably derived from the Egyptian Set, though in positive form. Certain parts of the Bible refer to Melchizedek as being, "like unto the Son of God," and "having neither the beginning of days, nor end of life." So it seems that I am coming close to this archetypal figure in the processes, but, as said, this will be dangerous at present.

An incident in waking life occurred at this time which I knew was connected with this figure of Melchizedek, and I think it would be of interest to relate it here.

I was sitting in my chair in the living room, reading Jung. Another person whom I will call P. was present. Suddenly, as we sat there quietly, I felt a force of spirit descend into the room from above and settle by the fireplace. This was not an ordinary ghost, but a very heavy force of "holy" spirit. The name Melchizedek jumped into my mind. Then, after a number of seconds, the force ascended again and left the room, but neither P. nor I said anything at all about this.

A little later, I took my dog for a walk, and P. decided to come with me. After a while, he said, "Do you know, earlier, when we sat in the living room, I felt a force of spirit come down into the room and settle in front of the fireplace." As I did not wish to become involved in long explanations at this time, I passed the incident off with some mundane remark, but in any case, how could I have explained all of the meaning that I have put into this book in a couple of sentences or so? But the fact remains, that a holy force, probably to do with Melchizedek, came down into the room that night, and both persons present experienced it, although neither said anything until later.

> Either God or His messenger speaks from the clouds, saying, "You may be too immature. If that is so, someone else will have to be chosen."

There is no need to say anything further here. Only that thoughts of Jane were engulfing me, the pressure being turned up by the instinctual depths. I also knew that if I gave up the work I would bitterly regret it one day. This was the greatest torture, and one dream had already compared this to being eaten by a crocodile.

> I am with a professor of archaeology, probably in Egypt, and we find an ancient, round shield with an emblem-symbol on it. The emblem is also round and is of a bird, but I have to explain to the professor what it means. "If you look closely," I say, "you will see that the bird is three birds curled up in one. Now, birds symbolize spirit, and when in flight are not earthed. When they come down from the sky, that is how we imagine spirit coming down to us. So these three birds in one signify the divine Trinity, the three-in-one deity."
>
> But the archaeologist looks at me suspiciously and walks away. He refuses to accept such nonsense in his rationalistic prejudice, though deep down he is much troubled.

Here again is the symbol of the Trinity. The dream puts the words into my mouth to convey its message, though modern man, like the professor, has forgotten how to listen to this music to his soul. He rejects these things consciously, but deep down, his soul stirs. This inner disturbance often causes fear of the unknown, just as St. Paul was driven to persecute the Christians because Christ, the Higher Self, unbeknownst to Paul, was stirring in his depths, and indeed, was ready to burst forth.

The professor is not part of myself, but represents the skeptical, disbelieving world of scholarship that I must convince. I have learned through 14,000-plus dreams that the old idea in psychology that when we dream of others, we are usually dreaming of aspects of ourselves, is almost always not the case. I used to think that way but then came to realize otherwise. In so believing, we are reducing a wider, non-personal unconscious to merely ourselves.

I once thought that a friend of mine, a slight shadow figure, only represented part of myself, my shadow, in dreams. Then I dreamt that he had a fight with a neighbor and thought that this was a conflict in which my shadow was involved in the unconscious. But a few days later, the real man came and told me of the actual fight. I have learned the same is true with other real figures, and this repeats what I said earlier about the personal unconscious being much less personal than we believe. But it is too involved to go into here.

> I am with a boy who is a sort of servant, and as we walk we come across a people, probably in India, who immediately fall to their knees to acknowledge the boy as king. This is because the boy, naked but for a loincloth, has a circular tattoo or mark on his body, perhaps on his forehead.

The boy is the divine child, the Self, and as such is king. This was the original idea of kingship in ancient Egypt, and why Christ was said to be king. It was not the strongest man or the cleverest who was king, but the one who represented the divine Son, a god, though in his human form on Earth. The Pharaohs themselves would not have brought forth the Higher Self, but the concept of Pharaoh was based on the mortal priest united with the immortal Self.

Yet such highness must be humble, for humility is the highest quality, and so the king must be a humble servant, which Pharaoh was said to be. This is also why Christ washes the feet of the disciples. The highest must humble themselves and become the lowest, for only those who choose to be the lowest can qualify to be the highest. Many a servant would love to be Pharaoh, but a Pharaoh who chooses to be the servant among the lowest in the land would be the highest and noblest soul.

The boy in the dream is a servant but has the mark of divine kingship, and the round symbol on the boy's forehead probably fits in with the shield and emblem in the last dream. It is like Christ who is born in a stable and becomes a humble carpenter, yet is true king, while Caesar and Herod, bloated and mad with worldly power in their palaces, count for nothing in the ultimate scheme of things.

> This dream is somewhat hazy, but I am on a mountaintop with rolling clouds above. Suddenly, lightning flashes and strikes me. I seem to "light up" with thousands of volts, yet I am not harmed. Then a voice speaks from the clouds, saying that I have been touched by God and can never be the same again.

I have developed and experienced the Higher Self and through him have experienced God—the Higher Self is always the intermediary and mediator. This is expressed as being touched by God, or struck by lightning. It is true that I can never be the same again because having experienced him and all of the contents of the processes, I can never doubt God again. It would be impossible. Whenever I hear other people discuss the "possible" existence of God I have to remain silent because I could not explain why I *know* God is real. When Jung was asked if he believed in God, on more than one occasion, he answered that he had no need to believe, but that "I know . . . I know."

> There is utter chaos in a city, with people running about wildly as though there are earthquakes and other catastrophes. I am attacked, accused of being a priest, but I fight off my assailants. Things are so bad, the chaos so great and utter, that I cry out, "Only God can help us now." As I look up at the evening sky, I see three balls of light; the rear two move forward to merge with the front one, so that the three become one.

I have had similar dreams in which I call to God to help mankind in its schizophrenic dissociation, and as in this one, the response is usually a three-in-one sign from Heaven. This may explain some of the sky sightings people have seen. For example, a retired Royal Air Force man saw the same formation of three lights in the sky, and though he stated that he does not believe in UFOs, that is what he nevertheless ascribed the lights to. It never occurred to him that they could have represented the Holy Trinity.

I see a baby boy lying on the floor. Next to him is a large, menacing python. I say, "Herakles strangled the serpent when he was a baby."

Once again the divine child is menaced by the serpent from the dark material depths. This motif is many thousands of years old, since man was first able to consciously make the journey through the unconscious. The earliest record of it, that I know of, is the myth of the Horus child, but it is probably much older. Horus is called "bruiser of the serpent," and stamps on it in one myth. The collective unconscious, which is a different reality from our physical one, is timeless and so produces the very same symbols across thousands of years.

It is not generally realized, but Herakles is born one of twins in the myths, which fits in with the fact that the Higher Self is actually twins. In the story, as the eight-month-old Herakles lay in the cradle with his twin, Iphicles, two serpents, sent by the goddess Hera, tried to suffocate and choke them. But Herakles instead seized them by the throat, and choked them. It is said that the origin and true nature of Herakles are unknown, but that he was probably a real-life hero. However, he is really also a Higher-Self figure, like Samson, and his mighty strength is that of the Self. Though not a religious figure, as such, he does institute a period of peace and culture, as savior figures do.

Herakles in the dream, or the child that I associate with him, does not allude to myself, but to the divine child, the infant Higher Self. Yet because I am connected to the Higher Self, in that way I am connected to the child.

I meet Jung in the grounds of his home in Switzerland. Also present is a young woman. I say to myself, "I will be Jung's heir, it seems."

Here again is the motif of the "wise old man" and the young girl. They express the two sides of a man's total psyche: spirit/meaning and soul/life; but also they express the full collective situation itself. As for being Jung's heir, all I can say is that my work on the unconscious adds to Jung's. Of course, I did receive the four gold keys from Jung just before he died, which seems to imply that it is an "official" position as far as the unconscious is concerned, my being "successor" to Jung.

> As I walk down the street everything seems to come together regarding myself and religion. "That is what I have aimed at all these years," I say, and I get a marvelous feeling spreading all over me. But then I feel wrong somehow, and I am told "It is not enough to be good rather than evil. You also have to be strong rather than weak."

This means that when consciousness aims for good, if it is too weak, the result is a split with the unconscious. Consciousness has not been strong enough to win over the "wilder" side of the unconscious, which then just goes its own opposite way. There is no need for me to try to explain this dream further.

> I hold a trident in my right hand and both I and the trident shake and vibrate violently because we are being "charged up" with spirit. Then I am with a man, E. We see a crocodile that has been badly burned, lying on its back though still alive. E. is now carrying the trident, so I say, "Put it out of its suffering." He throws the trident, but it does not hit the crocodile correctly and glances off, so I say, "You shouldn't have thrown it. You should have kept thrusting at it until it was dead."
> Suddenly, a large python appears and attacks the crocodile, though the latter is still able to fight, and, in fact, has no trouble tearing the python to pieces. Then three small snakes that were with the python slither away in fear. They retreat in formation; not in single file, but abreast and erect, like three vertical "S"s: SSS.

After more than twenty years of experience of the unconscious processes I am still not sure what the difference is between the crocodile and the serpent, the python especially. The crocodile was the seven-headed dragon-monster Sevekh for the Egyptians, and was not always evil; it was worshipped in a few cults, hated in others. The Apep serpent, however, was always evil. The spirit Mercurius was both serpent and dragon in certain aspects, and as a dragon, an earth-spirit, it sometimes had wings. But the serpent as the python is the great swallower, and represents the devouring aspect of the unconscious. In this dream, the crocodile, though severely injured, easily manages to tear up the python.

It is very significant that E. uses a trident as a weapon, as, being three pronged, it represents the trinitarian spirit with which it is charged up at the beginning of the dream, along with myself. An old engraving appears in Jung's *Psychology and Alchemy* of a dragon being speared by an adept with a trident, and in another of Jung's works, there is an illustration by one of Jung's patients of the very same thing. It is an archetypal motif, but Jung seems to have missed the significance of the trident representing trinitarian spirit. I have long suspected that E. is actually undergoing an unconscious individuation process himself. Whether I am trying to help him with this in the dream is unclear; maybe his and my processes are interconnected to a degree. Like the dream of my shadow figure, I know that it is E. himself of whom I dream because there is much evidence of this elsewhere. He does not represent part of myself, although I once thought that.

The hero's fight with the terrible dragon is known throughout mythology and legend, of course, and just as Marduk slays Tiamat in Babylonian myth, and Sigurd slays Fafnir in the Nordic legend, so Michael fights the dragon in Revelation. Sigurd's weapon is a magical sword (a sunbeam) which has the same meaning as the trident of Marduk; in some versions, both Sigurd and Marduk use arrows. The list of similar myths is long and not so varied, but whether it is sword/sunbeam, special arrows, trident, or thunderbolts, the meaning is the same: the defeat of chaos and the dark instinctual depths on behalf of the higher spirit, the weapon representing the light piercing the darkness.

All of mythology shows that though human life diversifies in consciousness into different races and cultures, it springs from the same roots in the unconscious. All life is unified and basically one, though it paradoxically has opposite, conflicting sides. This is not merely a religious ideal, but a definite fact in the unconscious. What the religions teach of the brotherhood of man, and of all life, is not merely a concept of conscious thinking, of reason, but the foundations of reality.

When Marduk fights the terrible serpent Tiamat, the weapon he uses, in certain interpretations, is a trident. He seems to be holding (on the stone depictions) a three-pronged thunderbolt, or lightning, which represents trinitarian spirit. The Epic of Creation says: "He seized the trident and burst her belly / He severed her inward parts, he pierced her heart."

There is a certain house in a certain street of which I usually dream when people I know die. Their spirits go to this house and pass through it to the afterlife. Why it is this particular house I have no idea. Now, my dog has just died in real life, and as I lie in my bed in the dream, he comes right up to my bed, as if to say his last farewell. He looks into my face for a few seconds, then turns and walks to the far end of the darkened room and then disappears. He then goes to that certain house to "pass over." This causes me to cry heavily, and my heart is in much pain. When I awaken, tears are streaming down my cheeks, so my dream crying was for real.

All animal life is made of the same clay as that of human life, and the spirit and soul also come from the same source. It is just more developed in humans. If the non-physical parts of humans return to the source, so too must those of lower animals. The dream says that it is so, anyway. My dog's spirit comes to me, as if to say his last farewell, and then goes to that certain house in order to pass over.

Why it is that certain house, I have no idea. Jung says that when a dream produces an exact copy of conscious reality, we must take it as the actual situation in conscious reality, which is the case with this dream. My bedroom in the dream is exactly as it is in real life, and in the same darkness, so I have no doubts that my dog's spirit had been to say his last farewells, and has now passed over. This is not my dog as the lower form of the Self here, but is actually Tino, my dog.

As to the house in the dream, there was a man I knew whose wife left him to live with another man. The first man, the husband, then died in very tragic circumstances. These people were not close to me so I thought no more about it. Some months later, I dreamt I was in that same house and found the husband hiding under some rugs. He said he wanted revenge on his wife and the other man, and so refused to "go over." So I had to convince him that, for the sake of his own soul, if for nothing else, he must return to the "other world." Finally he agreed to go. But why that certain house is involved remains a complete mystery to me.

I am taken up into a spaceship and questioned by alien beings, though I remember no details of this.

This has happened to me a number of times during the processes and it is probably what other people experience when they believe that it has happened to them as an external event. In other words, it is an occurrence of the collective unconscious, and the abductees believe it to be (or experience it as) an outer event. But is a dream not taken as reality when we are asleep, experiencing it? So these people may be having experiences through the unconscious but believe it is all happening in outer reality. This is not to say that the events, therefore, do not occur, only that they occur in a different dimension, one of spirit.

On the other hand, there are many instances on film of the manifestation of silver discs, lights, and so on, which seems to suggest the otherworldly powers are able to manifest themselves in physical reality. These would be *representations*, in the same way that certain ghosts manifest in certain representational forms. Many abductees claim that no worldly time had passed when they returned from the abductions, and all my experiences of the collective unconscious show that it is a timeless reality.

> I see a large, white bird, perhaps in flight; it is perhaps a mixture of a swan and a flamingo. Then I see a snake, probably a python, with brown markings on its head.

The swan-flamingo and the python symbolize the higher spiritual and lower material sides of the Self. They are extreme opposites, but as heads and tails of the same coin, so to speak, they belong together, though the hero must always defeat the serpent on behalf of the spirit. Further, we find the symbol combining the bird and serpent across the world from most ancient times.

The most obvious example is Quetzalcoatl, "the Plumed Serpent," who exemplifies the unification of spirit and soul. Quetzalcoatl, being a true Higher-Self figure, brings wisdom, truth, and higher culture to the people, though as often happens, they failed to understand his teachings and its implications, so that although civilization took a leap forward, it still remained warlike, cruel, and bloodthirsty.

> I go to my old teacher, Miss A. and say, "When you get the tension from all four sides (I use my hand to point to the four cardinal points, making a cross, with myself in the center), its center starts to rise up." As

I speak, a circle seems to rise up from the depths of me to my chest, and
it is the center of the four directions.

I am not the center of the four directions, the circle, or Self is. That
is why Christ on the cross symbolizes the Self. It rings a bell at the true
center of all human beings, and is the basis of the Gnostic symbol of the
cross within a circle, and of the Buddha in the center of his podium. In
fact, as it symbolizes the Self at the center of wholeness, it is known
more or less all over the world. Miss A. was head of the women teachers at school. She represents the feminine side of the Self, for as Jung
tells us, a teacher is one of the forms that the Self takes in dreams. The
tension is precisely that, the tension caused by the opposites from the
four directions in the processes. This causes the circle, the full Self, to
rise up.

I go to a hall where there is a debate taking place. This is about 1890
and all the great minds of the time are present, including Thomas Huxley
and H. G. Wells. The debate is about God, evolution, and religion, and
there is something ghostly about it all, as if it is a supernatural happening. In fact, it is taking place in another reality just above the earthly one.
Wells has just spoken but I say in reply to his remarks, "You are wrong.
God really does exist. Spirit is real. I know because I have experienced
them. I can prove it; at least, as near as anyone will ever be able to." Now,
Wells and the others are all great men, while I am just a small unknown
voice, yet Wells, who has been sitting high up at the back, comes down
to the front to look closely at me and to hear me better. He wants to hear
more of what I have to say.

It is difficult to know what to make of this dream. If it were only an
argument between religious experience and materialistic prejudice it
would be easier to understand; but the debate is a supernatural occurrence, as though I had stepped through the veil of time into another reality in the past. On the other hand, if it were happening now, in a spiritual
reality, the distinguished company should know much more about spiritual matters than I do. All I know is that the words I speak are true. God
and spirit can be experienced.

The dream illustrates that people in the afterlife are no more spiritually aware than we are on Earth; it would seem that the teachings of the

East, that only the saints win through to Heaven, are correct. Everyone else has to go to a somewhat lower realm, probably to be reincarnated. This is what the spirit of my father told me in an earlier dream. Yet why have not Wells and the others been reincarnated? On the other hand we should not limit the possibilities of spirit reality by our conceptions of what is possible from this earthly base.

In another dream, I was just above in the reality of the afterlife. But I was very disappointed that it was not spiritual (religious) and was no different than life on Earth. I realized in the dream that the right to attaining the numinous reality of spirit can only be achieved on Earth.

> **As I lie in my bed I see a horrible little creature, a cross between a crocodile and a leech, crawl up the bedpost. I jump up quickly and get out of its way.**

Flesh symbolizes matter and blood stands for spirit. The horrible little creature is part leech and will therefore suck the spirit out of me. As it is also part crocodile, this is all obviously the dark work of the dragon, the crocodile being an ancient symbol for the latter. A couple of nights ago I ate a fish in a dream that alluded to the assimilation of the Self as savior figure, or the beginnings of it. Now the dragon makes its destructive counterattack upon this development. The crocodile was evil in Egypt, though with positive aspects in certain cults, and it is the crocodile god, Sevekh, who rescues the limbs of Horus from the "Land of the Fish," the four limbs obviously symbolizing his four quarters or constituent parts, as the "god of the four quarters."

> **I seem to be an explorer of early North America, a sort of Daniel Boone. Going through a hole or half hidden opening in some rocks, I discover lands never before seen by man, including great mountains. When I look at these, I feel dizzy and ill and cannot bear to look farther. I have to lie down, closing my eyes to it all as it is so overwhelming and disturbing.**

The new lands never seen before by man are parts of unconscious or spirit reality which are as yet unexplored and unexplained. Mountains in dreams mean the spirit heights, here ones never experienced before, and it is this that makes me feel dizzy and ill. America is the New World, as is the virgin land I am to explore in the dream. Dreams which now follow continue this theme. This probably means that I am going beyond Jung's achievements now. He made the discoveries and laid the foundations, but only went so far with actual experience.

> I go into a cave and down a lot of stone steps until finally, in an underground chamber, I come to a pool of clear, pure water. The sides of the pool are white stone, which gives the effect of whiteness and cleanness to the pure water, though the cave itself is of brown stone.

In the previous dream I saw mountain ranges meaning spiritual heights and here now are their counterparts, the soul depths. A cave in dreams and visions mean the Earth-womb, the entrance and pathway to the feminine depths of the unconscious, the World Soul. The pool in these depths is extremely pure and clear and represents contents which are special and have the highest quality and value; they are soul depths in highest form. The white stone is also symbolic, reminiscent of the *albedo* state in alchemy which leads to the final stage of wholeness in the *rubedo*.

There were three, or sometimes four, stages in alchemy. The first was the *nigredo,* the blackening, which meant a state of psychic disorientation. The second stage was the *albedo*, the whitening, though the washing, the *ablutio*, had to take place for the *albedo* to occur. Some alchemists took the *albedo* as the completed stage, but others went further, to the *rubedo*. With this came the alchemical wedding of the *albedo* and *rubedo*, the red and white, which meant the marriage of the opposites of soul and spirit.

In ancient Egypt, the White Stone lay atop the sacred Mound, and the new initiate into the secret mysteries was given a white stone. We also find the white stone in Revelation, where it is said that he that overcomes shall be given the white stone.

> I have uncovered an ancient temple where I find a stele with hieroglyphs, figures, and scenes engraved upon it; these are carved on a stone wall. I find an ancient dagger, and with it I dig into the ground to uncover more of the stele which is sunk into it. There are professors of archaeology standing behind me, along with other kinds of experts, all watching me eagerly as I work.

> As I dig deeper, I uncover scenes which are of ancient Egypt and covered in gold leaf. They are scenes of Horus, perhaps; or maybe even of Iusa; or Iu-em-hetep, divine Son at Memphis; and Annu, the sacred center. I am a little concerned that the professors, being in positions of authority, will claim the credit for these discoveries, which are actually mine, but I decide not to let it worry me and carry on digging.
>
> I eventually come to a level of the stele which is blank, so that I think I have reached the bottom. However, this is not so, because as I dig lower still, I come to paintings of Egyptian corpses, all on top of one another, layer upon layer. I turn to the professors and say, "This obviously means that we are standing on an ancient Egyptian burial ground, which is extremely old. The treasures we will find here will be much more valuable than even those discovered in Tutankhamun's tomb." I see these layers upon layers of corpses partly unearthed before me.

A couple of dream-visions ago, I was an explorer and felt ill and dizzy as I looked at mountains never seen by man before. Then, in the last dream, I discovered the pure, clear water in the depths of the cave, the chthonic counterpart to the spiritual mountains. Now, in this dream, I find the roots of our spiritual life in the remote past of Egypt. This will reveal a great treasure, though of a spiritual nature, for as the alchemists stated, "Our gold is not the common gold."

The stele leads down to these roots, and as the Egypt of the Pharaohs is at a higher level than the corpses in the graveyard, then the roots must lie at an extremely ancient level. To continue the royal line of spiritual development through the unconscious, it is necessary first to return to its very beginning.

> I see a hare which I think is dead, but it then revives to become a small boy. The boy then becomes twin boys, and they extend out across other dimensions. They are related to me, as my counterparts, not in time but across time (or out of time and thus timeless).

The hare is a fairly well known symbol of the Higher Self in certain myths, and in the dream becomes the divine child, who then becomes twins, representing the dual aspects of the Self. I, as consciousness, am part of the Self in time, while the Self is my counterpart across those other dimensions and outside of time.

The hare was a symbol of Mercurius as guide through the work, that is, through the unconscious. As said previously, thousands of years earlier in Egypt, the hare was a symbol of Osiris, Lord of the Underworld, known as Un-nefer, the "Good Being," or "Beautiful Hare." Osiris is an excellent example of the lower part of the Self, and as such compares to Mercurius, who exemplifies the spirit of the unconscious. Osiris is twins with Set, and so my dream, with the hare and the twins, repeats the themes of Egyptian myths.

> I pray very hard, even frantically, for God to help our culture, which is in such a negative mess, and sinking further every day. Then later, as I walk down the street, I see flying saucers invading the Earth, descending from the sky. One in particular seems prominent. I lift my face to this and say, "Yes, I will talk with you."

The spaceships come in response to my pleas to God to help us, and they therefore represent spirit. Since this dream, I have become convinced that many of the UFOs being seen in the outer skies really are manifestations of spirit, coming through from the other reality in some way.

> I am in a building in the town just to the north of where I live. I have been captured by aliens from outer space who intend to operate on me. However, I climb through a window, though it was a very narrow escape.

To go north in dreams is to travel to the higher spirit side, and as I have said earlier, people who experience abductions by aliens are almost certainly being taken by spirit, which is not necessarily holy or pleasant. Man's development above the other animals may have been brought about by this spirit reality, acting in accordance with God's will. These powers may be the builders, watchers, and architects we find in early myths who are said to have built the first civilizations. When my father appeared in a dream and I said, "You can't be him, because he's dead," he changed into an alien. This is because spirit has no real form, and so can take on any that it wishes.

When we die, our spirits will enter the same formless state, but could presumably take on any shape when necessary as a representation, including that of an alien. My best friend died a few months ago, and he too changed into an alien in a dream to show that he is now spirit. So the aliens that people experience are pure spirit. In fact, they have been seen in so many forms that if they were aliens from other planets, they must have come from dozens of different ones.

Now the alien who first came in the guise of my "father" also informed me that man has a very dangerous gene that must be removed if man is to survive, and this could be why the aliens are going to operate on me in the dream. This could be the outcome of my prayer in the previous dream for God to help us; in other words, we can be helped by having the gene removed, though it may not be very pleasant for us, and we may not even like the result.

> I see an eagle swoop down to attack a little bear and start to eat it. This is very disturbing to me.

As a dove symbolizes the light and loving side of the Holy Spirit, so an eagle represents its more negative and savage side; at least, this is my interpretation. The bear is a well-known symbol of the soul depths, of Mother Earth, and is usually a sign of danger. In this dream the negative spirit starts to devour negative matter, or soul. The meaning may be that if man rejects God and the Holy Spirit, he will have to suffer the negative side of spirit, and, as in this dream, instead of a sacred marriage between the opposites, there will be violent division and war between them.

> I am by a canal where a net has been strung across, just above the water line. This net has caught a number of birds in it. Some ancient, very grand, Eastern-looking royal barges come along and stop when they reach me. Priests with shaved heads disembark, and with them is a boy of about twelve. He seems to be a god, and recognizing me, he points me out to the priests. Then strangely, the boy becomes a pope, and just as strangely, I too become a pope. What it amounts to is that the boy has recognized me as the spiritual leader of my people.
>
> The language the visitors use is foreign at first, but then I find that I can understand them. The empress of these strangers, who is probably the boy's mother, alights from her royal barge, and she presents me with a special ring that contains a large pearl, denoting my position as spiritual leader. She puts the ring onto the third finger of my right hand, a

man's marriage finger in Europe, though the ring is just a bit too large.
She then boards her royal barge again, which moves away, but as it does
so, she tells me, "Clear a way," referring to the canal possibly.

I remember seeing an illustration in a book on ancient Egypt of birds
caught in a net. The meaning was that spiritual contents must be
"caught" in the same way. The royal barges arrive, and the boy—a
prince, really a young god—recognizes me as the spiritual leader of my
people. Presumably, all the work that I have done on the processes to
bring forth the Higher Self has qualified me to be this, though I must
point out that it is the dream which says so, not my conscious thinking.
I would not care to presume this consciously. The divine boy is the lower
part of the Self, comparable to Osiris, as he comes with his mother the
Empress (the Great Mother), although the boy is still representative of
the total Higher Self.

From the empress I receive the ring with the large pearl—"the pearl
of great price"—and this, of course, alludes to the Higher Self, and the
to the authority that goes with it. Whoever brings forth the Self automatically has God's authority—again, this applies to the situation in the
unconscious. Joseph in Egypt receives such a ring from Pharaoh, and St.
Teresa of Avila was married to Christ when he placed a gold ring on her
finger.

As said in reference to an earlier dream, this is well known in religious and mythological accounts. However, the ring is a bit too large for
my finger, which means that I do not quite match up to such an exalted
position; at least, not at this precise moment in time. I have done the
work remarkably well and almost achieved the goal, but I still have one
or two worldly weaknesses, and in the end these could well cause me to
fail. The Buddhists state that there are always the ten thousand things of
the world which can pull us down from the spiritual path, and therefore
into temptation. The message of the Empress, "Clear a way," presumably
means clear a way through the unconscious. The ring, being a bit too
large, could mean that I need a bit more spiritual development, but I
doubt this interpretation. Whatever the case, the dream states how the
situation stands at the moment.

The words, "gold, frankincense, and myrrh" are spoken to me from
above as I sleep.

I have often wondered if these three gifts brought to the Christ child by the Wise Men represent the Holy Trinity. I believe that it is probable, and the meaning seems to be the same in the dream. Three angels appear to Abraham at Mamre, and declare that his wife shall bear a son, even though both Abraham and Sarah are now old and way past childbearing age. But the son-to-be is the Higher Self, which is ultimately, at the highest level of meaning, a divine child, and so the gold, frankincense, and myrrh here in the dream possibly relate to the same experience.

> I am in the street where I see people dashing about because they can see a spaceship in the sky, though it is a little hazy among the clouds. It has three fuselages which are interconnected, making it a three-in-one spaceship.

As I have said earlier, aliens, spaceships and so on, represent spirit in dreams, and this three-in-one craft can only refer to the Trinity, the three-in-one deity, repeating the message of the last dream with the gold, frankincense, and myrrh. God traditionally appears in the clouds, and if Moses, for instance, had been familiar with the concept of a spaceship, he may have experienced God's coming in that manner. This triadic spaceship is not just a symbol in a dream. This is God Himself coming forth, as a Trinitarian symbol, yet nevertheless *as an actual event*. We should all bow down before this because it is God. It may be taking place in another reality, but it is *real*.

> I am in a church, at a side wall, and there is a large golden cross on the wall—this is the Christian Cross with the horizontal bar high up on the vertical bar. Blood is coming out of it, flowing all over it. A few feet away the figure of a crucified man is on the wall; suddenly the two come together in the space between them. They then return to their original positions. I say to a certain woman, M., who is now present, "I have just had a vision where the cross and the figure came together and blood flowed forth." However, she believes that it was all due to hypnotism, or something similar. I then hear the old song, "My Happiness."

The flowing blood apparently refers to the Holy Spirit flowing forth, as water did from the hazy face of Christ in the house in Vienna in an earlier dream. Unless that is, it is the same as Christ's blood, God's essence, which is not quite the same as the Holy Spirit. Water in dreams usually refers to the lower depths of the unconscious, but not always so, as the earlier dream demonstrated. Christ's blood is redeeming, and Jung links the alchemical spiritual water, the *aqua permanens*, with this redeeming blood of the Church. He says the *aqua permanens* was a symbol for the unification of matter and spirit to the alchemists, and as the water of the Holy Ghost, had been of great importance to them since early times in the work. As the blood of Christ corresponded to this for the Christians, it is small wonder that the magical water was also termed *spiritualis sanguis* by the alchemists—the spiritual blood (1958).

A mixture of water and wine were sometimes used in the Mass, particularly in the Eastern Church—a little water is still added to the wine in the Catholic Mass today. This probably symbolized the unification of the higher spiritual and lower soul depths of the unconscious, as do my two visions. Christ changing water into wine has a similar meaning.

As one of the signs that he is acting on God's instructions, Moses is told: ". . . Thou shalt take the water of the river, and pour it upon the dry land: and the water which thou takest out of the river, shall become blood upon the dry land" (Exodus 4:9). This again has the meaning of matter, or its soul, being spiritualized, and John (19:34) says: "And one of the soldiers with a spear pierced his side and forthwith came there out blood and water." I have mentioned earlier that the Holy Grail legends are full of blood symbolism, so that the blood that flowed from Christ's side became almost more important than Christ himself. First, as the blood on the tip of the lance, then, caught in the Grail itself as it flowed from Christ, the Host—Christ's blood—is that most holy essence of God.

However, the vision in the dream seems to unify the crucified figure, perhaps the Higher Self, with the Christian cross. So the Higher Self has become Christianized, assimilated into the Western traditions and the specific meaning of the Christian cross. As for the woman, she would seem to be an aspect of my anima who refuses to accept all of this, rationalizing it to hypnotism, thereby denying the meaning and value of the vision, which is what modern man does all the time.

> I am with my mother and sister on a country walk when a lion comes dangerously close. So we go off across a field where we come on a lamb. The lion then arrives, and at first I am very afraid for the lamb; but my fears are unfounded because then the lion lies down with the lamb.

Isaiah 11:6 predicts: "The wolf shall dwell with the lamb, and the leopard shall lie down with the kid; and the calf and the young lion and the fatling together; and a little child shall lead them." This means that when all the opposites are united, the divine child will come forth—the infant Higher Self as savior. On the other hand, the lion symbolizes the lower spirit of the unconscious, Mercurius, in one form, while the Lamb is Christ as savior. So if the lion and the lamb lie down together, as in my dream, then my task in the unconscious is nearing completion, for the higher and lower spirits will then be united, Christ and Mercurius merged. On the other hand, the lion was also a symbol of Christ, and only last night I was looking at an illustration of an Egyptian stele which featured Horus as a lion. Iu-em-hetep, whom Jews later identified with Jesus, was frequently portrayed as a lion, though he was also the ass. All of these are Sun-gods and Higher Self figures. However, this probably refers to the lower aspect of the Sun-god, the lower Self of the Higher Self, as it were.

Jung said that the inner man in the West must be developed to parallel the outer Christ figure, and this is precisely what the dream now suggests. The crucified figure coming together with the cross in the last dream probably means the same thing, and in fact, the whole individuation process means this. As far as we know, this development has not happened in the West before, and therefore would mean the further development of Christianity and the evolution of the religious spirit which is extremely urgent in the modern world.

There is a little white poodle, wearing a lamb's woolen coat. It has a lovely face and seems to belong to me.

Here again, the poodle represents the Higher Self, who, wearing a lamb's coat, is assimilating itself to Christ the Lamb. The white poodle is the counterpart to Goethe's black poodle in *Faust*, and whereas I am bringing forth a figure of light, Faust brings forth Mephistopheles, a figure of darkness. Goethe was an alchemist and he said that Faust was the result of his dream processes stretching over decades. We are left with the conclusion that Goethe himself brought forth the Higher Self in the dark form of Mephistopheles. Jung stressed that neither Goethe nor others who dredged the great depths of the unconscious realized what a dangerous business it is. Alchemists such as Gerard Dorn and Christian

Rosencreutz who kept their work within the protective walls of religious traditions were wise. However, it is the morality of Christianity that is of utmost importance in the processes.

> A black octopus jumps off a wall and onto my head, where it settles curled up in a circle. It then injects a tentacle or feeler into my hand to feed off me.

The octopus perfectly symbolizes the lower, instinctual part of the Self, at quite a low level, in fact. Not only does it inhabit the depths of the sea, its shape also forms a mandala, the symbol of the Self known all over the world. The octopus, of course, has eight tentacles extending from a central body, which forms perhaps the most common form of the mandala. But whether the dream means that the creature is feeding off my personal ego-consciousness, or consciousness itself, is unclear.

> I am shown a large map of the world which has different colored areas according to the religion of each area. So, for example, the Far East is yellow for Buddhist, the Middle East blue for Islamic, and so on. When I look at the West (Europe and America) it is red; looking at the key at the bottom of the map, I expect red to be "Christian." However, it says "Atheist." Then, when I look at the full map again, I see that the red from the West is spreading as a poison all over the rest of the world.

This is the situation as the collective unconscious sees it. The atheism, materialism, and rationalism of the West constitute a poison that is affecting the whole world. Jung stated that the survival of Western civilization is extremely dubious, and we are pulling the rest of the world down with us because our influence is very strong and widespread. This is one of the main reasons I have persevered with the individuation processes, to do my bit to try and bring about the fundamental change in the way we think about and see reality.

> I am in an old church with a lot of people and we are making plans for an assault on the enemy. Suddenly, we hear enemy planes coming over and I say, "Surely they wouldn't attack a church," but as if in answer, the church is bombed and blown to bits. I put my hands over my

face as everything around is bombed. Fighter planes appear and riddle the site with machine-gun fire, but I manage to dodge the bullets.

Then torrents of water with flames from burning oil on the surface flood the place. This spreads rapidly towards me so that I have to escape by jumping onto a table that is floating past. The torrents of water that reach me do not have the burning oil on them yet; that is a little way away, but still spreading rapidly. Then I have an idea.

As the water floods through, it forms deep rapids, and if I jump into them, I will be quickly carried away from the threatening flames, which are catching up with me quickly. I may drown, but it is my only chance. So I jump into the rapids and am carried away from the flames. Then, lower down, I manage to scramble onto a bank, though I have to be wary of the broken glass and other debris lying about. A boy then appears who has special powers, and he helps me out of my difficulties. He is the divine child and takes me to a beautiful lagoon where the waters are still, and the surrounding land is decorated in lovely colors, mostly yellows and greens.

Everything seems to be catastrophic in the first part of the dream. The church is blitzed and obliterated by the dark opposing forces from the negative side of the spirit. Then the flood waters pour in, bringing fire, which I am lucky to escape. It was one of the main aims of alchemy to produce fire from the primal waters, which, they claimed, led to the production of the stone which symbolizes the Higher Self. The same could be happening in this dream, for the waters come pouring in bringing fire.

The divine child, the infant Higher Self, comes to help me, leading me to what must be the fulfilled stage of the Self, the Paradise of Peace. This is the lagoon where the waters are still and peaceful, and the land surrounding is all lovely yellows and greens. In my experience yellow (or gold) is the color of Christ, and green the color of the Holy Spirit—or of the countermatching *viridatis*, the verdant green of Mercurius. Incidentally, Jung and others, have had dreams and visions in which Christ appeared as yellow-green (or gold-green).

I see the divine child, and I and other people are filled with an intense religious feeling. We are on a hill and even the hill seems to be very holy.

To be on a hill in dreams and visions means to approach the religious and the holy. As we know from the Bible and other myths and religions, the prophet-hero is often said to go up a mountain to experience the divine; that is, God or spirit. I personally was struck by lightning on a hill in an earlier dream. The divine child here is holiness personified, which is why I, and the other people, have the intense religious feeling.

> I find myself in a sort of monastery on a higher plane of reality, and here I am met by Mahatma Gandhi. He informs me that, spiritually, I am a higher, greater soul than even he himself, and that I am held in great honor here. I then see two little beaverlike creatures who seem to bite everybody and everything in sight, and when I say that I cannot believe what Gandhi says about my being a great soul, he says, "It is true. These creatures have even bitten me, fetching blood, but notice, they do not bite you at all. You are the only one whom they will not bite."
>
> The scene then changes and I am on a skating rink doing a dance, going around in a clockwise circle. I say, "I am going to be a priest," but then I add, "or at least, I can be a priest for eighteen months, and then I can go back to leading a normal life."

It is true that I have spent a lot of years working on these processes, which are actually a religious task, but at no time have I ever considered myself to be a "great soul" to any degree, and even less so as time passes. I just try to do a job that I know desperately needs to be done; surely others must be working at the same problem. This is not false modesty on my part; I know myself only too well, my faults, limitations and weaknesses. My family and friends would fall over laughing if it were suggested to them that I am a "great soul."

All I can say is that I want to see a better, healthier, more decent society, one founded on religious meaning, and love and respect for God, but based on direct knowledge of the collective unconscious and the Higher Self. This would mean the further development of Christianity, the "evolution of the religious spirit" and the royal line that reaches back to ancient Egypt. I have thought this dream over a lot and would comment that I had been assessing it too much in terms of the world. I would not be considered a great soul in the eyes of the world as Gandhi was, but in the eyes of the unconscious I have achieved much in its processes. If we look at the inner processes of Moses, then I must have achieved something similar because of the same symbolism.

> I am at a symposium in Europe involving top scientists, including Jung. I am closely associated with Jung, perhaps as his top pupil and main collaborator, and I have provided certain material which he has studied. He now sends for me and I find him with the other experts gazing at a saucer on which a small, gold disc is spinning of its own volition. Jung is very excited, almost overwhelmed, as he watches, and he says, "Something is happening here." He says this because an unseen force is causing the disc to spin.
>
> Jung, the scientists, and I then look at a new planet that has been discovered, one that resembles Earth. I pick out a continent that looks like Africa. A young rationalist scientist has discovered this planet as an outer fact, but actually I had already discovered it before he did through the unconscious. The scientist has been widely acclaimed and honored for it, but Jung says to him. "I told you there is another, unseen reality running side by side with physical reality, and now we have proof of it." Though I have discovered this, no one takes any notice of me or recognizes I am there specifically, except as part of the crowd.

That there is the wider, spirit/soul reality behind the conscious, physical universe I am as certain as I am of the material world itself. All these dream processes are evidence of it; God and his Son, the Higher Self, are eternal realities of it, as is the Great Mother, the World Soul. But is this Jung himself here in the dream and if so, why did he need me to discover the "other reality" for him? Is it not possible to do so from where he now resides in the afterlife? Perhaps not, and is that why the world and human life are necessary? The spirit can only progress through life on Earth. In the "other reality," which is timeless, everything is static and cannot develop. This is why life, the world, the physical universe, were created: to help God grow and move through time, as He cannot do that in a timeless, spirit reality. The dream does not explain the significance of the new planet, but I may have heard of one being discovered around this time. A planet would not refer to the Higher Self, that would be symbolized by a star. However, the planet must in some way refer to the cosmic aspect of my experiences.

My father puts up some Christmas decorations. One contains the words, "New Testament," another says "Holy Trinity"; a third is an illustration of a fish.

It is in the New Testament that God develops and becomes the God of love, losing his wrathful side. He incarnates as his own good Son, and with the Holy Spirit, the two become the three of the Holy Trinity. However, as Jung points out, the Trinity actually reaches back to ancient Egypt as does the symbol of the savior as the fish, for Horus was the *An* fish, "the fish in the form of a man." This has occurred a number of times over the ancient world, for how else could we find the same symbolism throughout earlier mythology? However, here in the dream the fish alludes to Christ, as do the New Testament and Holy Trinity also mentioned.

A dragon-monster rises from the depths of the sea, holding a young woman in its jaws, whom it immediately takes back down to the depths again. The dragon rises up a second time, and it is not just a monster but also a god, and not just of the sea, but also of the sky.

Then it is a little later and a young man must have made an attempt to rescue the girl but failed, because the dragon rises up again with his body now in its jaws. I say that I represent Christianity, but do not feel at all confident in this, and smoke and fire come from the monster which hang in the air and form the word "lab."

This is the real stuff of myth and legend, and through this image we can see where and how it all originates. The dragon captures the maiden and the hero has to rescue her. The dragon represents the spirit of the lower unconscious, the Earth Mother, or her son, in terrible aspect; she is also goddess of the immediate sky because the immediate sky is included in the reality of the world. In Egypt, Nut was goddess of the immediate sky, and the Abyss, the depths, was the realm of Tepht, among others, and her seven-headed dragon son. (Nut was actually a goddess of the lower Waters herself and earlier was a female counterpart of Nun. In her celestial aspect, the constellation of the Plow was hers, as the "chair of Nut.") Only beyond the immediate sky, in Heaven, did Ra rule, although his female equivalent, Hathor, had her abode there.

The young woman in the jaws of the dragon seems to be the personal anima/soul, who is actually part of the World Soul, and she must be rescued in the processes. As for the part-word "lab," formed by the dragon's smoke and fire, it must remain a mystery, as I fail to understand just what the dragon is trying to express by it. One further point is that a dragon in a lake or the sea is a natural and common symbol of the unconscious, and accounts for the many lake monsters seen worldwide, including that of Loch Ness. Jung says that the sea monster Leviathan is "salted up" for the inhabitants of paradise, and that for the church fathers it signified the Devil.

> I see some tall skyscraper buildings, which have an extremely frightening effect, making me feel ill. They remind me of Babylonian ziggurats, and there is a bad, negative religious atmosphere about them. Modern man has gone badly wrong and is heading for destruction, it all seems to say.

What is implied by the skyscrapers and their resemblance to ziggurats is, of course, the Tower of Babel, which symbolizes man's inflated arrogance, corruption, and matter-worship. Modern man has gone the same way as the ancients in the Biblical account, which caused God to bring about their destruction. The Flood did not mean a real, physical one, but a deluge from the dark, negative side of the unconscious which flooded and overwhelmed conscious culture, causing its collapse. When man turns from religion, which forms the link with God and other realms of spirit, he soon falls into chaos.

For many centuries the tallest buildings in Christendom were the cathedrals and churches in every city, town, and village. What dominate now are the tall office blocks, cathedrals of business, erected for purely materialistic purposes, monuments to man's greed, arrogance, and stupidity. All of this makes me feel ill in the dream, and understandably so, because I know what the implications are.

The unconscious gives warnings of dire consequences, but also offers help. Only a few nights ago I dreamt of a Christian golden cross, but instead of the crucified Christ upon it, there was a lovely boy—the divine child, though not crucified. Such a child is, as the Higher Self, ultimately a Son of God. What are tower office blocks and the world of business compared to such holiness and meaning?

This is what we must worship, what must be the center of our thinking, not the wealth and power of the world, because the Self is the very center of ourselves. The savior/divine Son figure is always a symbol upon which we project our own "Christ within." Mankind has learned nothing of real wisdom since Biblical times. I am sorry to sound so negative here, but it is the collective unconscious itself pointing out all of this.

> A fish is lying on my bed, still alive, so I have to kill and eat it, although it has to be cooked first. This I do, but I may overcook it so that it is burnt.

The fish, as stated earlier, is the symbol of the Higher Self as savior, and to eat it is to assimilate the Self. Though a symbol from the lower half of the unconscious, which is why certain Son gods are depicted coming from the mouth of the Great Mother, the fish represents the total Higher Self. So yet again, the fish symbol, thousands of years old, is used by the unconscious to signify the Self in a specific way. It seems that when I am given the fish in various dreams, which is from the depths primarily, the symbol activates and brings forth the spirit counterpart. This is why Christ is both the Fish and the Lamb, soul and spirit aspects. As to overcooking the fish, it could mean applying too much of the spirit to it, too much of the heat of the sun. There is the retort in alchemy in which the *prima materia* had to be brought to the most intense heat, but I can find no reference to overheating, or overcooking. Christ cooked the fish (himself) for the disciples, and in this way was the "fish that fed the world."

> A voice from above tells me, "The Lamb was not revealed unto the Israelites because they would neither have accepted nor understood Him."

As we know, the Jews at the time of Jesus were expecting a warrior Messiah to free them from the yoke of Rome. This is probably the meaning behind the story of Barabbas—which means "Son of the Father"—the robber chosen by the Jews instead of Christ the Lamb. For many centuries the Jews had produced great prophets and holy men, and these had instituted the covenant with God, but the Jewish mentality at that time, by and large, could not comprehend the concept of the Messiah as the Lamb, let alone accept it. The Son of Man figures of Enoch, Ezekiel, and Daniel were Messiah figures brought forth in processes of the unconscious, and the earlier prophets, Abraham and Moses included, brought forth what amounts to the same figure, the Higher Self, but this was never understood by the Jews.

Some Jews did accept Christ, but they were by far the exception and not the rule. As it turned out, it was chiefly the European peoples who took up the cross—or the Fish and the Lamb for the first few centuries or so—the European psyche was apparently ready for the revelation because it had fallen into degeneracy and bestiality under the Roman Empire. It was therefore in much greater need of redemption than the Jewish psyche. Another dream I had stated that the phenomenon of Christ was caused by the degeneracy and power-madness of the Roman Empire. Christ proved a true civilizing force, and the Roman Empire was transformed into Christendom.

However, though we may accuse the West of never truly under-standing the Christ phenomenon, it is also true to say that the Jews understood it even less.

> Something about William Blake's poem "Jerusalem," and particu-larly his line, "and was the holy lamb of God in England's pleasant pas-tures seen." But it is Saturday night and I am due to go up to the pub for a few drinks.

I am coming to the culmination of the processes involving the Higher Self, but the trouble is, I like to have a few drinks on Saturday night with old friends and I usually get tipsy. This is not wrong in itself, and may even be a good thing for most people, if they are not involved in the work on the processes. Ground is lost so easily, and then the enemy, the dark side of the unconscious, may jump in and take over, so that the work has to be started all over again. The alchemists experienced this frequently.

It is obvious that I am not only close to the Higher Self, but to the Higher Self as the Lamb, and it needs one-hundred percent dedication. It is lonely, dangerous work, and as the rewards are the greatest possible (in a spiritual way), the sacrifices made must also be far beyond the normal.

> I go into a warehouse with my mother and sister where I am given a very large book which warms my heart. In it I find early Christian paint-ings, done in the most beautiful colors, but then something strikes me as

odd. In a number of them, there are expressions on the faces of the holy figures which greatly disturb me, probably because the faces themselves are full of fear. The name of St. John is very prominent. I show the book to my companions with mixed feelings of great pleasure and fear.

Why should there be such expressions on the faces of the holy figures? What is it they fear? The dream does not say. The name of St. John is very prominent, and perhaps this means John the Divine, therefore alluding to Revelation, which is quite fearsome in places; it has more of the vengeful ram rather than the gentle lamb. Is a terrible fate in store for mankind, thereby causing the holy figures to be full of fear? Is it the "end of days" for man? We are certainly destroying the planet, and big business rapes the Earth; but morally and spiritually we are in a great decline, a fall into chaos. Is this what the holy figures see?

I look at a Bible and then I pick up Goethe's *Faust*, and say, "This is the other side of it."

The Bible is nothing less than the revelation of God and of spirit/soul reality in man. It is the record of this experience in many individuals over a long period of time. Noah, Abraham, Moses, Daniel, Ezekiel, and many other figures in the Old Testament, Jesus and others in the New— most experience God through the collective unconscious, and all experience the Higher Self as intermediary. As far as I know, there is no other way it could have been done other than through the unconscious, even if this merges with outer reality in the waking state. When Christ says, "No man cometh unto the Father but by me," he speaks for all such experiences for all time.

The Self, at his highest level, is *mediator* between man and God because it contains both extremes within his nature, though the examples just given are all positive examples of the phenomenon.

In Goethe's *Faust*, the experience is inferior and negative. The Higher Self, containing all possibilities, always becomes what we develop it to be, what we forge it into, what we bring forth by our thoughts and actions. It contains all opposites and therefore all possibilities, and in the end we perhaps bring forth what we ourselves are, only a much larger version. I always aimed for the further development of Christianity in the processes because it is the highest treasure possible, as far as I can see, though it took the unconscious itself to reveal this to me. It is the continuance of the covenant with God through the unconscious, restoring true meaning and order to our world.

As to *Faust*, Goethe was an alchemist who spent decades on the work, depending largely on his dreams, but his goals were obviously inferior because the Higher Self he produced was Mephistopheles. Jung sees this (and Nietzsche's Zarathustra) as being due to the negative state of the collective German soul at that period of time, of which Goethe and Nietzsche were individual examples. Jung states that we must live by the higher Lord of Spirits, but that modern man has fallen into the dark, negative side of Mercurius, an aspect of which is Mephistopheles. Jung uses this term "Lord of Spirits," probably taken from Gnosticism though it is also found in the Book of Enoch. It exemplifies the higher spirit of Christ that must reign over not only the lower spirit Mercurius, but also, and perhaps even more importantly, over the light of man's reason.

> As I lie in my bed, a small creature comes through the window. This frightens me and I try to shoo it away, but when it comes up to me I see that it is a hare. It then lovingly licks the back of my hand, yet I am still afraid.

Here is the hare again, symbol of Osiris and Mercurius, and therefore of the lower Self. A window in dreams represents the division between this world and the other. The dream means I am visited by the higher immortal in the lower form of the hare; remember, the lower Self is ultimately part of the Higher Self. Licking the back of my hand means affection and gratitude, though I feel afraid probably because of the supernatural nature of it all. As said earlier, Un-nefer was Osiris as "the Opener," or "Good Being" with the head of a hare; the first ideograph in his hieroglyphic name is actually the figure of a hare.

> A rhinoceros comes up to me as I lie in bed. It fondly licks my hand.

The rhinoceros has been called a fitting symbol for the God of the Old Testament, who is sometimes said to be bad tempered like the rhinoceros. The Jesuit Nicolas Causin, writing in the seventeenth century, declared that God behaved like an angry rhinoceros until ". . . overcome by the love of a pure virgin, he was changed in her lap to the God of love."

In the last dream a hare, representing the lower spirit Mercurius, or the lower side of the Self, licked my hand. So if the rhinoceros in this dream represents the spirit of God, or the higher part of the Self, it means I have possibly united both higher and lower spirits, and completed the task most urgently on the agenda for modern man, according to Jung. This is in accordance with an earlier dream where the lion lies down with the lamb, Mercurius with Christ, or Osiris with Horus. If my interpretation is correct, the vastly different opposite sides of spirit and soul (the higher and lower spirits, as the alchemists call them) perform the same ritual act of licking my hand, showing a unity of purpose.

> I am secretly watching naked people at a black magic ritual. A naked woman lies across an altar ready to be sacrificed, the high priest standing over her. This priest has a goatee similar to my own, though while his is black, mine is gray-white. Suddenly, a youth shouts, "Death to the Christians." I reflect that he is a typical lout of the 1990's. Also, as I consider myself to be a Christian, they would surely kill me if they discovered me watching them.
>
> The scene then changes and I see a woman, M., walking along the street with a black cat as a familiar. As this means that she is joining the Satanists, I grab her by her hair and drag her along the pavement, away from it all.

There is evil here in this dream, and it is not just a part of my own psyche, but collective. Evil is gaining ground increasingly in the world, particularly in the West, and the "lout" is typical of some of today's youth, who are hopelessly lost to the shadow. But the woman, M., represents an aspect of my unconscious; conversely, she could refer to the soul of the real-life person and has been carried away by the influence of the evil. Her black cat is evidence of this, and just as the black dog has a sinister meaning and spells danger on the spirit side, so does the black cat on the soul side. M. is being led astray by this dangerous aspect, which is why I have to drag her away by force.

> I say to a group of friends, "Just as a second is part of eternity, so a person's soul is part of God's eternal structure. If that second were to break away from eternity and try to exist alone, denying all the rest of time, it would be lost, worthless, and meaningless. Yet this is exactly

what modern man does. He splits himself off from God and so becomes
an isolated fragment, lost and alone, surrounded by the void."

This must be the longest speech I ever made in a dream, and I
remembered it all afterwards. I have no need to comment further except
so say that the unconscious has expressed my conscious opinions perfectly.

> I see pagan hordes led by Attila the Hun riding across the Atlantic
> Ocean on a bridge from America to Britain and Europe. I am very sur-
> prised that the hordes are coming from the West, instead of from the
> East, as the Huns originally did. With them they carry the banner of the
> skull, here meaning the "Sign of the Pagan."

It would seem that negative, pagan forces are to invade Europe from
America, although we are already somewhat negative and pagan as it is.
The fact that the hordes are on a bridge means that they are not coming
solely from the depths of the unconscious itself, but the conscious culture of America is also involved. Exactly what forms these negative
forces will take is not clear, but they are apparently the same ones which
have affected American culture; they must be pagan and destructive in
nature if they are represented here by Attila and the Huns. I do not know
America personally, and Americans themselves are the best judge of the
ills of their society, but the forces are ones that may in the end destroy
all vestiges of Christian traditions, instituting a reign of barbarism that
may destroy the West.

Nazism, fascism, and communism were, as Jung says, only the first
step on the road to chaos. Rampant materialism, with its worship of
wealth, power, and worldly success, the very things that Christ and all
wise teachers of mankind warn against, is the current danger that takes
away the meaning and individuality of the human soul, though the
shadow that is overtaking younger people is equally destructive.

However, we in Europe are probably just as matter-possessed ourselves, even more so perhaps. Indeed, America may in some ways be
ready for a fundamental change that could not occur in Europe as yet.
Whatever the case, the invading pagan hordes in the dream are very disturbing, having the skull, a sign of destruction and death in this context,
as their emblem.

I saw a television program about Attila the Hun recently, and by the end he had been whitewashed so much that he was the shiny white knight, while it was the Christians who were the Scourge of God. This is part of the sickness of the West. While the light grows ever dimmer and cruelty and violence flourish, the dissociated intellectuals see only the dark side of our Christian heritage, and only the light side of its historical opponents, which were, in actual fact, usually cruel, ruthless, and barbaric. Even the marauding Vikings have become the saints, and the Christian monks they slaughtered are now the sinners. Yet the real spirit of Christianity represents an advance of higher consciousness and culture for the human race, though we so easily fall back into the barbarism and savagery again.

> I am in a carriage driven by an Indian or Pakistani man that takes me to a house where a lot of Asians live. The driver is playing Asian music, so when we stop and I get out of the carriage, I say, "I think the carriage should be playing traditional English music. Our culture is now very weak and should not be swamped by foreign ones." Then I add, "Now I study history and religions, so I know that Hindu and Muslim cultures are fine old ones, but they are not ours."

The loss of Christianity, our living myth, in the West is a devastating blow to our civilization, the full effects of which have now begun to show. The association between the conscious and unconscious worlds has been broken, and therefore between matter and spirit, causing a schizophrenic hiatus into which chaos and disease speedily rush. Christ and his mystery exemplify processes of the unconscious which involve the Higher Self; these have been constellated there for up to two thousand years, and thousands of years before that in prefigurations, so that when God "thinks" of Western man, it is in terms of the Christ phenomenon.

But Western man has now as good as lost this association, which has resulted in a culture-fall. In such a state of weakness, to be inundated by cultures that are of separate lines of religious development to the Western, is to pour water onto a drowning man. Those cultures and their religions are fine and admirable, as I say in the dream, but Western man is in a severe crisis of lost myth and lost soul, which ultimately causes the collapse of civilizations. He *must* recover his lost myth, the meaningful association with spirit reality, or die.

On the one hand, the foreign cultures may be pulled down into the same state of degeneracy and decadence that has afflicted the West. On the other, even if the foreign cultures manage to cling onto their own religious forms, which will be increasingly difficult for them with each new generation, those culture-forms do not speak the same mythic language as the collective Western soul in the unconscious.

The loss of living myth in the West is a malaise from which it may well be impossible to recover, because there is nothing appropriate upon which to base an association with the archetypal depths. The Higher Self is immortal and is ultimately part of God. Man in turn is part of the Higher Self, whether we know it or not, or like it or not, and only religion can express that mighty truth. But the Higher Self needs a savior figure to which he can attach himself, and though Vishnu and similar figures are just as valid as representations of the Self as Christ, they are not alive in the Western collective unconscious. As Jung states: ". . . the present tendency to destroy all (religious) tradition or render it unconscious could interrupt the normal development for several hundred years and substitute an interlude of barbarism" (1959a).

> **I see the white statue of a Greek god, Apollo probably, walk out of the sea and onto the beach.**

I have had a number of dreams concerning the Lamb, the coming of which is what is prophesied in Revelation. Jung writes somewhere that the birth of the divine child in Revelation is based on the Greek Leto and Apollo structure, in contrast to the Christian forms. Apollo was a Sun-god, and Christ was identified with the rising sun, as was Horus in Egypt, and all were sons of the High God. In other words, they are all based on the Higher-Self figure and that is the nature of the god in my dream, who comes out of the sea, i.e., the unconscious.

Apollo does, in fact, resemble Christ in many ways, both representing the Self as emanating from God above, whereas Dionysus is the lower counterpart to Apollo, representing the lower Self. We also see this distinction between Horus ("He who is above") and Osiris, Lord of the Underworld. True, Apollo in the dream comes from out of the sea, which usually refers to the lower depths of the unconscious, but here the sea represents the total "other reality," which is why Christ, the Ichthys is "drawn from the deep."

I feel somewhat ill and frightened as I travel to the realm of the afterlife. Everything is a haze with no scenery, as though in a fog, but there is a sort of large Ferris wheel, which is actually the Higher Self. It contains within itself its many lives. I contemplate this, and it seems that after so many good, or normal, lives, the evil side has to be incarnated in turn, and the world has to suffer for it. This is part of the divine plan. In my work on the unconscious processes I may now have to experience this evil part of the Self for a number of days. This will make me feel ill and will weaken me mentally for the duration, but it must be suffered and endured.

Thinking this dream over, it seems that the evil incarnation that has to occur every so often is nevertheless a human life. This is not the same as the dark twin of the Self, for if the light side parallels Christ, then the dark side must parallel the Antichrist—in other words, a super-human or godly power, though of darkness.

I am in an office with an old man and young woman, and on a desk is a sheet of paper or card with colored dots on it. Although the dots do not seem to mean anything as they are, when I hold the sheet up to the light, the dots form the villainous face of a man, with a long thin nose and thick lips.

Then, when I move the sheets about, different hats, hairstyles, and beards from different historical periods appear on the head, though it is always the same face. I say, "These must be the different incarnations of the evil part of the Self, as it has appeared in and through history."

This dream carries on from the previous one which said that the evil part of the Self must incarnate every so often in history. Evil must be born into the world just as the good and the normal must. There unfortunately has to be evil as well as good, to give a moral dimension in which we can maneuver to perfect our souls and to allow life to enact itself. Can we imagine a movie or novel without evil or disruption? We must hate evil and fight it incessantly, but we have to grudgingly admit it is necessary to Creation. The Higher Self has his evil aspect, as does God, who is the supreme totality of all opposites.

I was reading earlier in a newspaper where a child psychiatrist said that no child is ever born evil. That if it murders other children, or grows up to be a monster, then it is due to influences of the environment. This is nonsense, as the last couple of dreams demonstrate. Jung says, monsters are born into the world as children just as saints are. It may not be the fault of such children, monster or saint, for what choice do they really have? Each will follow its true nature, but the world will suffer for it to some degree with the former, and so must protect itself.

It is at times a relief to acknowledge the Devil because he at least has depth and real substance, a welcome change from the superficiality of modern thinking. We need to wake up, and sometimes it takes stark evil to shake us out of our blind complacency that assumes we can live without the gods and their blessings and terrors.

> As I lie in my bed, a golden Pharaoh (more like a god) is staring down at me. Though solid gold, he is alive, a living being, a god, but after a number of seconds he leaves and joins two other figures identical with him. He then lies in between them on the floor so that they form an SSS figure.

The figure reminds us of "Golden Horus," the Egyptian god and forerunner of Christ, and therefore of the Higher Self. When he joins the other two figures in my dream they form a Trinity, and again the Egyptian model of Ra, Horus, and Ka-Mutef was the forerunner of the Christian Trinity, as Jung points out. In the same way, Vishnu is the Second Person of the Hindu Trinity, the Trimurti.

I have also seen the opposite, chthonic trinity in dreams as three snakes in exactly the same SSS formation. Jung tells us that Mercurius is not only the lower counterpart to Christ, but to the whole divine Trinity, and is represented by three serpents. This is the origin of the caduceus, which later became a central rod entwined by two serpents.

> I am one of seven philosophers and statesmen in America, on the East Coast. There may also be a female one. We may have descended from the universe to Earth and have possibly come to do very important work. I think we smile at one another.

When mankind is in deep need of respiritualization, which usually means further spiritual development, it is because he has lost, outgrown, or for some other reason discarded his original spiritual orientation. This will mean the fall into matter and chaos and a deluge upon civilization if he fails to find further spiritual reorientation. This requires a leap forward to a higher level of religion, as the lower level has now become inadequate and cannot sustain the connection (the covenant) between the two realms of matter and spirit.

At such a time, spirit contents come through the collective unconscious from soul/spirit reality and could mean, if successful, a new incarnation of God as the Son, the Higher Self. Accompanying this will be such phenomena as the seven stars falling to Earth to help in the respiritualization. The savior-fish which comes from the sea (the unconscious), the star in the skies, the animals and conglomerations of different animals—these are all part of the processes which happen over time.

My dream-visions show that this is occurring now, and that I am involved in the phenomenon. It further seems that the "cure," the respiritualization, may well begin in America, as that is where the seven stars have fallen to. Possibly this is because it is leader of the Western world and because matter-worship is perhaps most extreme there.

We must also recall that in previous dreams stars have fallen onto Russia and America, possibly seven onto each, and with a probable feminine eighth. Those dreams were before Glasnost and the fall of communism in 1989, so they could partly allude to the actions of spirit which brought about the eventual reconciliation between the two sides split by the once Iron Curtain.

> I am in a palace in ancient Egypt where I am the son of Pharaoh. However, I am aware that Pharaoh is displeased with me and that I have been called to see him in his rooms (although I have also just passed him in a corridor).

Pharaoh was said to be Horus in his earthly aspect, Horus being the Higher Self. I, as son of Pharaoh in the dream, must also be connected to the Higher Self as one of his parts or emanations. In that way, I am the son of the Self, just as it in turn is the Son of God. In other words, Pharaoh here refers to the Higher Self and I am his human aspect. But it seems that Pharaoh, the Self, is displeased with me, which means that I must be doing something in life that is detrimental to the well-being of the total Self, causing disharmony and disturbance.

353

> I join my family, who is sitting in a darkened room. Suddenly, a golden crook, as carried by Pharaoh, appears in the air before us; it is like a light shining in the darkness.

The savior-gods in mythology are often the "Good Shepherds" because all of the flock, i.e., human souls, are gathered around them and are guided by them. This is in keeping with the facts of the unconscious processes, where all parts of the Higher Self must come together as its flock to be guided. The shepherd's crook is a specific symbol of this (as is the cross) for with it the shepherd pulls in the flock and keeps order, harmony. Furthermore, there is the classical metaphysical reference to the "Shepherd's Crook of the Second Person," this latter being Christ; but Horus is the Egyptian Christ, the Second Person to Ra and Ka-Mutef from a certain angle. This was perhaps the deeper meaning of the crook carried by Pharaoh (human form of Horus), and as such appears in my dream.

Pharaoh's crook was called the *hek*, and Pharaoh carried this in one hand and the flail in the other, his arms crossed across his chest. With these he would not only keep the "flock" in order, but drive them onwards in the way of righteousness to the spiritual goal. But the *hek* must have been a special symbol of the collective unconscious in early Egypt for it to be now so repeated in my dream.

> I am taking two, possibly three, lions up some stone steps to a class-room. The lions are humanized somehow, and walk upright. When we reach the classroom, it is filled with animal pupils, all of which sit in deep study at desks. Some even wear glasses, showing how studious they are.

The lion, as mentioned previously, is a symbol of Christ, Horus, Iu-em-hetep, and also, and most importantly, of Mercurius, the dual-sided lower spirit of the unconscious. In fact, it is most probably because the lower Self is symbolized by the lion, this being ultimately part of the Higher Self, that the above figures include the lion in their variety of symbols. There may be two lions in my dream which could allude to the dual nature of the lower Self, while three would mean the lower, Mercurial trinity.

The various studious animals would seem to be the animal parts of the World Soul brought together in harmony. This may now lead to a higher response from the opposite higher spirit. The whole purpose of the processes is to bring all of the opposites together in unification, and only man can accomplish this task and does so on behalf of spirit and soul realities. The unification would mean the sacred marriage between God and Sophia, wisdom.

> I see a very ancient sailing ship in the clouds, which I somehow know is connected with the ark of Flood legends. Then a very large Egyptian god appears, about eight feet tall, with a beard around his jaw, like the early depictions of certain gods; he carries an adze or an ax. When he sees me, he is going to poleax me with his weapon, but when I sing a Christian hymn, he stops and becomes friendly. Two male companions are with me, and we look up at the clouds again to see that the ark has become a nineteenth century sailing ship.

The ark in the sky reminds us of Noah's, but here is obviously Egyptian. As a matter of fact, as I show elsewhere, the Biblical Flood may well derive from an Egyptian one involving Ra and Nu, the latter building the ark for Ra who sends a deluge. Other gods of Egypt had arks (Horus, Osiris, Thoth, Num) and they usually had seven companions with them, matching Noah with his seven companions in the ark (his wife, his three sons, and their wives).

The god who appears in the dream is like one of the Egyptian Early Period depictions, though very large. He is going to destroy me with the ax until I sing the Christian hymn. This is because the god is a very early form of what Christ was later to represent: the archetypal Christ. The two were separated in time by thousands of years, yet were one in God, in timeless higher reality. My two companions in the dream represent the two auxiliary functions of my psyche that accompany me in these processes. However, why the ark changes into a nineteenth-century sailing ship is not clear, unless it alludes to Gerald Massey's works on Egypt, written in the nineteenth century.

There has long been debate as to what exactly the stone ax or adze signified in early Egypt. That it was the first sign or symbol of the gods seems clear, and the word *neter* (or *nuter*) refers to both the god and the ax. Certain scholars of the past ascribed the meaning of "power" to the symbol, though others disagreed, stating it meant "renewal." Still others claimed the ideograph for *neter* in the hieroglyphs was not an ax at all, but a scroll with the end turned over. Wallis Budge concluded it meant a being who had the power to create and maintain life; in other words, a god who possessed divine creative power. This seems to have been the true meaning.

The ideograph in the hieroglyphs is clearly an ax (or adze) with the head tied onto a handle (or short pole) probably with leather thongs. This is what the god in my dream is carrying. Wallis Budge says that such an ax is so ancient that it even preceded the stone knife as a weapon, though I doubt this. It is a very short step from using a sharp bone or stone as a knife to chipping one from stone, whereas tying a sharpened head on to a handle securely is a little more involved. But that is unimportant. What matters is that the stone ax or adze came very early to man and was used as a symbol in Egypt from the very earliest times as the symbol for the divine creative power of the gods, and indeed, for the gods themselves. We see the same sort of thing with Thor's hammer.

For his part, Gerald Massey says:

Now, as Darkness was the primal producer or parent, the first voice with which she spoke to man was thunder. Out of that darkness leaped the lightning, and the lightning was thought to deposit the thunder-ax, bolt, or stone from Heaven, the cloud-cleaver and Celestial *Celt*, which preceded and possibly *suggested* the manufactured weapon. For the Celt adze (named Anup) is the Nuter-sign of divinity, and this came from Heaven as lightning born of darkness. Such was the kind of *revelation* made by external nature to primitive man. The stone-ax gave him supremacy on earth, and that weapon was first hurled at him hot and hissing from the thunder-clouds of Heaven . . . *This was a form of the Ax which the Great Mother gives birth to in various American Myths as her First Child.* In Egypt it is identified with Set-Anup . . . Anup is a name of the Celt-ax. . . . Stone-Head is the name of the Serpent that guards the sixth of the Seven Halls of Osiris. . . . *the ideograph Nuter that was continued as a type of primordial Power which dwelt in darkness and manifested itself in death and destruction* as one of the Elementaries (1880).

Massey is speaking of the very earliest times, for although the stone ax may have been associated with death and destruction, ultimately it came to signify all the gods, their creative and destructive powers. (It is with this weapon that the god is at first going to "destroy" me.) In the hieroglyphs, the number of axes, or neters, signifies the number of gods.

> I am on a medieval battlefield with an army under attack. Knights on horseback and foot soldiers approach, and just behind me is Christ crucified on the cross; somehow Christ is white. I have a large, two-handed sword and I face the enemy to protect Christ. This is the large, heavy sword that can only be lifted with two hands—hence "two-handed sword." A knight in black armor riding a white horse, charges at me, but I now have a lance and knock the black knight off his horse, being careful not to harm the horse. In this way I defend Christ.

I have seen the crucified Christ a number of times in dreams. He represents the Higher Self, or divine Son, appearing in accordance with our Christian traditions and in the act of suffering and self-sacrifice. However, the "cross of death" is also the "cross of life" and there are ancient depictions of Christ "hanging on a tree" as the scriptures put it, surrounded by fruit also hanging from the Tree of Life. We find this earlier with Joseph in Egypt, where Pharaoh's baker is also hung on a tree, though Pharaoh's butler has dreamt of grapes which means life for him, rather than death.

Christ on the cross symbolizes the "god of the four quarters," the fourfold structure of the Higher Self, but much earlier in Egypt, Horus exemplified this with his four sons, Quebhsennuf, Tuamutef, Hapi, and Amset. These had been his four brothers previous to his attaining divinity. The tree was likewise a great symbol in Egypt, and the Egyptian image of the Tree on the Mound is possibly the basis of the cross on the Hill of Golgotha. Golgotha means "the place of the skull" and just as Christ is resurrected, so the skull of Osiris was the most important part of his reconstituted body in his resurrection. The tree was both fourfold and sevenfold, expressing the nature of the Higher Self and the realm of the god. The head or skull was always the "vessel of transformation" throughout the esoteric Mysteries, the "Children of the Golden Head," Baphomet, the head of John the Baptist, all following from the head of Osiris. Jung says that the head of Osiris crossing the waters means the resurrection itself.

357

Be that as it may, it seems that here I defend Christ (Christianity and all it involves), while I also defend the light side of the Higher Self in the processes (who is white) against the forces of darkness led by the black knight. I accomplish this to a degree by unseating the black knight, though taking care not to harm the horse.

Again, on the one hand this is because it would cause me much distress to harm any animal either in real life or in dreams, and the unconscious knows it, but on the other hand, the horse has a symbolic meaning. In old legends the sun rides upon the moon as a horse. These exemplify the solar god, the Higher Self (Horus) upon the moon god, the lower Self (Osiris), and means the unification of the opposites. The horse, being four-legged, is an apt symbol for the fourfoldness of the Earth, as is the true cross. Here in the dream, however, the horse carries the dark side of the Higher Self, the black knight. It is not therefore the lower Self (the horse) that I must stop, but the corresponding dark side, the black knight.

> I may be with another person, though this is not certain. What is sure is that an angel with spread wings appears just above. For some reason, perhaps because of previous dreams, I am a little wary as to whether the angel is of the light or dark, but whichever, I am told that there is the penultimate level in the unconscious-spiritual process, and then the highest ultimate level. The former is perhaps represented by the Buddha, so the dream intimates, but the latter, final stage, symbolized by Christ, requires total self-sacrifice.

The levels of attainment in the esoteric processes are said to be sevenfold, and so the Buddha would represent the sixth degree of attainment, while Christ is the seventh. On this, Blavatsky (1888) comments: "It is not correct to refer to Christ—as some Theosophists do—as Buddhi, the sixth principle in man. The latter per se is a passive and latent principle, the Spiritual Principle of Atma, inseparable from the manifested Universal Soul. It is only in union and in conjunction with Self-consciousness that Buddhi becomes the Higher Self and the Divine, discriminating Soul. Christos is the seventh principle, if anything."

Blavatsky further comments: ". . . Christos, or Logos, or the Spirit of true Divine Wisdom . . . [is] distinct from the spirit of intellectual or mere materialistic reasoning—the Higher Self in short" (1888).

As I stand in front of the sink in the kitchen, I see two spiders come up out of the pipe, and so I try to swill them down again with the water. As this happens, the figure of Christ stands just behind me, so that there is a very heavy atmosphere over the whole scene.

The spiders seem to be twins from the lowest level of the soul depths, and Christ behind me must represent the corresponding heights of the processes, the Higher Self in that specific form. But the heavy atmosphere is not from the spiders, rather from the divine presence of the figure behind me. The presence of the Higher Self is not permanent here, but when he does merge with the human individual it may well be permanent, as in the case of Elijah, Enoch, and Jesus.

Here in this dream, the Higher Self is present as a Christ figure. As I said, this is not a permanent presence, and in fact, it is some while since it occurred and I have experienced no similar presence since. But the processes continue and who knows what will happen in the future? Jung says somewhere that it is enough to know that the Higher Self exists and is there, and that total unification with him is unnecessary, and may even be undesirable, at least, from our everyday view.

My individuation processes illustrate the phenomenon of the Higher Self and all of the connected contents in and through the unconscious, even God and the World Soul. They also demonstrate how the denial by Freud and other reductionists that dreams contain divine revelation in any way, and indeed, their denial that the divine itself and the collective unconscious exist, are wrong and invalid.

There is a group of people, perhaps all women, and they give me a fish ready to eat. Not only is the fish battered, someone also salts it for me.

Here is the symbolic fish again, covered in batter and ready to be eaten, which places it not only with the edible fish of the alchemists, but also with the Ichthys (fish) that was Christ. The alchemical, and indeed, the mythological, fish was required to be edible because the archetypal content was then in a form that could be assimilated to consciousness, whereas an inedible fish could not be assimilated, and would in fact be highly dangerous.

The fact that the fish is salted for me is highly meaningful, for salt meant the *Sapientia* (wisdom) most sought after by the "sons of the philosophers." This was the *sal* that was said to be the begetter of the spirit Mercurius which symbolizes the greater unconscious. It was even said that salt alone could conquer sulfur, the Devil: "Verily, sulfur is the true black devil of hell, who can be conquered by no element save by salt alone." The alchemist Johann Glauber (1658), who wrote these words, referred also to Christ as the *sal sapientiae*, which Jung calls a symbol of the Higher Self.

It was further said by the alchemists that in "lead" was the "shining white dove" (the salt), and that this was the "pure, chaste, wise, and rich Queen of Sheba." As I say elsewhere, the Queen of Sheba was the feminine wisdom of the unconscious experienced and gained by Solomon. Salt was the soul of the *anima mundi*, which again equates it with the Queen of Sheba; with Zipporah and her sisters who come to Moses at the well of Midian; and with Beersheba, the "well of seven" of Abraham (*sheba* means seven). This "salt of the wise" was the arcane substance that could unite the opposites and produce the alchemical stone, a symbol of the Higher Self, for in the salt, it was said, lay the whole "magistery" of the work.

Salt was not only sometimes equated with the Anthropos, but even with the higher Christ, so that the body "salted" by Christ became incorruptible. In this way, the salt was the wisdom that was Christ, and the fish in my dream is also connected with Christ, the Ichthys. The Old Testament (Leviticus 2:13) states that salt must be added to all meat offerings, obviously for similar symbolical reasons; the New Testament (Mark 9:50) tells us: "Salt is good. . . . Have salt in yourselves and peace in one another."

> I go to a lake, and as I do so Christ's spiritual presence descends from the sky and rests behind the lake, as though becoming united with it. Though I know that this is happening, I do not actually see Christ, but nevertheless know he is there. I walk to an old church where people are singing my favorite Christmas carol, "Silent Night," and as I walk, I pass an elderly woman, who is like an old schoolmistress of much authority.

Christ in the dream signifies the Higher Self in highest and ultimate aspect, as the divine Son unified here with the feminine soul depths, represented by the lake. The elderly woman of authority is the personification of the collective feminine soul, or World Soul. The church intimates the sacred marriage of Christ with matter. Though a church is the "House of God," it nevertheless enfolds the whole Christian mystery, which includes the feminine soul side, with Mary equaling Sophia, the "Shining Mother." She and the birth of the divine child are most beautifully expressed by the carol "Silent Night."

> I see the model of a church that has a large stained-glass window. This contains Christ as his actual living presence and not just as a depiction. A large fish is in front of the window; by now the church and everything else has become life-size and real. Outside the church is a youth with golden, curly hair; he is somehow associated with a sheep—perhaps he carries one. This causes me to think of the Good Shepherd.

This dream continues the previous one, and now Christ is in the church, part of the stained-glass window. This means the Higher Self in the form of Christ has become assimilated to our Christian traditions. So too has the fish, which represents the lower part of the Self from the watery depths (although the fish symbolizes the total Higher Self, as son of the Father).

The youth with the golden curls seems to mean the Good Shepherd, which reaches back before Christ to most ancient times. Osiris and Horus were both Good Shepherds and Christ was the continuance of their royal line. It also seems that the Christ figure in the above dream follows on from these early images: the Higher Self as divine Son and Good Shepherd.

> I see the southeastern states of America from above, and these are almost white with illumination. However, there are points dotted all over that are even brighter, shining like stars, but also pulsating. It is as though the earth in those states had been implanted with stars, had been impregnated by them, so that the whole area is now aglow, and what it perhaps signifies is that the earth there is spiritualized.

Some while ago, I saw the seven stars fall onto this area, and these in another dream became seven philosophers—the seven sages known all over the ancient world—and I was one of them. There may also have been a female eighth, fitting in with the ancient archetype of 1 + 7 (in one form, Sophia with her Seven Sons). All this seems to be continued with this dream, and things seem to be following a divine plan over the years, which includes my own development and bringing forth of the Higher Self. But according to the dream, not England but these states in America will be affected. This is what the dream processes strongly suggest.

The flood myths of the world represent the second part of the unconscious processes; the first part is building up the Higher Self in some individual. It is when this fails to take root in the sick and ailing society, not merely in consciousness, but in the souls of the people, that the floods of chaos break out in full force and deluge the culture. Higher culture with its spiritualizing effects has then been rejected, and although this happens mostly unconsciously, the Devil is nevertheless still unchained. We see all of this threatening the West at this moment, for the darkness has become very attractive and man is falling to his shadow. However, it is not merely man's own shadow that is involved, but more devastatingly, the dark side of the collective, or eternal, forces. It is these which drown and destroy a culture.

> I am on the top of a grassy hill where I see Christ crucified upon the cross. The whole scene is close-up, so I do not see anything else. One or two other people may be present at the side. I am told that when I die and leave this world, I will join the Christ figure that is now on the cross, though this is not too pleasing to me in the dream.

This is the Higher Self as a Christ equivalent. All of my years of processes have been heading toward this, if shakily at times. If taken to the ultimate levels, the initiate may unite with the Higher Self, so that God becomes man and man becomes God. This may occur during the initiate's lifetime—it almost happened with me at one point in my processes—but usually the unification is meant to occur in the afterlife.

This may not appear entirely attractive from our conscious standpoint, for we think of our loved ones, whom we would naturally like to be with again in the afterlife. Our view from the worldly standpoint is extremely limited, for we cannot know what the ultimate truth is and how other planes of reality are structured. We cannot know what full reality really is, what the Higher Self is, or even what a human being is. Nevertheless, it has become apparent that the Higher Self is not just a single figure, but a much wider, fuller, eternal truth containing *all* opposites within its nature. Who knows what is possible with such an immortal being?

> I am with a female companion, M., in an old Catholic Church, where a nun, clad in white, or very light gray habit leads us through some rear rooms. We pass through a small room, where we see some small statues in white marble, about a yard or so high. These are a goddess—or several goddesses—in various poses. As we then go into a much larger room, the nun tells us that the twelve statues are of the Virgin Mary. This is very interesting to me, and so I go back to have another look, though there seem to be fewer than twelve statues. Maybe these are just some of them. I then rejoin M. and the nun in the larger room.
>
> The nun takes us to an altar, before which is a large metal trapdoor set in the floor, which the nun causes to rise by pulling a rope. As it opens, I see a pebbled path leading down to the dark depths below, where I know there is water, perhaps a lake or even the sea, though it is in darkness. I can also see a very old brick bridge, which has been entirely covered up by the building of the later church. Suddenly, I have received a large charter in yellowed parchment folded to make double pages. I have received this charter from the depths below.

I was expecting a dream such as this in complement to the one of the Christ figure on the Cross, and here it is. This is the response from the feminine depths, the World Soul, intimated by Mary as a twelvefold goddess. The Sun Woman in Revelation, who gives birth to the divine child, wears a crown of twelve stars, and so twelve now seems to be the number of the Great Mother (in the ancient world it was usually seven). Christ has his twelve disciples in the Gospels, but in Revelation it becomes sevenfold in several ways; and in the Old Testament, Joseph is the seventh legitimate son, but is also one of twelve. These are just a couple of examples of twelve and seven symbolism that appear in the Bible, and indeed, throughout mythology. Along with the three of spirit and the four of matter (soul), seven and twelve are the numbers of the processes in the divine drama experienced through the unconscious. However, why I seem to see less than twelve statues of Mary, when there should be twelve, is a mystery at the moment.

The church in the dream is built over the feminine waters of the World Soul, which countermatches Christ on the hill in the previous dream. It is a nun who leads me to the hidden depths, so everything is feminine here. The Catholic Church does represent the feminine principle far more so than the other churches, and Jung saw the recognition of the Assumption of Mary by the Catholic Church in 1950 as a tremendously important step in the divine drama, paving the way for the birth of the divine child. In this dream I receive the charter from the fathomless depths, which appears to mean that I have its sanction, although what this entails is not stated.

It is significant that the pathway leads *under* the bridge, for a bridge usually leads *over* to somewhere. Psychologically and mythologically a bridge can lead over to the higher plane of spirit, which can be dangerous, as my early dream demonstrates, in which I became mentally disorientated when I almost crossed over too soon. However, that was to the higher spirit, and here under the bridge leads down to the lower soul depths, which, incidentally, may be just as dangerous in certain circumstances as going over.

The bridge in the dream is also a solid support for the church, as the church is built over it. The Church itself needs this solid support from the depths for then it will have solid foundations in lower soul reality, as well as in the higher spirit. I get the feeling in the dream that this bridge, as an arch, can support literally anything. As I say, the Catholic Church is somewhat feminine in any case—indeed, it is the Bride of Christ—and this is all to the good, as masculine spirit and feminine soul are then combined in religious totality.

Earlier, I mentioned the vision of the Virgin covered in stars seen by a group of children in Pontmain, France, in 1871. Her son, Christ, then appeared beside her on the cross in a deep red color. This is the same theme as my last two dreams where Christ and the feminine World Soul are united. It is the reason the divine son sometimes incestuously marries his mother in mythology—Horus marries Isis, for instance—but it means that divine spirit and soul have been unified at highest level. A lot of popular books claim that Jesus married Mary Magdalene and that their offspring became European monarchs, but the Gnostic myths have the real answer, where Christ marries the Virgin, or Sophia, in spiritual union; the *hieros gamos,* or Sacred Marriage.

We see this situation exemplified in early Egyptian mythology. In *Gods of Eden,* Andrew Collins writes of what are perhaps the most archaic myths of Egypt. These have much relevance to my dreams of

Christ crucified on the hill and the watery realm to be reached beneath the church. Collins takes his information from a book by female archaeologist, E. A. E. Reymond, *The Mythical Origin of the Egyptian Temple*. Ancient Egyptian texts tell of a temple that came down from Heaven near Memphis, the architects of which were said to be Imhotep (a contraction of Iu-em-hetep) and his father, Kanefer. This substantiates what I say elsewhere about the mythical temple built by Iu-em-hetep, the divine Son and Higher Self figure. In other words, this temple represents the Higher Self descending from the spirit realm. Imhotep, who was a real person, can be taken as the initiate who brought forth the Higher Self, Iu-em-hetep.

However, other records which remain on the walls of a much later, real temple at Edfu, Egypt, speak of the time in the very remote past when the sacred Mound, known then as the Island of the Egg, arose from the Nun, the Primeval Waters. The creator gods here had various names, including the "Eight Shebtiu," who equal the Ogdoad gods (who are 1 + 7). The Shebtiu construct a temple, known as the "Mansion of Wetjeset-Neter" (neter means god), and, after a threatening flood is vanquished, the Shebtiu sail away to continue their creative work across the Earth in other lands. These Shebtiu, then, are the builders, potters, carpenters, watchers, etc., known to many mythologies, and are essentially the Higher Self with the seven powers. They are the basis, in fact, of the Elohim of the Bible: God is El, while the accompanying Elohim number seven. (Also of Noah, with his seven companions in the ark.)

There are many other details involved in the archaic myths at Edfu, but the above constitutes the creation myth of the First Time. This is the same in essence as the creation myth of the very ancient sacred center at Annu, and indeed, of those found at different cult centers all over Egypt. The Shebtiu are almost certainly the Shebt-Iu, Shebt being possibly a form of *hept*, and *hept* being the earlier form of *hetep*, which means both peace and seven. In other words, the eight Shebtiu are the same as Iu-em-hetep, the savior son who comes to Earth not only as "peace," but as "seven," or perhaps more correctly, as 1 + 7. Again, this is the Higher Self with the seven powers. Collins and Reymond both say that the temple on the Mound referred to at Edfu must have been near Memphis, forgetting that this is precisely where Imhotep's temple was said to descend from Heaven, though Imhotep's temple is actually Iu-em-hetep's mythical temple of the Higher Self.

The Mound, or Island of the Egg, was closely associated with the Underworld, usually known as the Duat (or Tuat) though being more correctly as Amenta. (Massey says that the Duat was only the first part of Amenta.) Connected with the Island of the Egg, the Underworld was known as the Underworld of the Soul, situated beneath the Island. This subterranean realm was called *bw-hnm*, which Reymond interprets as "Place of the Well" (or perhaps lake). It was reached by going down a long, descending passageway. So these myths of the First Time again repeat the ones of Iu-em-hetep, where Hetep itself, the sevenfold Paradise of Peace above, was countermatched by the twelvefold Amenta Underworld below. Indeed, another name for the Island of the Egg was the Island of Peace.

Here is another thread linking Egypt to my two dreams. The first pyramid built by Imhotep for pharaoh Djoser, although appearing six-stepped today, was originally seven-stepped with the platform on top. Beneath it is a very large chamber complex. I do not know for sure at this moment, but I am willing to bet that this underground chamber complex beneath the pyramid is, or was originally, or was intended to be (maybe unfinished) twelvefold in structure, because above and below would then match the seven-stepped Mound above and twelvefold Amenta below. Further, the mythical temple built by Iu-em-hetep rested upon seven pillars, and he was helped in his task by Aft (or Tepht), goddess of the watery deep. This meant again the coming together of the higher and lower realms of the unconscious. Be that as it may, when Iu-em-hetep is equated with the Shebtiu gods it shows that Iu-em-hetep is far more ancient than usually taken to be, and that there is far more to all of this than his merely human architect Imhotep with his earthly architectural designs.

Now let us connect all of these myths to my dream of Christ crucified on the hill and the following one of the underground realm of the waters below the church. We can see that the symbolism is the same. The sevenfold temple, or even the seven-stepped Mound, with the Shebtiu or Iu-em-hetep, correspond to Christ on the hill in my dream. The subterranean watery depths below (the Underworld of the Soul) correspond to the watery depths revealed to me by the nun, and which lay beneath the church. In both the myths and my dream, this lower realm is reached by a long, descending pathway. It is implied in my dream that Mary is the twelvefold goddess of these depths, matching the ancient realm of the soul depths, and as I say above, the Underworld of Amenta was twelvefold.

So the very first myths of Egypt and my latest dreams, though separated in outer reality by thousands of years, are saying the same things. The only differences are that the Higher Self in the ancient accounts, whether seen as the temple, the Shebtiu, or Iu-em-hetep, is 1 + 7, whereas in my dream, Christ on the Cross is 1 + 4. However, the Higher Self, historically, is both 1 + 7 and/or 1 + 4. This is why Christ in the Gospels has seven fishermen disciples in one account and four in another. The other difference is the sevenfold nature of the goddess in the ancient world as compared with the twelvefold of Mary in my dream, though the lower realm itself is twelvefold in both the ancient myths and my dream. However, some of the statues of Mary were missing, and I would say that this did leave about seven. So both seven and twelve would be connected with Mary in my dream.

Returning to Imhotep and Iu-em-hetep, there is something very strange here. There are hieroglyphic texts which tell of Imhotep as high priest, architect, and physician to pharaoh Djoser, who honored him greatly. Yet, the myths of Iu-em-hetep (and of the Shebtiu) building the sevenfold temple are apparently much older; the attributes of architect, builder, physician, and healer are ascribed to many gods, stretching from the Americas to the Far East, and from the Egyptian Ptah, the "grandfather of the gods," up to Christ. It would seem that Imhotep's construction of the first step-pyramid for Djoser was merely the *outer* expression of the latest instance of the building of the inner, spiritual temple, and that Iu-em-hetep, possibly as the Shebtiu was considerably older. Indeed, Iu as divine Son of Ptah is probably exceedingly ancient.

Afterword:
Restoring Reality in the Light of the Spirit

If we look back to the first part of this book, to the Prelude, where I am lost, depressed, and in a state of disorientation, it will be realized just how far I have journeyed with the dreams. Everything has been completely transformed, not only my own personality, but the whole of reality itself. I now inhabit a universe that is not limited to mere matter, but one that is part of a vast, eternal, religious complex, where the God of Spirit and the Goddess of Soul are the ultimate truths.

When I reflect on the state that I was formerly in, where the universe was cold, frightening, and meaningless, I can only marvel at the difference now. My original fears that Nietzsche was right died many years ago, when I felt myself undergoing transformation to a new and different way of being. This was gradual change to the age-old way of religious orientation as a matter of direct knowledge—gnosis rather than belief. It was as though a light had been switched on in the whole universe, the light of the spirit, restoring reality to how it always was for man until quite recent times. As I know these things for certain, I have naturally been happy with the nature of full reality for all these years. What is now so depressing is the dissociated and disoriented way man generally thinks and exists today.

I have been privileged to make the heroic quest through the unconscious, and my dreams have revealed archetypal contents. In the depths

I found my own individuation and transformation. Rather than seeing the world as the big thing and spirit reality as something vague (if existing at all), spirit, being real and permanent, now becomes true reality, while the world, with its constant change and impermanence, becomes less real in that sense. Yet I live with the definite knowledge that the spirit, as well as being eternal, is nevertheless part of every day reality. We all walk under the eye of God because we are psychically attached, and for me this is a living reality. On the other hand, despite the gnosis gained in my processes, I remain my simple self, for no matter what great things we experience, we nevertheless remain what we are, and must be thankful for it. Let God be great and man be small, and then the world is in its right order.

The eternal feminine spirit, the Great Mother of All, as She has frequently been termed, is forever there as counterpart to God. As She tells us in Proverbs, when God laid the foundations of the world She was at His side. The sacred marriage between God and the Great Mother produces the ultimate divine son, and this is the form the Gnostic Trinity takes; Father/Mother/Son. The Church Trinity, however, is exclusively male; Father/Son/Holy Spirit. Nevertheless, both Trinities are equally valid as archetypal structures. Furthermore, the Catholic Church has virtually made a goddess of Mary, and when she is added, the Holy Trinity structure becomes 3 + 1, the quaternity of wholeness that Jung writes about so frequently. Likewise though conversely, when the Holy Spirit is added to the Gnostic Trinity, the quaternity is reached again.

When the Devil is added to the Holy Trinity he becomes the "recalcitrant fourth," and another quaternity is formed, or perhaps I should say realized. This archetypal pattern runs from man to God, so that man, Higher Self, and God are 3 + 1 in nature, all having a recalcitrant fourth. There are also lower, chthonic, countermatching trinities and quaternities, as my processes have further demonstrated. These were explored and experienced by the alchemists and hermetic philosophers over many centuries.

The reason I mention all of this is that man is connected to these archetypal patterns through the unconscious. To be dissociated from them means danger to the personal psyche, and if it is the general situation, to the whole culture. The purpose of my book is to demonstrate that our connection to these forces is real and direct, and that we must live within a framework of religious orientation where they are our highest truths and values.

Christianity exemplifies the mystery of the divine incarnation in a special way because it is based so solidly upon love. The Old Testament and Egyptian prefigurations were also dependent upon morality and righteousness, but not so much on love in the way that Christianity is. It has been pointed out many times that such mythical gods as Dionysus, Mithras, and even Cernunnos, are resurrecting gods, but we must understand that these are lower, more primitive versions of the phenomenon.

Jung calls Christianity a great advance in man's conscious awareness, so that God incarnates in highest form. The Christian version has a special beauty that is not so evident with the others. The World Soul becomes a simple, pure and decent woman, and the divine child is born in a humble stable—God would not be known in Caesar's palace where power-madness reigns. This exemplifies the fact that in the individuation process the adept must empty himself of what the world considers of greatest value in order to develop the inner man in his most positive form.

It is a fact that only when man is at his humblest and most perfect, will God incarnate in highest form. Can we imagine the true Christ craving worldly wealth and power? Yet many modern books claim just that; that Jesus craved the Jewish throne and that such was the purpose of his mission. (In certain versions Christ, like Mithras, is born in a cave, the Earth-womb," which means the feminine depths of the unconscious, but this does not alter the truth of what I say about the stable.)

The world draws farther and farther away from these greatest of all truths—the truths of the soul—and this withdrawal was predicted by the Bible texts. However, when the science fiction writers of the early twentieth century wrote of the future, they invariably saw the main dangers to culture as loss of freedom and censorship. None foresaw the opposite danger, too much freedom and no censorship, resulting in a fall into the abyss. Yet myths from the earliest times show this to be Man's greatest peril; loss of the gods, loss of soul, and loss of morality and right order. None of the later writers seem to have foreseen that the great danger would be the symbolical Noah's Ark all over again.

A report in the British press recommends we should get rid of Easter altogether as a religious festival, that it no longer reflects the realities of our times; indeed, neither does religious instruction generally. However, the report fails to add that many schools no longer teach Christianity at all in any case, and that they want to take away what little is left. But as my processes show, the Christian Mystery is still very much alive in the collective substrata of the Western mind, and to cut children off from this is to cause a dissociation in the psyches of those children. This is another nail in the coffin of Western civilization, or, put differently, part of the gradual eating-away of its foundations.

Of course, and as my processes show, the Christian Mystery is a more complex phenomenon than the Church may be aware of. But we could not expect little children, or even some adults, to understand the deeper complexities of the inner truths (though the Bible is actually the record of archetypal processes). Yet children need to develop in a religious milieu in order to make basic connections with the symbolical nature of unconscious reality—of full reality. It is also important to show that moral truth has deeper foundations than the somewhat shallow concepts of mere intellect, which blow hither and thither in the wind when limited to themselves, when they are not anchored in the deeper archetypal layers. The science fiction that now obsesses the young is a poor and dangerous substitute for religious training, for essential indoctrination to put them into harmony with their deeper selves. Religious teachings speak to the unconscious, to the soul, even though consciousness rejects them.

Can any science fiction equal the symbolical star or magical fish that heralds the coming of an immortal savior? Can any match the holy meaning of the wine in the cup that is Christ's blood, the very essence of God Himself? Can any feature of science fiction equal the fact that part of God may descend into a human individual as an act of direct incarnation? Religions have always been needed to express these greatest of truths that are *facts* of the spirit. The soul has a religious function, and Jung tells us that adults should be educated to the fact that the God-image resides in each human being. But it also is good for children to grow up with the magical image of Christ and all of the miraculous tales that surround Him.

So the Christian myth in the modern world is much in need of deeper understanding in terms of the archetypal symbolism, but the simpler Bible stories are more suitable for little children, as indeed, for certain adults, though the symbolic meanings could also be included to a degree. It can only be beneficial to know that when Christ feeds the five thousand with the loaves and fishes it is symbolical of deeper truths. Indeed, if the people were only fed physically, then it would merely be an act of physical magic. But Christ the fish who feeds Himself to the whole world as an act of spirit through the unconscious is a true miracle; for then, the divine essence of God is received.

The churches will always be necessary in the West for the same reason that temples are needed in the East, for though Hinduism and Buddhism are known to be based upon inner unconscious structures, temples are nevertheless required as outer expressions of them, and as physical structures in which the people can worship. Some will not need the Church, though it is the nature of Man to worship together with others, the flock under the guidance of the Good Shepherd. However, there is no reason why churches should not also be temples of learning. That is, unless we become a completely soulless and spiritually alienated society, a fate that has threatened mankind from his beginnings, as Jung has told us. But as one of my dreams, where the nun shows me the soul depths beneath the church demonstrates; the Church represents not only the lofty heights of spirit, but also the feminine depths of soul that must be unified with the spirit.

Jung began as a young psychiatrist treating the mentally sick, but gradually came to realize that much of the sickness was being caused by psychic/spiritual dissociation. As he progressed, he found that the unconscious is not just personal but connects to another reality, and that we must be in harmony with it for psychic health. Consequently, he had no option from his earlier works onwards but to connect psychology up with religion, simply because the human psyche leads to other levels of spirit and soul. Ancient cultures had this relationship developed to high degree. So whether in a primitive tribal environment or in our modern schools, children must be grounded in this relationship. Religion works on the unconscious even though the conscious mind is unaware of the relationship, whether it is the minds of children or adults. Thousands of years of religious experience form layers in the unconscious, a Royal Line, that descends and ascends to eternity, and we must be integrated with that line.

One thing is sure: The world cannot continue along its current destructive path. Everything must be changed and fundamentally so. Jungian depth psychology is the means and the first step to this. Everything will grow from there. I have witnessed the individuation process—the spiritualizing process—at work in at least a dozen people, though it was mostly unconsciously. These people had never heard of

Jung and were not outwardly highly intelligent or religious personalities, but were somewhat mesmerized, though a little disturbed, because they were having strange dreams and felt disoriented. At least two said that God had spoken to them in a dream, and a number had seen Christ.

We call these phenomena unconscious individuation processes, but it is all the workings of the Holy Ghost. As we become ever more dissociated and tumble farther into the morass, the spirit gets to work in us to try to bring about an imperative reorientation. If it fails, then the culture collapses. If I have seen this process at work in so many people I know, how many others are being affected across the whole of Western civilization?

The trouble is, most will not understand what is taking place, and so the attempt by the spirit may fail. This is why the works of Jung are so vital to us. People must be educated to understand what is happening to them, and it is not so much a matter of psychology but of religion, the soul depths as well as the spirit heights. Here are a few examples of men and women who are understanding this truth.

A friend told me a couple of weeks ago about a magical severed head that appeared in a dream, and several nights ago he found himself in an underground chamber which had strange archaic inscriptions all over the walls. He has also dreamt of a black raven and tombstones. These are age-old symbols in alchemy and other esoteric mysteries, of the unredeemed and somewhat dangerous state of the lower Earth spirit. (One meaning of the raven is that it signifies the beginning of the *nigredo*, the black melancholia at the start of the processes.) It all needs to be brought to the light and Christianized, and then the black raven may become the white dove of the Holy Spirit. This is their meaning in the story of Noah.

The friend is a very strong Christian consciously, but the lower spirit is kicking back, wanting recognition and development. A lot of people will not be suited to the work, but this man has the chance to taste of the Holy Grail on his quest, to experience God. As I have advised him, he will need to study Jung in depth if he wants to be sure to gain understanding. Though we may look upon these processes as ones of psychology from the human angle, in themselves they are ultimately holy processes of God.

The daughter of another friend is also having archetypal dreams and tells me she dreamt of a land in utter chaos, but that she just managed to make it to a church where there was safety. Then God spoke in her dream, stating that certain people are infertile and cannot have children, but that certain others can have children, including her. This refers to those who are able to develop the inner Self through the processes, which involves the divine child, and those who are not. The young woman is not a religious person, though with dreams such as these, could well become one, and is meant to. (Her brother, incidentally, recently dreamt of a fish, knowing nothing of the inner mysteries or depth psychology.)

Another young woman I know is suffering badly with her nerves and is taking medication to put her into a happier state of mind. This is false and will do nothing to help resolve the conflict within her soul, which will only become even more repressed and negative. I knew this woman as a girl and she was very sensitive and intelligent. But she has spent her adult life, since she was a young teenager, completely in the pursuit of worldly wealth and success. Her soul has not developed in the magical world of archetypal reality, which a personality such as hers especially needs, and so she remains in the same undeveloped state as when she first left childhood. The result is always a neurosis, which can become quite painful, and even life-destroying, for in such a state we are dissociated from the true nature of both ourselves and ultimate reality. She would be amazed if I told her that her cure lies in readjustment to a religious attitude towards life.

The fate of our civilization, and ultimately that of the whole world, depends upon these processes that are taking place within certain people, perhaps millions all told. This is what Jung meant when he said the human individual is the makeweight that tips the scales. It is human beings that are causing the sickness to the world, and so the cure for the world must take place within the human soul.

Yet it would be a mistake to believe that these inner processes are due solely to the individual soul being in need of development. In a disoriented age like our own, when fundamental change to the sick culture is called for, the Spirit is hard at work to try to bring the change about, for the Holy Ghost is the force that heals. Jung also said that the Holy Ghost descends into the human personality and in this way Father, Son, and Man share in the Holy Ghost. Jung says this happens as a definite action, and my processes demonstrate that this is so. However, the infusion of spirit grows with the processes. It may come as a shock to the people who are experiencing these strange dreams and disturbances within themselves, that in addition to needing to develop their own psychic depths, they are ultimately experiencing the workings of the Holy Ghost.

The divine child may be born within us all potentially, but very few, if any, will develop him to the level of a Christ figure. This would be undesirable in any case. This is why Jung said that the stamping out of the early Gnostic groups was desirable and necessary overall. More than one Christ would have confused the issue somewhat. Only one symbolic figure is needed in which all of the people may share, on which to project the Great Man. It is enough for most to know that we all connected to the Higher Self and that we must think in a religious way to be in harmony with it. This is why it is essential to teach religion to children in school, to make early contact with their religious depths and to accustom their conscious minds in that mode of thought. It is incalculably dangerous not to do so.

A few decades ago the communist world was heavily criticized for turning people into soulless automatons, and yet we are now doing precisely the same thing. In the first few pages of this book I told of the recent dream where I am a small boy again, holding hands with my sister as we sing "There's a Friend for Little Children above the Bright Blue Sky." As I comment, the dream makes me feel tremendously secure in a world belonging to God, where what is right must win in the end. Do we really want to take this away from little children?

My mother used to tell me of a recurring dream I would have when I was very small. I remember it only vaguely, but I would dream that a church was following me everywhere I went. Jung tells us that these earliest dreams are always archetypal, and this is because the conscious ego-personality has not really been formed yet, and so what is speaking in the dreams are the archetypal layers of the psyche, and beyond, involving the Higher Self. The church in my recurring dream represents the Self in a specific form, revealing how I should be attached to it and should develop my life accordingly. Jung says that these dreams can predict our future because we will be directed in life by that archetypal pattern, or should be. It is when, in fact, we act contrary to that pattern that all sorts of neuroses set in.

I mentioned the Jewish girl earlier who had the soul of a saint, but who was neurotic because of the loose and atheistic modern way in which she was living her life. Her father, a rich banker, had rejected the faith of his forefathers and had brought up his daughter accordingly. She had wealth, beauty, intelligence, and could boast a long line of lovers, but of what use are these things to the soul of a saint? She too had been brought up with no religious groundings, within a materialistic, over-intellectualized framework of orientation.

I dreamt recently that God has planted His good seed upon the Earth, and time will tell what will grow from that monumental event. The seed may fail to take root as much as the possibility that it will grow and flourish. Certainly, God's direct intervention is needed as much as the workings of the Holy Ghost to bring about the fundamental change in us. Nothing less will suffice, for only experience of religious phenomena has any lasting effect upon man. It was not political movements of any type that evolved and civilized man into his cultures; it was ultimately the workings of the spirit through the unconscious. As I needed a bucketful of blood myself to bring about transformation, so too does mankind.

We see this exemplified in the story of Ebenezer Scrooge, which we all know and love, but which is much more than a lovable old Christmas tale. The message is that Scrooge is killing his soul with worship of business and profit. All of his thinking is directed towards those gods. He is consequently in dire need of inner transformation, His soul needs salvation. It would be of no use for him to find his cure in anything but the Spirit, for only the opposite to matter can be its antidote. This is why the three spirits visit him, for only the spirit is truly able to bring transformation to the ailing soul.

The royal bloodline of spirit that runs through the Western collective unconscious has been developed to a degree by my inner processes, and it is now the task to unite this knowledge with traditional Christianity, to help bring to the latter its deeper roots and meaning. What I visualize is a new flowering of the religious spirit, based upon the new knowledge and experience of the psychic depths, for the unconscious is the gateway to God Himself. Essential to this, as said, are Jung's discoveries, for in connecting us to our own spiritual aspects and foundations, Jung helps do the work of the Holy Ghost.

The psychic foundations are also religious foundations, and the human individual is at bottom a religious complex that is part of the eternal religious complex. That is our true nature. We can never alter the fact, though we can grow away from it and corrupt its meaning. A new order is needed in the world, though that new order is really the further development of the lost ancient one. Each layer of a skyscraper is dependent upon all of the levels beneath, and this is especially so with man's religious and cultural growth. The false developments that began to take hold of the West after the second World War (though their beginnings reach back much farther) must be wiped out. We must go back and develop everything anew, along lines laid down by the spirit through the unconscious, which is really the royal bloodline of our traditional heritage. This is what most of us want deep down within ourselves. Only perverse personalities would wish to live in a soulless world of chaos, because they would be at home in it.

Yet the great danger is not limited to such destructive personalities. The forces of chaos masquerade also, and even especially, under seemingly progressive and enlightened banners. Jung says that man must be guided by the light of the Lord of Spirits, not by the light of his own reason, which is not so bright a light. What light would the Earth have if the sun ceased to shine? If the Age of Reason, when man pulled down God from his throne and set up the guillotine, taught us anything, it is that man displays little reason when his thinking is limited to mere intellectual concepts of ego-consciousness.

Last night I dreamt I was walking with a bishop's crook. This was about six feet high with a very ornate hook at the top in gold, with gold also at the center and lower tip. It is really the development of the rod of the prophet, with the added meaning of the crook of the Good Shepherd, who hooks in the flock and guides them on the right path. It is the authority from the higher powers above. To my left in the dream were factories and a "normal" working life. To my right was a road where I would meet a lot of women. But my true road was neither of these; it was a different path where I was to symbolically carry the bishop's crook. This fits in with my first dreams as a child of the church following me. As a young man I was very far from this path, and I became ill and lost, but finally, after many years, I was where I should be. Not so much in the outer world, but within myself and the unconscious, where it really counts.

I have experienced great things, and because of this know that all I say is true, (though Jung said much the same earlier) I carry on with my simple life, hoping that the change to the new order will come. I have the tremendous certainty that God is real, that spirit and soul are real, and that anything is ultimately possible with these eternal powers. But even then, so much depends upon us.

For myself, I was never happy, never at home working for any worldly aims or authority, and in fact, always felt completely lost with them. Then, in the inner processes, I experienced the Higher Self and God and thereby found my true authority. This was it; this is where I belong; this is home. I could not now serve any worldly authority and would probably become ill if I tried to. Serving God, as I try to in my own way, I am at where I should be.

Yet this is ultimately true of us all. Every human being gains enormously when God is his or her authority, and the world itself is a better place. Then man is integrated and properly balanced, and the pomposity of worldly power deflates to nothingness, because there is nothing to support it. Every human being gains true freedom with God in authority, although the self-indulgent freedoms are lost. We can no longer act selfishly or irresponsibly. Nevertheless, the soul gains tremendously. If anyone disbelieves my words, or disagrees, I say, go to the unconscious and spend years in the processes, and then your opinions will be changed. You too will have gnosis.

Nietzsche said, "God is dead. God remains dead. And we have killed him." However, Nietzsche was hasty in these conclusions, and I can now report most emphatically that God is alive; God remains alive; and will be around for quite some time to come!

REFERENCES

Angelucci, Orfeo. 1955. *The Secret of the Saucers*. Amherst, Wisconsin: Amherst Press.

Augustine, St. 1943. *The Confessions*. Translated by Francis Joseph. London: Sheed.

Aurora Consurgens contained in *Artis Auriferae*. 1593. Basel.

Baigent, Michael and Richard Leigh. 1989. *The Temple and the Lodge*. London: Jonathon Cape.

Blavatsky, H. P. 1888. *The Secret Doctrine*. London and New York: The Theosophical Publishing House.

Bonaventure, St. 1937. *The Fransiscan Vision, a Translation of St. Bonaventure's Itinerarium Mentis in Deum*. Translated by Father James. London: Burns, Oates, and Washbourne.

Budge, A. E. Wallis. 1904. *The Gods of the Egyptians*. London: Methuan.

Campbell, Colin. 1912. *The Mysterious Birth of King Amen-Hotep III*. Edinburgh and London: n.p.

Dorn, Gerard. 1659. *Congeries Paracelsicae Chemicae*, in *Theatrum Chemicum Britannicum*. London: Elias Ashmole.

Eckhart, Meister. 1924. *Works of Meister Eckhart*. Translated by C. de B. Evans. London: J. M. Watkins.

Epiphanius. 1868. *Against Heresies*, in *The Writings of Irenaeus*. Translated by A. Roberts and W. H. Rambaut. Edinburgh.

Glauber, Johann. 1658. *Tractatus Natura Salium*. Amsterdam.

Hancock, Graham. 1995. *Fingerprints of the Gods*. London: William Heinemann.

Hippolytus. 1921. *Philosophumena; or, Refutation of All Heresies, Formerly Attributed to Origen.* . . . Translated by Francis Legge. New York: Macmillan.

Honorius of Autun. 1844. *Expositio in Cantica Canticorum*, in *Patorlogiae Cursus Completus*. Paris: P. L. Migne.

I Ching. N.p., n.d.

James, Montague Rhodes, translator. 1924. Acts of Peter in *The Apocryphal New Testament*. Oxford: Clarendon Press.

Jennings, Hargreave. 1884. *Phallicism*. London: George Redway.

Jung, C. G. 1958. *Psychology and Religion: West and East*. London: Routledge and Kegan Paul.

———. 1959a. *Aion*. London: Routledge and Kegan Paul.

———. 1959b. *The Archetypes and the Collective Unconscious*. London: Routledge and Kegan Paul

———. 1963a. *Memories Dreams Reflections*. London: Collins and Routledge.

———. 1963b. *Mysterium Coniunctionis*. London: Routledge and Kegan Paul.

———. 1964. *Civilization in Transition*. London: Routledge and Kegan Paul.

———. 1968. *Alchemical Studies*. London: Routledge and Kegan Paul.

Jung, Emma and Marie-Louise von Franz. 1960. *The Grail Legend*. Zurich and Stuttgart: Raschler.

Massey, Gerald. 1883. *The Natural Genesis*. London: Williams and Norgate.

———. 1907. *Ancient Egypt, the Light of the World*. London: T. F. Unwin.

Ostanes. 1887. In *Collection des Anciens Alchemistes Grecs*. Paris: Marcellin Berthelot.

Pererius, Benedictus. 1598. *De Magia*. Cologne: n.p.

Plato. *Phaedrus*. N.p., n.d.

Ripley, Sir George. 1602. *Duodecim Portarum Axiomata Philosophica*, contained in *Theatrum Chemicum*. Strasbourg.

Rosararium Philosophorum, contained in *Artis Auriferae*. 1593. Basel: n.p.

Rundle-Clark, R. T. 1959. Pyramid Texts quoted in *Myth and Symbol in Ancient Egypt*. London: Thames and Hudson.

Tertulian. 1869. *De Carne Christi*. Translated by Sydney Thelwall. Edinburgh: n.p.

Theatrum Chemicum. 1622. 6 volumes. Strasbourg: n.p.

Wilson, Colin. 1997 *From Atlantis to the Sphinx*. London: Virgin.

———. 1998. *Alien Dawn*. London: Virgin.

Zosimos. 1593a. In *Rosinus ad Sarratantam Episcocum*, in *Artis Auriferae*. Basel: n.p.

———. 1593b. In *Turba Philosophorum* in *Artis Auriferae*. Basel: n.p.

INDEX

ABOUT THE AUTHOR

 Robert B. Clarke, after a materially and educationally poor but spiritually rich youth in central England, became an independent scholar who delved deeply into the realms of philosophy, religion, and psychology, seeking evidence of some greater meaning beyond day-to-day life. Severely depressed and disillusioned—having lost the inner certainty of his childhood—Clarke accidentally stumbled onto the teachings of the great psychologist Carl Jung, and there found the path to the understanding he had sought. Today, he lives only a few streets away from his birthplace, in Stoke-on-Trent, England.

Hampton Roads Publishing Company

... for the evolving human spirit

Hampton Roads Publishing Company
publishes books on a variety of subjects,
including metaphysics, health, integrative medicine,
visionary fiction, and other related topics.

For a copy of our latest catalog, call toll-free
(800) 766-8009, or send your name and address to:

Hampton Roads Publishing Company, Inc.
1125 Stoney Ridge Road
Charlottesville, VA 22902

e-mail: hrpc@hrpub.com
www.hrpub.com